D1131668

Palgrave Advances in Behavioral Economics

Series Editor

John Tomer
Co-editor, Journal of Socio-Economics
Manhattan College
Riverdale
USA

MF

This groundbreaking series is designed to make available in book form unique behavioral economic contributions. It provides a publishing opportunity for behavioral economist authors who have a novel perspective and have developed a special ability to integrate economics with other disciplines. It will allow these authors to fully develop their ideas. In general, it is not a place for narrow technical contributions. Theoretical/conceptual, empirical, and policy contributions are all welcome.

More information about this series at
http://www.springer.com/series/14720

Sherzod Abdukadirov
Editor

Nudge Theory in Action

Behavioral Design in Policy and Markets

Editor
Sherzod Abdukadirov
Mercatus Center at George Mason University
Arlington, Virginia, USA

Palgrave Advances in Behavioral Economics
ISBN 978-3-319-31318-4   ISBN 978-3-319-31319-1   (eBook)
DOI 10.1007/978-3-319-31319-1

Library of Congress Control Number: 2016951439

Cover illustration: © Zoonar GmbH / Alamy Stock Photo

Printed on acid-free paper

This Palgrave Macmillan imprint is published by Springer Nature
The registered company is Springer International Publishing AG Switzerland

FOREWORD

The issues surrounding "Nudge" are some of the most important in all of economics. The simplest models of economics take preferences as given, but nudge ideas suggest that we can be moved, steered, and in some cases manipulated. Given these behavioral propensities, how do markets actually work? How does politics work? How *should* politics work and what should policymakers do? How much can government take advantage of its nudging capability to bring about a better world?

Should we be more suspicious of private sector nudge or public sector nudge?

I am myself never quite sure how to answer the above question. On one hand, I fear the greater competency of private sector nudge. I know that a talented team of marketers is working overtime to try to get me to buy the product, take out a loan, or participate in a charitable cause. Furthermore, a competitive process winnows out the market players who are less good at nudging and elevates those who are better at nudging.

A lot of this nudging is good for me. If Spotify recommends some new music, there is a pretty good chance I'll like it. If Whole Foods advertises a special, and puts it prominently on display, they figure I have the potential to become a regular buyer and enjoyer of the good. These nudges help me navigate the world.

In many other cases I am less sure, especially when the transaction is not likely to be repeated. I don't trust doctors and dentists who try to intimidate me into scheduling more work and more procedures. I can't trust the claims which most nonprofits make on behalf of their effectiveness. And at times I wonder if higher education is really all it is cracked up to be or rather simply something one must do to avoid not having a degree. Harvard does such a good job of making the lawn look nice when the parents visit for graduation.

Private sector nudge is highly problematic, and I would say it is often worst in those areas we tend to feel best about: health care, education, and charity. In those cases, our guard is most likely to be let down, even if we are highly educated. Or should I say *because* we are educated?

What about public sector nudge? Well, the good news is that a lot of what government does is simply send money around through transfer programs. In this regard, its potential for manipulating us is fairly limited. Furthermore, government is extremely bureaucratic and usually it does not have top tier marketing talent. Most of the time I just don't find my government very persuasive. Is there really anything the DMV can talk me into that I wouldn't otherwise want to do?

But can I then relax? Can I stop worrying about public sector nudge? I am not so sure.

The biggest costs in human history come from wars, and very often the public sector—especially the executive branches in various countries— nudges us into wars. I don't hear enough discussion of this topic in the nudge literature.

Government also has nudged us into believing that more government regulation is the answer to many of our problems. This is a supposition created in part by government rhetoric, coming from Congress, the president, and of course, from the regulators themselves. Too often we see more regulation as the proper default, yet I believe that overall the American economy is too regulated in most areas. Government is partly to blame for that. Even if government agencies do not have the most effective marketers, they have information advantages which they use to promote a mentality of "let's pass a law," or "let's pass a regulation," as the best response to a lot of social problems.

Finally, I worry about how private sector and public sector nudge interact. Nudges from the television news, and its coverage of crime stories, convince many Americans that rates of crime are rising when in fact they are falling. That's a private sector nudge to be sure, and the private sector is doing the marketing, with great skill I might add. But how does it interact with the public sector? Well, prosecutors send more people to jail and for longer periods of time. Arguably we have ended up with too many people in jail, and there are then public sector unions which take a dim attitude to working too hard to close some jails. The problem, in broadest terms, is that the public sector often piggybacks upon the marketing efforts of the private sector. The private sector marketing, taken alone, probably would be far less harmful, but it can be combined with the coercive powers of the public sector.

On the brighter side, sometimes public sector nudge helps us. The campaign to cut back on the number of Americans smoking for instance has mostly been a big success, with big gains.

I find these to be some of the most important and interesting issues today. The essays in this book are but one part of a broader movement to see just where the "Nudge" concept leaves us. I hope you will enjoy them, and I hope this preface gives you just the slightest nudge toward proceeding further.

Tyler Cowen

Holbert L. Harris Chair of Economics at
George Mason University and
General Director of the Mercatus Center at
George Mason University, Arlington, VA, USA

ACKNOWLEDGMENTS

I wish to personally thank the Mercatus Center at George Mason University for its generous support of the project. Specifically, I wish to thank James Broughel, program manager at the Mercatus Center, whose tireless efforts moved this project forward and ensured its fruition. I wish to thank Jamil Khan for providing administrative support, and Garrett Brown, director of publishing, for his help in navigating through the publishing process. Finally, I wish to thank Joe Kennedy and anonymous reviewers for their thoughtful comments. All errors are the sole responsibility of the authors.

Sherzod Abdukadirov

CONTENTS

xi

About the Contributors

Sherzod Abdukadirov is a research fellow in the Regulatory Studies Program at the Mercatus Center at George Mason University. He specializes in the federal regulatory process, behavioral economics, and health policy. Abdukadirov has prepared numerous policy briefs on regulatory issues, has written for *USA Today*, and *US News & World Report*, and is a contributing author for *The Hill*. He published in *Constitutional Political Economy*, *William and Mary Policy Review* and *Regulation*. Abdukadirov received his PhD in public policy from George Mason University and his BS in information technology from Rochester Institute of Technology.

Jodi N. Beggs is a lecturer at Northeastern University, where she teaches behavioral economics to undergraduate and graduate students. In addition, Beggs is the economics expert for About.com and a consultant to a number of technology companies and textbook publishers. Via her own company, Economists Do It With Models, Beggs provides online educational content in various formats to both help students directly and help instructors present economics in a way that is timely, relevant, and fun. Beggs has an AM in Economics from Harvard University as well as graduate and undergraduate degrees in Computer Science and Mathematics from the Massachusetts Institute of Technology.

Jessica Carges is a masters student in the Department of Economics at George Mason University. She is currently a second-year MA Fellow with the Mercatus Center, where she works as a graduate research assistant focused on health policy. She has interned with Health and Human

Services, HHR Strategies, and the U.S. Trade Representative Office. Carges graduated from George Mason University with a BS in economics in 2015.

Tyler Cowen is Holbert L. Harris Chair of Economics at George Mason University and serves as chairman and general director of the Mercatus Center at George Mason University. With colleague Alex Tabarrok, Cowen is coauthor of the popular economics blog *Marginal Revolution* and cofounder of the online educational platform Marginal Revolution University.

A dedicated writer and communicator of economic ideas who has written extensively on the economics of culture, Cowen is the author of several books and is widely published in academic journals and the popular media. He writes the Economic Scene column for the *New York Times;* has contributed extensively to national publications such as the *Wall Street Journal* and *Money;* and serves on the on the advisory boards of both *Wilson Quarterly* and *American Interest.* His research has been published in the *American Economic Review*, the *Journal of Political Economy, Ethics*, and *Philosophy and Public Affairs.*

In 2011, *Bloomberg Businessweek* profiled Cowen as "America's Hottest Economist" after his e-book, *The Great Stagnation*, appeared twice on the *New York Times* e-book bestseller list. Columnist David Brooks declared it "the most debated nonfiction book so far this year." *Foreign Policy* named Cowen as one of 2011's "Top 100 Global Thinkers," and an *Economist* survey counted him as one of the most influential economists of the last decade. Cowen graduated from George Mason University with a BS in economics and received his PhD in economics from Harvard University.

Robert Graboyes is senior research fellow and health care economist at the Mercatus Center at George Mason University. Author of "Fortress and Frontier in American Health Care," his work asks, "How can we make health care as innovative in the next 25 years as information technology was in the past 25?" Previously, he was health care advisor for the National Federation of Independent Business, economics professor at the University of Richmond, regional economist/director of education at the Federal Reserve Bank of Richmond, and Sub-Saharan Africa economist for Chase Manhattan Bank. His work has taken him to Europe, Africa, and Central Asia. An award-winning teacher, he holds faculty appointments at Virginia Commonwealth University and the University of Virginia. Previously he taught at George Mason University and the George Washington University.

His degrees include a PhD in Economics from Columbia University; master's from Columbia University, Virginia Commonwealth University, and the College of William and Mary; and a bachelor's from the University of Virginia. He chaired the National Economists Club, Richmond Association for Business Economics, and National Association for Business Economics Healthcare Roundtable. He won the Reason Foundation's 2014 Bastiat Prize for Journalism, an international competition for "writing that best demonstrates the importance of individual liberty and free markets with originality, wit, and eloquence."

Brian F. Mannix is a research professor at the George Washington University Regulatory Studies Center. He is a recognized national expert on energy and environmental policy and regulation. From 2005 to 2009 he served as the Environmental Protection Agency's Associate Administrator for Policy, Economics, and Innovation; earlier he served as Deputy Secretary of Natural Resources for the Commonwealth of Virginia. He has held appointments at a number of other federal and state agencies, and has held research positions at several public policy think tanks. From 1987 to 1989 Mannix was the Managing Editor of *Regulation* magazine at the American Enterprise Institute. He earned AB and AM degrees from Harvard University in Mathematics and Chemistry and an MPP from the Harvard Kennedy School of Government.

Michael Marlow is a professor of economics and distinguished scholar at California Polytechnic State University, San Luis Obispo. His research examines numerous issues associated with spending, taxation and regulatory policies of government. His most recent research focuses on public health economics. Prior to coming to Cal Poly in 1988, he was a senior financial economist at the U.S. Treasury and taught at George Washington University. He is a Phi Beta Kappa graduate of George Washington University where he was awarded a BA in Economics. He received his PhD in economics from Virginia Tech.

Sofie E. Miller is a senior policy analyst at the George Washington University Regulatory Studies Center. Her research portfolio includes use of benefit-cost analysis by agencies, retrospective review of existing rules, economic analysis of energy efficiency standards, quantitative analysis of regulatory benefits, and the regressive effects of regulation. Miller has drawn on this research to submit over twenty public comments to federal agencies on proposed rules spanning the topics of energy and environment, consumer safety, transportation, reducing regulatory burdens, and enhancing competition through regulatory policy. Miller has published articles in academic journals of public policy and administrative law and her work has also appeared in the Washington Post, Bloomberg BNA, Morning Consult, Reuters, the Chicago Tribune, and The Hill. Miller serves as Editor in Chief of the Regulatory Studies Center's weekly Regulation Digest, which reaches over 1,300 subscribers with weekly updates on regulatory developments in agencies, think tanks, the media, and academia. Miller has a master's degree in public policy with a concentration in regulatory policy from the George Washington University.

Mario J. Rizzo is a professor of economics at New York University, director of the Program on the Foundations of the Market Economy, and co-director of the Classical Liberal Institute at the NYU Law School. He received his PhD. in economics from the University of Chicago. He was a law and economics fellow at Yale Law School and the University of Chicago Law School. He teaches a yearly seminar at the NYU Law School called "Classical Liberalism."

Professor Rizzo's major fields of research has been law and economics, ethics and economics, and most recently behavioral economics and paternalism. He is the author of *Austrian Economics Re-examined: The Economics of Time and Ignorance* published in 2015 by Routledge. This is an expanded version of *The Economics of Time and Ignorance*. He is the author of many law-review and other scholarly articles. He is also the co-editor with Lawrence White of a Routledge book series called Foundations of the Markets Economy. There are now 33 books in this series. He is currently finishing a book for Cambridge University Press on rationality, behavioral economics and new paternalism.

Adam C. Smith is an associate professor of economics and director of the Center for Free Market Studies at Johnson & Wales University. He has published peer-reviewed articles in the *Journal of Economic Behavior & Organization*, the *European Journal of Political Economy, Social Choice & Welfare*, and *Public Choice*, as well as popular pieces in *Forbes, US News & World Report, Charlotte Business Journal*, and *Regulation* magazine. He is also a visiting scholar with the Regulatory Studies Center at George

Washington University, and co-author with Bruce Yandle of *Bootleggers and Baptists: How Economic Forces and Moral Persuasion Interact to Shape Regulatory Politics* (Cato Press, 2014).

Adam Thierer is a senior research fellow with the Technology Policy Program at the Mercatus Center at George Mason University. He specializes in technology, media, Internet, and free-speech policies, with a particular focus on online safety and digital privacy. His writings have appeared in the *Wall Street Journal*, the *Economist*, the *Washington Post*, the *Atlantic*, and *Forbes*, and he has appeared on national television and radio. Thierer is a frequent guest lecturer and has testified numerous times on Capitol Hill.

Thierer has authored or edited eight books on topics ranging from media regulation and child safety issues to the role of federalism in high-technology markets. His latest book is *Permissionless Innovation: The Continuing Case for Comprehensive Technological Freedom*. He contributes to the *Technology Liberation Front*, a leading tech policy blog. Thierer has served on several distinguished online safety task forces, including Harvard University's Internet Safety Technical Task Force and the federal government's Online Safety Technology Working Group. Previously, Thierer was president of the Progress & Freedom Foundation, director of telecommunications studies at the Cato Institute, and a senior fellow at the Heritage Foundation. Thierer received his MA in international business management and trade theory at the University of Maryland and his BA in journalism and political philosophy from Indiana University.

Steve Wendel is a behavioral social scientist who studies financial behavior, and how digital products can help individuals manage their money more effectively. He serves as Head of Behavioral Science at Morningstar, a leading provider of independent investment research, where he leads a team of behavioral scientists and practitioners to conduct original research on saving and investing behavior.

Wendel is the author of *Designing for Behavior Change* (November 2013) and *Improving Employee Benefits* (September 2014). The first book gives step-by-step instructions on how to develop products that help users take action: from exercising more to learning a new language. His second book examines why employees fail to use their benefits and how behavioral economics can help. Wendel also founded the non-profit Action Design Network, which hosts an annual conference and monthly events in seven cities for over 5,000 practitioners applying behavioral research to product development and communications. Wendel holds a BA from the University of California at Berkeley, an MA from the Paul H. Nitze School of Advanced International Studies at Johns Hopkins University, and a PhD from the University of Maryland, where he analyzed the dynamics of behavioral change over time.

Mark D. White is chair and professor in the Department of Philosophy at the College of Staten Island/CUNY, where he teaches courses in philosophy, economics, and law. He has published widely in the intersections of these areas, including five authored books, over 50 journal articles and book chapters, and many edited and co-edited volumes.

Richard Williams is director of the Regulatory Studies Program, and a senior research fellow at the Mercatus Center at George Mason University. He is an expert in benefit-cost analysis and risk analysis, particularly associated with food safety and nutrition. Williams has testified before the US Congress and addressed numerous international governments, including those of the United Kingdom, South Korea, Yugoslavia, and Australia. His media appearances have included NPR, Reuters, Bloomberg, the *New York Times* and the *Wall Street Journal*.

Before joining the Mercatus Center, Williams was the director for social sciences at the Center for Food Safety and Applied Nutrition in the Food and Drug Administration (FDA). He also was an adviser to the Harvard Center for Risk Analysis and taught economics at Washington and Lee University. He is a US Army veteran who served in Vietnam. Williams received his PhD and MA in economics from Virginia Tech and his BS in business administration from Old Dominion University.

Todd J. Zywicki is Foundation Professor of Law at George Mason University School of Law, Executive Director of the Law and Economics Center, and a senior scholar of the Mercatus Center at George Mason University. He specializes in bankruptcy, contracts, commercial law, business associations, law and economics, and public choice and the law. Zywicki has testified before Congress on consumer bankruptcy and consumer credit, and he frequently commentates in print and broadcast media, including the *Wall Street Journal*, the *New York Times*, the *Washington Post*, *Forbes*, the *Atlantic*, *Nightline*, *NBC Nightly News*, *PBS Newshour*, Fox Business, CNN, CNBC, Bloomberg News, BBC, ABC Radio, and

The Diane Rehm Show. He writes for the legal blog the *Volokh Conspiracy* and is an editor of the *Supreme Court Economic Review.*

Previously, Zywicki was director of the Office of Policy Planning at the Federal Trade Commission (FTC) and taught at Vanderbilt University Law School, Georgetown University Law Center, Boston College Law School, and Mississippi College School of Law. Zywicki received his JD from the University of Virginia, his MA in economics from Clemson University, and his BA in economics from Dartmouth College.

Introduction: Regulation versus Technology as Tools of Behavior Change

Sherzod Abdukadirov

For a long time in human history, the world was relatively simple. Our hunter-gatherer ancestors faced few choices.[1] They hunted when they ran out of game and ate whatever they could hunt or gather—watching their diet or exercising was hardly a concern. They ate their kill within days to avoid the meat getting spoiled; they could not save any of it for future consumption. They did not plan out their future careers. They did not save for old age. In the extraordinarily violent world of hunter-gatherers, few individuals lived past their prime years. Surprisingly, they enjoyed quite a bit of leisure time. While life was no picnic, it put few cognitive demands on hunter-gatherers' brains.

Modern life could not be more different. We are bombarded with choices in our daily lives: a cornucopia of cereal brands and flavors; dozens of investment funds with varying degrees of risk; and a seemingly endless selection of TV shows, apps, books, clothing, and so on.[2] We have to make complex decisions that require considerable mental capacity but also patience to weed through all the details; just take mortgages, credit card agreements, or college financial aid applications. We have to plan for events that are years and even decades in the future, like saving for

S. Abdukadirov (✉)
Mercatus Center at George Mason University, Arlington, VA, USA

1

children's college tuition or our own retirement. Most importantly, every day we have to exert substantial willpower to stick with those decisions in the face of all the other enticing choices.

Yet, despite the ever-multiplying demands on our cognitive abilities and self-control, our brain's capacity to handle these requests remains quite limited. Behavioral economists Sendhil Mullainathan and Eldar Shafir compare our brain capacity to a computer's bandwidth.[3] Each new task that requires individuals to process more data or exert self-control depletes the brain's capacity. For example, studies show that students are more likely to cheat on tests given later in the day as their capacity for self-control—the ability to resist temptation—gets depleted through the course of the day.[4] Similarly, subjects preoccupied with money or their diets perform worse on cognitive tests.[5]

This scarcity of cognitive capacity and self-control often leads consumers to make biased decisions.[6] Consumers fail to make the rational choice, meaning they fail to select the option that is clearly more cost beneficial and would improve their welfare. For example, many overweight and obese individuals understand the harms of extra weight to their health and want to lose weight, but they find it extremely difficult to resist the immediate gratification of a tasty but unhealthy snack in favor of long-term health. Many employees procrastinate and fail to set up contributions to their 401(k) plans, despite the obvious need to save for retirement. Many patients with chronic health conditions forget to take their pills or do not comprehend the need to complete the full course of medication to prevent future hospitalization and expensive treatment.

Scholars refer to these biased decisions as behavioral failures, and the impact of these decisions can be substantial.[7] For example, some estimates show that more than half of Americans are not saving enough for retirement.[8] Over two-thirds of Americans are either overweight or obese,[9] which may lead to a host of major health problems.[10] Failure of chronic patients to adhere to medication leads to an estimated $100–300 billion in additional medical expenditures each year.[11]

Note that when discussing behavioral failures in the context of policy, we are not talking about deviations from the caricature *perfect* rationality that expects consumers to purchase the most cost-beneficial cup of coffee. Rather we are talking about *reasonable* rationality that many of us exhibit by graduating from college, staying on track with retirement plans, or watching what we eat. What elevates some behavioral failures to the level of public policy concern is that the harms caused by these behavioral biases can be severe and often irreversible.

Faced with these concerns, policymakers have increasingly sought to counter behavioral biases through regulations. For example, in 2015, President Obama issued an executive order that encouraged federal agencies to employ behavioral insights to design more effective government policies and programs.[12] The order directed all agencies to develop strategies for greater use of behavioral sciences. It further directed the recently created Social and Behavioral Sciences Team to issue guidance to help agencies implement the order. These efforts follow in the footsteps of the Behavioral Insights Team—better known as the Nudge Unit—established within the UK government.[13]

In most cases, these regulatory remedies take the form of paternalistic policies. These nudges aim to correct consumer errors by either limiting consumer choices or replacing consumer decisions with those of policymakers. For example, fuel efficiency standards force consumers to purchase more efficient vehicles in an effort to save consumers money through lower fuel costs. Financial regulations attempt to discourage consumers from using overdraft protection and incurring substantial fees for the service; they instead aim to get consumers to use cheaper alternatives. Sugary drink taxes try to encourage consumers to switch to less caloric and more nutritious drink alternatives.

What often escapes the notice of policymakers and academics that advise them is the crucial role that markets play in generating products and services that would help consumers overcome their biases. When market efforts do come up in the discussion, advocates of policy nudges either dismiss markets as insufficient to solve problems or assume they will exploit consumers' weaknesses rather than correct them.[14]

In this volume, we attempt to remedy this shortcoming of the nudge literature by comparing and contrasting the two primary tools for behavior change: regulations and technology. As the chapters in this volume discuss, there is a wide array of products on the market that aim to help consumers make better decisions and improve their lives. Financial advisors and personal finance apps help consumers stay on track with their finances. Numerous diets and recently popular wearable technology tools help consumers reduce the negative impacts of excess weight. Similar to policy nudges, these tools increasingly incorporate behavioral insights to become more effective in helping consumers overcome their biased decision-making.

Given the competing role played by government regulations and private behavioral technologies in their attempts to help consumers make better choices, the two approaches warrant a closer examination. Regulators and private firms designing nudges face similar problems. They often lack the information they need to measure the underlying consumer bias and to design effective mechanisms to counter it. They also face thorny ethical issues when it comes to their ability to manipulate consumer behavior. Yet, regulators and private firms address these issues differently, which has significant impact on the effectiveness of each approach.

Part one of the book reviews each method and considers the ethical challenges that arise with both government and market nudges. In the opening chapter, Mark White provides a brief overview of behavioral economics and its use in public policy. White further summarizes the greatest challenges to the government's pursuit of policy ends through nudges, which he groups into epistemic, ethical, and practical categories. The main epistemic challenge stems from the policymakers' inability to determine whether a consumer's choice reflects true preference or biased decision-making. The main ethical challenge derives from the fact that by imposing a choice on consumers, nudges threaten their autonomy. On a practical level, White questions whether nudges can actually deliver the outcomes they promise.

Following the theme of epistemic challenges, Mario Rizzo's chapter outlines four necessary conditions for policymakers to be able to craft effective nudges. First, the policymakers have to know exactly what constitutes a rational choice for consumers under given circumstances. Second, they have to empirically demonstrate that consumers systematically deviate from the rational choice. Third, they need to be able to devise effective policies to counter consumers' biases. Fourth, these policies should not impose excessively high costs on consumers' welfare or freedom. Yet as Rizzo demonstrates, at each point, policymakers face substantial, if not insurmountable, epistemic challenges to satisfying these conditions.

Adam Thierer's chapter highlights uncertainty of a different kind— the long-term impact of nudge policy. In a cross-disciplinary overview, Thierer notes the crucial role that failure and learning play in advancing human progress. He expresses concern that a nudge policy framework that aims to eliminate all individual failure may have the unintended consequence of depriving individuals of critical life lessons and the ability to build up resilience in response to adverse circumstances. Thierer acknowledges that some failures may be catastrophic and genuinely warrant policy intervention. However, he points out the current academic literature fails to clearly delineate the cases that would justify policy intervention.

In contrast to preceding chapters, Steve Wendel turns attention to the private sector's use of behavioral technologies to help consumers change their behavior. He gives a brief overview of the private nudge industry that frequently aims to help consumers correct the same individual failures as public policy. Wendel outlines several challenges that face the private sector for nudges. First, high-quality behavioral research is uncommon and many studies are incomplete or contradictory. Second, the secrecy that typically surrounds product development in the private sector can hamper knowledge sharing among nudge practitioners. Third, the high level of sensitivity of nudges to specific context, implementation, and population characteristics often makes it difficult to apply behavioral research findings in a different context.

Going beyond the epistemic issues, Jody Beggs addresses the potential ethical challenges that may arise when private firms seek to change consumer behavior. Since private firms pursue profits rather than consumer welfare, their attempts to change consumer behavior may not necessarily benefit consumers. Beggs identifies two types of nudges. In the first category, which she calls Pareto nudges, the interests of consumers and companies align, and therefore, private nudges typically help consumers. In the second category are rent-seeking nudges in which companies benefit by exploiting consumers' biases. These nudges may help the company's bottom line but generally harm consumers. Yet, whether a nudge falls under one or the other category is not always clear. Given heterogeneity of consumer preferences and biases, the same nudge could help some consumers but harm others.

Finally, Sherzod Abdukadirov compares the private and public sectors in their ability to deal with epistemic challenges in order to produce effective nudges. Given the embryonic state of behavioral research and uncertainty that exists with regard to most behavioral intervention mechanisms, nudge designers have to rely on a trial-and-error process to weed out bad ideas and refine the promising nudges. While most private firms set up flexible innovation processes that allow for experimentation, the rigid regulatory process that governments have to follow makes the necessary experimentation extremely difficult. Consequently, regulatory nudges are more likely to fail.

Part two of the book includes four case studies that examine the effectiveness of government and market nudges in specific policy areas.

Michael Marlow discusses the use of nudges to counter the growing obesity epidemic. Given the many difficulties facing government and market nudge designers, Marlow finds that nudges are a rather blunt instrument to encourage consumers to lose weight. Yet comparing the two, Marlow tentatively concludes that market nudging efforts may provide a more promising avenue for helping consumers make better dietary choices.

In a chapter devoted to nudges in the consumer finance sector, Adam Smith and Todd Zywicki question the quality of evidence for some common consumer biases that provoked regulatory responses. Echoing Thierer's concerns, Smith and Zywicki argue that markets are the product of an unguided evolutionary process, and consumer choices, even if not strictly rational, may represent adaptive behavior in response to circumstances. The authors refer to this as ecological rationality. They further point to a great deal of incentives for private firms to provide consumers with tools for better financial decision-making, leading them to question the rationale for regulatory interventions.

In their chapter, Sofie Miller and Brian Mannix examine the case for perhaps the most extensive government nudge policy—energy and fuel efficiency standards. Federal agencies imposing the standards justify them on the grounds that the standards correct present biased consumer behavior and ultimately save consumers money in future energy costs. In their critique, Miller and Mannix point out that a single standard cannot effectively serve the goals of consumers with varying preferences and discount rates. They note that the negative impacts of energy efficiency standards may fall disproportionately on the low-income consumers.

In the final case study, Robert Graboyes and Jessica Carges examine the impact of behavioral insights in healthcare. The authors point out that the field of healthcare is unique since the insights of behavioral economics merge with the two existing dominant streams of thought in healthcare: medical paternalism and progressivism. Medical paternalism refers to the longstanding tradition within the medical profession to discount patients' wishes and decision-making capacity, while progressivism refers to the bias toward government as opposed to market solutions in healthcare. The result is a highly precautionary environment where policymakers do not simply ignore market efforts to improve healthcare but actively restrict and forestall some of these solutions.

In the concluding chapter, Richard Williams makes the following observations with regard to the unbridled enthusiasm displayed by some government nudge advocates. Not all behavioral failures require government intervention; failure is frequently a useful learning mechanism that helps consumers make better decisions in the future. Heterogeneity among consumers makes it difficult to design nudges that would help broad segments of society. And the unintended consequences that frequently accompany most policies increase the potential cost of centralized intervention. In contrast, private firms designing nudges, while facing their own set of challenges, may be able to produce more effective and targeted nudges at a considerably lower cost than regulators.

A Note on Terminology

Given considerable disagreements over the role that behavioral economics ought to play in public policy, it is useful to define some of the common terms. In this book, discussions of paternalism refer specifically to new paternalism. New paternalism describes cases where governments enact policies that attempt to help individuals achieve goals that they set for themselves.[15] It is different from traditional paternalism in that the new paternalists do not attempt to impose their own views and agendas on individuals. Although, as later chapters explain, the distinction between the two often get blurred, since even with new paternalist policies it is typically the regulators who decide what goals are in consumers' best interest.

Antiobesity policies are a typical example of new paternalism. Most overweight and obese individuals want to lose weight and keep it off, but they find it extremely difficult to stick with the diet and exercise regimen given all the temptations that surround them. Policies like soda taxes or calorie disclosures attempt to help people who want to lose weight choose a better diet and achieve the long-term weight goals they set for themselves. In contrast, the ban on alcohol sales imposed during Prohibition is an example of traditional paternalism. In this case, paternalists imposed a policy that they thought was best for the American people, even if many Americans disagreed.

Some scholars make a further distinction between soft and hard paternalism. For example, behavioral economists, Richard Thaler and Cass Sunstein, popularized the term *nudge* in their influential book with the same title to refer to behaviorally informed government policies.[16] In that book and other works, the authors advocated for what they call libertarian paternalism.[17] The key feature of soft or libertarian paternalism is the ability of consumers to opt out of the paternalistic policy. In contrast to hard paternalism, which relies on coercion to push consumers toward better choices, soft paternalism exploits behavioral quirks to steer consumers in the right direction. For example, policymakers can exploit the natural human tendency to procrastinate to nudge them toward a given choice by setting it as a default. While consumers can easily opt out of the nudge and make a different choice, pervasive behavioral biases ensure that few consumers do.

In practice, the distinction is often blurred. Both soft and hard paternalism rely on a similar mechanism: they make bad choices more costly compared to good choices. The main difference is that in the case of soft paternalism, the costs attached to bad choices are considerably lower than in the case of hard paternalism. For example, opting out of a default choice requires consumers to exert mental effort—a relatively minor cost. In contrast, opting out of the mandatory energy efficiency standard would be very costly.

Yet, in some cases, the line between soft and hard paternalism is not clear. Consider the example of New York City's failed attempt to ban large-sized sodas.[18] The policy would prevent consumers from purchasing soda in 64 ounce containers. But consumer could still purchase two 32 ounce sodas to circumvent the ban. Whether the cost of opting out—the slightly higher price and added inconvenience—would qualify the policy as soft or hard paternalism is unclear. While some of the measure's proponents viewed it as a nudge,[19] Thaler emphatically disagreed.[20]

More to the point, many paternalist policies inspired by Thaler and Sunstein's influential book take both a soft and a hard paternalistic approach. As chapters in this volume discuss, energy standards often coexist with energy labeling requirements and sugar taxes go hand in hand with calorie disclosure requirements. To cover the full range of policies attempting to deal with consumer biases, this book will discuss both soft and hard paternalistic policies and refer to all behaviorally informed regulations as nudges.

Finally, the discussion of behavioral economics in policy often conflates the concepts of new paternalism and behavioral design.[21] Both use behavioral insights into the psychology of human decision-making but they employ these insights for different purposes. Behavioral design does not seek to achieve a particular goal. Its aim is to make consumer products or government policies more efficient by designing them with consumer behavior in mind. It does so by removing friction from the process and making it as effortless as possible.

For example, in the UK, Her Majesty's Revenue and Customs department partnered with the Behavioral Insights Team to develop mechanisms to improve tax debt collection.[22] In one field experiment, they sent letters to taxpayers informing them that most people in their neighborhood have already paid their taxes. Thus, the department exploited the power of social norms to improve tax return compliance. The program did not seek to improve consumer welfare, be that from the point of view of consumer or regulators, but rather to improve the effectiveness of a government program. While this is certainly an important area for discussion, this book will focus mainly on the use of behavioral economics toward paternalist goals.

NOTES

1. Marshall David Sahlins, *Stone Age Economics* (New York: Aldine de Gruyter, 1974); Richard Barry Lee, "What Hunters Do for a Living, or, How to Make Out on Scarce Resources," in *Man the Hunter*, ed. Richard Barry Lee and Irven DeVore (New York: Aldine de Gruyter, 1968), 30–48.
2. See Sheena Iyengar, *The Art of Choosing* (New York: Twelve, 2011).
3. Sendhil Mullainathan and Eldar Shafir, *Scarcity: The New Science of Having Less and How It Defines Our Lives* (New York: Times Books, 2013).
4. Maryam Kouchaki and Isaac H. Smith, "The Morning Morality Effect: The Influence of Time of Day on Unethical Behavior," *Psychological Science* 25(1) (January 1, 2014): 95–102; Brian C. Gunia, Christopher M. Barnes, and Sunita Sah, "The Morality of Larks and Owls: Unethical Behavior Depends on Chronotype as Well as Time of Day," *Psychological Science* 25(12) (December 1, 2014): 2272–2274.
5. Anandi Mani et al. "Poverty Impedes Cognitive Function," *Science* 341(6149) (August 30, 2013): 976–980; Louise Vreugdenburg, Janet Bryan, and Eva Kemps, "The Effect of Self-Initiated Weight-Loss Dieting on Working Memory: The Role of Preoccupying Cognitions," *Appetite* 41(3) (December 2003): 291–300.
6. Richard H. Thaler and Cass R. Sunstein, *Nudge: Improving Decisions About Health, Wealth, and Happiness* (New Haven: Yale University Press, 2008); Saugato Datta and Sendhil Mullainathan, "Behavioral

Design: A New Approach to Development Policy," *Review of Income and Wealth* 60(1) (2014): 7–35.

7. e.g. Cass R. Sunstein, *Why Nudge?* (New Haven: Yale University Press, 2014); Jason F. Shogren and Laura O. Taylor, "On Behavioral-Environmental Economics," *Review of Environmental Economics & Policy* 2(1) (January 2008): 26–44.

8. Alicia H. Munnell, Wenliang Hou, and Anthony Webb, *NRRI Update Shows Half Still Falling Short*, Center for Retirement Research, Boston College Issue Brief 14–20 (Boston, MA, December 2014), Boston, MA, http://crr.bc.edu/briefs/nrri-update-shows-half-still-falling-short/

9. Centers for Disease Control and Prevention, *Health, United States, 2014*, Centers for Disease Control and Prevention Report DHHS 2015–1232 (Washington, DC, May 2015), 215, Washington, DC, http://www.cdc.gov/nchs/data/hus/hus14.pdf

10. John B. Dixon, "The Effect of Obesity on Health Outcomes," *Molecular and Cellular Endocrinology* 316 (2010): 104–8.

11. Meera Viswanathan et al. "Interventions to Improve Adherence to Self-Administered Medications for Chronic Diseases in the United States: A Systematic Review," *Annals of Internal Medicine* 157(11) (December 4, 2012): 785–795.

12. "Executive Order 13707: Using Behavioral Science Insights to Better Serve the American People," *Federal Register* 80(181) (September 18, 2015): 56365–56367.

13. David Halpern, *Inside the Nudge Unit: How Small Changes Can Make a Big Difference* (London: Ebury Publishing, 2015).

14. See e.g. Sunstein, *Why Nudge?*

15. Mario J. Rizzo and Douglas Glen Whitman, "The Knowledge Problem of New Paternalism," *Brigham Young University Law Review* (4) (2009): 905–968.

16. Thaler and Sunstein, *Nudge*.

17. Ibid.; Richard H. Thaler and Cass R. Sunstein, "Libertarian Paternalism," *The American Economic Review* 93(2) (May 1, 2003): 175–179.

18. The New York City Obesity Task Force, *Reversing the Epidemic: The New York City Obesity Task Force Plan to Prevent and Control Obesity* (New York, NY, May 31, 2012), New York, NY, http://www.nyc.gov/html/om/pdf/2012/otf_report.pdf

19. Oliver Burkeman, "How Bloomberg's Soda Ban Is a Classic Example of 'Choice Architecture,'" *The Guardian*, July 10, 2012,

http://www.theguardian.com/commentisfree/oliver-burkemans-blog/2012/jul/10/bloomberg-soda-ban-new-york-freedom

20. Richard H. Thaler, "To State the Obvious: A BAN Is Not a NUDGE. The Opposite in Fact. So Don't Blame Bloomberg's Ban on Large Soda Cups on Us.," Twitter, @R_Thaler, May 31, 2012, https://twitter.com/R_Thaler/status/208273339507150849

21. In fact, Thaler and Sunstein are guilty of this as well. One of their most cited examples is about the use of defaults to increase organ donation—a policy designed to promote a societal, not personal welfare. See Thaler and Sunstein, *Nudge*.

22. Behavioural Insights Team, *Applying Behavioural Insights to Reduce Fraud, Error and Debt* (London, UK, February 2012), London, UK, https://www.gov.uk/government/uploads/system/uploads/attachment_data/file/60539/BIT_FraudErrorDebt_accessible.pdf

PART I

Theory

Overview of Behavioral Economics and Policy

Mark D. White

As philosophers have long recognized, human beings are imperfect and often make bad choices that have a negative impact on themselves and other people. Sometimes we recognize our own mistakes, and sometimes other people bring them to our attention. In the best case scenario we learn from our mistakes, but sometimes we need institutions to guide us to better ones, whether those come in the form of mentors to give us advice on how to live better lives or the state enforcing laws to protect citizens from each other.

In recent years, however, the emphasis of these institutions has changed in two significant ways. First, the focus has shifted from choices and their consequences to how we make those choices in the first place. Psychologists and economists have subjected the process of decision-making to new scrutiny, and their innovative and fascinating research revealed quirks and anomalies in how we process information and weigh options. Idealized models of "rational choice" are gradually being replaced by new conceptions of decision-making that incorporate empirical evidence of psychological imperfections. Put simply, we seem to know more about *why* we make bad choices as well as *how* we might make better ones.

M.D. White (✉)
College of Staten Island/CUNY, Staten Island, NY, USA

© The Editor(s) (if applicable) and The Author(s) 2016
S. Abdukadirov (ed.), *Nudge Theory in Action*,
DOI 10.1007/978-3-319-31319-1_2
15

Second, policymakers in government absorbed this new research and began to incorporate it into regulation and policymaking itself. Some uses were oriented toward public policy ends, such as making recycling bins more attractive (to promote proper disposal of waste) and painting flies in urinals (to reduce clean-up costs in public restrooms).[1] But policymakers also began to use behavioral insights to help people make better decisions for *themselves*, which can be characterized as paternalistic and is therefore subject to disagreement from those who believe a government's proper role is to protect citizens from others, not from themselves.

As Gerald Dworkin defines it, paternalism is "the interference of a state or an individual with another person, against their will, and defended or motivated by a claim that the person interfered with will be better off or protected from harm."[2] While this definition covers paternalistic acts by individuals, the focus of this chapter is on paternalistic interventions on the part of the state. The canonical statement against paternalism was provided by John Stuart Mill in what came to be known as the "harm principle":

> The only purpose for which power can be rightfully exercised over any member of a civilized community, against his will, is to prevent harm to others. His own good, either physical or moral, is not a sufficient warrant. He cannot rightfully be compelled to do or forbear because it will be better for him to do so, because it will make him happier, because, in the opinions of others, to do so would be wise, or even right.... The only part of the conduct of any one, for which he is amenable to society, is that which concerns others. In the part which merely concerns himself, his independence is, of right, absolute. Over himself, over his own body and mind, the individual is sovereign.[3]

However, the new psychological insights into decision-making have led academics and policymakers to doubt that people regularly make decisions reliably in their own interests, which in turn motivated a more active role of government in helping people pursue those interests.[4]

In this chapter, I will summarize the development, key results, and main applications of the new behavioral science to government paternalism. Then I will offer several criticisms of this new brand of paternalism, focusing on the lack of knowledge among policymakers regarding people's true interests and the nature of the manipulation inherent in such behavioral interventions. Lastly, I will survey private uses of these psychological insights, including private alternatives to government interventions, the topic of many of the chapters in this book.

BEHAVIORAL SCIENCE AND CHOICE

For decades, mainstream economics enjoyed a broad consensus regarding its model of individual decision-making, known as *expected utility maximization* or *constrained preference-satisfaction*.[5] This standard choice model allowed economists to explain and predict typical economic behavior such as consumption, production, and investment decisions, in addition to noneconomic topics such as marriage and childbearing decisions, criminal activity, and discriminatory hiring.[6] This model consists of several simple elements, which I will describe briefly before introducing recent behavioral critiques of them.

First, a person has a set of preferences, a ranking of states of the world over which he or she has some choice, such as which size of laundry detergent to buy, which company to invest in, and which job to take. These preferences are normally assumed to be "given" to the individual and do not change (an assumption arising less from a principled conviction and more from a desire for parsimony, as well as humility regarding our knowledge of the nature of preference change).[7] Furthermore, they are substantively empty: rather than stemming from a psychological state such as desire or need, they are ideally taken to be "revealed" by behavior, whatever their ultimate source may be. As long as a person's preferences meet basic formal conditions such as consistency and completeness, they can be represented by a "utility function" that represents to what degree the person's preferences are satisfied.[8]

Second, persons are faced with certain constraints that limit satisfaction of their preferences. These normally take the form of material resource constraints, such as scarcity of wealth or capital, or limitations on the time available to "spend" on various activities (such as in labor supply decisions). Like preferences, constraints are often assumed to be exogenous, although some can be based on earlier choices; for instance, wealth is based both on initial endowments and later choices about work and investment.

Third, individuals are assumed to have sets of beliefs over the likelihood of various uncertain states of the world. These include beliefs about themselves, such as which options will satisfy their preferences, as well as beliefs about external events, such as whether it will rain on their cousin's wedding day. Sometimes the two types of beliefs combine, such as whether a person will be able to adjust comfortably to living in a new city where she is considering taking a job. These probabilities, often based on subjective judgment about uncertainty rather than precise objective risk, are used in the decision-making process to discount the amount of utility a person will derive from each state of the world.

These three elements together define decision-makers' "problem": maximizing their expected utility, based on their preferences and beliefs, within their constraints. This model grounded nearly the entirety of microeconomic theory until theoretical and empirical research by decision theorists and psychologists questioned its real-world applicability. For example, in the 1950s, Herbert Simon introduced the concept of *bounded rationality*, which encapsulated the imperfections of and limitations on human rationality. As Simon described the standard model of choice, the agent

> is assumed to have knowledge of the relevant aspects of his environment which, if not absolutely complete, is at least impressively clear and voluminous. He is assumed also to have a well-organized and stable system of preferences, and a skill in computation that enables him to calculate, for the alternative courses of action that are available to him, which of these will permit him to reach the highest attainable point on his preference scale.[9]

As an alternative, Simon introduced the concept of *satisficing*, in which an individual facing a difficult choice lacks either the time or the mental capacity to select the perfectly optimal decision, and instead optimizes these scarce resources by making a decision that is "good enough" (or satisfactory).[10] In this way, the person meets some internal threshold of preference-satisfaction even though it may not be the choice he or she would make with infinite time and computing power. Now a significant topic of study by economists, psychologists, and philosophers alike, Simon's concept of satisficing was the first major challenge to the standard economic model of choice, which was revealed to be an abstract mathematical ideal that neglected to consider or incorporate the limited decision-making capacities of real human beings.[11]

Simon's bounded rationality emphasizes the limits of our deliberative and executive faculties: that our rationality and willpower are limited and do not always operate as predicted by textbook models of decision-making. Later, psychologists led by Daniel Kahneman and Amos Tversky added details and nuance to Simon's ideas, supported by years of psychological experiments.[12] These researchers identified a number of common cognitive biases, dysfunctions, and heuristics that cause decision-making processes to differ from the ideal textbook depictions. For example, the *endowment effect* describes the phenomenon by which people place more value on an item when it is in their possession than when it is not. This is also related to *loss aversion*, by which people feel more harmed by a loss of given magnitude than they are helped by an identical gain. So we would rather give up $100 that we never received than lose $100 we have, and we would demand more money to part with an item we owe than we would have paid to get it in the first place. Also, *hyperbolic discounting* explains why our preferences seem to change over time, and why an unpleasant event (such as a root canal) that a person has no problem scheduling six months from now seems much worse the day before it is set to happen; this is very useful to modeling weakness of will, especially with regard to procrastination.[13]

These cognitive biases affect our preferences, from which, in the traditional model of choice, values are derived. Other findings from behavioral research address how we incorporate new information into our set of beliefs. Instead of simply updating our beliefs with any new information we acquire, we do so in a way that privileges some information over other. For example, *confirmation bias* implies that we give more attention and weight to new information that confirms our current beliefs (and less attention and weight to information that challenges them); this can be seen in choices of news sources, in which people often choose cable news stations that confirm their preexisting political positions. *Optimism bias*, as the name suggests, describes our propensity to maintain exaggerated beliefs about ourselves and our futures; this can be illustrated by the "it can't happen to me" effect when hearing mortality rates about smoking, and the statistic that well over 50 % of people think they are above average drivers (which is unlikely if we assume a fairly symmetrical distribution of driving skill).

Most relevant for the discussion of nudges, behavioral studies also demonstrate the power of *framing* in influencing how we make choices, which implies quirks in how both our preferences and information are affected. For example, patients are more optimistic when told that a procedure has a survival rate of 90 % than when they are told that it has a mortality rate of 10 %, a result that reflects the emotional impact of how a choice is framed. We see this also when there is a widely publicized plane crash and more people take road trips, despite the much higher mortality rate on the highway, because of the visceral impact of the news. Finally, marketers are testaments to framing effects, expert at promoting products in order to increase sales.[14]

BEHAVIORAL ECONOMICS AND NUDGE POLICY

In recent years, *behavioral economists* have been incorporating the numerous insights of Kahneman, Tversky, and their colleagues into standard models of choice and experiments of their own. One of the pioneers of behavioral economics, Richard Thaler, explained a number of "anomalies" in economic behavior with the new behavioral science, and also developed the area of *behavioral finance*, showing how financial decision-making is affected by psychological quirks that interfere with the flawless mathematical precision previously assumed to be the hallmark of finance.[15] Other behavioral economists examined how procrastination arises from rational actors acting under the influence of various cognitive flaws and dysfunctions.[16] Finally, experimental economists such as Vernon Smith have tested the predictions of many mainstream models of choice and observed results consistent with behavioral economics, particularly when it comes to the pursuit of self-interest. In the realm of game theory, for instance, participants in situations such as the Ultimatum game are "supposed to" reveal self-interest but instead display altruistic behavior, even toward other players who are strangers and are not expected to reciprocate.[17]

It did not take long for the models of behavioral economics to be applied to the policy realm, initiated by legal scholars working in the hybrid field of *behavioral law and economics*.[18] Scholars in this field studied not only how the various cognitive biases and dysfunctions identified by psychologists affected legal outcomes, such as jury decisions, contract formation, and even judges' opinions, but they also suggested ways that those same decision-making anomalies could be harnessed to *improve* outcomes in all areas of policy, including both general outcomes, such as recycling efforts and organ donation, as well as more individual-focused efforts, such as retirements savings and weight loss.

In 2008, behavioral economist Richard Thaler and legal scholar Cass Sunstein published their book *Nudge*, presenting their earlier academic work on behaviorally based policy interventions to a broader audience.[19] According to them:

> It is legitimate ... to try to influence people's behavior in order to make their lives longer, healthier, and better. In other words, we argue for self-conscious efforts, by institutions in the private sector and also by government, to steer people's choices in directions that will improve their lives.[20]

interesting

In this spirit, Thaler and Sunstein advocate for *nudges*, which they define as "any aspect of the choice architecture that alters people's behavior in a predictable way without forbidding any options or significantly changing their economic incentives."[21] As opposed to traditional paternalist tools such as mandates, bans, taxes, and subsidies, which affect the material availability or price of choices, nudges are changes to the choice environment (or *choice architecture*) around options, using the same cognitive biases and dysfunctions that motivate them to steer people toward choices that better serve their interests. Because choices themselves are not affected, nudge advocates regard their brand of paternalism as "libertarian" in the sense that it is more respectful of individual autonomy and liberty because people are free to make the same (allegedly inferior) choices they would have made without the nudge.

Thaler and Sunstein give many examples of nudges in their academic and popular work, but there are several well-known examples they emphasize throughout. In one, a manager of a cafeteria in an office building is tasked with arranging the food items.[22] To promote healthy eating among the workers in the building without foreclosing any options, the manager chooses to put healthier options at the front of the shelf and in the best light, to take advantage of people's propensity toward laziness and the illusion of well-lit items as being tastier. While customers are free to take the poorly lit and hard-to-reach puddings, the manager takes advantage of their behavioral quirks to guide them toward healthier choices.

In another example, employers (or policymakers acting through them) are concerned that employees are not saving enough for retirement—in particular, they are not taking advantage of 401(k) plans, contributions to which are not only tax exempt but are often matched by employers.[23] The forms that new employees fill out at human resources typically require active choice to enroll in such a program; in other words, the default choice is nonenrollment (also known as "opt-in"). Because studies show that people often defer to the default choice on a form (either through active or passive choice), employers who want to promote savings can switch the default choice to enrollment (also known as "opt-out"). In doing so, they leverage people's unthinking acceptance of the default choice by switching the default to the option that they believe is in people's best interests.

Other nudges take the form of providing information, which works on several levels. One popular instance of this is mandatory nutritional labeling in restaurants. On the one hand, this provides information, which does not make use of cognitive biases or dysfunctions but rather enhances rational deliberation over choices. On the other hand, the specific nutritional details that are emphasized are implied to be the most important, triggering the *availability bias* that gives more weight to readily available information; a focus on fat content, for instance, may distract a food consumer from carbohydrate content, which he may regard as more important. A related example is the familiar nutritional labels on packaged food products, listing the amount of fat, carbohydrate, and other contents, which health advocates argue should be made more prominent and colorful, making use of cognitive biases behind framing effects to both grab consumers' attention and make information easier to digest.[24]

Problems with Nudges

The reasons to be concerned about nudges can be split into three categories: epistemic, ethical, and practical. These categories overlap to some extent, and the epistemic problems are the primary ones that lead to the most significant ethical and practical problems. All three, however, combine to paint a different picture of nudges than the one offered by advocates of this new brand of paternalism.[25]

(a)   The epistemic problem with nudges derives from the inability of policymakers to know the true interests of the people being nudged. Certainly, nudge designers have some idea of the interests they wish to promote with behavioral interventions: in Thaler and Sunstein's examples, cafeterias are designed to promote healthy eating and default enrollment in retirement plans is meant to promote savings. Policymakers do not know, however, if these nudges promote the true interests of any given individual, much less that of the population in general. Health and wealth are of interest to all in a very general and trivial way, but each person interprets them and combines them in different ways with other important interests, reflecting a complexity about which policymakers have no knowledge. Based on economic models of choice which normally posit a single end or goal, policymakers have a narrow, myopic view of interests that individuals pursue, which in turn limits the goals of nudges.

Whereas nudges focus on promoting one vague interest, such as health or wealth, individuals have a multiplicity of interests that combine in various ways according to the context of each choice situation. They care about material prosperity in some way, but each has his or her own goals with respect to wealth as well as ways they prefer to pursue it; the same goes for health or any other general goal assumed by policymakers.

Furthermore, they have other interests that coincide or compete with pursuing their individual conceptions of wealth or health. Some are very personal interests, such as other individual goals that may represent success more than wealth does, or simply a desire to live life to the fullest, even if that compromises a single-minded focus on simpler goals. People also have interests in other people's well-being, happiness, and success, and often sacrifice their own personal interests to help others. Finally, individuals have interests in principles and ideals, whether personal or societal. People limit their pursuit of self-interest according to their moral codes, refusing to lie or steal even when it would benefit them (or others). They also sacrifice their own well-being—and sometimes even their lives—in the service of ideals such as justice, equality, or freedom. The variety of interests that individuals pursue reflects their multifaceted nature, and the ways that they combine in different circumstances shows their overall complexity. While people may have many interests of different kinds, they do not necessarily pursue all of them in every decision-making context. Sometimes they make decisions according to simple preferences, and other times they take the wider social impact of the decisions into account.

As a result of the multifaceted and complex nature of interests, nudges designed to promote one interest, even if it is an interest held by an individual, will have unintended and possibly adverse effects on other interests that the individual may value just as much—if not more—than the one targeted by the nudge. Interventions to increase retirement savings, for example, may negatively affect individuals' other goals, financial or otherwise. Nudges to lower fat intake may end up increasing individuals' consumptions of sugar, which may be of greater concern to them. It is easy to say that people can simply avoid nudges that are not in their interests, but the subtle way that nudges work makes this difficult (as we will discuss below). Without an appreciation of the complexity of individuals' interests, a policymaker cannot anticipate how a nudge in one area will affect other parts of their lives.

Even if policymakers did appreciate the complex and multifaceted nature of interests, they have no access to information regarding them because interests are inherently subjective. Choices that they see as imprudent or "mistaken" may very well advance the true interests of the people making them. People themselves are often unaware of the full range of their interests; many recent studies suggest that people are poor estimators of their own well-being or of how much satisfaction they will derive from various choices.[26] Nonetheless, individuals have a firmer grasp on the various interests on which they make decisions than an outside observer does, especially disinterested ones such as researchers or policymakers who have no way to know any person's true interests. John Stuart Mill put this well when he wrote:

> The strongest of all the arguments against the interference of the public with purely personal conduct is that, when it does interfere, the odds are that it interferes wrongly, and in the wrong place. On questions of social morality, of duty to others, the opinion of the public, that is, of an overruling majority, though often wrong, is likely to be still oftener right; because on such questions they are only required to judge of their own interests; of the manner in which some mode of conduct, if allowed to be practiced, would affect themselves. But the opinion of a similar majority, imposed as a law on the minority, on questions of self-regarding conduct, is quite as likely to be wrong as right; for in these cases public opinion means, at the best, some people's opinion of what is good or bad for other people.[27]

Because of this ignorance of people's true interests, policymakers who judge that people's choices are "mistaken" are basing this judgment on interests they have decided are appropriate or "obvious." Furthermore, these are the same interests that form the basis for nudges designed to "correct" these bad choices, interests that are defined vaguely enough to be of *some* possible relevance to most people but closely correspond to no one's true interests, much less to the degree that they matter to any one person.

This imposition of interests is one of the key ethical problems with nudges: it violates a core principle of modern democracies, *liberal neutrality*, which maintains that individuals have the right to pursue their own ideas of the good life, provided they do not wrongfully interfere with the rights of others to do the same. Again, John Stuart Mill provided the definitive statement:

> As it is useful that while mankind are imperfect there should be different opinions, so it is that there should be different experiments in living; that free scope should be given to varieties of character, short of injury to others; and that the worth of different modes of life should be proved practically, when any one thinks fit to try them. It is desirable, in short, that in things which do not primarily concern others, individuality should assert itself.[28]

At its most essential, liberal neutrality implies a person's right to make choices in his or her own interests as the person understands them, not as

a policymaker defines them. Paternalism of any type violates liberal neutrality and the personal autonomy it protects; as philosopher Dan Brock
wrote,

> Paternalistic interference involves the claim of one person to know better
> what is good for another person than that other person him- or herself
> does. It involves the substitution by the paternalistic interferer of his or her
> conception of what is good for another for that other's own conception of
> his or her good. If this involves a claim to know the objectively correct con-
> ception of another's good—what ultimate values and aims define another
> competent individual's good, independent of whether that other accepts
> them—then it is ethically problematic.[29]

This is widely recognized as a criticism of traditional paternalist policies
such as bans or taxes that limit or modify choices, but nudge advocates
argue that it does not apply to mere alterations to choice architecture,
such as changing arrangement of options or default choices that do not
foreclose choices.

However, this argument ignores the way that nudges work: by making
use of the same cognitive biases and dysfunctions that motivated them in
the first place. For example, enrolling new employees in retirement plans
by default is effective at increasing savings because default choices have
an outsized impact on choices, not because it inspires better decision-
making. Another choice is still possible, but the cognitive defects on which
nudges rely make other choices more difficult to make. Furthermore, this
is not an incidental effect of nudges but the basis on which they operate,
as demonstrated by their success in altering choices. For example, Thaler
and Sunstein point to the enormous increase in 401(k) enrollment under
an opt-out plan.[30] This cannot be taken as evidence that people are making
better choices in their true interests, but merely a testament to the effectiveness of designed defaults at influencing choice.

In this way, nudges threaten autonomy on two different scales: by
imposing policymaker's idea of interests for people's own, thereby interfering with people's long-term pursuit of their vision of the good life,
and also by influencing their smaller day-to-day decisions and the way
people make them. While traditional paternalism may affect choices, such
as by increasing the cost of certain options, it leaves people free to make
their choice without interfering with their decision-making process itself.
Nudges do not engage people's rational deliberative faculties, however,

but instead subvert them, relying on cognitive biases and dysfunctions to circumvent rational choice. The cafeteria manager's rearrangement of food items is not meant to convince her customers of the importance of making healthy choices; it relies on subtle psychological effects to steer them toward choices she thinks are better for them. This can be seen even more directly in the manipulation of default choices, which takes advantage of simple laziness and inertia to guide choice rather than inspiring deeper consideration of the various options. In this way, the interference with choice is not simply in terms of results but also process, which, as we will see, has longer-term ramifications for our cognitive abilities themselves.

Finally, the epistemic problem implies that, in practical terms, nudges cannot do what they claim: to help people make better choices in their own interests. Policymakers may sincerely want to help people improve their lives along some general measures such as health or wealth, but they cannot promote the true complex and multifaceted interests of which they have no knowledge. As Mario Rizzo and Glen Whitman wrote, comparing the knowledge problem in nudge policy with Friedrich von Hayek's arguments against government planning based on similar issues:

> If well-meaning policymakers possess all the relevant information about individuals' true preferences, their cognitive biases, and the choice contexts in which they manifest themselves, *then* policymakers could potentially implement paternalist policies that improve the welfare of individuals by their own standards. But lacking such information, we cannot conclude that actual paternalism will make their decisions better; under a wide range of circumstances, it will even make them worse.[31]

Furthermore, by promoting the interests they have chosen, policymakers are interfering with individuals' pursuit of their own interests in ways that cannot easily be resisted, given the subtle methods by which nudges operate.

This failure of nudges to achieve their stated aim is their most basic practical shortcoming, but it is not the only adverse effect of nudges, the most important of which may be their long-term impact on deliberative processes.[32] As we have discussed, the goal of nudges is to steer people toward better choices, not to improve their faculties of decision-making. As legal scholar and federal judge Richard Posner wrote of nudge paternalists, "all their suggestions for legal reform are of devices for getting around, rather than dispelling, our irrational tendencies."[33] As stated above, altering the choice architecture does not engage the rational deliberation but rather subverts it by steering individuals' choices, often without people being aware of the nudge. Rather than acting to lessen the impact of cognitive biases and dysfunctions and bring decision-making closer to the textbook model of rationality, nudges rely on these cognitive anomalies to achieve the policymaker's desired outcome without addressing the core cause of the problem.

Furthermore, the inability of people to make mistakes when nudged into "better choices" denies them the benefit of learning from one's mistakes, an essential tool of cognitive development of which every parent is well aware. Furthermore, the stagnation of decision-making processes will lead to more "bad choices" and therefore, the continued "need" for nudges, as legal scholars Jonathan Klick and Gregory Mitchell explain:

> Research on self-fulfilling prophecies warns that regulated parties are likely to become the weak decision-makers envisioned by paternalistic policy makers, as paternalistic regulations undercut personal incentives to invest in cognitive capital and the regulated parties conform to the expectancies of the paternalist.[34]

The reasonable alternative is to help people to overcome their decision-making flaws to make better choices in their own interests; as another legal scholar, Jeffrey Rachlinski, writes, "The role of individual learning and adaptation ... cannot be ignored in assessing the need for paternalism. Simple experience might, in some contexts, be a much better cure for cognitive missteps than adopting a paternalist intervention."[35]

BEHAVIORAL SCIENCE IN THE PRIVATE SECTOR

To this point, we have discussed behavioral interventions and nudges mostly in the context of government policymakers acting in their idea of their citizens' interests. However, such tools are used not only by the state but also by private parties for their own purposes. In this section, I will introduce two general ways in which private parties use behavioral insights (each of which will be discussed at length in other chapters in this book): firms using them on consumers in order to increase profits and individuals using them on themselves to circumvent their own cognitive flaws and dysfunctions.

Profit-Maximizing Behavioral Interventions

Long before the advent of modern behavioral research, private companies—especially retailers, advertisers, and marketers—relied on intuitive behavioral insights to sell their products.[36] Advertisers use emotional appeals to make products as banal as soda seem like the key to popularity and esteem. Experts who design the floor plans for supermarkets strategically place the most profitable items around the periphery of the store and impulse purchases near the checkout line. Contracts for large purchases or loans are written to obscure details to which consumers may object while drawing attention to the low price or interest rate. If government nudges are to be characterized as manipulative, subverting people's rational faculties to obtain a desired result, private companies may be the masters at the practice.

Despite the similarities in the manipulative tactics employed by both, there is a critical difference in the use of behavioral interventions by the government and private companies: their purpose or goal. Despite their psychological subtlety, the underlying ethical problem with government nudges is the same as with traditional state paternalism: the attempt to influence people's behavior *in their own interests*, whether policymakers have knowledge of those interests or not. When people's choices are steered in their own interests (or policymakers' idea of them), they are blocked from making those choices themselves. As John Stuart Mill pointed out, the proper role of government is to protect citizens from each other, not from themselves; a person's well-being and other interests are the concern and legitimate domain of that person only.

Behavioral interventions on the part of private companies, however, are not designed to benefit their customer's interests, but those of the owners of the company, interests which are usually assumed to be primarily to increase profit. Advertising companies do not cast young beautiful people in their beer commercials simply to make their customers feel good about themselves and the product—they want to make their customers feel good so they will buy more beer. Supermarkets are designed the way they are to exploit well-known cognitive biases and dysfunctions among shoppers to maximize the store's profit. In other words, private companies are not acting paternalistically when they use behavioral insights to change consumers' behavior; firms do not assume any interests on the part of the consumers because they are using behavioral interventions to promote their own.

Ironically, the self-serving nature of behavioral interventions among private companies makes them less problematic than when government policymakers nudge people ostensibly in their own interests. The element of manipulation is the same, but this is not the primary concern with government nudges anyway; for instance, nudges designed to promote collective goals such as recycling or organ donation are less troubling than nudges designed to help people eat better for their own health because they assume no knowledge of individuals' own interests.[37] The critical issue with public nudges is paternalism, the presumptive usurpation of decision-making autonomy in people's own interests, an aspect that is absent from behavioral interventions used by companies to increase profit. Manipulation that impairs people's use of their full rational faculties is a concern when anyone engages in it, but even more so when it is used to steer people's choices in interests that were chosen for them.

Furthermore, people *expect* private companies—again, especially retailers, advertisers, and marketers—to use whatever means they can to sell their products (outside of fraud). Customers are conditioned to be skeptical of outrageous claims, and they expect subtle psychological techniques to be used. There is room for criticism of the manipulation involved, but no one is surprised that companies intent on making a profit use whatever means they can, within the law, to do that—and if they do not like the manipulation they perceive, they are free to take their business to competitors they believe are less manipulative. But most people, regardless of their views on the size and scope of government, do not expect their government to practice manipulation, especially when designed to promote their own interests. (Also, unlike the private case, there is often no competitor that citizens can switch to in order to avoid government manipulation.) As Edward Glaeser wrote, using the word "persuasion" in the sense of subversion of rational deliberation, "Persuasion lies at the heart of much of [nudge policy], and it is not obvious that we want governments to become more adept at persuading voters or for governments to invest in infrastructure that will support persuasion."[38]

Individual, Self-Focused Nudges

The other way in which private agents can make use of behavioral insights is to improve their own lives by countering or leveraging their own cognitive biases and dysfunctions to make better decisions in their own interests.[39] This can take various forms, including self-motivated correctional behavior, cooperation involving a number of people, or commercial products that help people better manage their decision-making.

In the first case, people can recognize common flaws in their own decision-making and take measures to either combat them or make use of them. This can take the form of simple steps, such as the common advice not to go grocery shopping while hungry when one would be more likely to succumb to temptation to buy junk food. Other examples include the procrastinator who spends too much time surfing the Internet instead of completing projects and so takes steps to minimize her distractions before starting work (such as finding a spot with no Internet connection), or the person who wants to exercise first thing in the morning and so lays out his workout clothes the night before, exploiting his natural tendency toward laziness and giving him one less excuse to put it off. All of these examples involve individuals recognizing circumstances that interfere with pursuing their own goals, particularly "in the moment," and then taking steps to avoid them before those circumstances occur, or leveraging them—as government nudges do—to help further their goals.

These efforts are often more successful when engaged in with other people. Individuals can all too easily make excuses to themselves for why they did not exercise or work as planned, but they may feel more obligation to other people with whom they promised to exercise or work. For example, common advice for people trying to maintain a regular exercise schedule is to commit to work out with a friend; writers who need help making deadlines often form reading groups to which they are responsible to share something at regular meetings. This type of *social scaffolding* to help combat lack of willpower can also be organized by nonprofits, such as support groups for recovering addicts, or be commercialized, as in the case of programs such as Weight Watchers.

Weight Watchers is also an example of third-party initiatives to help people overcome cognitive biases or dysfunctions. For example, many firms offer monitoring devices, such as FitBit and word count trackers, that allow individuals to keep track of their progress toward a goal (such as exercise and writing) and provide an incentive to maintain or increase the level of effort. The wealth of information counters many biases that are enabled by ignorance, such as confirmation and optimism biases that take advantage of limited information, and the regular notices or updates these products provide to counter natural tendencies to procrastinate or rationalize their failures of willpower. Some also provide rewards for reaching a short-term goal, such as a daily target for physical activity or a medallion for a certain length of sobriety, which satisfies individuals' desires for encouragement and recognition of progress.

Many of these private uses of behavioral science to further goals involve some element of manipulation, but the justification for the manipulation is much different than in the case of government nudges. As opposed to state paternalism, these private behavioral mechanisms are chosen voluntarily by individuals who seek out help making better decisions to further their interests. As with all decisions, people make good ones and bad ones, and this includes the choice to seek help making decisions. But the epistemic problem implies that individuals have better information regarding their own interests and failures to pursue them effectively, so self-initiated efforts to improve their decision-making are more likely to be helpful than government nudges imposed by policymakers based on interests assumed on behalf of individuals. Of course, this does not preclude the state from *offering* products and programs to help people make better decisions, just as firms and nonprofit firms do, but it does imply, as explained above, that forcing nudges on people without their knowledge or consent is not in their true interests and raises serious concerns regarding autonomy.

CONCLUSION

This chapter introduced and summarized some of the ethical and practical aspects of behavioral interventions on the part of the government as well as private parties such as individuals and firms. In the rest of this book, other scholars will explore these issues in more depth, starting with private efforts to improve decision-making, the extent of manipulation in marketing, and government efforts to influence choice in areas such as health care and consumer finance. While the subversion of rational processes of deliberation is an important issue to consider with respect to all behavioral interventions, it is the government's use of these measures to steer people's choices in their own interests that uniquely invokes the dangers of paternalism and the denial of personal autonomy to pursue one's idea of the good life. Behavioral interactions that are initiated and directed by decision-makers themselves, however, allow people to make better choices, either by overcoming or by leveraging their cognitive biases and dysfunctions, and more important, to do so in their own true interests.

NOTES

1. For a survey of such policy initiatives and the behavioral science relevant to them, see Peter John et al. *Nudge, Nudge, Think, Think: Experimenting with Ways to Change Civic Behaviour* (London: Bloomsbury Academic, 2011).
2. Gerald Dworkin, "Paternalism," *Stanford Encyclopedia of Philosophy*, June 4, 2014, at http://plato.stanford.edu/entries/paternalism/
3. John Stuart Mill, *On Liberty*, ed. D. Spitz (New York: W.W. Norton, 1975), 10–11.
4. For recent defenses of paternalism in general based on behavioral insights, see Cass Sunstein, *Why Nudge? The Politics of Libertarian Paternalism* (New Haven: Yale University Press, 2014), ch. 1; Sarah Conly, *Against Autonomy: Justifying Coercive Paternalism* (Cambridge: Cambridge University Press, 2013), 20–23. For a defense of Mill against their criticisms, see Mark D. White, "The Crucial Importance of Interests in Libertarian Paternalism," forthcoming in Klaus Mathis and Avishalom Tor (eds), *Nudging: Possibilities, Limitations and Applications in European Law and Economics* (Dordrecht: Springer, 2016), 21–38.
5. For a thorough treatment, see Shaun Hargreaves Heap et al. *The Theory of Choice: A Critical Guide* (Oxford: Blackwell, 1992).
6. Much of this work started with Gary Becker, *The Economic Approach to Human Behavior* (Chicago: University of Chicago Press, 1976).
7. On this, see Till Grüne-Yanoff and Sven Ove Hansson, *Preference Change: Approaches from Philosophy, Economics and Psychology* (Dordrecht: Springer, 2009).
8. Note, however, that the empty nature of preferences renders this concept of utility empty as well; it bears no relationship to meaningful concepts of utility as used as philosophers such as Jeremy Bentham or John Stuart Mill. See John Broome, "Utility," in *Ethics Out of Economics* (Cambridge: Cambridge University Press, 1999), pp. 19–28.
9. Herbert Simon, "A Behavioral Model of Rational Choice," *Quarterly Journal of Economics* 69 (1955): 99–118, at 99.
10. Herbert Simon, "Rational Choice and the Structure of the Environment," *Psychological Review* 63 (1956): 129–138. More recently, the idea of limitations on decision-making capacity suggests

the possibility of "too much choice," which has been emphasized by Barry Schwartz, *The Paradox of Choice: Why More Is Less* (New York: Harper, 2004), and Sheena Iyengar, *The Art of Choosing* (New York: Grand Central, 2010).

11. In a broader sense, satisficing may represent optimal decision-making in that it makes the best use of scarce decision-making resources, but in the narrower sense, it is still considered an alternative to optimizing.

12. Collections of this work include Daniel Kahneman, Paul Slovic, and Amos Tversky (eds), *Judgment Under Uncertainty: Heuristics and Biases* (Cambridge: Cambridge University Press, 1982); Kahneman and Tversky (eds), *Choices, Values, and Frames* (Cambridge: Cambridge University Press, 2000); and Thomas Gilovich, Dale Griffin, and Daniel Kahneman (eds), *Heuristics and Biases: The Psychology of Intuitive Judgment* (Cambridge: Cambridge University Press, 2002). For a recent summary, see Kahneman, *Thinking, Fast and Slow* (New York: Farrar, Straus and Giroux, 2011).

13. George Ainslie, *Breakdown of Will* (Cambridge: Cambridge University Press, 2001), and "Procrastination: The Basic Impulse," in Chrisoula Andreou and Mark D. White (eds.), *The Thief of Time: Philosophical Essays on Procrastination* (Oxford: Oxford University Press, 2010), 11–27.

14. For a summary, see Erik Angner, *A Course in Behavioral Economics*, 2nd edn (New York: Palgrave Macmillan, 2016). For an engaging popular treatment of these various cognitive biases, dysfunctions, and heuristics, see Dan Ariely, *Predictably Irrational: The Hidden Forces That Shape Our Decisions* (New York: Harper Perennial, 2010).

15. See Thaler's books *The Winner's Curse: Paradoxes and Anomalies of Economic Life* (Princeton: Princeton University Press, 1994), *Quasi-Rational Economics* (New York: Russell Sage Foundation, 1994), and his edited books, *Advances in Behavioral Finance* (New York: Russell Sage Foundation, 1993) and *Advances in Behavioral Economics, Volume II* (Princeton: Princeton University Press, 2005).

16. See George Akerlof, "Procrastination and Obedience," in *Explorations in Pragmatic Economics* (Oxford: Oxford University Press, 2005), 209–231; and Ted O'Donoghue and Matthew Rabin, "Doing It Now or Later," *American Economic Review* 89 (1999): 103–124 (the first of several papers by O'Donoghue and Rabin on the topic).

17. See, for instance, Charles R. Plott and Vernon L. Smith, *Handbook of Experimental Economics Results, Volume 1* (Amsterdam: North-Holland, 2008).

18. For seminal early work, see Cass Sunstein (ed.), *Behavioral Law & Economics* (Cambridge: Cambridge University Press, 2000), and Francesco Parisi and Vernon L. Smith (eds.), *The Law and Economics of Irrational Behavior* (Stanford: Stanford University Press, 2005).

19. Richard Thaler and Cass Sunstein, *Nudge: Improving Decisions About Health, Wealth, and Happiness* (New Haven: Yale University Press, 2008); their earlier academic work includes Sunstein and Thaler, "Libertarian Paternalism Is Not an Oxymoron," *University of Chicago Law Review* 70 (2001): 1159–1202, and Thaler and Sunstein, "Libertarian Paternalism," *American Economic Review Papers and Proceedings* 93 (2003): 175–179. Other work at the same time that advocated similar ideas includes Russell B. Korobkin and Thomas S. Ulen. "Law and Behavioral Science: Removing the Rationality Assumption from Law and Economics," *California Law Review* 88 (2000): 1051–1144; Colin Camerer et al, "Regulation for Conservatives: Behavioral Economics and the Case for 'Asymmetric Paternalism,'" *University of Pennsylvania Law Review* 151 (2003): 1211–1254; and Christine Jolls and Cass Sunstein, "Debiasing Through Law," *Journal of Legal Studies* 35 (2006): 199–241.

20. Thaler and Sunstein, *Nudge*, 5.

21. Ibid., 6.

22. Ibid., 1–3; Sunstein and Thaler, "Libertarian Paternalism Is Not an Oxymoron," 1164–1166.

23. Thaler and Sunstein, *Nudge*, ch. 6; Sunstein and Thaler, "Libertarian Paternalism Is Not an Oxymoron," 1172–1173.

24. See Ezekiel J. Emanuel, "Healthy Labels, Not Stealthy Labels," The New York Times, March 5, 2012, available at http://opinionator.blogs.nytimes.com/2012/03/05/healthy-labels-not-stealthy-labels/

25. For more detail on these problems, see Mark D. White, *The Manipulation of Choice: Ethics and Libertarian Paternalism* (New York: Palgrave Macmillan, 2013); for similar points, see also Riccardo Rebonato, *Taking Liberties: A Critical Examination of Libertarian Paternalism* (New York: Palgrave Macmillan, 2012).

26. See, in general, Daniel Gilbert, *Stumbling on Happiness* (New York: Vintage, 2005); for more detail, see George Loewenstein and David

Schkade, "Wouldn't It Be Nice? Predicting Future Feelings," in Daniel Kahneman, Ed Diener, and Norbert Schwarz (eds), *Well-Being: The Foundations of Hedonic Psychology* (New York: Russell Sage Foundation, 1999), 85–105; and Daniel Gilbert and Timothy D. Wilson, "Miswanting: Some Problems in the Forecasting of Future Affection States." in Joseph P. Forgas (ed.), *Feeling and Thinking: The Role of Affect in Social Cognition* (Cambridge: Cambridge University Press, 2000), 178–197.

27. Mill, *On Liberty*, 78.

28. Ibid., 54.

29. Dan W. Brock, "Paternalism and Autonomy," *Ethics* 98 (1988): 550–565, at 559.

30. Thaler and Sunstein, "Libertarian Paternalism Is Not an Oxymoron," 1172–1173.

31. Mario Rizzo and Glen Whitman, "The Knowledge Problem of New Paternalism," *Brigham Young University Law Review* (2009): 905–968, at 910; see also Friedrich von Hayek, "The Use of Knowledge in Society," in *Individualism and Economic Order* (Chicago: University of Chicago Press, 1948), 77–91.

32. For instance, see Jonathan Klick and Gregory Mitchell, "Government Regulation of Irrationality: Moral and Cognitive Hazards," *Minnesota Law Review* 90 (2006): 1620–1663.

33. Richard Posner, "Rational Choice, Behavioral Economics, and the Law," *Stanford Law Review* 50 (1998): 1551–1575, at 1575.

34. Klick and Mitchell, "Government Regulation of Irrationality," 1626–1627.

35. Jeffrey J. Rachlinski, "The Uncertain Psychological Case for Paternalism," *Northwestern University Law Review* 97 (2003): 1165–1225, at 1214.

36. See Martin Lindstrom, *Brandwashed: Tricks Companies Use to Manipulate Our Minds and Persuade Us to Buy* (New York: Crown, 2011) and *Buyology: Truth and Lies About Why We Buy* (New York: Crown, 2008); Ellen Ruppel Shell, *Cheap: The High Cost of Discount Culture* (New York: Penguin, 2009); William Poundstone, *Priceless: The Myth of Fair Value (and How to Take Advantage of It)* (New York: Hill and Wang, 2010); and Eduardo Porter, *The Price of Everything: Solving the Mystery of Why We Pay What We Do* (New York: Portfolio, 2011).

37. For more evidence regarding this use of nudges, see John et al. *Nudge, Nudge, Think, Think*; for skepticism regarding the ability of nudges to address large-scale social problems, see Evan Selinger and Kyle Powys Whyte, "Nudging Cannot Solve Complex Policy Problems," *European Journal of Risk Regulation* 1 (2012): 26–31.
38. Edward Glaeser, "Paternalism and Psychology," *University of Chicago Law Review* 73 (2006): 133–156, at 135.
39. This was the focus of Dan Ariely's follow-up to *Predictably Irrational* (see note 14), titled *The Upside of Irrationality: The Unexpected Benefits of Defying Logic at Work and at Home* (New York: Harper, 2010).

The Four Pillars of Behavioral Paternalism

Mario J. Rizzo

In the past 15 years there has been a great deal of discussion, both scholarly and popular, about behavioral economics, irrationality, and "new paternalism." But to my knowledge, no one has clearly presented the *structure of the argument* that links the failure of individuals to be rational in the standard economics sense to the desirability of paternalist policies. The purpose of this article is to fill that gap and to demonstrate the inability (thus far) of paternalists to make their case.

I shall organize the discussion around four propositions that must be advanced in order to make the overall argument for new paternalism based on behavioral economics. Each proposition is necessary to make the paternalist case. The failure to demonstrate any one of the propositions breaks the link, and at that point, the argument is lost. While initially some readers may think that this requirement is too stringent, careful consideration of the logical steps involved will show that this is not the case. The advocates of new paternalism, both scholarly and popular, have incorrectly led many to believe that the case is far simpler than it really is. In fact, there are many complexities that are often overlooked.

M.J. Rizzo (✉)
New York University, New York, NY, USA

© The Editor(s) (if applicable) and The Author(s) 2016   37
S. Abdukadirov (ed.), *Nudge Theory in Action*,
DOI 10.1007/978-3-319-31319-1_3

These are the four propositions or pillars on which the case for new paternalism rests.

1. There is a set of general normative criteria for "rational" or welfare-increasing behavior, with respect to both judgment and preferences.
2. Real-world behavior significantly departs from these criteria.
3. Policymakers have the ability to craft policies that move people toward more welfare-enhancing behavior.
4. Policies can be carried out without unacceptably high costs in either welfare or freedom.

focus of law review article [handwritten note in left margin, bracketing item 3]

The first proposition is the heart of the entire case. Without a set a normatively persuasive criteria for rational behavior, neither cognitive nor preference biases can be defined and established. We shall see that both behavioral and standard economics have misconstrued the rationality axioms of economics. This misconstrual has elevated technical norms into prescriptive norms. The second proposition must be maintained by the behavioral paternalist to make the case for policy intervention in principle. However, from the perspective I am advancing, this may or may not be important. Even assuming the abstract persuasiveness of norms, the question to ask is: Do they apply in the real world? If not, then empirical violations—to the extent they occur—are not important from the perspective of the real-world agent. The third proposition is critical but often overlooked in simplified stories of irrational behavior and their possible remedies. In a world of complex and interacting biases whose general quantitative magnitudes are unclear, crafting efficacious policy is no simple matter. The fourth proposition relates to the claims made by behavioral paternalists that their policies are mild or moderate, requiring only "nudges" or other soft inducements. But these claims are belied by the arguments of other behavioral economists that nudges are not enough. They are also belied by the inherent expansive potential of policies in a world where benchmarks are ambiguous.

As the reader can see, *each* of the propositions is necessary to make the case. I could stop the analysis after showing that any one of them has not been adequately supported. Nevertheless, the full force of the anti-paternalist case cannot be seen without covering the entire ground. It is also important to understand that we are not dealing with the normative desirability of new paternalism per se. We are making an "impossibility" claim. If a policy framework is neither coherent nor possible, it cannot be desirable. Ought presupposes can.

PILLAR ONE: NORMATIVE CRITERIA

Behavioral economics starts from the assumption that the real-world individual is, in essence, a neoclassical agent who is predictably and systematically disturbed by psychological shocks (Bernheim and Rangel 2007). In the absence of these shocks, all of the standard axioms about preferences and judgments would be correct. For example, agents would have complete, transitive, and stationary preferences. In conditions of uncertainty modeled as risk, they would be expected utility maximizers and they would learn about the world through Bayesian updating. This basic assumption is not an empirical conclusion. It is a maintained, nonfalsifiable core proposition that provides a framework for analysis. It is part of a research program (Lakatos 1970). In this research program, anything that systematically interferes with the "normative" operation of the agent is construed as a psychological shock, and therefore, in a technical sense, a "bias."

The proposition that in the absence of psychological shocks the individual would exhibit neoclassical rationality characteristics is also treated, perhaps oddly, as a normative proposition. These are the characteristics the individual *should* have (Whitman and Rizzo 2015).[1] Not surprisingly there appears to be some resistance to saying this outright in plain language since the normatively required characteristics, as we shall see, are not persuasive. Nevertheless, it is the inconsistencies of choice as well as other rationality violations that "can justify the need for paternalistic policies" (Camerer et al. 2003, 1218). The aim of paternalistic policies is to create "'as if' rationality" (Sunstein 2014, 154). The logic of behavioral economics is that in the absence of violations of standard rationality there is no "decision-making failure" and no need for public policies aside from the ones often inferred from standard economics (e.g., externalities, public goods, monopoly, and, in some cases, inadequate information).

Nevertheless, the norms with respect to which shocks and biases are defined are not what most people, including economists, think they are. They are not, at least in the first instance, *prescriptive* standards. To clarify this claim I refer to a distinction made by the philosopher, John Searle (1969). There are two kinds of norms: constitutive and prescriptive. Constitutive norms refer to the rules of the game or endeavor. Think of playing chess. There are rules that constitute the game of chess. At some point, violation of these rules is not playing chess badly, it is not playing chess. We can take standard chess pieces and play by the rules of checkers.

No one would say simply that we are playing chess badly. On the other hand, a driver who violates traffic rules on a road is still driving but he is driving poorly. The poorness of his driving is likely to put either his own safety or that of others at risk. A case can be made for reforming his driving. The traffic rules are prescriptive norms. In the first case, it is not clear at all that not playing chess is a bad thing. It might be if the individual's well-being depended on it—say, if he were involved in a tournament in which he stood to make a great deal of money. But the case would have to be made.

Analogously, the norms of economic rationality are constitutive norms. *If* you want to be rational in a technical sense, you must obey the standard axioms of rationality. And that is it.

The rationality axioms were originally developed to give a firm logical foundation to the utility-function construct. As part of the attempt to rid economics of the hedonic psychology that was associated with the term "utility" and to clarify just how minimal the necessary assumptions for utility-function analysis were, a set of rationality axioms was developed (Mas-Colell et al. 1995). From these (completeness and transitivity of preference ordering were the main ones), the economist could derive a utility function that would summarize the preferences an agent might have. This is the logical foundation of a key economics construct. The utility function, in turn, is the core of economic models that explain aggregate behavior. The preference axioms thus became the constitutive norms of economic models and rationality. Unfortunately, certain ambiguities appeared right at the outset. In the hands of "welfare economics," it was asserted that, on the basis of these norms, the impact of policy on the welfare of agents could be determined. What was missed was the proviso that *if* agents behaved in accordance with the axioms, then their welfare could be assessed in relation to the axioms. There was no defended claim that agents *should* behave in accordance with the axioms.

Later, some economists tried to show that if people did not behave in accordance with the transitivity axiom they would be vulnerable to a money pump (Tullock 1964). This is a variant of the so-called Dutch book argument. An alert agent would—somehow—notice that an "irrational" individual had the following preference ordering: A is preferred to B, B is preferred to C, but C is preferred to A. Let an individual be in possession of C. The Dutch bookie offers him B if he will pay $C + \varepsilon$. The individual accepts. Then the bookie offers A in exchange for $B + \varepsilon$. Again the individual accepts. At this point, noticing the intransitive preferences, the bookie offers C in exchange for $A + \varepsilon$. Our irrational fellow accepts and is back where he started from but missing 3ε. If this process is continued a "sufficient" number of times, the individual will be out of resources and effectively out of economic existence.

In one sense, the money-pump argument is too good. It effectively bans such individuals from existence. And yet, at least according to experimental research, such people seem to exist. But the argument also presupposes that the agent not only has intransitive preferences but also is oblivious to the money pump. After the first complete round, he apparently still does not see what is going on. To succeed, the Dutch bookie would have to be facing not only a person with intransitive preferences but a person with an extreme case of myopia. The individual does not see that, in effect, the separate offers are really just one offer: You give me C plus 3ε and I will give you C. This is not all. To what does the abstract Dutch bookie correspond in the real world? Suppose I have intransitive pair-wise preferences among three people I might date. Is the Dutch bookie supposed to be some malevolent character who wishes to rid me of my date money? Suppose I have intransitive preferences among products in a store. Does the store owner money-pump me? If so, do I go back?[2]

Of course, it is possible in principle to construct examples in which behaving contrary to the standard rationality axioms produces bad results from the point of view of the agent. In those cases, the constitutive norms would also be prescriptive norms. The point is that *one would have to make the case that behaving in a specific way in a specific environment reduces the welfare of the agent as he sees it.*

Before concluding this section, it will be useful to examine a little more carefully the kinds of perfectly reasonable behavior that give rise to violations of the constitutive norms of standard economics. While these illustrations do not demonstrate that all violations must be reasonable, they do demonstrate that the axioms are not necessary conditions for reasonable purpose-enhancing—or at least not self-defeating—behavior. [3]

Violation of Completeness

To be "rational" the agent must be able to completely order the options he faces before any choices are made. There must be a complete preordering of the preference field. This means that an agent who simply does not know or is not sure if he prefers A to B does not behave as a rational agent.[4] Complete self-awareness in the form of internal omniscience is a requirement of rationality. It should be clear, however, that this requirement is entirely derived from its necessity in constructing a standard utility function. But utility function analysis, convenient though it may be, is not the only way to think of making choices. The individual can follow heuristics or rules. For example, in intertemporal choice if an individual cannot adequately distinguish the subjective value of consuming $50 today from the subjective value of consuming $55 in six months, he may use a heuristic like choosing the option that is sooner or the option that is greater in amount (Manzini and Mariotti 2006). An individual following such a heuristic is purposeful, consistent, and rational in any broad meaning of the word. There is nothing here to repair or to call a bias.[5]

are those sufficient conditions?

Violation of Independence of Irrelevant Alternatives

Another important criterion of economic rationality is that expression of preferences is independent of "irrelevant alternatives." This is closely connected with the idea that the framing of an option should not matter. If an individual preferred *A* over *B* when both were available, she ought not to prefer *B* over *A* when *C* is also available.[6] Pair-wise preferences cannot be reversed by expansion (or contraction) of the preference set. This is because, by assumption, the set of options itself cannot convey information that might change behavior. The axiom explicitly excludes that possibility.

To see how easily this is violated, consider a polite conservative lady who has not seen a relative for a long time and has been invited to tea (Sen 1993). Initially, she is posed with the simple option of going to tea (*A*) or not going to tea (*B*). Her preference is to go to tea. Now the invitation is elaborated. She is offered the options of going to tea, going to smoke cocaine with the relative (*C*), or not going at all. She decides not to visit the relative at all. Why? The answer is that, contrary to the axiom, the additional option conveys information about the kind of person her long-lost relative really is. If he would want to smoke cocaine, then she doesn't even want to have tea with him. This is no doubt reasonable. Examples such as these make obvious that the rationality of preference ordering is a different kind of rationality than we would normally uphold as a prescriptive standard.[7]

Violation of Transitivity

Transitivity of preferences is sometimes thought of as akin to transitivity of propositions in logic, but it is not. We must distinguish the transitivity of preference from the transitivity of logical implication (Read 1995, 251). An example of the latter is the syllogism: *From "if A then B" and "if B then C" then we can infer "if A then C."* Note that the consequent of each step in this chain is used as the antecedent in the next step. This is the "transitivity of proof." In contrast, the relation of preference is not a logical one ("if A then B") but an evaluative one ("x is at least as good as y"). Whether an evaluative chain is transitive depends on the basis of the evaluation.

Again, a violation of the transitivity of preferences is easy to produce. A person is presented with a bowl of three pieces of fruit: a large apple, a small apple, and an orange. Her order of preferences is: A large apple is preferred to an orange; an orange is preferred to a small apple. So as between a large apple and a small apple she should prefer the large apple. However, the host presents her with a choice between a large apple and a small apple. She chooses the small apple. Why? Because she considers it impolite to take the bigger of the two apples presented to her. Old-fashioned manners are clearly not irrational in any reasonable prescriptive sense.

While the above examples of axiom violations may seem trivial, they illustrate a nontrivial point. The axioms of rationality in standard economics are not prescriptive; they are constitutive of a certain kind of behavior that is useful for technical purposes.

Axiom Violations and Arbitrary Norms

It is one thing to show that behavior violates one of the axioms of rational choice; it is quite another to decide what better behavior would be. To see this, let us explore the implicit axiom of stationarity that underlies most of the normative literature on intertemporal choice. The standard neoclassical agent applies a single discount rate to all of the future flows of income that he can choose among regardless of when they occur. Thus, if he just barely prefers the option of $100 today to $105 in one year, he will also just barely prefer the option of $100 in three years to $105 in four years.[8] The discount rate is independent of when the one-year delay occurs. It is well known that there are many violations of the axiom (Read 2004).

One of the most interesting violations, from the perspective of behavioral economics, is what is misleadingly called "preference reversal." Consider again the individual above. He prefers $100 today to $105 a year from now. But in our revised story, he also prefers $105 in four years to $100 in three years. He is time inconsistent. The second delay—in the farther future—is not discounted by the same amount. The individual appears less impatient with respect to the second option than the first. In itself this might be thought of as a curiosity or as a technical problem. However, behavioral economists have interpreted the phenomenon in a special way that makes it appear to be a kind of substantive irrationality. The first decision is often viewed as indicative of a present bias rooted in transient psychological states or defects. While almost all of the experimental evidence on preference reversal relates to hypothetical choices about money, some of the interpretations are more like this: A very hungry individual is faced with an attractive steak now or a multicourse fancy dinner tomorrow. He cannot control his urges so he grabs the steak now. On the other hand, if the same individual is faced with the option of a steak in three months when hungry or a multicourse fancy dinner in three month and a day, he may choose the later, better meal. He will say I can control my hunger then and wait a day. The implication of this (not directly tested) is that when three months have elapsed and the future becomes the present, he will switch and grab the steak. Here it is visceral factors that explain the present bias (Loewenstein 1996, 272–292). Similar arguments—though not visceral in nature—have been made about why people plan to save but then do not. The new clothes in the store on payday are just too tempting.[9]

The implicit assumption being made is that the immediate decision is contaminated by some sort of psychological distortion while the decision for the farther future is being made rationally and without distortion. As plausible as this may seem, it is not supported by any fair reading of the full range of literature on temporal discounting. No rate of discounting—immediate or long-run—is free from either affective or cognitive influences. Let us assume for the moment that the psychological state that impels present consumption is a distortion relative to some ideal. So we shall, for the sake of argument, label the earlier, higher rate of discount affectively biased. What about the second, lower rate of discount?

We must take a small detour on how the farther future tends to be envisioned by human beings. The passage of a given amount of calendar time (one month, one year, and so forth) is not always *perceived* as being of the same length. For example, a year is not perceived as the equivalent of four three-month periods. From a psychological perspective, the first three-month segment is longer than one quarter of a year. The rest of the year gets compressed relative to the first segment. As the agent looks to the farther future, the passage of calendar time is increasingly compressed.

Delays will appear to be shorter. The individual will have to be paid less for waiting a given amount of calendar time in the more distant future. Thus, a lower and lower discount rate will be applied to the successive periods.

From the perspective of behavioral economics, this would be considered a cognitive bias. Recall that the normative standard applied by behavioralists is the neoclassical ideal. Neoclassical man is a creature who lives solely in calendar time. For that reason alone, the second, later discount rate is "contaminated." It is too low.[10]

In another related approach, Read (2001) has shown that intertemporal choices are subadditive. This means that the average compounded discount rates applied over short segments are higher than the rate applied over a long segment. In our example above, the individual appears to be less impatient in the choice of $105 in four years over $100 in three years. But take the delay between the present and three years and divide it into smaller intervals or segments (say, of three or six months each). The average of the individual shorter interval discount rates will be higher—often significantly—than the discount rate applied to the undivided full interval.[11] Thus, the discounting of the smaller, sooner reward (in the second option) will be greater. In the typical case, the preference reversal will disappear. A proposed psychological basis for this is that the salience of the events over shorter intervals is greater than that over longer intervals. Thus, the value of what is being sacrificed by delay *is seen more precisely*. Discount rates go up. Unless behavioral economists want to argue that less salience is normative, it is hard to escape the conclusion that—as usually measured—long-term discount rates are too low relative to omniscience. From this it follows that the divergence of discount rates and preference reversal is not the simple temptation-cool planning phenomenon it is alleged to be. All discount rates are "distorted" relative to omniscience. The behavioral economist has no good reason for choosing the long-run rate as the uniquely normative one.

PILLAR TWO: REAL-WORLD BEHAVIOR

The purpose of this section is not to contest that there are many violations of the standard rationality axioms in the real world. My point is that we should never have expected the real world to behave in accordance with those axioms.[12] Indeed Leonard Savage (1954), who had a significant role in developing the axiomatic approach in economics, made a useful distinction between small worlds and large worlds. Only the former have clearly defined options with definite probabilities. Large worlds, on the other hand, are characterized by ambiguity, imprecision, and true uncertainty rather than risk. The standard rationality axioms make sense only in a closed, carefully circumscribed, and delimited small world.[13] An agent acting like neoclassical man in a large world would be acting irrationally. He would not be adapted to his environment; he would not be ecologically rational.[14]

Standard economics is filled with analyses of optimal courses of action. This of course can make perfect sense in a small world where if there is "uncertainty" it is purely risk. The future may not be known but its stochastic structure is or, at least, the agent has some stochastic structure in mind. So (subjective) expected utility maximization is the way to go. In my view, economists have overinvested in this form of analysis. In large worlds people use fast and frugal heuristics to make judgments and choices (e.g., Gigerenzer 2008). Heuristics are shortcuts. They economize on the use of data and actually suppress the consideration of certain factors. They are not used because people are stupid—and not only because people are "boundedly rational." In fact, they can yield the best results in a particular environment.

Amos Tversky and Daniel Kahneman (1974, 1124–1131) created a "heuristics and biases" literature that is quite different from the ecological rationality framework of Gerd Gigerenzer. Heuristics and biases are the basis of most behavioral economics. For the behavioralists the main issue is the cognitive limitations of the human mind. As we have seen above, behavioral economists believe that (a) the real-world individual is basically a neoclassical agent who is disturbed by psychological shocks and (b) the normative standard for his behavior is technical rationality. Therefore, in this view, heuristics are necessarily inferior instruments in dealing with the world. Since, however, the errors made by using heuristics are systematic and predictable to the behavioral analyst (although not to the agent), there is the possibility that decision-making can be improved by informed policy interventions. Unfortunately, these conclusions rest on the unsupported idea that the environment in which people act is the equivalent of Savage's small world. All of the relevant data for optimal or rational decision-making is allegedly out there but boundedly rational people cannot see it or process it, or act in accordance with it.

This analysis is seriously incomplete and one-sided. Herbert Simon (1990, 7) believed that human rationality "was shaped by scissors whose two blades are the structure of the task environment and the computational capabilities of the actor." In their appropriate environments heuristics are not only an economical way to make judgments and decisions, but they are also more successful than trying to use small-world decision-making techniques. For example, instead of engaging in complex and expensive optimization of an investment portfolio, a simple rule of allocating funds equally across n standard mutual funds outperformed almost all of 15 other strategies. But more significantly, no other single strategy could consistently outperform the $1/n$ rule (DeMiguel, Garlappi and Uppal 2009).

Take-the-best (TTB) is another heuristic that has been used for tasks that involve identifying properties of a particular object: which city has the higher population, which firm has the highest profit prospects, which of two suspects is more likely to have committed a murder, and so forth. This heuristic requires the decision-maker to choose cues (characteristics), rank them in order of their perceived validity, and then check off if the candidate object satisfies the cue or not. The heuristic is lexicographic so as the decision-maker goes down the list of cues the first object to satisfy a cue while the others do not is chosen. For example, if we are trying to find out which of two cities has the greater population, we might check if the city is the capital of the country. If neither, we go to the second cue: Does it have a soccer team? If A does and B does not, we choose A. If both (or neither) have one, we go on to the third cue. The first time either A or B has the characteristic and the other does not, we stop and choose the one that has it. In a competition with standard "integration strategies" like multiple regression analysis, TTB was superior to all the others in this population task (Gigerenzer and Goldstein 1996).

This does not mean that TTB is a superior decision-making method for all problems. It is a context-specific tool that economizes on information and cognitive effort. Accordingly, people do not always use the heuristic but in many environments where it is appropriate they do. This appropriateness depends not only on the cognitive limitations of the individual but also on the structure of the environment. For example, even when people experienced a *reduction* in cognitive load, they did not shift away from TTB to more complex strategies (Bröder 2012). In fact, the effect of high cognitive load was to prevent people from moving away from a more complex strategy when it was inferior to TTB. Thus the idea that heuristics are less effective ways of coping with the environment than various optimizing strategies is incorrect. In an environment that does not satisfy the small-world criteria, heuristics can be a better instrument. Under such circumstances, the greater the individuals' cognitive capacity, the more heuristics will be used. We should not regret that individuals do not satisfy the standard rationality requirements of economic theory.

Pillar Three: The Knowledge Demands of Policy[15]

The purpose of a new paternalist policy is to bring out the inner neoclassical agent.[16] To accomplish this, the policymaker must first uncover people's "true preferences." These are the preferences individuals would have if they were not subject to psychological distortions such as imperfect computational ability, imperfect appreciation of information, and no lack of willpower (Thaler and Sunstein 2003, 175).

The purpose of this section is to ask whether the findings of behavioral psychology and economics are sufficiently robust and precise to serve as a basis for policy. Keeping in mind that the fundamental policy requirement of new paternalism is to enhance the individual's satisfaction of her true preferences, the task is not simply changing behavior. It is changing behavior relative to a particular standard. Sometimes this is ignored or downplayed, as when a certain activity—say, smoking—is socially disapproved. Other times as when there is discussion of proper diet and nutrition for young children, parents presumably do not care about the children's true preferences. Parents may simply want to act as "old paternalists" in what *they* perceive to be the children's best interests. Nevertheless, what is supposed to be unique about new paternalism is that it rests on the identification of what individuals want—down deep.

Let us take the case of "undersaving." People claim that they would like to save more. Many behavioral economists believe them.[17] However, behavioral economists must know to what extent people are saving less because of *present bias or time-inconsistent impatience.* Time-*consistent* impatience is just the ordinary, normatively "legitimate" expression of time preference between consumption today and consumption in the future. There is nothing irrational about that. Present bias, on the other hand, is the application of a higher discount rate in the short term than in the longer term. It can result in the abandonment of savings plans as the future becomes the present. For example, suppose an individual planned to save $100 next month in exchange for a return of $110 in one month and a year. And yet today when faced with the opportunity to sacrifice $100 today for $110 a year from now, he chooses the $100 today. The same time delay is being priced differently (inconsistently) for the nearer future than for the more distant future. This is incompatible with the standard rationality axioms.[18]

Suppose a policymaker wanted to make savings more attractive in order to offset present bias. He could propose a tax on consumption or a subsidy on savings. How much should it be? He would have to know, not simply that people have present bias, but the quantitative extent of that bias. This requires that he distinguish between ordinary time-consistent impatience and present bias. Too high a subsidy must be avoided because it could result in welfare losses that are just as great (or even greater) due to oversaving. The problem is that empirical estimates of discount rates have an extraordinarily high variance. There is a "spectacular disagreement among dozens of studies" (Frederick et al. 2002, 389) and "sometimes even within studies" (393). The following graphic shows the variation in the measurements of discount factors by the year of their publication (Fig. 1).[19]

While it is not possible to go into details here, it is quite clear that measured discount rates vary as a result of (Weatherly 2014):

1. The method of elicitation. Three of the most common methods are to require individuals to make binary choices, multiple choices, or to fill in the blank. Different rates of impatience are found for each. The binary choice method, for example, usually reveals greater impatience than the others.
2. How the outcomes are framed. Is the intertemporal option framed as money won or as money owed? Money owed is less heavily discounted, sometimes significantly.

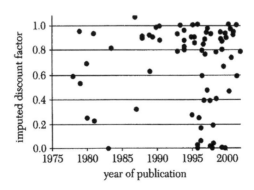

Fig. 1   Discount Factor by Year of Study Publication (Source: Frederick et al. (2002, 380))

3. Magnitude effects. Holding time delays constant, the greater the magnitudes involved, the less heavily people discount the future. In other words, as the amounts at stake at all time periods become more significant, people become less impatient.
4. Money versus other outcomes. It appears that people discount money options differently from, say, health options. There is more discounting in the money case.

Perhaps the most serious of these problems is the elicitation method since there does not seem to be a good theoretical reason to choose one over the others.

The difference in measured discounted rates gets compounded because the effect on conventionally determined welfare can be magnified. For example, in a study of "optimal sin taxes," that is, taxes on products or activities that paternalists believe are not good for people, there is an enormous variation in the policy prescriptions depending on smaller variations in measured discount rates. The point is rather striking:

> If half of the population is fully self-controlled while the other half of the population has a very small present bias of ... 0.99, then the optimal tax is 5.15 %. If instead the half of the population with self-control problems has a somewhat larger present bias of ... 0.90 – which is still a smaller present bias ... than is often discussed in the literature – the optimal tax is 63.71 %. (O'Donoghue and Rabin 2006, 1838)[20]

This and similar considerations are very significant for the determination of whether paternalist policies will make things better or worse from the perspective of helping people satisfy their true preferences. I stress that too high a tax can be worse, in this view, than no tax at all. Even if the policy is not to formulate a sin tax but to construct a "nudge" toward more savings—say, making automatic enrollment the default in the case of employer-sponsored retirement plans—these problems of estimation are important. How do we know when the nudge is enough?[21] What is the measure of success?

Before concluding this section, I would like to briefly analyze another important difficulty for paternalist policy that arises out of the multiplicity of interacting biases. In the discussion above about oversaving I assumed that the only relevant bias was the overvaluation in immediate decisions of present consumption. However, behavioral economists also claim that individuals overestimate their *future* consumption needs (Rabin 1999). Clearly, these biases move in opposite directions. The first can lead to undersaving while the second can lead to oversaving. Corrective policy would need reasonably accurate quantitative estimates of the two conflicting biases. The data on discounting is quite unreliable as we have seen. I do not know of reliable quantitative estimates of overestimation bias.

There are also the alarming and vivid commercials about the health effects of cigarette smoking. These supposedly exist because certain biases restrict the effects of informational advertising and because risk narratives like these commercials elicit a further offsetting bias. The argument goes like this: If we were simply to give people information of the dangers of smoking, they would probably not fully absorb this information due to lack of full attention. Furthermore, people are victims of "optimism bias," whereby they accept the scientific information about the probabilities of a bad health outcome but believe that they are "magically" protected from these effects. To offset this, frightening narratives can be presented, which take advantage of people's "availability bias"—the effect of vivid, present events (like plane crashes) on exaggerating the likelihood of the particular danger involved. Thus, the behavioralist seeks to fight one set of biases with another. However, the problem is more complex. Cigarette smokers, even before all of the advertising of this nature, believed that cigarette smoking is more dangerous than it really is (Antoñanzas et al. 2000; Viscusi 1990).[22]

To determine whether risk narratives improve welfare in the behavioral calculation requires quantitative knowledge beyond what is available. First, the analyst needs to know the extent to which inattention and optimism bias result in people thinking cigarette smoking is safer than it really is. Second, that must be quantitatively counterbalanced by the belief that cigarette smoking is more dangerous than it really is in order to get the appropriate *perceived* probability of health risks. Third, then we must determine how much availability bias enhances the perception of risk—assuming of course that the target audience is suitably attentive to the risk narratives. At this point, the analyst would be able to ascertain the resulting perceived probability of harm. If this is correct (i.e., equal to the true probabilities), then the individual would be able to correctly determine the optimal course of action: to smoke or not to smoke.

Behavioral economists have not come to terms with this kind of problem. But they must. Recall that what is unique about behavioral paternalism—new paternalism—is that the standard of making individuals "better off" is the *true preferences of the individuals themselves*. Since smoking has obvious benefits, the optimal amount of smoking is not zero in a diverse population. This cost-benefit calculation is complicated since even behavioral economists allow that consistent impatience, rather than present bias, is allowable in intertemporal decisions (smoking pleasure today versus possible health consequences later).

In the actual world of policymaking, however, the behavioral criterion does not matter. As the examples of sin taxes and risk narrative show, the measure of success for behavioral economists is elusive. So the practical standard of success will be the (nonoptimal) obliteration of the suspect activity. This sets part of the stage for the final pillar of paternalism.

PILLAR FOUR: "UNINTENDED" COSTS OF POLICY EXPANSION[23]

It is often difficult to say whether certain outcomes are intended or not. Policies are usually advocated by many people with different agendas. I do not doubt that this is true about new paternalist policies. Some advocates may welcome the transformation of soft policies into harder policies. For my purposes here what is important are the claims made by certain of the advocates. Richard Thaler and Cass Sunstein (2008) in particular have pushed the point that they advocate only soft interventions—nudges. *The Economist* referred to new paternalist policies as embodying the "avuncular state" in contrast to the more severe "paternalist state" (April 6, 2006). In this respect, Thaler and Sunstein are tacitly admitting that certain types of highly restrictive government intervention may be undesirable. This is especially evident in Sunstein's more recent book *Why Nudge?* (2014).[24]

Not all new paternalists are so reluctant. George Loewenstein and Peter Ubel (2010) have argued that nudges are not strong enough. In general they are insufficient to effect the appropriate change in behavior. For example, they argue that the real problem underlying obesity is not lack of information. Less healthful and processed foods have fallen in relative price. This is a powerful incentive to consume them. Calorie postings are too puny a policy tool. They claim government needs to consider taxes. This more expansive approach also gains traction from the problem we discussed in the previous section. When success or failure of a policy is difficult to ascertain empirically (even if its theoretical standard were clear), there is a special opportunity to push out the range of restrictions. This is in part because the public thinks in dichotomous terms—obesity is bad, smoking is bad; ideally, there should be none of each. Policy can easily fail because the optimum amount of a suspect activity is practically unobservable and is probably not meaningful to the public in any event.

From the perspective of behavioral economics, if ordinary people are subject to biases—say, present bias—it is hard to see that policymakers would not also be. It is therefore instructive to explore the effect of present bias in the political process. Most public choice economists agree that the incentives of the political system are such that rational, unbiased actors will be focused on policies that promise short-term gains even at the expense of greater long-term costs. In the first place, unless there are short-term gains the politician is not likely to be around for the long run. Secondly, most politicians are not in fact around for the long run and by that time the public is likely to have forgotten which policy caused which outcomes. Atop all of this is the effect of policymaker present bias and time-inconsistent planning. To illustrate, consider a sin tax on foods that are high in fat, salt, sugar, or other refined carbohydrates. Paternalists usually find that consumption of these foods is excessive. Recall that the excess consumption is not due to time-consistent impatience but to the extra kick of present bias. Thus, a paternalist who takes "a careful, cautious, and disciplined approach" (Camerer et al. 2003, 1212) will want, as best he can, to limit the tax to offsetting present bias and not more. Such a tax will lead the individual to incorporate in the upfront costs of consumption the "correct" (unbiased) present value of the future health risks. Ideally, the present bias problem will then be solved; people will, on average, consume the optimal amount of junk food. However, paternalists are not the only actors in the political system. There are those who want additional tax money to support whatever their projects are. Having established a sin tax on food, the mechanisms are all in place and the public is acclimated to their existence.[25]

Let us assume that the paternalist policymaker is aware of all this. He sees the threat of expansion. He is determined to resist the hijacking of the policy for other purposes that will also reduce the welfare of the now optimally controlled consumer by reducing consumption still further. The future possibility now becomes a present possibility. How does a present-biased paternalist react? He sees the cost of decreased welfare because consumers will not be able to optimally enjoy junk food. But he excessively discounts these costs at the moment of his promised resistance. Oh well, it is not so bad—he tells himself—it is better to conserve political resources for use in some other area of paternalist policy advocacy or

Thaler + Sunstein admitted this

implementation. This phenomenon is exacerbated by the fact that there is no bright-line rule, no clear optimum that can act as at least a conceptual bulwark against sliding into unintended expanded policies.

Even without biases on the part of policymakers, the policy discussed above has expansionary potential. One of the leading behavioral justifications for junk-food taxes is consumer myopia in various forms. Present bias is just one form of this phenomenon. Another is the failure to look at circumstances in a wide-enough frame of reference. When a tax is placed on foods with high refined sugar content or other foods deemed to contribute to the obesity, people will adjust presumably by eating less of this food. But they also may adjust by engaging in less exercise like walking or by not restricting by as much the quantity of food they eat. There are many personal inputs into the overall objective of weight control. The policy only targets one of them. Since, by assumption, people have not changed their overall weight objectives, it is quite plausible that they will perceive lower consumption of sugary drinks as "permission" to eat more or exercise less. This reaction will offset, to some degree at least, the initial effect of the fat tax. However, myopic individuals focus more on subgoals (eating more healthily) and less on superordinate goals (losing weight) (Fishbach et al. 2006).[26] Progress toward the satisfaction of a subgoal can cause people to disengage from the overall picture of controlling weight and thus induce a reduction in *all* of the inputs into weight control. [27] This may result in even less exercise or portion control than in the case without biases. Therefore, initial tax rates on sugary foods are fairly certain to rise because these adjustments will make the previous policy inadequate. The more myopically biased individuals are, the more substantial will be this effect.

The final expansionary tendency in new paternalism that I wish to discuss here is not a quantitative issue but a qualitative one. Behavioral economists have a peculiar relationship with information. One of the obstacles to fully rational choice is supposedly incomplete information (Thaler and Sunstein 2003, 175). However, economists in the rational choice tradition have incorporated incomplete information in their models for many decades without jeopardizing the rationality of the agents. As we have seen, behavioral economists find that there are obstacles to the full appreciation or absorption of information even where in some sense it may be complete. Some philosophers, even before the development of behavioral economics, have argued that, for an individual to be completely informed, the information must be the focus of attention, maximally vivid, and there must be no doubt about its truth (Brandt 1979, 111–112). This requirement raises some important issues. Just as complete information about the dangers or risks of one activity may not be properly absorbed (as in the case of simple declarative warnings about cigarette smoking), so too information that is too vivid or too much the focus of attention might not be properly processed. Sunstein and Thaler (2003, 1183) claimed: "In the face of health risks, for example, some presentations of accurate information might actually be counterproductive because people might attempt to control their fear by refusing to think about the risk at all." This type of argument has been used to question whether people can be trusted to properly absorb, process, or utilize information about the relative risks of different products.

Recently a manufacturer of smokeless tobacco products petitioned the FDA for a modification of the required warning label on its product "snus." Swedish Match AB wanted at least part of the label to read that its product carries "substantially lower risks to health than cigarettes."[28]The FDA Advisory Panel rejected the petition. In an article reporting this *The New York Times* said "One big worry is whether labels that indicate lower risk may tempt people, particularly young people, to use tobacco products that they might not have tried otherwise" (Tavernise 2015). In an editorial on the same subject, the *Times* further claimed that "snus might lead some nonsmokers to take up the nicotine habit, and progress on to cigarette smoking, when abstention would be the safest approach" (NYT, April 23, 2015). This argument is made despite the fact that "most panelists agreed that snus appears less harmful than cigarettes when used by smokers who switch" (Clarke 2015).

This development should be troubling from an ethical and legal perspective. The influence of behavioral psychology on policy has created a gradient from the inadequacy of simple truthful disclosure to the inappropriateness of truthful disclosure. Statements of facts which are true can be forbidden on labels, even though they are of obvious relevance to consumers. It appears that the operative criterion is whether the statements further the outcomes that the FDA wants rather than whether they inform consumers. Clearly, the evaluation of new paternalism must include an assessment of the autonomy-limiting implication for consumer information.

Conclusions

The structure of the new paternalist arguments presented here allows us to examine step by step the claims that must be supported to make the case for this new direction in regulatory policy. Too often the case for new

paternalism is made, especially in the popular press, as simply a psychologically aware, soft-touch approach to producing socially affirmed outcomes.
"We all know that Americans are too fat so here is a clever new idea to
change that," is the essence of the popularized version. However, new
paternalism is more than that.

The foundation of new paternalism is the idea that people have "true
preferences," which for a variety of "psychological" reasons they are
unable to satisfy. Behavioral economists claim that they have new tools
that enable them to discover what these preferences are. They then claim
that by a series of behavioral manipulations (sometimes called "nudges"),
selective or processed information disclosures, taxes, mandates, and so
forth the policymaker can change that behavior. The change is supposed
to be toward the greater fulfillment of the individual's true preferences.
In most stylized presentations, the complications of interacting biases or
other information complexities are abstracted from. Thus, the appropriate
policy seems clear and straightforward. In fact, given the limitations of
the data available, the difficulties are quite significant. Furthermore, new
paternalists rarely pay significant attention to the institutional or policy-
logic tendencies that their ideas generate. Indeed elsewhere Rizzo and
Whitman (2009a, 738) call this set of ideas a "paternalism-generating
framework."

The development of new paternalism has added a whole new dimension to the increasing power and reach of the state. It creates the impres-
sion that areas of behavior which were previously in the domain of private
individual behavior can be brought under the domain of state concerns
with only minimal restrictions on liberty and autonomy. But this is an
illusion. When serious analysis is applied to the problems of new paternalism, especially its epistemic problems, it is easy to see that the dynamic
of paternalist arguments leads to the expansion of control of individual
behavior.

Notes

1. Generally speaking, inferring from what would be under certain conditions to what ought to be is analytically little different than inferring
   from what is to what ought to be. In itself this is known as the "natu-
   ralistic fallacy."
2. For a detailed analysis of Dutch book arguments, see Vineberg
   (2011).

3. Certain biases may be considered a violation of one or more axioms either simultaneously or alternatively. The reader should not place a great deal of emphasis on exactly which axiom is being violated.
4. It is necessary to distinguish the absence of a complete preference ordering from indifference. An agent can prefer A to B or B to A or be indifferent between the two. All of this counts as a preference ordering. Incompleteness means that the agent simply does not know how he feels about the options.
5. This particular heuristic can give rise to inconsistent intertemporal preferences because it implies that sometimes the agent chooses the sooner amount and other times the agent chooses the larger amount. In such a case, the agent would not have a consistent complete preference ordering. Behavioralists usually consider the first possibility (smaller sooner) a present bias.
6. The Strong Axiom of Revealed Preference mirrors this. If A is revealed preferred to B, B can never be revealed preferred to A.
7. Some economists have tried to distinguish between seeming violations and actual ones (Burkett 2006, 139, n. 4). The seeming violation occurs because the agent gets some new information from the additional option. But the "seeming" violation is an actual one. As I argue above, the claim that there is new information generated by the set of alternatives is contrary to the assumption of the axiom so if there *is* such new information, the axiom is ipso facto violated. If, however, we allow that information generated by the set of alternatives can save the axiom (along Burkett's lines), then the axiom will never be violated unless behavior is simply random. It is hard to imagine what else could cause the axiom to be violated as long as we stay in the domain of purposeful behavior. An axiom that can never be violated cannot serve as a behavioral welfare norm.
8. There are many assumptions behind this statement. The most important of these assumptions is that there are no capital markets on which to borrow or lend. It is also assumed that the money is consumed when it is obtained. For a complete list of assumptions, see Read (2004, 424–43).
9. It should be pointed out that the experimental evidence on preference reversal has been almost entirely from latitudinal (cross-sectional) studies. Subjects are asked about their various intertemporal preferences at a single point in time. On the other hand, preference reversal really refers to a change in preferences over time from larger

later to smaller sooner. Therefore, the existence of the phenomenon should be ascertained by a longitudinal study. Do people actually reverse their decisions over the passage of time? When such a study is carried out, there does not seem to be a systematic tendency toward preference reversal. There are as many patient shifts ("negative preference reversal") as there are impatient shifts. See Read et al. (2012).

10. But we can go further. This analysis calls into question the interpretation of the initial discount rate as the result of temptation or viscerally induced impatience. The real issue is how people perceive the passage of time.

11. "...discounting over an interval is greater when it is calculated in 'installments' than when it is done in one operation" (Read 2001, 9).

12. Fritz Machlup (1974) argued that the assumptions of economic theory were simply analytical devices to make predictions about the direction of change of market or aggregate outcomes in response to exogenous changes. For this limited purpose, they may succeed in many cases.

13. Savage (1954, 16) was referring to subjective expected utility theory and said it would be "utterly ridiculous" to apply it to large worlds. See also Volz and Gigerenzer (2012).

14. For a discussion of the small- and large-world distinction in the context of ecological rationality, see Brighton and Gigerenzer (2014).

15. A more in-depth analysis of some of the issues in this section can be found in Rizzo and Whitman (2009b).

16. I attribute this exact expression to Robert Sugden in conversation. However, the idea had been percolating in my own mind for some time and is implicit in Bernheim and Rangel (2007).

17. Saving involves an opportunity cost of present consumption. Whether people really have a preference to save more *and consume less* is a different question. Having more resources later for consumption is an economic good and therefore we all have positive attitudes toward that. But at what cost? It should also be noted that the benefit-cost structure of saying things (e.g., for social approval or because of a feeling that something is right) is different from the benefit-cost structure of doing things. This is one reason why many economists are dubious about the expression of preferences through talk.

18. A rational individual would apply the same discount rate over the nearer and farther future.

19. Discount factors vary inversely with discount rates. A discount factor of 1.0 means that there is no discounting and anything above that is negative discounting. The lower the discount factor, the more impatience there is.

20. Present bias is measured as a discount factor, that is, the percent of the future outcome that is brought forth to its present value. Thus, the lower the discount factor, the higher the discount rate and the higher the level of impatience.

21. The psychology of nudges is murky. Can there be too much of a nudge? Suppose, for example, that the mechanism by which a nudge works is to focus the individual's attention on an issue. If attention is a scarce resource with opportunity costs, is the increased focusing due to the policy suboptimal? Perhaps the individual should be focusing on another problem. Furthermore, if the problem is status-quo bias, then, regardless of the default, there will be people "stuck" in the wrong option (Tergesen 2011). As the reader can see, nudges do not obviate the need for quantitative estimates of the relevant parameters.

22. Viscusi (2002–2003, 63) discusses the offsetting effects of present bias and overestimation of cigarette health risks. He also discusses optimism bias (60).

23. A more in-depth analysis of the themes in this section can be found in Rizzo and Whitman (2009a).

24. "Suppose that freedom of choice is part of what people care about. Suppose too that if people are denied freedom of choice, they will suffer loss in welfare, in part because they feel frustrated and mistreated. To the extent this is so, there will be a legitimate and potentially forceful objection, on grounds of welfare, to hard paternalism..." (128). However, "there are many opportunities for improving welfare without intruding on freedom of choice" through nudges (23). Much of this freedom-of-choice claim is sustainable only by ignoring legal impositions on those who are not the direct beneficiaries of paternalism. For example, when restaurants are required to post calories, they are coerced even if customers are not forced to consume low-calorie food.

25. These general effects are what Volokh (2003, 1039–51) calls incentive-altering slippery slopes and attitude-changing slippery slopes.

26. Obese individuals are often assumed to be myopic in the sense that they consider the near (present) pleasure of eating but not the distant (future) benefits of good health.

27. Economists would call this a scale effect and the previous adjustment a substitution effect.

28. See Jacob Sullum, "Snus and E-Cigarettes Are Indisputably Safer Than Smoking, Contrary to What The New York Times Wants You to Think" http://reason.com/blog/2015/04/24/snus-and-e-cigarettes-are-indisputably-s

BIBLIOGRAPHY

Antoñanzas, Fernando, W. Kip Viscusi, Joan Rovira, Francisco J. Braña, Fabiola Portillo, and Irineu Carvalho. 2000. Smoking risks in Spain: Part I – Perception of risks to the smoker. *Journal of Risk and Uncertainty* 21(2): 161–186.

Bernheim, B. Douglas, and Antonio Rangel. 2007. Behavioral public economics: Welfare and policy analysis with non-standard decision makers. In *Behavioral economics and its applications*, eds. Peter Diamond and Hannu Vartiainen, 7–84. Princeton: Princeton University Press.

Brandt, Richard B. 1979. *A theory of the good and right*. Oxford: Oxford University Press.

Brighton, Henry, and Gerd Gigerenzer. 2012. Are rational actor models 'rational' outside small worlds? In *Evolution and rationality: Decisions, co-operation and strategic behavior*, eds. Samir Okasha and Ken Binmore, 84–109. Cambridge: Cambridge University Press.

Bröder, Arndt. 2012. The quest for take-the-best: Insights and outlooks from experimental research. In *Ecological rationality: Intelligence in the world*, eds. Peter M. Todd, Gerd Gigerenzer, and ABC Research Group. Oxford: Oxford University Press.

Burkett, John P. 2006. *Microeconomics: Optimization, experiments, and behavior*. Oxford: Oxford University Press.

Camerer, C., S. Issacharoff, G. Loewenstein, T. O'Donoghue, and M. Rabin. 2003. Regulation for conservatives: Behavioral economics and the case for 'Asymmetric Paternalism'. *University of Pennsylvania Law Review* 151(3): 1211–1254.

Clarke, Toni. 2015. FDA panel votes against label change to Swedish Match Snus. *Reuters*, April 10, 2015 (http://www.reuters.com/article/2015/04/10/us-swedish-match-fda-idUSKBN0N11VP20150410).

DeMiguel, Victor, Lorenzo Garlappi, and Raman Uppal. 2009. Optimal versus naïve diversification: How inefficient is the 1/N portfolio strategy? *Review of Financial Studies* 22(5): 1915–1953.

Fishbach, Ayelet, Ravi Dhar, and Ying Zhang. 2006. Subgoals as substitutes or complements: The role of goal accessibility. *Journal of Personality and Social Psychology* 91(2): 232–242.

Frederick, Shane, George Loewenstein, and Ted O'Donoghue. 2002. Time discounting and time preference: A critical review. *Journal of Economic Literature* 40(2): 351–401.

Gigerenzer, Gerd. 2008. *Rationality for mortals: How people cope with uncertainty*. Oxford: Oxford University Press.

Gigerenzer, Gerd, and Daniel G. Goldstein. 1996. Reasoning the fast and frugal way: Models of bounded rationality. *Psychological Review* 103(4): 650–669.

Lakatos, Imre. 1970. Falsification and the methodology of scientific research programmes. In *Criticism and the growth of knowledge*, eds. Imre Lakatos and Alan Musgrave, 91–196. Cambridge: Cambridge University Press.

Loewenstein, George. 1996. Out of control: Visceral influences on behavior. *Organizational Behavior and Human Decision Processes* 65(3): 272–292.

Loewenstein, George, and Peter Ubel. 2010. Economics behaving badly. *The New York Times*, July 14.

Machlup, Fritz. 1974. Spiro Latsis on situational determinism. *British Journal for the Philosophy of Science* 24: 271–284.

Manzini, Paola, and Marco Mariotti. 2006. A vague theory of choice over time. *Advances in Theoretical Economics* 6(1): 1–27.

Mas-Colell, Andreu, Michael D. Whinston, and Jerry R. Green. 1995. *Microeconomic theory*. New York: Oxford University Press.

New York Times editorial. 2015. The perils of smokeless tobacco. *The New York Times*, April 23.

O'Donoghue, Ted, and Matthew Rabin. 2006. Optimal sin taxes. *Journal of Public Economics* 90(10–11): 1825–1849.

Rabin, Matthew. 1999. Comment on 'what me worry? A psychological perspective on economic aspects of retirement,' by George Loewenstein, Drazen Prelec, and Roberto Weber. In *Behavioral dimensions of retirement economics*, ed. Henry Aaron, 247–251. Washington, DC: Brookings Institution Press.

Read, Stephen. 1995. *Thinking about logic: An introduction to the philosophy of logic*. Oxford: Oxford University Press.

Read, Daniel. 2001. Is time-discounting hyperbolic or subadditive? *Journal of Risk and Uncertainty* 23: 5–32.

———. 2004. Intertemporal choice. In *Blackwell handbook of judgment and decision making*, eds. Derek J. Koehler and Nigel Harvey, 424–443. Malden: Blackwell Publishing.

Read, Daniel, Shane Frederick, and Mara Airoldi. 2012. Four days later in Cincinnati: Longitudinal tests of hyperbolic discounting. *Acta Psychologica* 140: 177–185.

Rizzo, Mario J., and Douglas Glen Whitman. 2009a. Little brother is watching you: New paternalism on the slippery slopes. *Arizona Law Review* 51: 685–739.

———. 2009b. The knowledge problem of new paternalism. *Brigham Young University Law Review* 2009(4): 905–968.

Savage, Leonard J. 1954. *The foundations of statistics.* New York: Wiley.

Scullum, Jacob. 2015. Snus and e-cigarettes are indisputably safer than smoking, contrary to what *The New York Times* wants you to think. *Hit & Run Blog*, April 24. http://reason.com/blog/2015/04/24/snus-and-e-cigarettes-are-indisputably-s. (It looks like the URL has been truncated).

Searle, John R. 1969. *Speech acts: An essay in the philosophy of language.* Cambridge: Cambridge University Press.

Sen, Amartya. 1993. Internal consistency of choice. *Econometrica* 61(3): 495–521.

Simon, Herbert A. 1990. Invariants of human behavior. *Annual Review of Psychology* 41: 1–19.

Sunstein, Cass R. 2014. *Why nudge?* New Haven: Yale University Press.

Sunstein, Cass R., and Richard H. Thaler. 2003. Libertarian paternalism is not an oxymoron. *University of Chicago Law Review* 70(4): 1159–1202.

Tavernise, Sabrina. 2015. Swedish Company asks F.D.A. to remove warnings from smokeless tobacco product. *The New York Times*, April 8.

Tergesen, Anne. 2011. 401(k) law suppresses saving for retirement. *The Wall Street Journal*, July 7.

Thaler, Richard H., and Cass R. Sunstein. 2003. Libertarian paternalism. *American Economic Review* 93(2): 175–179.

———. 2008. *Nudge: Improving decisions about health, wealth, and happiness.* New Haven: Yale University Press.

Tullock, Gordon. 1964. The irrationality of intransitivity. *Oxford Economic Papers* 16: 401–406.

Tversky, Amos, and Daniel Kahneman. 1974. Judgment under uncertainty: Heuristics and biases. *Science* 185(4157): 1124–1131.

Vineberg, Susan. 2011. Dutch book[ie?] arguments. In *The stanford encyclopedia of philosophy*, ed. Edward N. Zalta. http://plato.stanford.edu/archives/sum2011/entries/dutch-book/

Viscusi, W. Kip. 1990. Do smokers underestimate risks? *Journal of Political Economy* 98(6): 1253–1269.

———. 2002–2003. The new cigarette paternalism. *Regulation* 25: 58–64.

Volokh, Eugene. 2003. The mechanisms of the slippery slope. *Harvard Law Review* 116(4): 1026–1137.

Volz, Kirsten G., and Gerd Gigerenzer. 2012. Cognitive processes in decisions under risk are not the same as in decisions under uncertainty. *Frontiers of Neuroscience* 6: 105. http://doi.org/10.3389/fnins.2012.00105

Weatherly, Jeffrey N.   2014. On several factors that control rates of discounting. *Behavioral Processes* 104: 84–90.

Whitman, Douglas Glen, and Mario J. Rizzo.   2015. The problematic welfare standards of behavioral paternalism. *Review of Philosophy and Psychology* 6(3): 409–425.

Failing Better: What We Learn by Confronting Risk and Uncertainty

Adam Thierer

INTRODUCTION

Nudge advocates seek to improve decisions about health, wealth, and happiness by applying insights from human psychology and behavioral economics to public policy decision-making.[1] The chapters in this collection address the trade-offs associated with determining optimal default rules and devising laws and regulations that seek to engineer better "choice architecture."

Critics of nudge theory often attack this reasoning by noting the informational deficiencies faced by policymakers when making such decisions.[2] Those problems are valid, but an equally compelling critique of nudge theory attacks the underlying assumption that better choices must be "architected" at all to avoid undesirable outcomes. That is, advocates of either "soft" or "hard" paternalistic interventions often fail to appreciate the enormous value in allowing experiments—personal, organizational, and societal—to run their course and to "learn by doing."[3] Accordingly, this chapter addresses how nudge theory often ignores or devalues how ongoing experimentation and experience—including the possibility of

A. Thierer (✉)
Mercatus Center at George Mason University, Arlington, VA, USA

65

S. Abdukadirov (ed.), *Nudge Theory in Action*,
DOI 10.1007/978-3-319-31319-1_4

failure—facilitates greater learning, innovation, resiliency, and progress.[4] Put simply, when we fail, we can learn a great deal from it.

Policymakers and regulatory proponents often seek to short-circuit that process of ongoing trial-and-error experimentation, believing that they can anticipate and head off many mistakes through preemptive, precautionary steps. No amount of behavioral theorizing can substitute for the experiential value gained through ongoing real-world trials and errors, however.[5]

When it comes to human health, wealth, and happiness—and to social progress and prosperity more generally—there is no static equilibrium, no final destination. There is only a dynamic and never-ending learning process.[6] Learning from experience provides individuals and organizations with valuable informational inputs regarding which methods work better than others.[7] Even more importantly, learning by doing facilitates social and economic resiliency that helps individuals and organizations develop better coping strategies for when things go wrong. Behavioral theorists and nudge advocates often fail to incorporate these insights into their analysis and policy proposals.

A BETTER WAY TO THINK ABOUT RISK

To more fully appreciate what we learn by failing, the way we think and talk about risk must be reconsidered. Risk is often mistakenly conflated with harm itself when, in reality, risk represents only the *potential* for harm[8] or the "potential for an unwanted outcome."[9]

But even that definition is too limiting because *risk often involves the potential for desired outcomes as well as unwanted ones.*[10] Every thrill-seeker knows this. For example, someone who skydives from an airplane realizes that the potential for grave harm exists, but they also derive tremendous satisfaction from what they regard as a thrilling experience. Importantly, while it is somewhat easier to value the former (i.e., the loss of life or danger of extreme injury), the latter (happiness or utility) is harder to value. This can lead to an overestimation of the catastrophic (but unlikely) danger and a devaluing of the subjective (but almost certain) reward.

Much the same holds true for anyone who has ever started a business. Saint Thomas Aquinas once noted that, "If the highest aim of a captain were to preserve his ship, he would keep it in port forever."[11] Of course, no captain does so because they have higher aspirations. Like captains of ships, businesspeople know the possibility of failure exists when they "take a risk" with a new venture or investment, but so too does the potential for enormous reward. That is why they steer the ship of industry out of port and into the brave unknown (and potentially quite risky) waters. If they didn't, progress would never occur and society would suffer. As Sir Alfred Pugsley, one of the foremost modern experts on structural engineering, once noted, "A profession that never has accidents is unlikely to be serving its country efficiently."[12]

Generally speaking, therefore, we can think of two types of potential benefits associated with taking a chance. One is static in that unless you (1) take a risk you have no chance of a good outcome. For instance, if you don't buy a lottery ticket, you are not going to win. The second benefit is (2) dynamic and implies learning. If you take a risk and fail, you might learn something that allows you or someone else to improve the probability distribution next time around.

This way of thinking about risk can be applied in more mundane ways. For example, anyone who uses a knife or ladder in their home or office to complete a task understands the potential for both harm and benefit associated with those tools. But countless tasks would be made more difficult—perhaps even impossible—without them. The static benefit, therefore, is that nothing is ever going to get done easily in the kitchen or garage without a knife handy. The dynamic benefit is that, when mistakes are made with knives, we learn how to use them better the next time around to get those tasks done more effectively and safely.

For these reasons, risk must be thought of as a two-sided coin involving the potential for both harm and benefit with learning-by-doing being the core benefit of the process.

WHY EMBRACE FAILURE? THE BENEFITS OF LEARNING BY DOING

The idea of embracing failure may seem bizarre and defeatist at first, but its benefits are numerous, and were perhaps best summarized by the novelist and playwright Samuel Beckett, who once counseled: "Ever tried. Ever failed. No matter. Try Again. Fail again. Fail better."[13]

The value of "failing better" is often overlooked in public policy debates, and especially in discussions of behavioral economics and nudge theory. Individuals, organizations, and nations all benefit from the knowledge they gain from making mistakes. "Humiliating to human pride as it may be," the Nobel prize-winning economist Friedrich Hayek once wrote, "we must recognize that the advance and even preservation of civilization are dependent upon a maximum of opportunity for accidents to happen."[14]

What both Beckett and Hayek were alluding to was that there is enormous value tied up with learning to confront and cope with risk through ongoing experimentation. Progress and prosperity are inextricably linked to trial-and-error experimentation, including the freedom to fail in the process. "We could virtually end all risk of failure by simply declaring a moratorium on innovation, change, and progress," notes engineering historian Henry Petroski.[15] But the costs to society of doing so would be catastrophic. "The history of the human race would be dreary indeed if none of our forebears had ever been willing to accept risk in return for potential achievement," observed H.L. Lewis, an expert on technological risk trade-offs.[16] Somewhat paradoxically, therefore, we must tolerate a certain amount of short-term failure if we want long-term success.[17]

Again, consider basic tools we use almost every day. Most of us suffered a few cuts or burns while learning to use fire or sharp knives to prepare meals. But these failures taught us important life skills and helped us develop a sense of personal responsibility. Likewise, firms learn important lessons when their business plans fail and the public rejects their goods or services.[18] The economist Joseph Schumpeter famously described the "perennial gales of creative destruction" that constantly renew capitalist economies.[19] If we disallowed risk-taking and propped up every failing business model, society would never discover new and better ways of innovating and satisfying consumer needs.

These lessons seem self-evident yet are often ignored in the public policy arena. Indeed, if there is a unifying feature associated with much modern policymaking, it is the seemingly insatiable impulse to preemptively eliminate the potential for failure through well-intentioned regulations—including nudges.[20] Despite the best of intentions, those preemptive safeguards are typically counterproductive and even dangerous to long-run economic growth and social prosperity.[21]

The benefit of allowing individuals, organizations, and society more generally to fail freely is that (a) we learn how to do a thing better the next time around and (b) we develop better coping skills in the process of facing adversity, helping us to better adjust to future failures.[22] In other words, it's about building resiliency.[23] "Regular, modest failures are actually *essential* to many forms of resilience—they allow a system to release and then reorganize some of its resources," note Andrew Zolli and Ann Marie Healy, authors of, *Resilience: Why Things Bounce Back*.[24]

Nudge advocates often claim that various supposed cognitive deficiencies among consumers or companies can be preemptively diagnosed and remedied through policy interventions. But positive feedback and learning cannot occur without the possibility of failure. "The role of individual learning and adaptation, however, cannot be ignored in assessing the need for paternalism," argues Jeffrey J. Rachlinski. "Simple experience might, in some contexts, be a much better cure for cognitive missteps than adopting a paternalist intervention."[25] The problem with nudges, Jonathan Klick and Gregory Mitchell note, is that they, "interfere with information searches, educational investments, and feedback that would occur in the absence of paternalistic interventions and that are important to the individual's development of effective decision-making skills and strategies."[26]

This gives rise to "cognitive hazards" or cognitive deficiencies of a different sort than those which concern nudge advocates. Again, seeking to head-off failure in the short-term creates the potential for more serious failures in the long-run because individuals aren't learning how to cope with those failures and advance their knowledge because, as the case studies below will illustrate, "learning may be greatest in response to negative or unfavorable outcomes."[27] And this is equally true for even softer forms of paternalism, including minor nudges meant to gently push individual decision-making in even slightly different directions.[28]

Again, this learning by doing (and failing) process creates powerful feedback loops in both the individual and institutional contexts.[29] Indeed, its importance scales up to the entire economy. "Once failure is recognized as being just as important as success in the market process," note economists Steven Horwitz and Jack Knych, "it should be clear that the goal of a society should be to create an environment that not only allows people to succeed freely but to fail freely as well."[30]

WHY PRECAUTION OFTEN DICTATES POLICY

Unfortunately, in the context of public policy, many factors conspire to make "failing freely" very challenging. Lawmakers and regulators are naturally risk-averse because they fear the political ramifications associated with short-term setbacks. As a result, they sometimes slow the pace of innovation, or directly restrict certain types of economic and social experimentation, to avoid unwanted outcomes for which they might be blamed.

These policymakers are engaged in "precautionary principle" thinking and rulemaking activities.[31] The precautionary principle generally holds that, because a new idea or innovation could pose some theoretical danger or risk in the future, public policies should control or limit the development of such innovations until their creators can prove that they won't cause any harms.[32] The classic articulation of the principle was set forth by a collection of environmental activists in the 1998 "Wingspread Consensus Statement," which stated that, "When an activity raises threats of harm to human health or environment, precautionary measures should be taken even if some cause and effect relationships are not fully established scientifically."[33]

The problem with letting such precautionary thinking guide policy is that it poses a serious threat to technological progress, economic entrepreneurialism, social adaptation, and long-run prosperity.[34] If public policy is guided at every turn by the precautionary principle, innovation is hindered based on fear of the unknown; hypothetical worst-case scenarios trump all other considerations.[35] Social learning and economic opportunities become far less likely, perhaps even impossible, under such a regime. In practical terms, it means fewer services, lower quality goods, higher prices, diminished economic growth, and a decline in the overall standard of living.[36]

Political scientist Aaron Wildavsky identified the problem with precautionary principle thinking when he described it as "trial *without* error" reasoning. Wildavsky argued that real wisdom is born of experience and that we can only learn how to be wealthier and healthier as individuals and a society by first being willing to embrace uncertainty and even occasional failure:

> The direct implication of trial without error is obvious: If you can do nothing without knowing first how it will turn out, you cannot do anything at all. An indirect implication of trial without error is that if trying new things is made more costly, there will be fewer departures from past practice; this very lack of change may itself be dangerous in forgoing chances to reduce existing hazards. ... Existing hazards will continue to cause harm if we fail to reduce them by taking advantage of the opportunity to benefit from repeated trials.[37]

More recently, Nassim Nicholas Taleb has highlighted the benefits that flow from "using error as a source of information. If every trial provides you with information about what *does not* work," he notes, "you start zooming in on a solution—so every attempt becomes more valuable, more like an expense than an error. And of course you make discoveries along the way."[38] This notion that "success is the culmination of many failures"[39] was perfectly captured by inventor Thomas Edison when he famously noted of his 10,000 failed light bulb experiments: "I have not failed 10,000 times. I have not failed once. I have succeeded in proving that those 10,000 ways will not work. When I have eliminated the ways that will not work, I will find the way that will work."[40] In this sense, as one expert on innovation policy recent noted, "Failure is lesson, not loss; it is gain, not shame."[41]

The lesson here is that the ongoing process of experimentation and failure helps bring us closer to ideal states and outcomes (not just more innovation but also more wealth, better health, etc.). *But we will never discover better ways of doing things unless the process of evolutionary, experimental change is allowed to continue.* Individuals and institutions must be at liberty to keep trying *and keep failing* in order to learn how to move forward and prosper.[42] As the examples discussed below make clear, the big leaps forward in societal learning and economic progress came about as a result of what we learned following various failures, even catastrophes. Precautionary principle reasoning and policymaking makes that process less likely, perhaps even impossible. Living in constant fear of worst-case scenarios—and premising public policy upon them—means that best-case scenarios will never come about.[43] As the old saying goes, "Nothing ventured, nothing gained."[44]

WHY FAILURE IS VITAL TO PROGRESS IN ENGINEERING

Let us consider some instructive examples of this process in action. First, consider what we can learn about the importance of "learning by doing"—and failing—from the history of structural and mechanical engineering. Structures such as skyscrapers and suspension bridges, and machines such as ships and airplanes, are remarkably sophisticated contraptions. What's more remarkable, however, is the fact that so few of them fail today. Of course, that has everything to do with the fact that previous iterations of each *did* fail and that we learned so much from those failures.

"It is both a sad and happy fact of engineering history that disasters have been powerful instruments of change," notes technological historian Edward Tenner. "Designers learn from failure. Industrial society did not invent grand works of engineering, and it was not the first to know design failure. What it did do," Tenner says, "was develop powerful techniques for learning [from??] the experience of past disasters."[45]

Henry Petroski, author of *To Engineer Is Human: The Role of Failure in Successful Design*, has noted that the entire history of engineering has been one of learning from occasional failures, including buildings and bridges falling down and ships and planes sinking or crashing.[46] But,

> were we not willing to try the untried, we would have no exciting new uses of architectural space, we would be forced to take ferries across many a river, and we would have no trans-Atlantic jet service. While the curse of human nature appears to be to make mistakes, its determination appears to be to succeed.[47]

Thus, while it is true that "disasters that do occur are ultimate failures of design," Petroski notes that "the lessons learned from those disasters can do more to advance engineering knowledge than all the successful machines and structures in the world." He concludes that, "to understand what engineering is and what engineers do is to understand how failures can happen and how they can contribute more than successes to advance technology."[48]

This explains how failure teaches us how to not only cope with adversity but also become far safer in the long run. "The importance of past tragedy (whether of natural or human origin) for safety suggests a positive corollary of Murphy's Law," notes Tenner. "It is that sometimes things can go right only by first going very wrong."[49]

This uncomfortable reality will not sit well with many safety-conscious regulatory advocates who might suggest that past failures simply mean that society must redouble our efforts to find preemptive, precautionary solutions and avoid similar accidents and calamities in the future. But, again, that ignores the fact that strict application of that principle would mean many life-enriching, and even life-saving, innovations would ever come about.[50]

THE PROBLEM OF "SURPLUS SAFETY" ON THE PLAYGROUND

Just as engineers benefit from "learning by doing," and by failing, so too do individuals in their everyday lives—even children.

Recall, as noted earlier, how we benefit in the long run by learning how to use basic tools such as knives and ladders early in life—even with some cuts and falls suffered in the process. Similarly, any parent who has witnessed with great anxiety the first time their child rode a bike without training wheels well understands that "falling down is part of growing up."[51] If the training wheels never came off, the experience of riding a bike would never be truly mastered.[52] But the secondary effects of prohibiting the learning process would be even more profound. People would not learn to ride their bikes better or faster. They would not go as far on them. They also might not be willing to use even more sophisticated machines out of fear of the potential dangers associated with them.

If this sounds like a far-fetched hypothetical, consider a powerful real-world case study of this phenomenon in action: the recent push for greater playground safety. Individuals who grew up before the 1980s can remember a time when every playground had jungle gyms and other tall structures for kids to climb and explore. Then, over the course of the following two decades, those tall playground structures started disappearing.[53] Today, it is difficult to find many playgrounds—and almost none near schools—where tall climbing structures exist for kids.[54] "The old tall jungle gyms and slides disappeared from most American playgrounds across the country in recent decades because of parental concerns, federal guidelines, new safety standards set by manufacturers and—the most frequently cited factor—fear of lawsuits," notes John Tierney of *The New York Times*.[55]

Those safety-conscious moves were motivated by the best of intentions. Plenty of kids were injured falling off tall structures through the years, so tearing down those structures or regulating them to be lower in height decreased the danger associated with playground accidents—at least those accidents associated with falls from tall, man-made structures. Limitations or bans have been imposed on playgrounds in some communities, not only due to increased regulation by local governments and the US Consumer Product Safety Commission[56] but also by fear of lawsuits following injuries to some children. Incidentally, the same process unfolded for high diving boards at swimming pools over the past two decades, and today it is happening again with snow sledding down large hills.[57]

But, again, risk is a two-sided coin and something valuable is being lost when we eliminate all these things from childhood or severely restrict them out of an abundance of caution. When tall climbing structures are highly regulated or removed from playgrounds, for example, children lose the chance to experience the thrill of pushing limits and learning from that process. "Children need to encounter risks and overcome fears on the playground," observes Dr. Ellen Sandseter, a professor of psychology at Queen Maud University in Norway.[58] She notes that,

> Climbing equipment needs to be high enough, or else it will be too boring in the long run. Children approach thrills and risks in a progressive manner, and very few children would try to climb to the highest point for the first time they climb. The best thing is to let children encounter these challenges from an early age, and they will then progressively learn to master them through their play over the years.[59]

Sandseter and her colleagues cite a wealth of academic studies showing that experimentation and experience builds resiliency into children that can help them develop vital coping skills that will help them later in life.[60] As Tierney summarizes:

> While some psychologists—and many parents have worried that a child who suffered a bad fall would develop a fear of heights, studies have shown the opposite pattern: A child who's hurt in a fall before the age of 9 is less likely as a teenager to have a fear of heights.[61]

In other words, an overly cautious approach to playground safety is counterproductive. It potentially creates life-long anxieties and phobias that discourage normal play, experimentation, learning, and enjoyment. "Overprotection might thus result in exaggerated levels of anxiety [for children]," Sandseter concludes.[62] "Overprotection through governmental control of playgrounds and exaggerated fear of playground accidents might thus result in an increase of anxiety in society. We might need to provide more stimulating environments for children, rather than hamper their development."[63]

There are other secondary effects associated with what some have referred to as "surplus safety" on playgrounds.[64] If creative exploration on playgrounds is discouraged or forbidden, it certainly will not help alleviate the growing problem of childhood obesity.[65] A recent study of 34 daycare centers by five pediatric researchers confirmed that "[s]ocietal priorities for young children—safety and school readiness—may be hindering children's physical development."[66] In particular, those researchers found that "[s]tricter licensing codes intended to reduce children's injuries on playgrounds rendered playgrounds less physically challenging and interesting.

... Because children spend long hours in care and many lack a safe place to play near their home, these barriers may limit children's only opportunity to engage in physical activity."[67]

Reduced playground time might also affect the sociability of youth by diminishing interaction opportunities and the resulting learning experiences.[68] It also might limit the ability of children to explore and learn from nature.[69]

The lesson here can be applied more generally beyond playgrounds. Tim Gill, author of *No Fear: Growing Up in a Risk Averse Society*, puts it best:

> It is worth reminding ourselves of two truths about how children grow up to be confident, resilient, responsible people. First, they have to be given the chance to learn from their mistakes. Second, the best classroom for learning about everyday life is indisputably the real world, beyond home and school. Rather than having a nanny state, where regulation, control and risk aversion dominate the landscape, we should embrace a philosophy of resilience.[70]

THE EU, RISK-AVERSE CULTURE, AND THE IMPACT ON ENTREPRENEURIALISM

Finally, let's consider a case study that involves entire continents and large economies. When a country or continent's policymakers decide to institute precautionary principle-based policies in an attempt to head-off any number of perceived worst-case scenarios, the results can be devastating for consumers, innovators, competitiveness, and living standards.

Consider the real-world experiment that has played out on either side of the Atlantic over the past two decades in terms of how the European Union and the USA dealt with the rise of the Internet and the data-driven, digital economy.

Many economists and other observers have documented Europe's ongoing struggle with chronic unemployment and general economic malaise.[71] Writing in November 2014, *The Wall Street Journal*'s Matt Moffett noted that, "Scarce capital, dense bureaucracy, a culture deeply averse to risk and a cratered consumer market all suppress startups in Europe."[72] Moffett cited results from the Global Entrepreneurship Monitor, which surveys startup activity, finding that early-stage entrepreneurial activity in 2013 was just 5 % in Germany, 4.6 % in France, and 3.4 % in Italy, compared with 12.7 % in the US. Moffet noted that many academics and business analysts had attributed this to "a deeply ingrained fear of failure that is a bigger impediment to entrepreneurship on the Continent than in other regions."[73]

Europe's risk-averse culture and "fear-of-failure" policies have also likely held back digital innovation. Beginning in 1995 with the adoption of its Data Protection Directive, the European Union has instituted highly restrictive policies governing online data collection and use. The EU's approach has been shaped by precautionary principle thinking at every turn, based largely on concerns about privacy and data security.

Meanwhile, the USA adopted a very different disposition that favored risk-taking and "permissionless innovation," or the general notion that experimentation with new technologies and business models should generally be permitted by default.[74] Disruptive technologies were embraced (or at least permitted) in the USA and it resulted in the explosive growth of the Internet and America's information technology sectors (computing, software, Internet services, etc.) over the past two decades.[75] Those sectors have ushered in a generation of innovations and innovators that are now household names across the world, including in Europe.[76]

The results of this real-world experiment have been striking. Analysts at the economic consultancy Booz & Company release annual surveys of the world's most innovative companies and, over the past decade, America's info-tech sectors have dominated the top 10 list. For example, the firm's 2013 list revealed that 9 of the top 10 most innovative global companies are based in the USA and that most of them are involved in computing, software, and digital technology.[77] No European company has made the list since 2010. Another recent survey revealed that the world's 15 most valuable Internet companies (based on market capitalizations) have a combined market value of nearly $2.5 trillion, but none of them are European while 11 of them are US firms.[78]

Many European officials and business leaders are waking up to this grim reality and are wondering how to reverse this situation. Danish economist Jacob Kirkegaard of the Peterson Institute for International Economics notes that Europeans "all want a Silicon Valley. ... But none of them can match the scale and focus on the new and truly innovative technologies you have in the United States. Europe and the rest of the world are playing catch-up, to the great frustration of policy makers there."[79]

Again, attitudes toward risk and failure account for these differences. German economist Petra Moser notes that Europeans are "trying to recreate Silicon Valley in places like Munich, so far with little success," because "[t]he institutional and cultural differences are still too great" and "In Europe, stability is prized" above all else, she says.[80] In a recent *New York Times* essay on this trans-Atlantic clash of visions, James B. Stewart noted that:

> Often overlooked in the success of American start-ups is the even greater number of failures. "Fail fast, fail often" is a Silicon Valley mantra, and the freedom to innovate is inextricably linked to the freedom to fail. In Europe, failure carries a much greater stigma than it does in the United States.[81]

Moreover, he notes, "Europeans are also much less receptive to the kind of truly disruptive innovation represented by a Google or a Facebook."[82]

What European regulators fail to appreciate is, as Daniel Castro and Alan McQuinn of the Information Technology and Innovation Foundation observe, that "Innovation is about risk, and if innovators fear they will be punished for every mistake … then they will be much less assertive in trying to develop the next new thing."[83]

Unsurprisingly, many European officials are unhappy that American operators enjoy these competitive advantages and they are now looking to force their more restrictive policies on US-based digital innovators.[84] The easier way to "level the playing field" between digital rivals on either side of the Atlantic would be for Europe to relax its restrictive, risk-averse policies to give their innovators a better chance of learning from marketplace experimentation. Of course, that would mean that European policymakers would need to be willing to embrace the possibility that many of those firms would fail, or to the extent they succeeded, that traditional privacy regulations and other regulations might need to change.

Thus far, most European officials have shown little willingness to embrace that option. In fact, within the so-called sharing economy, European governments have moved aggressively to limit or shut down ride-sharing provider Uber. Following a major strike by French taxi drivers during the summer of 2015, France went so far as to arrest two Uber executives.[85] (Ironically, downloads of Uber's mobile app increased following the arrests.[86]) There's even talk in Europe of creating an EU-wide super-regulator, mostly to address concerns about US-based tech companies.[87]

Such moves are motivated by a fear of disruption and change. Whether it is economic or social norms, failure is literally not an option in some European countries; public policies will protect industries, organizations, professions, or even just cultural norms that are threatened by technological change. The irony, however, is that the more overzealously European officials seek to avoid the possibility of various short-term failures, the more prone the continent is to potentially far more dangerous and systemic failures in the long term.[88]

EPISTEMIC IGNORANCE PERPETUATES THE PRECAUTIONARY PRINCIPLE PROBLEM

These examples make it clear that there is immense value in embracing "risk" and learning from failing often in the process. We can now marry this insight to the more predominant critique of paternalistic nudges, which is identified in other chapters of this book: behavioral theorists and nudge advocates spend so much time focused on the supposed irrationality of consumers or organizations that they ignore the irrationality or ignorance of those who (incorrectly) believe they are in the best position to solve every complex social or economic problem through paternalistic policy solutions.

Policymakers simply do not possess the requisite knowledge to perfectly plan for every conceivable outcome and they also frequently ignore the unintended consequences of well-intentioned policies.[89] Unfortunately, like most other humans, regulators suffer from what Taleb calls "epistemic ignorance" or hubris concerning the limits of our knowledge. "We are demonstrably arrogant about what we think we know," he says.[90] "We overestimate what we know, and underestimate uncertainty."[91]

Maureen K. Ohlhausen, a commissioner at the Federal Trade Commission, has succinctly explained why the paternalistic, precautionary mindset is dangerous when enshrined into laws or regulations, especially when used to regulate new, fast-moving technologies:

> It is ... vital that government officials, like myself, approach new technologies with a dose of regulatory humility, by working hard to educate ourselves and others about the innovation, understand its effects on consumers and the marketplace, identify benefits and likely harms, and, if harms do arise, consider whether existing laws and regulations are sufficient to address them, before assuming that new rules are required.[92]

In light of the limits of our ability to plan or predict the technological future, we must recognize the dangers associated with top-down, fear-of-failure thinking. We must push back against what Tim Harford, author of *Adapt*, calls the "God Complex," which refers to the general belief that within our own specialized areas of expertise we know everything there is to know about a subject.[93] More broadly, it is important to avoid what economist Harold Demsetz referred to as the "Nirvana approach" to policy, or the comparison of real-world phenomena and results with hypothetically perfect alternatives, which are logically impossible.[94]

This is true even for minor policy nudges aimed at correcting for supposed consumer biases. After all, regulators and policymakers bring their own biases to the table when seeking to supposedly correct the biases of others and, as Wright and Ginsberg note, "behaviorist proposals frequently assume that the social costs of cognitive error are large and presumptively greater than the cost of the regulatory solution designed to reduce them."[95] They conclude:

> In short, not all errors imply irrationality because perfect decisionmaking would be costly. To miss subtle distinctions between rational and irrational decisionmaking will almost certainly lead to erroneous conclusions about legal policy. The data required to distinguish rational mistakes from irrational mistakes, much less to estimate the magnitude of any welfare loss caused by the latter, are significant and may be unavailable.[96]

Moreover, "[b]ecause regulation often represents the preferences of high-income households and reduces the disposable income of low-income households, regulation has a regressive effect."[97] Thus, regulation—especially nudges—may simply substitute the values and priorities of some groups for others and diminish overall welfare in the process.[98]

WHEN SHOULD PRECAUTION PREVAIL?

Of course, a certain amount of precautionary regulation *might* make sense when the potential harm being considered is so immediate, tangible, highly probable, and potentially catastrophic in nature that "learning by doing" simply isn't practical or wise. For example, almost all countries prohibit the private possession of uranium, bazookas, and tanks. These things are banned because it is generally acknowledged that their unrestricted use would have disastrous consequences. But most cases aren't like this. Instead, we generally allow citizens to freely experiment with technologies, and even engage in risky behaviors, unless a compelling case can be made that precautionary regulation is necessary.[99] And this is equally true of many items that individuals may unintentionally harm themselves with, as was already discussed in the case of knives, ladders, and so on.

How is the determination made regarding when precaution makes sense? This is where the role of benefit-cost analysis (BCA) and regulatory impact analysis is essential to getting policy right.[100] BCA represents an effort to formally identify the trade-offs associated with regulatory proposals and, to the maximum extent feasible, quantify those benefits and costs.[101] BCA generally cautions against preemptive, precautionary regulation unless all other options have been exhausted—thus allowing trial-and-error experimentation and "learning by doing" to continue.

At the federal level in the USA, regulatory policymaking and the BCA process are directed by various presidential executive orders and guidance issued by the White House Office of Information and Regulatory Affairs (OIRA).[102] As part of any BCA review, OIRA demands "a clear explanation of the need for the regulatory action, including a description of the problem that the agency seeks to address."[103] As part of this step, OIRA specifies, "Agencies should explain whether the action is intended to address a market failure or to promote some other goal."[104] Second, "[a] clear identification of a range of regulatory approaches" is required "including the option of not regulating."[105] Agencies must also consider other alternatives to federal regulation, such as "State or local regulation, voluntary action on the part of the private sector, antitrust enforcement, consumer-initiated litigation in the product liability system, and administrative compensation systems."[106] Agencies are supposed to assess the benefits and costs of all these alternatives.[107] If federal regulation is still deemed necessary, flexible approaches are strongly encouraged by OIRA.[108] Finally, "[a]n estimate of the benefits and costs—both quantitative and qualitative" is required.[109] The quantification of benefits and costs is strongly encouraged but, when that is impossible, agencies are required to describe them qualitatively and make a clear case for action.[110]

Unfortunately, regulators often ignore those requirements, or at least do not take them seriously enough.[111] Worse yet, many agencies are neither required to conduct BCA nor have their rulemaking activities approved by OIRA. This is like giving regulators a free pass to meddle with new innovation without any serious oversight.

All new proposed regulatory enactments—even nudges of a "soft" nature—should be subjected to strict BCA and, if they are formally enacted, they should also be retrospectively reviewed to gauge their cost-effectiveness and continued need.[112] Better yet, sunsetting guidelines should be applied to make sure outdated regulations are periodically removed from the books so that innovation is not discouraged.

Of course, every effort should be made to exhaust all other options before even entertaining a discussion about the need for new regulations and restrictions. Less-restrictive approaches based on transparency, education, and empowerment are almost always preferable to precautionary prohibitions.[113] Whether it is health and safety regulation or economic policy, giving the public more information and helping them make decisions for themselves is usually the superior option when compared to more restrictive regulatory approaches. Education and empowerment-based strategies leave more breathing room for continuous learning and innovation through trial-and-error experimentation. Common law legal remedies—contract and property law, torts, and so on—are also more sensible alternatives when compared to paternalistic controls. Such ex post remedies allow for experimentation to continue and then let courts identify more serious harms as they develop.[114]

Conclusion: Avoiding Failure Leads to Failure

If we hope to prosper both as individuals and as a society, we must preserve the general freedom to "learn by doing," and even to fail frequently in the process. Both individuals and institutions learn how to do things better—both more efficiently and safer—by making mistakes and dealing with adversity. Facing up to challenges and failures is never easy, but it helps us learn how to cope with change and continuously devise new systems and solutions to accommodate those disruptions.[115]

For these reasons, we should embrace failure as an essential ingredient to the success of a free and prosperous society and not try to "nudge" it out of existence.[116] "Success may be grand, but disappointment can often teach us more," Petroski noted of the history of engineering.[117] Much the same can be said of economic and social experience and experiments more generally. Rigid precautionary principle thinking and policymaking, by contrast, interrupts this learning progress and leaves us *more* vulnerable to the most serious problems we might face as individuals or a society. Paradoxically, then, we can conclude that individuals, institutions, and countries that overzealously seek to avoid the possibility of certain short-term failures are actually prone to potentially far more dangerous and systemic failures in the long term.[118]

NOTES

1. Richard H. Thaler and Cass R. Sunstein, *Nudge: Improving Decisions About Health, Wealth, and Happiness* (Yale University Press, 2008). A concise overview of behavioral economics—and critique of its applications—can be found in: Christopher Koopman and Nita Ghei, "Behavioral Economics, Consumer Choice, and Regulatory Agencies," *Economic Perspectives*, Mercatus Center at George Mason University, August 27, 2013, http://mercatus.org/publication/behavioral-economics-consumer-choice-and-regulatory-agencies

2. *See generally*, Joshua D. Wright and Douglas Ginsberg, "Behavioral Law and Economics: Its Origins, Fatal Flaws, and Implications for Liberty," *Northwestern University Law Review* 106(3) (2012); Joshua D. Wright, "Behavioral Law and Economics, Paternalism, and Consumer Contracts: An Empirical Perspective," *NYU Journal of Law & Liberty* 2(3) (2007); James C. Cooper, "Behavioral Economics and Biased Regulators," Mercatus Center, *Mercatus on Policy*, November 21, 2013, http://mercatus.org/publication/behavioral-economics-and-biased-regulators

3. Jonathan Klick and Gregory Mitchell, "Government Regulation of Irrationality: Moral and Cognitive Hazards," *Minnesota Law Review* 90 (2006): 1626. ("research from developmental psychology indicates that individuals improve their decision-making skills over time through a 'learning by doing' process, and that paternalistic policies threaten interference in this self-regulatory process.").

4. Sim B. Sitkin, "Learning Through Failure: The Strategy of Small Losses," in Michael D. Cohen and Lee S. Sproull (eds.), *Organizational Learning* (Thousand Oaks: Sage, 1996): 541–578, ("There is substantial consensus that successful innovation requires risk-taking, experimentation, and failure.").

5. Wright and Ginsberg, "Behavioral Law and Economics," at 1044–5. ("many (but not all) of the behaviorists' findings are fragile and disappear when exposed to market discipline and the profit motive, which create incentives for participants to specialize and to learn to reduce their errors. These incentives are not present in the laboratory.").

6. Mary Douglas and Aaron Wildavsky, *Risk and Culture* (Berkeley: University of California Press, 1983): 195. ("Relative safety is not a static but rather a dynamic product of learning from error over time.... The fewer the trials?? and the fewer the mistakes to learn from, the more error remains uncorrected.").

7. Ibid., 14. ("much new knowledge must be acquired through experimentation or learning by doing; implementation often involves a long feedback loop where each incremental improvement in the technology requires new skills, which make further improvements feasible...").

8. Institutional Review Board for the Social and Behavioral Sciences (IRB-SBS) at the University of Virginia, "Defining Risk," [last accessed December 20, 2014], http://www.virginia.edu/vpr/irb/sbs/resources_guide_risk_define.html

9. Department of Homeland Security, Risk Steering Committee, *DHS Risk Lexicon*, (September 2008): 24, https://www.dhs.gov/xlibrary/assets/dhs_risk_lexicon.pdf

10. Mary Douglas and Aaron Wildavsky, *Risk and Culture* (Berkeley: University of California Press, 1983): 22. ("Risk is also opportunity.").

11. Thomas Aquinas, *Summa Theologica*, I-II, q. 2, art. 5.

12. Quoted in Henry Petroski, *To Engineer is Human: The Role of Failure in Successful Design* (New York: Vintage, 1992): 221.

13. Samuel Beckett, "Worstward Ho," (1983).

14. F. A. Hayek, *The Constitution of Liberty* (1960): 29.

15. Henry Petroski, *To Engineer Is Human: The Role of Failure in Successful Design* (New York: Vintage, 1992): 170.

16. H. W. Lewis, *Technological Risk* (New York: WW. Norton & Co., 1990): x.

17. Megan McArdle, *The Up Side of Down: Why Failing Well Is the Key to Success* (New York: Viking, 2014), 206. ("Normal accident theory tells us that we often have to live with some background rate of disasters. But no one wants to be at the mercy of the universe. Identifying mistakes and culprits tells us that we can control those accidents, and make them not-so-normal.").

18. An extensive literature exists in the fields of business management and organizational communication regarding what firms and other organizations can learn from their own past failure or the failure of other organizations. *See*, e.g., Sim B. Sitkin, "Learning Through

Failure: The Strategy of Small Losses," in Michael D. Cohen and Lee S. Sproull (eds.), *Organizational Learning* (Thousand Oaks: Sage, 1996): 541–578; Philippe Baumard and William H. Starbuck, "Learning from Failures: Why It May Not Happen," *Long Range Planning* 38 (2005): 281–298; Mark D. Cannon and Amy C. Edmondson, "Failing to Learn and Learning to Fail (Intelligently): How Great Organizations Put Failure to Work to Innovate and Improve," *Long Range Planning* 38 (2005): 299–319; Dean A. Shepherd, "Educating Entrepreneurship Students about Emotion and Learning from Failure," *Academy of Management Learning & Education*, 3(3) (2004): 274–287; Rita Gunther McGrath, "Failing by Design," *Harvard Business Review*, April 2011, https://hbr.org/2011/04/failing-by-design

19. Joseph Schumpeter, *Capitalism, Socialism and Democracy* (New York: Harper Perennial, 1942, 2008) 84.

20. Daniel Castro and Alan McQuinn, "How and When Regulators Should Intervene," Information Technology and Innovation Foundation Reports, (February 2015): 1, http://www.itif.org/publications/how-and-when-regulators-should-intervene. ("[I]nnovation by its very nature involves risks and mistakes—the very things regulators inherently want to avoid.").

21. Nathan Rosenberg and L. E. Birdzell Jr., *How the West Grew Rich: The Economic Transformation of the Industrial World* (New York: Basic Books, 1986), 29. ("Uncertainty runs throughout the process of innovation. ... The only known device for resolving the uncertainties surrounding any given innovation proposal is experiment, up to and including the manufacture and marketing of a product. Such experiments are costly; on the other hand, the failure to undertake them precludes the possibility of innovation. And the consequences of successful experiments are economic growth.") Joseph Epstein, "ObamaCare and the Good Intentions Paving Co.," *Wall Street Journal*, December 31, 2013, http://online.wsj.com/news/articles/SB10001424052702304020704579276942556236158, ("Unfortunately, when it comes to public policy, good intentions are only slightly better than bad intentions, and not always even that.").

22. Aaron Wildavsky, *Searching for Safety* (New Brunswick: Transaction Books, 1988), 103. ("Allowing, indeed, encouraging, trial and error should lead to many more winners, because of (a) increased wealth,

(b) increased knowledge, and (c) increased coping mechanisms, i.e., increased resilience in general.") Mary Douglas and Aaron Wildavsky, *Risk and Culture* (Berkeley: University of California Press, 1983): 197. ("If some degree of risk is inevitable, suppressing it in one place often merely moves it to another. Shifting risks may be more dangerous than tolerating them, both because those who face new risks may be unaccustomed to them and because those who no longer face old ones may be more vulnerable when conditions change.").

23. Mary Douglas and Aaron Wildavsky, *Risk and Culture* (Berkeley: University of California Press, 1983): 196. ("Resilience is the capacity to use change to better cope with the unknown; it is learning to bounce back.").

24. Andrew Zolli and Ann Marie Healy, *Resilience: Why Things Bounce Back* (New York: Free Press, 2012): 13.

25. Jeffrey J. Rachlinski, "The Uncertain Psychological Case for Paternalism," *Northwestern University Law Review* 97, (2003): 1165. *Also see* Jonathan Klick and Gregory Mitchell, "Government Regulation of Irrationality: Moral and Cognitive Hazards," *Minnesota Law Review* 90 (2006): 1629. ("Through education, experimentation, experience, and observation, individuals learn which options are most likely to produce desirable outcomes and develop competence in the ability to compile and rank-order options, and then select the option that will lead to the most favorable outcome.").

26. Ibid., 1626.

27. Ibid., 1636.

28. Ibid., 1632. ("Softer forms of paternalism may also adversely affect learning by altering the individual's representation of the choice setting and how she encodes feedback about success or failure in a given situation. The individual does not exert the same level of control in compiling and assessing options in the presence of soft paternalism, and verbal feedback about even a soft paternalistic situation should cause the individual to discount her own role in achieving a particular outcome.").

29. For an overview of the literature on learning by doing in the context of organizational management, see: Barbara Levitt and James G. March, "Organizational Learning," in Michael D. Cohen and Lee S. Sproull (eds.), *Organizational Learning* (Thousand Oaks: Sage, 1996): 516–540.

30. Steven Horwitz and Jack Knych, "The Importance of Failure," *The Freeman* 61(9) (November 2011), http://www.fee.org/the_freeman/detail/the-importance-of-failure#axzz2ZnNlpqHQ

31. Adam Thierer, "Technopanics, Threat Inflation, and the Danger of an Information Technology Precautionary Principle," *Minnesota Journal of Law, Science & Technology* 14(1) (2013): 309–386.

32. *See*, e.g., John Frank Weaver, "We Need to Pass Legislation on Artificial Intelligence Early and Often," *Slate*, September 12, 2014, http://www.slate.com/blogs/future_tense/2014/09/12/we_need_to_pass_artificial_intelligence_laws_early_and_often.html

33. "Wingspread Conference on the Precautionary Principle," January 26, 1998, http://www.sehn.org/wing.html

34. Jonathan H. Adler, "The Problems with Precaution: A Principle Without Principle," *The American*, May 25, 2011, http://www.american.com/archive/2011/may/the-problems-with-precaution-a-principle-without-principle

35. Cass R. Sunstein, *Laws of Fear: Beyond the Precautionary Principle* (Cambridge: Cambridge University Press, 2005).

36. Adam Thierer, "Who Really Believes in 'Permissionless Innovation'?" *Technology Liberation Front*, March 4, 2013, http://techliberation.com/2013/03/04/who-really-believes-in-permissionless-innovation

37. Aaron Wildavsky, *Searching for Safety* (New Brunswick: Transaction Books, 1988): 38.

38. Nassim Nicholas Taleb, *Antifragile: Things That Gain From Disorder* (New York: Random House, 2012): 71.

39. Kevin Ashton, *How to Fly a Horse: The Secret History of Creation, Invention, and Discovery* (New York: Doubleday, 2015): 67.

40. As quoted in Nathan Furr, "How Failure Taught Edison to Repeatedly Innovate," *Forbes*, June 9, 2011, http://www.forbes.com/sites/nathanfurr/2011/06/09/how-failure-taught-edison-to-repeatedly-innovate

41. Kevin Ashton, *How to Fly a Horse: The Secret History of Creation, Invention, and Discovery* (New York: Doubleday, 2015): 66.

42. Bruce Schneier, "Our Decreasing Tolerance to Risk," *Forbes*, August 23, 2013, http://www.forbes.com/sites/bruceschneier/2013/08/23/our-decreasing-tolerance-to-risk. ("We need to relearn how to accept risk, and even embrace it, as essential to human progress and our free society.").

43. *See generally* Adam Thierer, *Permissionless Innovation: The Continuing Case for Comprehensive Technological Freedom* (Arlington: Mercatus Center at George Mason University, 2014). *Also see* H. W. Lewis, *Technological Risk* (New York: WW. Norton & Co., 1990): 119. ("there is never such a thing as a worst case.... Risk without probability is, as the French say, like a meal without wine or day without sunshine. Yet worst-case planning pervades our society.... There is an almost hypnotic appeal to thinking that if you have covered the worst case, you have covered everything. But it isn't true.").

44. Mary Douglas and Aaron Wildavsky, *Risk and Culture* (Berkeley: University of California Press, 1983): 28. ("Would people voluntarily subject themselves to a lower standard of living and less safety? That is what proponents of risk taking—nothing ventured, nothing gained—believe will follow from what they deem excessive concern with avoiding risks. To them, today's avoidance of tomorrow's risk is the greatest danger.").

45. Edward Tenner, *Why Things Bite Back: Technology and the Revenge of Unintended Consequences* (New York: Vintage Books, 1996): 23.

46. Henry Petroski, *To Engineer Is Human: The Role of Failure in Successful Design* (New York: Vintage, 1992): viii. ("I believe that the concept of failure—mechanical and structural failure in the context of this discussion—is central to understanding engineering, for engineering design has as its first and foremost objective the obviation of failure.").

47. Ibid., at 105. ("Technology has advanced by our constantly seeking to understand the hows and whys of our own disappointments, and we have always sought to learn from our mistakes lest they be repeated. But failures do and will occur... and there is little indication that innovation will ever be abandoned completely for the sake of absolute predictability. That would not seem to be compatible with the technological drive of Homo faber to build to ever greater heights and to bridge ever greater distances, even if only because they are there to be reached or spanned.").

48. Henry Petroski, *To Engineer Is Human: The Role of Failure in Successful Design* (New York: Vintage, 1992): viii.

49. Edward Tenner, *Why Things Bite Back: Technology and the Revenge of Unintended Consequences* (New York: Vintage Books, 1996): 24.

50. Peter Huber, "Exorcists vs. Gatekeepers in Risk Regulation," *Regulation*, November/December 1983, 28–9. ("The paradox of

risk regulation is that too much of it makes life more dangerous. Not just more expensive, not just less convenient, but *more dangerous*.").

51. Henry Petroski, *To Engineer Is Human: The Role of Failure in Successful Design* (New York: Vintage, 1992): 11.

52. H. W. Lewis, *Technological Risk* (New York: WW. Norton & Co., 1990): x. ("Risk is part of the price we pay for growth, as nearly all parents know.").

53. Tom Norquist, "Climbing Trends on the North American PLAYground," *GameTime News*, August 26, 2013, http://www.gametime.com/news/entry/climbing-trends-on-the-north-american-playground1. ("I'm sure I'm not the only one who remembers from my college Play classes seeing pictures of the original gymnastic play equipment that populated our schools and parks at the turn of the century. This equipment tended to be well over 10' tall, often as high as a two-story building/ Injuries from falls onto a hard surface all but eliminated this type of equipment. Today, if you ask children what they want, and we do, they tell us the taller the better.").

54. Kevin Rossignol, "The Changing Shape of America's Playgrounds," *City Parks Blog*, November 20, 2013, ("If you venture out to a park with a newly built playground, what you'll find is a multi-colored configuration lined with a soft rubber padding that seems slightly out of place amongst the grass and trees. The iconic playground structures adults remember growing up with, such as see-saws, jungle gyms and tall slides, will almost certainly seem smaller and modified, if they are present at all.").

55. John Tierney, "Can a Playground Be Too Safe?" *New York Times*, July 18, 2011, http://www.nytimes.com/2011/07/19/science/19tierney.html?_r=0

56. U.S. Consumer Product Safety Commission, *Public Playground Safety Handbook*, November 2010, http://www.cpsc.gov/page-files/122149/325.pdf

57. Scott McFetridge, "Liability concerns prompt some cities to limit sledding," *AP: The Big Story*, January 4, 2015, http://bigstory.ap.org/article/4190016301c14b37bee5747373353be5/liability-concerns-prompt-some-cities-limit-sledding

58. Ibid.

59. Ibid. at D3.

60. Ellen Beate Hansen Sandseter and Leif Edward OttesenKennai, "Children's Risky Play from an Evolutionary Perspective: The Anti-

Phobic Effects of Thrilling Experiences," *Evolutionary Psychology* 9 (2011): 257–284.

61. Ibid.
62. Ibid., at 275.
63. Ibid.
64. *See* Shirley Wyver et al. "Ten Ways to Restrict Children's Freedom to Play: The Problem of Surplus Safety," *Contemporary Issues in Early Childhood* 11 (2010): 263, 277.
65. *See* Alice G. Walton, "New Playgrounds Are Safe—and That's Why Nobody Uses Them," *The Atlantic*, February 1, 2012, http://www.theatlantic.com/health/archive/2012/02/new-playgrounds-are-safe-and-thats-why-nobody-uses-them/252108
66. Kristen A. Copeland et al. "Societal Values and Policies May Curtail Preschool Children's Physical Activity in Child Care Centers," *Pediatrics* 129 (2012): 265.
67. Ibid. at 265, 270.
68. Ibid. at 266, 269.
69. Ibid. at 268 (explaining that exposure to nature is a possible benefit of kids being outside).
70. Tim Gill, "Cotton Wool Revolution: Instilling Resilience in Children Is a Vital Lesson but Only Makes Sense in a Supportive Society," *The Guardian*, October 30, 2007, at 30.
71. Adam Thierer, "Europe's Choice on Innovation," *Technology Liberation Front*, December 3, 2014, http://techliberation.com/2014/12/03/europes-choice-on-innovation
72. Matt Moffett, "New Entrepreneurs Find Pain in Spain," *Wall Street Journal*, November 27, 2014, http://www.wsj.com/articles/new-entrepreneurs-find-pain-in-spain-1417133197
73. Ibid.
74. Adam Thierer, *Permissionless Innovation: The Continuing Case for Comprehensive Technological Freedom* (Arlington: Mercatus Center at George Mason University, 2014); Adam Thierer, "Why Permissionless Innovation Matters," *Medium*, April 24, 2014, https://medium.com/tech-liberation/why-permissionless-innovation-matters-257e3d605b63
75. *See* Bret Swanson, "The Exponential Internet," *Business Horizon Quarterly* (Spring 2014): 40–47, http://www.uschamberfoundation.org/sites/default/files/article/foundation/BHQ-Spring12-Issue3-SwansonTheExponentialInternet.pdf

76. Ibid., at 46. ("The entrepreneurship and investment that has sustained such fast growth for so long is due, in substantial part, to light-touch government policies (at least compared to other industries. ... There have been mistakes, but for the most part, scientists, entrepreneurs, and big investors have been allowed to build new things, try new products, challenge the status quo, cooperate, and compete. They have also been allowed to fail.").
77. Booz & Company, "The Top Innovators and Spenders," http://www.strategyand.pwc.com/global/home/what-we-think/innovation1000/top-innovators-spenders#/tab-2013
78. Larry Downes, "Europe's Innovation Deficit Isn't Disappearing Any Time Soon," *Washington Post*, June 8, 2015, http://www.washingtonpost.com/blogs/innovations/wp/2015/06/08/europes-innovation-deficit-isnt-disappearing-any-time-soon
79. Quoted in James B. Stewart, "A Fearless Culture Fuels U.S. Tech Giants," *New York Times*, June 19, 2015, http://www.nytimes.com/2015/06/19/business/the-american-way-of-tech-and-europes.html
80. Quoted in Ibid.
81. Ibid.
82. Ibid.
83. Daniel Castro and Alan McQuinn, "How and When Regulators Should Intervene," Information Technology and Innovation Foundation Reports (February 2015): 2 http://www.itif.org/publications/how-and-when-regulators-should-intervene
84. Tom Fairless and Stephen Fidler, "Europe Wants the World to Embrace Its Internet Rules," *Wall Street Journal*, February 24, 2015, http://www.wsj.com/articles/europe-wants-the-world-to-embrace-its-data-privacy-rules-1424821453
85. Romain Dillet, "Uber France Leaders Arrested for Running Illegal Taxi Company," *TechCrunch*, June 29, 2015, http://techcrunch.com/2015/06/29/uber-france-leaders-arrested-for-running-illegal-taxi-company
86. Dan Primack, "Uber Downloads in France Hit All-Time High after Strike," *Fortune*, June 30, 2015, http://fortune.com/2015/06/30/uber-downloads-in-france-hit-all-time-high-after-strike
87. Tom Fairless, "Europe Looks to Tame Web's Economic Risks," *Wall Street Journal*, April 23, 2015, http://www.wsj.com/articles/

eu-considers-creating-powerful-regulator-to-oversee-web-plat-forms-1429795918

88. *See* Adam Thierer, "How Attitudes About Risk & Failure Affect Innovation on Either Side of the Atlantic," *Medium*, June 19, 2015, https://readplaintext.com/how-attitudes-about-risk-failure-affect-innovation-on-either-side-of-the-atlantic-b5f0f41c3466

89. Sherzod Abdukadirov, "The Unintended Consequences of Safety Regulation," Mercatus Center at George Mason University, *Mercatus Research*, June 3, 2013, http://mercatus.org/publication/unintended-consequences-safety-regulation

90. Nassim Nicholas Taleb, *The Black Swan: The Impact of the Highly Improbable* (New York: Random House, 2007): 138.

91. Ibid., 140.

92. Maureen K. Ohlhausen, "The Internet of Things and the FTC: Does Innovation Require Intervention?" Remarks Before the US Chamber of Commerce, Washington, D.C., October 18, 2013, http://www.ftc.gov/speeches/ohlhausen/131008internetthingsremarks.pdf

93. Tim Harford, *Adapt: Why Success Always Starts with Failure* (New York: Farrar, Strauss and Giroux, 2011): 124–7.

94. "The view that now pervades much public policy economics implicitly presents the relevant choice as between an ideal norm and an existing 'imperfect' institutional arrangement. This *nirvana* approach differs considerably from a *comparative institution* approach in which the relevant choice is between alternative real institutional arrangements." Harold Demsetz, "Information and Efficiency: Another Viewpoint," *Journal of Law and Economics* 12(1) (April 1969): 1 (italics in original).

95. Josh Wright and Douglas Ginsberg, "Behavioral Law and Economics: Its Origins, Fatal Flaws, and Implications for Liberty," *Northwestern University Law Review* 106(3) (2012): 1048.

96. Josh Wright and Douglas Ginsberg, "Behavioral Law and Economics: Its Origins, Fatal Flaws, and Implications for Liberty," *Northwestern University Law Review* 106(3) (2012): 1048–9.

97. Diana Thomas, "The Effects of Regulation on Low-Income Households," Testimony Before the House Committee on the Judiciary, July 9, 2013, http://mercatus.org/publication/effects-regulation-low-income-households

98. Diana Thomas, "Regressive Effects of Regulation," Mercatus Center Working Paper, No. 12-35, November 27, 2012, http://mercatus. org/publication/regressive-effects-regulation. *Also see* Henry I. Miller, "When Bureaucrats Get Away with Murder," Hoover Institution, *Defining Ideas*, July 1, 2015, http://www.hoover.org/research/when-bureaucrats-get-away-murder. ("Although it is difficult to quantify precisely the relationship between mortality and the deprivation of income, academic studies suggest as a conservative estimate that approximately every $7 million to $10 million of regulatory costs will induce one additional fatality through this indirect 'income effect.' Because unnecessary deaths are the real costs of regulators' 'erring on the side of safety,' excessive regulation has been dubbed 'statistical murder.'"); Robert W. Hahn, Randall W. Lutter, and W. Kip Viscusi, "Do Federal Regulations Reduce Mortality?" (Washington, DC: AEI-Brookings Joint Center for Regulatory Studies, 2000), http://law.vanderbilt.edu/files/archive/ 011_Do-Federal-Regulations-Reduce-Mortality.pdf

99. This section is adapted from: Adam Thierer, "Technopanics, Threat Inflation, and the Danger of an Information Technology Precautionary Principle," *Minnesota Journal of Law, Science & Technology* 14(1) (2013): 356–64.

100. John Morrall and James Broughel, "The Role of Regulatory Impact Analysis in Federal Rulemaking," Mercatus Center at George Mason University, April 10, 2014, http://mercatus.org/publication/ role-regulatory-impact-analysis-federal-rulemaking

101. *See* Susan E. Dudley and Jerry Brito, *Regulation: A Primer*, 2nd ed. (Arlington: Mercatus Center at George Mason University, 2012), 97–98 ("The cost of a regulation is the opportunity cost—whatever desirable things society gives up in order to get the good things the regulation produces. The opportunity cost of alternative approaches is the appropriate measure of costs. This measure should reflect the benefits foregone when a particular action is selected and should include the change in consumer and producer surplus."); Jerry Ellig and Patrick A. McLaughlin, "The Quality and Use of Regulatory Analysis in 2008," *Risk Analysis* 32(855) (2012).

102. See Richard B. Belzer, "Risk Assessment, Safety Assessment, and the Estimation of Regulatory Benefits," Mercatus Center Working Paper (Arlington: Mercatus Center at George Mason University, 2012), 5, http://mercatus.org/publication/risk-assessment-safety-assessment-and-estimation-regulatory-benefits

103. White House, Office of Information and Regulatory Affairs, *Regulatory Impact Analysis: A Primer* (2011), 2, http://www.whitehouse.gov/sites/default/files/omb/inforeg/regpol/circular-a-4_regulatory-impact-analysis-a-primer.pdf
104. Ibid.
105. Ibid.
106. Ibid.
107. Ibid., 7.
108. Ibid., 2, 5.
109. Office of Information and Regulatory Affairs, *Regulatory Impact Analysis*, 3.
110. Ibid., 3–4.
111. Robert W. Hahn and Patrick M. Dudley, "How Well Does the U.S. Government Do Benefit-Cost Analysis?" *Review of Environmental Economics and Policy* 1(2) (Summer 2007): 192–211; Jerry Ellig and Patrick McLaughlin, "The Quality and Use of Regulatory Analysis in 2008," *Risk Analysis* 32(5) (May 2012): 855–880, http://onlinelibrary.wiley.com/doi/10.1111/j.1539-6924.2011.01715.x/abstract
112. Cass R. Sunstein, "Regulation in an Uncertain World," Speech Before the National Academy of Sciences Government-University-Industry Roundtable Meeting, Washington, DC, June 20, 2012, https://www.whitehouse.gov/sites/default/files/omb/inforeg/speeches/regulation-in-an-uncertain-world-06202012.pdf. ("Retrospective analysis has long been recommended by those interested in empirical assessment of regulations.") Randall Lutter, "Regulatory Policy: What Role for Retrospective Analysis and Review?" *Journal of Benefit-Cost Analysis*, March 2013, http://mercatus.org/publication/regulatory-policy-what-role-retrospective-analysis-and-review
113. Adam Thierer, "The Pursuit of Privacy in a World Where Information Control Is Failing," *Harvard Journal of Law & Public Policy* 36 (2013): 409–55.
114. James Broughel, "OMB 2014 Draft Report to Congress on the Benefits and Costs of Federal Regulations and Unfunded Mandates on State, Local, and Tribal Entities," Mercatus Center at George Mason University, *Public Interest Comment*, September 2, 2014, http://mercatus.org/sites/default/files/Broughel-OMB-2014-PIC-090214.pdf. (Outlining a set of "Principles for Regulation of New Technologies in the Face of Uncertainty.").

115. Petroski, *To Engineer Is Human*, at 62. ("No one *wants* to learn by mistakes, but we cannot learn enough from successes to go beyond the state of the art.").
116. Will Yakowitz, "Why You Need to Embrace Failure," *Inc.*, December 16, 2013, http://www.inc.com/will-yakowicz/if-youre-not-failing-youre-not-succeeding.html
117. Petroski, *To Engineer Is Human*, at 9.
118. Mary Douglas and Aaron Wildavsky, *Risk and Culture* (Berkeley: University of California Press, 1983), 196. ("The ability to learn from errors and gain experience in coping with a wide variety of difficulties, has proved a greater aid to preservation of the species than efforts to create a narrow band of controlled conditions within which they would flourish for a time...").

Behavioral Nudges and Consumer Technology

Steve Wendel

Neat Tricks

A cap for medicine bottles that glows to remind you when to take medication.[1] A report that shows you when your neighbors are spending less than you are on electricity, and nudges you to spend less as well.[2] A subtle change to your Facebook feed that triggers a positive or negative emotion.[3] Countless tiny experiments every day on websites around the world to measure the effects of colors, images, and small changes in wording on driving you to purchase something online.[4]

Almost without public notice, the last few years have seen the explosive growth of behavioral nudges applied to consumer products. The examples above cover merely a few of them. Many of these new applications are clearly beneficial to consumers—in fact, consumers pin their hopes on these tools to help them where they have struggled to meet their own goals. Some, however, are clearly more problematic.

In this chapter, we take a look at how private sector companies are applying behavioral interventions or "nudges" to consumer products, especially with digital technology.

S. Wendel (✉)
Morningstar, Chicago, USA

© The Editor(s) (if applicable) and The Author(s) 2016   95
S. Abdukadirov (ed.), *Nudge Theory in Action*,
DOI 10.1007/978-3-319-31319-1_5

- We start off by asking: how are behavioral nudges—until recently the domain of academic researchers—making their way into consumer products?
- Then, we examine products that employ behavioral nudges, with a particular focus on two areas where they have been most notably applied: finance and health.
- Next, we take a step back and categorize the underlying behavioral biases these nudges attempt to address—from consumer inattention to procrastination.
- Finally, we examine the limited, though growing, information about the effectiveness of these behavioral nudges in practice, and how companies are learning to iteratively improve that impact in novel ways.

While no comprehensive survey of behavioral nudges in consumer products appears to exist, and creating one is beyond the scope of this chapter, our goal is to provide a framework for thinking about these nudges and introduce core concepts that both practitioners and academics can ask about their purpose, theoretical backing, and empirical impact.

How Behavioral Techniques Are Reaching Private Sector Products

Before we look at how behavioral nudges are being applied in private sector products, let us consider how behavioral nudges are reaching the private sector at all. Much of the research on behavioral nudges comes from the academic fields of behavioral economics and psychology, especially the psychology of judgment and decision-making. Academic researchers working at universities and colleges, especially in the USA, have literally created these fields. It is only through recent and popular books like *Nudge* (Thaler and Sunstein 2008), *Predictably Irrational* (Ariely 2008), and *Thinking Fast and Slow* (Kahneman 2011) that this wave of behavioral research, and the nudges based on that research, have entered the mainstream. All of those books were authored by leading researchers in the field and draw heavily on peer-reviewed publications written by the authors and other academic researchers.

One might reasonably assume that similar academic researchers are bringing behavioral nudges into private sector products. Instead, people whose daily work involves building products—designers and product managers like Deena Rosen of Opower and Kelvin Kwong of Jawbone—

appear to be the most active users of behavioral nudges in consumer products. The main reason is that there are relatively few behavioral economists in the country,[5] and the product design community (especially) has a long-standing interest and practical training in consumer psychology.[6] Behavioral economics has been incorporated into existing product design approaches as simply another, popular, way of understanding users, as seen in design toolkits like Dan Lockton's *Design with Intent* (2013) or Stephen Anderson's *Mental Notes* (2013). While there are a few high-profile examples of behavioral scientists who work directly with private companies—Dan Ariely's role as the Chief Behavioral Officer at the startup Timeful being one such example—that doesn't appear to be the norm.

By and large, behavioral techniques appear to reach the private sector via three routes:

- *Books.* In this author's admittedly nonscientific survey of private sector companies,[7] the majority of companies that apply behavioral techniques do so based on the three popular press books mentioned above: *Thinking, Fast and Slow* (Kahneman 2011), *Nudge* (Thaler and Sunstein 2008), and *Predictably Irrational* (Ariely 2008). Others draw upon user interface design books like *Seductive Interaction Design* (Anderson 2011) and *Evil by Design* (Nodder 2013), written by designers who themselves build upon the academic literature.
- *Behavioral scientists training practitioners.* From BJ Fogg's Bootcamp to Dan Ariely's Startuponomics, researchers are helping entrepreneurs, product managers, and designers learn behavioral techniques that they can apply to their products.[8] The Action Design Network, Habit Design Meetup, and the London Behavioural Economics Network each hold monthly public events that bring together researchers and practitioners to learn new techniques.[9]
- *Consulting.* Some behavioral scientists also consult directly with private companies; BJ Fogg and Dan Ariely's *Irrational Labs* and Brian Wansink's *Slim by Design*, for example, each advertise consulting services.[10] New behavioral consulting companies such as ideas42 and The Greatest Good Group in the USA and the quasi-governmental Behavioral Insights Team in the UK also work with clients around the world to solve problems using behavioral techniques.[11] Finally, some marketing agencies have hired behavioral scientists to provide services to their clients, for example, Ogilvy Change, Brain Juicer, and FCB.[12]

The manner in which behavioral techniques reach the private sector matters for how those techniques are applied. One challenge facing private sector companies is that the lessons from behavioral research are often divorced from the processes by which they were developed. Companies apply behavioral interventions—like loss aversion[13] or peer competitions—in contexts completely foreign to the original academic settings. As we will discuss later in this chapter, context matters—and thus, shapes whether behavioral nudges actually have their intended effect.

Another challenge is that without a strong, direct link between private sector practice and academic research, practical lessons from the private sector don't appear to be reaching the deeper and more theoretical discourse in the academic literature. In interviews for this book chapter, the author found that consulting companies and marketing agencies that apply behavioral techniques for their clients and assess their impact are often under nondisclosure agreements about their work—they can't share lessons publicly, and certainly not for academic publication. While some lessons may filter back to the academic world via informal conversations, the process is unlikely to be either systematic or complete.

This chapter is an initial attempt at shedding light on private sector applications of behavioral nudges, especially in consumer technology, so that practitioners and academic researchers alike can better understand the current state of the field and learn from each other. Let us start with two of the most active and exciting areas of application: health and finance.

Examples of Behavioral Nudges in Consumer Products

Health Applications

Who hasn't seen—or owned—a wearable exercise band like those from Jawbone, FitBit, or Nike, or a smart watch by Pebble, Motorola, or Apple? Consumers bought an estimated 33 million of them in 2014 alone, up from virtually none in 2010 (Danova 2015).[14] They appear to be everywhere; they are also one of the most obvious examples of behavioral nudges in consumer technologies.

Companies like Jawbone explicitly use behavioral research to help their users do things like exercise more and sleep better (Kwong 2015). In practice, that means they do two things. First, they read the academic literature and find effective *behavioral interventions* like peer comparisons that they then implement in their user interfaces. Second, they use *behavioral research methods* to verify the impact of their products and, often, to iteratively improve them.

Here's an example. Lots of people have difficulty following through on their desire to get a good night's sleep. At the beginning of the day, it makes sense—we all know a regular eight hours (or so) of sleep is important to our health, mood, and so on. But, when the time comes to either go to sleep or watch another episode of TV, our willpower breaks down. The team at Jawbone read the behavioral research literature and decided to try a principle known as "commitment and consistency" to help people follow through on their desire to sleep well; commitment and consistency refers to our tendency to follow through on an action (and related actions) once we've made even a small personal commitment to it—without penalties or incentives being applied (Cialdini 2007). In the mobile application that accompanies Jawbone's exercise and sleep tracker, they added a little pop-up message—asking people whether they would go to sleep earlier. They tested the impact of the message on actual sleep using a randomized control trial (the primary method that behavioral researchers use to measure the impact of their nudges). They found that a simple nudge to encourage commitment and consistency made participants 72 % more likely to go to bed early enough to get seven hours of sleep (Kwong 2015).

RCTs, do you buy them? primary strength/ weaknesses

In the wearable space overall, behavioral nudges appear to be quite common. For example, many exercise bands have accompanying mobile applications that facilitate the setting of specific, actionable goals, provide feedback on performance, and create peer networks that support those goals. They also employ intelligent defaults to allow the user to focus on more challenging and interesting tasks. Take FitBit's exercise bands and mobile applications as an example:

- FitBit automatically defaults users into a reasonable (and standard) goal of 10,000 steps per day.
- Progress toward the goal is visible on the band and via the mobile and online applications.
- Users have the option to connect with friends and colleagues who also have a FitBit, can see and share progress, and get encouragement (or friendly jabs) through the interface.

Automation is also a core technique used across multiple products, where exercise bands automatically track exercise (such as the number of steps taken) to remove drudgery; many also automatically track heart rates and sleep times. Each of these techniques, from goal-setting to providing feedback on progress, has been well studied in the broad behavioral research literature and found to be effective under the right circumstances.[15] In addition to physical wearables, fitness apps such as Moves, RunKeeper, and Motivate use similar nudges of automation, peer support, and commitment devices to encourage exercise.

Beyond the wearable space, behavioral techniques appear to be common in three other health and wellness areas. First, we find them in medication adherence. Over 50 % of patients with chronic conditions don't take their medicines as prescribed (Brown and Bussell 2011), leading to significant complications and medical risks for patients. Vitality's Glowcaps, the glowing caps on medicine bottles mentioned above, are a clever behaviorally informed solution to this problem.[16] Other interventions range from Abiogenix's uBox pill reminder to lottery-based incentives for adherence (Volpp et al. 2008) to apps that provide tracking capabilities along with reminders and other nudges (e.g., My-Meds. com). A 2014 survey found 160 medication adherence smartphone apps alone (Dayer et al. 2013).

Employee wellness programs are another area in which we find behavioral interventions for health. Companies like Keas use the social psychology of competitions and points (aka gamification) to encourage exercise and good diet among employees (Keas 2015). Employees are given a list of specific actions, like undertaking a health risk assessment, which will earn them points that are compared to peers and can trigger incentive dollars. Virgin Health lists ten behavioral techniques at work in its employee wellness program: from financial incentives to social support to feedback about progress (Turgiss 2014). Omada Health, for example, employs behavioral counseling based on the NIH's Diabetes Prevention Program in its application, to help employees avoid diabetes (Omada Health 2014).

And, of course, there are mobile dieting programs. There are 55 apps in the official "weight loss" category on the Apple App store, and over 5000 search results for "diet."[17] Many of these apps, like DietBet, use competitions or social support to "reward" dieters. Weight Watchers applied the work of BJ Fogg, head of the Stanford University Persuasive Technology Lab and pioneer in the field, to redo its interface to be more behaviorally effective (Kosner 2012). Fogg's behavioral model focuses on three core components (Fogg 2009): the motivation to act (which is often already present), the ability to act (in which a myriad of frictions and barriers can block action), and a trigger to act now (such as an email from the application reminding people to plan out their meals).

Noom's mobile phone–based weight loss application combines BJ Fogg's Motivation-Ability-Trigger model with Ryan and Deci's Self Determination Theory (2000) to focus on and remove points of friction that hinder people from taking action (Petakov 2015). For example, the app automatically predicts and fills out meal descriptions in a diet log since much of eating behavior is habitual. In another example, Brian Wansink, head of the Cornell Food and Brand Lab and author of *Mindless Eating* and *Slim by Design*, explicitly puts his research findings on food psychology and choice architecture into simple checklists that people can interact with online to help them "mindlessly" lose weight (Wansink 2015b).[18]

Applications in Finance

In finance, there has been a similar flowering of behavioral innovations to help consumers manage their money more effectively. In fact, behavioral finance, the study of how people interact with money and the common biases we face when making financial decisions (e.g., Thaler 2005), is one of the earliest and best established research traditions in behavioral economics. In terms of digital technology, one set of applications that employs behavioral nudges is focused on investments and another is focused on day-to-day money management.

In the investment arena, companies like Betterment explicitly apply behavioral lessons to help investors avoid common mistakes (Egan 2015). For example, during market downturns, investors often become anxious and remove their money from the market—an understandable but terrible thing to do, since their investments are then at their *lowest value*. Betterment conducted a randomized control trial in which they added a "tooltip" (icon for more information) that warned individuals when they were about to withdraw money. It provided information about the dangers of hasty withdrawals and resulted in a 10 % decrease in withdrawals (Egan 2015).[19] Betterment's Director of Behavioral Finance and Investments, Dan Egan, applies lessons from the behavioral literature and conducts new experimental tests of behavioral interventions like those in their product (Egan 2015). Similarly, leading investment research provider Morningstar has recently formed a new advisory board with prominent behavioral scientists to develop and field test interventions in their products that can help everyday investors (Morningstar 2015).[20]

In personal finance, HelloWallet[21] has been a leading proponent of behavioral science for better money management. HelloWallet uses behavioral techniques such as peer comparisons, default options, and reframing, all to improve savings rates. SaveUp uses sweepstakes with big prizes (based on behavioral research into variable rewards) to encourage increased savings through their application. Popular personal money management tools like Mint.com also apply behavioral techniques such as providing descriptive norms ("75 % of Americans establish a savings account to plan for their future") and targeted personalization ("Hi, I'm Vince, and I'm a Product Manager here at Mint. I noticed you…") in their products to encourage people to take actions in their application that support savings behavior (Maniago 2014).[22]

The US Household Finance Initiative, part of the international development agency Innovations for Poverty Action, is explicitly working to spread the application of behavioral science in consumer financial products. They provide grants to companies ranging from Prospera to The Financial Clinic, and then pair the companies up with behavioral scientists who can help them implement effective behavioral nudges in their products.[23] Another innovation program for financial technology, by the Center for Financial Services Innovation (CFSI), supplies grants for new ideas in financial services; some of which, like Clarifi and Doorways to Dreams, apply behavioral techniques to help users save for the future.[24]

Broader Applications

Looking beyond health and finance applications, where can behavioral nudges be found? We can see them scattered across many industries and technologies. In the digital realm, we see products such as Stickk.com, which uses commitment devices to encourage people to follow through on self-specified goals (Blanding 2014). Users set their goal, and then decide on an amount of money they will lose if they fail to fulfill their goals; the money can go to a charity they like, or more interestingly, to a one they dislike—further encouraging them not to fail. We also see companies like Facebook, which reportedly conducted hundreds of experimental tests (Albergotti 2014), from a nudge to mobilize voters (Bond et al. 2012) to an ill-fated nudge to induce positive (or negative) moods by tweaking the content users saw on their site (Meyer 2014; Kramer et al. 2014). Companies such as Automatic and GreenRoad provide feedback on driving history and fuel efficiency to encourage better driving habits. It is difficult to generate an exhaustive list, however, especially since many companies refuse to talk about the particular techniques applied in their products.

In nondigital consumer products, Opower's energy reports are one of the most prominent examples. Opower, mentioned at the start of this article, uses cleverly crafted peer comparisons to highlight how much one's neighbors spend on energy, in order to encourage efficiency. Also in the energy space, Ambient's Energy Joule provides clear immediate feedback on energy prices, glowing red when prices are high and providing a digital readout with information about household consumption, to nudge consumers to spend less on electricity.

In terms of physical environments, there are a few often-cited examples. Wansink's Food and Brand Lab has redesigned the layout and display of food in cafeterias around the world to encourage healthier eating—putting unhealthy foods behind frosted glass, making water bottles easier to reach, and so on (see Kuang 2012; Wansink 2015b). Another famous example was reported by Richard Thaler and Cass Sunstein (2008): at the Schiphol International Airport in Amsterdam, an economist decided to "etch an image of a black house fly onto the bowls of the airport's urinals, just to the left of the drain." The result: Spillage declined 80 percent.

Uncertainty around What Really Is a Nudge

When you look broadly out at the field, behavioral nudges seem to be almost everywhere. However, things become fuzzy very quickly.

For example, behavioral researchers have studied the impact of reminders to encourage people to follow up on a previously committed action (they are surprisingly effective). Such external reminders are believed to "work" because of failures in the standard economic model: that is, limited attention and limited planning ability hinder our efficient pursuit of our self-interest. Researchers have developed models of the decision-making process, which can forecast the impact of such reminders (e.g., Karlan et al. 2011). Does that mean that any application that reminds people to take action is actually applying behavioral nudges? That seems extreme—especially since people used reminders long before "behavioral" research even existed.

In the digital design community, there is a refrain that all designs are inherently persuasive (e.g., Redstrom 2006; Fabricant 2010) and that the point of design is to shape behavior. In fact, one can reasonably argue that nudges are literally everywhere because products often seek to shape consumer behavior and leverage behavioral techniques. Facebook encourages us to log in habitually using random rewards—updates and references from friends. Rosetta Stone nudges (or pushes) us to learn languages effectively using structured feedback and goal setting. Our online calendars nudge us to remember appointments. Ads for everything from shoes to cigarettes use techniques like social proof (testimonials) and scarcity (limited time offers) to nudge us to buy. And so forth. When we expand our sights to our physical environment, everything from the design of chairs to the placement of stairs affects our behavior.

Unfortunately, "behavioral nudges are everywhere, in everything" is not a very useful way to analyze nudges. To draw the line between "products that apply behavioral nudges" and those that don't, there are a few different questions we might ask, such as:

1. How was the technique developed? Was it invented or at least extensively studied by behavioral scientists?
2. How is the technique applied? Are behavioral scientists involved, either directly or through published research?
3. Is the product intended to change behavior?

There's no "right" answer to these questions, of course, nor any universal definition of what constitutes a nudge. As a practical matter, this author focuses on cases where behavioral scientists have developed or otherwise researched a technique and that research is intentionally used to change behavior. Admittedly, this definition is still messy, however, because it means that context matters in determining whether something is a "behavioral nudge":

- Simple reminders, for example (like sending an email), often aren't behavioral nudges. But, if a behavioral researcher develops a nuanced model of decision-making and inattention, and then tests it in the field using experimental methods, that probably qualifies (at least under the definition that this author uses).
- When Homer wrote about the mythical Odysseus asking his crew to tie him to the mast of his ship so that he could not answer the siren's call, he wasn't describing a behavioral nudge (a proto-nudge, perhaps). When behavioral scientist Dean Karlan helped develop Stickk.com using precommitment and a theoretically grounded model of decision-making (e.g., Byran et al. 2010)[25]—he designed the product to nudge.

Throughout this chapter, we've focused on nudges that are explicitly part of the behavioral research canon: actions that intentionally shape user behavior using a theoretically grounded understanding of decision-making from the behavioral literature. Each of these nudges addresses one or more behavioral biases or quirks of the decision-making process that researchers have identified. Let us now turn our attention to those biases.

What Types of Interventions Are Used?

As we've seen, the scope and variety of behavioral nudges in consumer products is vast. One useful way to structure an analysis of the space is to look not at the particular products themselves but at the underlying behavioral biases they seek to overcome or, in some cases, exploit. There are literally over a hundred behavioral biases that researchers have identified which can be turned into behavioral nudges (e.g., see Richards 2015), but these biases fall into a few straightforward categories.

We can think about the range of behavioral biases as a chronicle of our fundamental cognitive limitations, and how our minds use clever tricks to overcome them. On the one hand, we are sadly limited in our attention, our willpower, and our memory. Holding more than seven[26] unrelated numbers in our memories is too much for most of us to handle (Miller 1956), and within only a few hours after breakfast, our ability to make complex decisions is radically diminished (Danziger et al. 2011; Baumeister and Tierney 2011). On the other hand, we're remarkably good at recognizing similar situations and judging them based on past experience in a blink of an eye, and at guessing whether something is right for us based on social cues—that is, using intuitive heuristics and our automatic pattern recognition systems.[27]

Wendel (2014) uses the CREATE model, below, to organize and understand the various cognitive limitations and biases that individuals may encounter. Each letter of the acronym represents an obstacle that individuals may face to taking action (like exercising), for which researchers have found potential behavioral nudges. Specifically (Fig. 1):

Cue   ✗ ask for personal examples of how CREATE has been used

Some techniques are designed simply to capture or retain our limited attention by cueing us to pay attention.

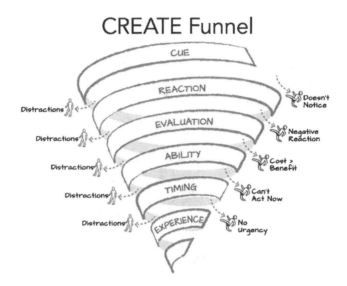

CREATE Funnel

Fig. 1 The CREATE Model, a simple tool to remember the major cognitive limitations and biases that researchers have identified. From Wendel (2014)

For example, asking people to take a survey about overdraft fees increases the salience of the fees in their minds and the attention they pay to them for up to two years—significantly affecting behavior and decreasing the fees individuals pay (Stango and Zinman 2011).

Other techniques to attract attention include reminders, visual contrast, movement, or embedding cues in our environment (like a wearable on our wrist reminding us to exercise).

Reaction

Other techniques are designed to work with our implicit ("fast") decision-making system: how we *react* to our environment and consumer products.

For example, researchers found that a sign posted near elevators informing viewers (correctly) that most people took the stairs increased stair usage by seven percentage points and had a continued effect even after the sign was removed (Burger and Shelton 2011). The technique, called social norms, builds on one of the most basic heuristics that people use when deciding what to do: do what most other people are doing.[28]

Other techniques that can overcome obstacles in how people implicitly react to a product or action include personalized messaging, design that conveys professionalism and evokes trust, and designs that build on existing positive associations and emotions, for example, the use of flags to evoke patriotism and a sense of duty, as seen in President Obama's (and many other candidates') online platform asking for campaign volunteers.

Evaluation

Researchers have also developed techniques that work through our deliberative ("slow") decision-making system, and how we consciously *evaluate* the costs and benefits of an action. They may push us to think consciously instead of merely reacting, or try to work around our conscious minds' fundamental limitations, like our limited mathematical skills.

For example, researchers worked with the Internal Revenue Service (IRS) to design communications that would increase the usage of *free* cash benefits to low-income individuals via the Earned Income Tax Credit (EITC) program. They would do that by simplifying the information presented, and by clearly expressing the benefits of the program, they could significantly increase uptake (Bhargava and Manoli 2013).

Other techniques include incentives highlighting that something is free, using a price comparison to show an item is "moderately priced," priming a particular interpretation of the benefits of action, using competitions or social status to create additional (nonmonetary) incentives, or increasing monetary incentives to act; see Volpp et al. (2009) on how GE used cash incentives to encourage people to stop smoking.

Ability

Techniques designed simply to make it easier to act, or to boost our belief in our own ability to succeed at taking action (i.e., self-efficacy).

For example, researchers ran an experiment with a private company's flu vaccination program, in which they asked workers to write down the specific time and day they would get vaccinated. Even though no penalties were installed if people did not follow through, that simple request to make specific plans increased the vaccination rate by 4.2 percentage points (Milkman et al. 2011). This technique, known as implementation intentions, makes it easier to follow through because the cognitive "work" (when, how, etc.) has already been completed.

Other techniques include removing frictions in the user interface like additional pages to click through or form fields to complete, using defaults, or decreasing the number of options involved in a complex choice.

Timing

Techniques designed to overcome our inherent tendencies to procrastinate or ignore the nonurgent.

For example, researchers took photographs of participants and showed them an aged version of themselves to encourage them to save money for retirement; participants saved more than twice as much as a control group. The images helped people overcome the common tendency to procrastinate on retirement savings[29] and made the future (their future selves) more vivid and real (Hershfield et al. 2011). The technique was later applied by Merrill Lynch for the same purpose—retirement savings.

Other techniques include focusing on present benefits instead of future ones, using scarcity, or providing a focal date or deadline for action.

Experience

Techniques designed to overcome our vividness and availability biases in particular, and the overwhelming power of recent prior experiences (especially negative ones).

Techniques include avoiding associations with past (negative) experiences by using different imagery and content, or intentionally linking to positive, loosely related prior experiences by creating a narrative that combines the past and current actions (Wilson 2011).

The CREATE Model thus is one way in which we can identify and categorize the particular techniques that a company uses in its products; Wendel (2015) demonstrates how the model can be used as a checklist to audit a product design.[30] Even if we clearly understand what techniques are used, however, that does not mean that the techniques are actually effective—a question that we address next.

DO NUDGES IN CONSUMER PRODUCTS ACTUALLY WORK?

Naturally, every company that uses behavioral nudges in its products does so with the hope that the techniques actually work. Companies will often have anecdotal or correlational evidence about how users of their products have succeeded—at losing weight, eating better, and so on. The scientific evidence on whether their products, and the particular behavioral nudges they employ, in fact work is considerably less robust.

The gold standard for assessing impact is the randomized control trial (RCT), in which one set of randomly selected individuals receives the product (or particular behavioral intervention within the product), another set does not, and outcomes are compared across the two groups (e.g., see Gerber and Green 2012). RCTs are the primary tool used to prove the efficacy of pharmaceuticals (Junod 2014) and are increasingly used to measure impact in diverse realms, from political campaigns (Issenberg 2012) to international development (Karlan and Appel 2011). RCTs are also the behavioral scientist's tool of choice to measure the impact of nudges on behavior, because of their rigor and because behavioral scientists have learned that what people *say* they do doesn't necessarily align with what they actually do.

Behavioral nudges developed by academic researchers, by and large, have been tested and found to be effective via RCTs. A wide range of academic studies have shown the efficacy of techniques from automating and streamlining the Free Application for Federal Student Aid (FAFSA; Bettinger et al. 2009) to peer groups for savings (Kast et al. 2012). These are often accompanied—or buttressed—by theoretical models that attempt to explain *why* people act that way, and how people make decisions (see DellaVigna 2009 for a review).

When we look at how behavioral techniques are applied in consumer products, they fall into two broad categories. First, there are companies that employ RCTs to directly test the efficacy of their specific consumer products and behavioral interventions. Opower is a notable leader in the field, having subjected their interventions to numerous RCTs over time—with initial, positive results that gained caveats and nuance over time.[31] In the initial accounts, Opower's energy reports caused a reduction in energy usage of roughly 2 % (Allcott 2011). In addition to third-party academic studies, companies like HelloWallet conduct RCTs of their effectiveness (and have found positive results), often in partnership with third-party academics, but publish through popular press whitepapers (Fellowes and Spiegel 2015).[32]

In the second category, many companies use *techniques* that have been tested and validated in previous field experiments, but do not test the particular implementation of those techniques in their own products. As noted above, Stickk.com uses commitment devices to encourage people to follow through on their goals; commitment devices have been found to be effective in studies by Gine et al. (2010) and others.[33] Omada Health's online Prevent product applies a clinically proven diabetes prevention program (2014). The gamification techniques used by Keas, the weight loss competitions of DietBet, the feedback and goal-setting techniques used by wearable products like FitBit, and many others all draw upon previously tested techniques. However, in these examples and many more, there do not appear to be any publicly accessible RCTs about their impact.[34]

Unfortunately, it is not clear that impactful *techniques* translate into impactful *products*—in the next section, we examine why we should be cautious.

The Challenges of Implementing Behavioral Techniques in Products

When companies apply behavioral techniques that were tested in academic studies to their products, we have good reason to doubt that those techniques do, in fact, have the desired impact. The potential disconnect between proven techniques and unproven products occurs for four reasons:

1. *The details matter.* One of the core lessons of behavioral research is that the details matter immensely. Small changes in wording and presentation have outsized influence on behavior. Rarely are the precise implementations of techniques studied in the academic literature applied in consumer products.[35]
2. *Untested user interfaces.* Even if they *were* applied precisely as intended, the rest of the user interface is often wildly different than the ones used in prior research. We know that seemingly irrelevant details of presentation that are outside of the intended scope of the intervention, but nevertheless part of the product (like the questions asked of the user on prior screens), can influence behavior—by setting a numerical anchor that people base their answers on or priming people to think about a question in a particular manner.
3. *New contexts.* The user interface is one part of a much larger change in context that occurs from (most) academic studies to their private sector implementations. Whereas most academic studies involved environments free of irrelevant distractions, the daily lives and environments of users for commercial products are quite the opposite—with distrac-

tions of family, work, and so on. It's not clear what impact these additional demands on our cognitive resources have and how they might interact with a particular behavioral intervention.

4. *Uncertain generalizability.* It's unclear that impactful successful techniques can be generalized even within their original context. Since each population is different, with its own personal experiences and patterned responses, it's quite possible that what works with one population won't work with another. Preliminary experimental evidence by HelloWallet, in which behavioral interventions like reminders were tested across diverse worker populations, indicates that nongeneralizability is quite common.

The result is that, without rigorous and specific testing, apart from a few cases, we simply don't know whether specific products and their nudges actually work as promised. We can give them the benefit of the doubt when they use experimentally tested techniques, but doubt should remain until actual evidence is gathered. It warrants notice that the same problems likely plague applications of behavioral techniques from the academe in public policy—without direct testing, we should doubt they actually work and are worth the effort.

A Way Out: How Companies Effectively Apply Nudges

The bright spot in impact testing, if it is to be called that, lies in the marketing realm. Marketing optimization specialists spend their careers specifically fine-tuning communications and materials for their impact on sales. The best of them rigorously use RCTs, also known as A/B or Split tests to measure the final causal impact of a particular change in wording or design (see Hubspot 2015), aided by tools such as Adobe Target, Optimizely, Eloqua, or Apptimizer. While many of the results of these marketing experiments are kept private, you can find a remarkable, and publically accessible, collection of hundreds of experimental tests at WhichTestWon.com.

The marketing optimization process is straightforward, and we can learn the following lessons from these companies:

1. *Identify potential changes* to a product or communication that the company believes will improve performance. For example, changing the "call to action" (the specific request that is made of the user to do

something, usually on a clickable button), from "Learn More" to "Get Free Weight Loss Tips."

2. *Experimentally test* those changes on the smallest subset of the available population (or for the shortest time period) to get a clear statistical signal. For example, for traffic to a website, devote 5 % of the traffic for one month or 50 % of traffic for a few days to the new call to action ("Get Free Weight Loss Tips").

3. *Immediately apply the lessons* to the rest of the population.

4. *Iterate*, and test as many possible impactful changes as possible (repeat steps 1–3). For example, test the call to action, then the header, then the design, and then the time of day of the communication. Or, test all of them simultaneously—a technique known as multivariate testing (see Optimizely 2015).

5. *Invest* in the technology to make that iterative process as inexpensive as possible, by using tools like Adobe Target where the design and execution of an experiment literally only requires dragging and dropping elements on a screen, without any technical or statistical knowledge.

In short, the solution to the problem that "we don't know if techniques studied by researchers will work in a particular product" is simply to test it, and test as many as possible techniques as quickly and efficiently as possible. It is from this approach that marketers have shown impact—in specific areas.

Where to Expect Impact

The marketing optimization process is effective (and has the experimental data to prove it), it works for a particular goal—driving sales. If there is a more general lesson to be learned about where behavioral techniques improve consumer outcomes (and we know they can do so), it is this: look wherever private sector incentives are aligned with the presumed behavioral impact of the intervention on consumers, and wherever iterative testing is possible.

In marketing optimization, incentives are aligned to drive sales—behavioral interventions are deployed to increase click through rates, decrease disengagement, and drive more dollars to the company. Marketers also have powerful tools for iterative testing—as mentioned above. Outside of the marketing arena, those incentives aren't as neatly aligned. No consumer wearable technology company, for example, is paid based on the *measured impact* of its product. Rather, these companies drive sales based on the presumption of impact, which is a fundamentally different goal. It sadly means that applying behavioral techniques and marketing them heavily is often good enough.[36] Some companies choose to rigorously test and improve the impact of their products for the good of their end users, but those companies appear to be relatively rare.

Clearly then, impact remains one of the big open questions in the field. We have answered the question "do behavioral nudges in consumer products (sometimes) work": yes. We have also answered the question "do they (always) work": no. The remaining question is simply one that we cannot answer in the abstract: "does a particular product and its behavioral nudge work?" We know techniques that *can* work, but, we're never quite sure whether they actually do work in a particular context with a particular population until they have been experimentally tested there.

CONCLUSION

Over the last decade, we have witnessed the remarkable intersection of behavioral science and consumer products. A new crop of products explicitly uses behavioral "nudges" to help their users with difficult tasks—from dieting (MyFitnessPal) to exercising more (Jawbone) to improving their finances (HelloWallet). In fact, behavioral techniques have spread far beyond these obvious examples. Leading technology companies such as Facebook, Google, and Intuit have teams of behavioral scientists running experiments on user behavior, and nudges are increasingly at the center of modern digital marketing efforts (e.g., WhichTestWon).

As their use has become widespread, there has been remarkably little publicity[37]—until very recently with negative examples from Facebook and OKCupid (e.g., Meyer 2014; Wood 2014; Lupkin 2014). As these techniques grow in public awareness, naturally we should wonder: what exactly are these products doing, and do these techniques work?

With this chapter, we've traced the path that behavioral nudges have taken from the academy to consumer products in the field:

- Overall, nudges are reaching private sector products indirectly—through popular books for product managers and designers; behavioral scientists themselves rarely work on these products directly.
- Nudges are particularly prominent in the health and finance space, though examples can be found in wide ranging areas from energy

usage (Opower, Energy Joule) to driving behavior (Automatic, GreenRoad).

✳ • We can categorize nudges according to the underlying behavioral biases and cognitive limitations they address—from inattention to innumeracy to procrastination—summarized by the CREATE model (cue-reaction-evaluation-ability-timing-experience).

• We should be skeptical that behavioral nudges will work the same (or at all) once they are translated from an academic environment into consumer products, because of core lessons in the behavioral literature itself—that the details of implementation and decision-making context matter immensely.

• While a few companies have subjected their products and behavioral nudges to rigorous RCTs, most companies appear to rely on previously published research about the techniques and have not directly tested them as expressed in their products.

• In one domain, there is diligent and thoughtful attention to the impact of behavioral nudges and how to improve them—digital marketing optimization. In the digital marketing realm, incentives align to iteratively develop and test nudges in the field.

• Outside of marketing, we can learn from the optimization process and overcome the challenges of applying academic nudges to consumer products by following the methods of marketers: clear outcome metrics, rigorous testing, and rapid iteration.

Behavioral nudges in consumer products are still quite new, and we still have a great deal to learn about their impact, best uses, and dangers. Exciting times are ahead.

NOTES

1. Vitality's Glowcaps. See http://www.vitality.net/glowcaps.html
2. Opower generates such a report. See http://opower.com/solutions/energy-efficiency
3. See Goel (2014)
4. For example, Microsoft was conducting 200 concurrent experiments per day on the Bing site in 2013 (Kohavi et al. 2013). See also WhichTestWon.com, a repository of the results of such online digital experiments.

5. There appears to be no conclusive data about the size of the field, but we do have proxies that give us orders of magnitude. As of 2012, there were 16,900 economists of all types employed in the USA, roughly 45% of whom work for government (and are thus unlikely to consult in the private sector) (BLS 2015a), and behavioral economists are a small subset of economists. By comparison, there were over 1000 attendees for a single (digital) interaction designer conference in 2015, Interaction2015, featuring speakers like Opower's Rosen on how to apply behavioral techniques to design (IxDA 2015). There are also over 259,000 graphic designers in the USA, though the subset of whom apply nudges is unclear (BLS 2015b).

6. See, for example, Carnegie Mellon's Bachelor of Design program.

7. Based on interviews for this book chapter and two prior books on the topic (Wendel 2013, 2014).

8. This author also hosts such workshops (SXSW 2014).

9. See http://www.actiondesigner.net/; http://www.meetup.com/habitdesign/; http://www.meetup.com/London-behavioural-comms-monthly-informal-drinks/. Note: This author is the president of the nonprofit Action Design Network.

10. See http://www.bjfogg.com/how.html; http://irrationallabs.org/work-with-us/; http://www.slimbydesign.org/contact/

11. See http://www.ideas42.org/; http://tgggroup.com/; http://behaviouralinsights.co.uk/

12. See http://www.ogilvychange.com/; http://www.brainjuicer.com/; http://www.instituteofdecisionmaking.com/our-team/

13. Loss aversion refers to the tendency of people to strongly prefer (and expend effort) to avoid losing something that they already have to gaining something of equivalent value. In a nudge that uses loss aversion, a company might frame inaction as losing out, rather than framing action as a gain. For example, describing a trip to the gym as not losing the money one's spent on the gym, rather than gaining the value from it.

14. Estimates vary wildly in terms of growth of the sector; but major reports from Juniper, ABI, and Business Intelligence all show rapid growth from 2010 onward (Business Insider 2013). GfK, for example, estimated that 17.6 million smartwatches and health and fitness bands were sold worldwide in 2014 (see GfK 2015).

15. Goal setting: See, for example, Locke et al. (1981), Locke and Latham (2002). Feedback: See Kluger and DeNisi (1996) and Hattie and

Timperley (2007), noting that feedback can have a positive or negative impact depending on the design. Peer effects: See Smith and Christakis (2008) or Christakis and Fowler (2007) on the similarly two-sided nature of peer effects and health.

16. See http://www.glowcaps.com/. Glowcaps, along with other interventions, are currently being studied in a randomized controlled field trial for their effectiveness: see ClinicalTrials.gov (2015).

17. Author search on April 25, 2015, based on counting the apps under the "health & fitness: weight loss" category and by searching for the word "diet" in the App Store.

18. See SlimByDesign.org, for example. Wansink is developing a mobile application as well (Wansink 2015a).

19. This is an application of just in time decision-making aids, promoted by researchers such as Daniel Fernandes and John Lynch (Fernandes et al. 2014).

20. The author currently works at Morningstar and leads the behavioral science team there.

21. The author previously worked at HelloWallet and led their behavioral science efforts.

22. See Steverman (2014) for a quick survey of 11 products applying behavioral nudges to financial behavior.

23. See http://www.poverty-action.org/ushouseholdfinance/projects

24. See http://www.cfsinnovation.com/Financial-Capability-Innovation-Funds.aspx

25. Or, an older tradition of analysis seen in Elster's aptly named book, *Ulysses Unbound* (2000).

26. Or perhaps as little as four (Cowan 2010)

27. See Kahneman's *Thinking, Fast and Slow* (2011) and Malcolm Gladwell's *Blink* (2005). The first is a detailed look at our automatic (fast) thinking and the latter is a lighter read.

28. Another often-cited example comes from the Behavioural Insights Team (then part the UK government), which employed a simple normative message: "9 out of 10 people in your town pay their tax on time." See Behavioural Insights Team (2012).

29. And the inherent lack of urgency: it does not matter if one starts saving more on a given day or a day later. It only matters when we procrastinate repeatedly.

30. See Cugleman (2015) for another useful way to "audit" the behavioral techniques used in products.

31. See Allcott (2011) and Ayres et al. (2012) for two of the RCTs on Opower with positive results. See Allcott (2012) for a caveat.
32. Additional academic publications are in press or under development.
33. See Bryan et al. (2010) for more information on Commitment Devices, and Stickk.com for the particular product.
34. Nor, based on private discussion with companies in the field, do most companies run nonpublic RCTs on their products.
35. This problem is not unique to behavioral nudges, of course. As Abdukadirov discusses earlier in this volume building on Hippel (2006), the implementer of an idea may not have all of the "sticky" knowledge required to be effective—the small details that undermine effectiveness if ignored or not transferred effectively.
36. One could argue that if a product is not effective at impacting user behavior (in a beneficial way, beyond simply sales), then users would stop buying it (i.e., that the ultimate test of impact is market success). That is a testable hypothesis—but one that the history of diet fads and get rich quick schemes would seem to contradict. Humans are very good at weaving stories of success out of random noise—also known as the narrative bias.
37. Brief articles about selected techniques have appeared in major newspapers (Simon 2010) and magazines (Olson 2015). *Designing for Behavior Change* (Wendel 2014) provides a limited overview of commercial applications but does not attempt to provide a comprehensive look across industries. In addition, *Seductive Interaction Design* (Anderson 2011) and *Evil by Design* (Nodder 2013) provide many examples of behavioral science applied to consumer products but focus particularly on the UX design issues.

Bibliography

Albergotti, Reed. 2014. Facebook experiments had few limits. *Wall Street Journal*, July 2, sec. Tech. http://www.wsj.com/articles/facebook-experiments-had-few-limits-1404344378

Allcott, Hunt. 2011. Social norms and energy conservation. *Journal of Public Economics* 95(9–10): 1082–1095.

———. 2012. Site selection bias in program evaluation. Working paper. National Bureau of Economic Research, September. http://www.nber.org/papers/w18373

American Library Association. 2015. Number employed in libraries, April. http://www.ala.org/tools/libfactsheets/alalibraryfactsheet02. Accessed 1 May 2015.

Anderson, Stephen. 2013. Mental notes card deck. http://getmentalnotes.com/

Ariely, Dan. 2008. *Predictably irrational: The hidden forces that shape our decisions.* New York: HarperCollins.

Ayres, Ian, Sophie Raseman, and Alice Shih. 2012. Evidence from two large field experiments that peer comparison feedback can reduce residential energy usage. *Journal of Law, Economics, and Organization* 29(5): 992–1022.

Baumeister, Roy F., and John Tierney. 2011. *Willpower: Rediscovering the greatest human strength.* New York, NY: Penguin Press.

Behavioural Insights Team. 2012. Applying behavioural insights to reduce fraud, error and debt. *Cabinet Office*, London.

Bettinger, Eric P., Bridget Terry Long, Philip Oreopoulos, and Lisa Sanbonmatsu. 2009. The role of simplification and information in college decisions: Results from the H&R block FAFSA experiment. Working paper. National Bureau of Economic Research, September. http://www.nber.org/papers/w15361

Bhargava, Saurabh, and Dayanand Manoli. 2015. "Psychological frictions and the incomplete take-up of social benefits: Evidence from an IRS field experiment." *The American Economic Review* 105(11): 3489–3529.

Blanding, Michael. 2014. The business of behavioral economics. *Forbes*, August 11. http://www.forbes.com/sites/hbsworkingknowledge/2014/08/11/the-business-of-behavioral-economics/

Bond, Robert M., Christopher J. Fariss, Jason J. Jones, Adam D.I. Kramer, Cameron Marlow, Jaime E. Settle, and James H. Fowler. 2012. A 61-million-person experiment in Social influence and political mobilization. *Nature* 489(7415): 295–298.

Brown, Marie T., and Jennifer K. Bussell. 2011. Medication adherence: WHO cares? *Mayo Clinic Proceedings* 86(4): 304–314.

Bryan, Gharad, Dean Karlan, and Scott Nelson. 2010. Commitment devices. *Annual Review of Economics* 2(1): 671–698.

Bureau of Labor Statistics. 2015a. Economists : Occupational outlook handbook: U.S. Bureau of Labor Statistics. http://www.bls.gov/ooh/life-physical-and-social-science/economists.htm

———. 2015b. Graphic designers: Occupational outlook handbook: U.S. Bureau of Labor Statistics. http://www.bls.gov/ooh/arts-and-design/graphic-designers.htm

Burger, Jerry M., and Martin Shelton. 2011. Changing everyday health behaviors through descriptive norm manipulations. *Social Influence* 6(2): 69–77.

Business Insider. 2013. CHART: Just how big will the new mobile market for wearable devices become? *Business Insider Australia*, April 30. http://www.businessinsider.com.au/how-big-will-mobile-market-for-wearable-devices-2013-4

Christakis, Nicholas A., and James H. Fowler. 2007. The spread of obesity in a large social network over 32 years. *New England Journal of Medicine* 357(4): 370–379.

ClinicalTrials.gov. 2015. GlowCaps adherence randomized control trial, February 27. https://clinicaltrials.gov/ct2/show/NCT01756001

Cowan, Nelson. 2010. The magical mystery four: How is working memory capacity limited, and why? *Current Directions in Psychological Science* 19(1): 51–57.

Cugelman, Brian. 2015. Psychology for digital behavior change. Workshop toolkit. http://www.alterspark.com/training/psychology-for-digital-behavior-change. Accessed 9 Oct 2015.

Danova. 2015. THE WEARABLES REPORT: Growth trends, consumer attitudes, and why smartwatches will dominate. *Business Insider*. http://www.businessinsider.com/the-wearable-computing-market-report-2014-10. Accessed 25 Apr 2015.

Danziger, Shai, Jonathan Levav, and Liora Avnaim-Pesso. 2011. Extraneous factors in judicial decisions. *Proceedings of the National Academy of Sciences* 108(17): 6889–6892.

Dayer, Lindsey, Seth Heldenbrand, Paul Anderson, Paul O. Gubbins, and Bradley C. Martin. 2013. Smartphone medication adherence apps: Potential benefits to patients and providers. *Journal of the American Pharmacists Association: JAPhA* 53(2): 172–181.

DellaVigna, S. 2009. Psychology and economics: Evidence from the field. *Journal of Economic Literature* 47(2): 315–372.

Egan, Brian. 2015. Interview with Brian Egan. Phone, March 27.

Elster, Jon. 2000. *Ulysses unbound: Studies in rationality, precommitment, and constraints*. New York: Cambridge University Press.

Fabricant, Robert. 2010. Design with intent. Design observer, September 11. http://designobserver.com/feature/design-with-intent/14338

Fellowes, Matt, and Jake Spiegel. 2015. *Financial wellness—The future of work*. http://www.hellowallet.com/research/financial-wellness-future-work/

Fernandes, Daniel, John G. Lynch, and Richard G. Netemeyer. 2014. Financial literacy, financial education, and downstream financial behaviors. *Management Science* 60(8): 1861–1883.

Fogg, BJ. 2009. A behavior model for persuasive design. *Proceedings of the 4th International Conference on Persuasive Technology*, 40: 1–40: 7. Persuasive '09. New York: ACM.

Gerber, Alan S., and Donald P. Green. 2012. *Field experiments: Design, analysis, and interpretation*. New York: W. W. Norton.

GfK. 2015. Gfk forecasts 51 million wearables will be bought globally in 2015, March 2. http://www.gfk.com/news-and-events/press-room/press-releases/pages/gfk-forecasts-51-million-wearables-sold-globally-2015.aspx

Giné, Xavier, Dean Karlan, and Jonathan Zinman. 2010. Put your money where your butt is: A commitment contract for smoking cessation. *American Economic Journal: Applied Economics* 2(4): 213–235.

Gladwell, Malcolm. 2005. *Blink: The power of thinking without thinking*, 1st edn. New York: Little, Brown and Company.

Goel, Vindu. 2014. Facebook tinkers with users' emotions in news feed experiment, stirring outcry. *The New York Times*, June 29. http://www.nytimes.

com/2014/06/30/technology/facebook-tinkers-with-users-emotions-in-news-feed-experiment-stirring-outcry.html

Hattie, John, and Helen Timperley. 2007. The power of feedback. *Review of Educational Research* 77(1): 81–112.

Hershfield, Hal E., Daniel G. Goldstein, William F. Sharpe, Jesse Fox, Leo Yeykelis, Laura L. Carstensen, and Jeremy N. Bailenson. 2011. Increasing saving behavior through age-progressed renderings of the future self. *Journal of Marketing Research* 48(SPL): S23–S37.

Hippel, Eric von. 2006. *Democratizing innovation*. Cambridge, MA: The MIT Press.

Hubspot. 2015. An introduction to using A/B testing for marketing optimization. Whitepaper. http://cdn2.hubspot.net/hub/53/file-13221855-pdf/docs/ebooks/introduction_to_ab_testing_for_marketing_optimization.pdf

Interaction Design Association. 2015. Interaction15 schedule. http://interaction15.sched.org/directory/attendees/1. Accessed 1 May 2015.

Issenberg, Sasha. 2012. Obama does it better. *Slate*, October 29. http://www.slate.com/articles/news_and_politics/victory_lab/2012/10/obama_s_secret_weapon_democrats_have_a_massive_advantage_in_targeting_and.single.html

Junod, Suzanne White. 2014. Overviews on FDA history—FDA and clinical drug trials: A short history. WebContent, July 7. http://www.fda.gov/AboutFDA/WhatWeDo/History/Overviews/ucm304485.htm

Kahneman, Daniel. 2011. *Thinking, fast and slow*, 1st edn. Farrar, Straus and Giroux: New York.

Kaiser Family Foundation. 2015. Total professionally active physicians, March. http://kff.org/other/state-indicator/total-active-physicians/

Karlan, Dean, and Jacob Appel. 2011. *More than good intentions: Improving the ways the world's poor borrow, save, farm, learn, and stay healthy*. New York: Penguin.

Karlan, Dean, Margaret McConnell, Sendhil Mullainathan, and Jonathan Zinman. 2011. Getting to the top of mind: How reminders increase saving. National Bureau of Economic Research working paper. http://www.dartmouth.edu/~jzinman/Papers/Top%20of%20Mind%202011jan.pdf

Kast, Felipe, Stephan Meier, and Dina Pomeranz. 2012. Under-savers anonymous: Evidence on self-help groups and peer pressure as a savings commitment device. Working paper. National Bureau of Economic Research, September. http://www.nber.org/papers/w18417

Keas. 2015. Keas launches health management platform to integrate health benefits. *Reuters*, March 18. http://www.reuters.com/article/2015/03/18/keas-launches-idUSnPn8nxMtR+85+PRN20150318

Kluger, Avraham N., and Angelo DeNisi. 1996. The effects of feedback interventions on performance: A historical review, a meta-analysis, and a preliminary feedback intervention theory. *Psychological Bulletin* 119(2): 254–284.

Kohavi, Ron, Alex Deng, Brian Frasca, Toby Walker, Ya Xu, and Nils Pohlmann. 2013. Online controlled experiments at large scale. *Proceedings of the 19th ACM SIGKDD International Conference on Knowledge Discovery and Data Mining* 1168–1176. KDD '13. New York: ACM.

Kosner, Anthony Wing. 2012. Weight watchers 360: Mobile apps can break hard habits with easy-to-follow steps. *Forbes*, December 27. http://www.forbes.com/sites/anthonykosner/2012/12/17/weight-watchers-360-mobile-apps-can-break-hard-habits-with-easy-to-follow-steps/

Kramer, Adam D. I., Jamie E. Guillory, and Jeffrey T. Hancock. 2014. Experimental evidence of massive-scale emotional contagion through social networks. *Proceedings of the National Academy of Sciences* 111(24): 8788–8790.

Kuang, Cliff. 2012. In the cafeteria, google gets healthy. *Fast Company*, March 19. http://www.fastcompany.com/1822516/cafeteria-google-gets-healthy

Kwong, Kelvin. 2015. A smart coach by your side. *The Jawbone Blog*, January 28. https://jawbone.com/blog/smart-coach-side/. Accessed 1 May 2015

Locke, Edwin A., and Gary P. Latham. 2002. Building a practically useful theory of goal setting and task motivation: A 35-year Odyssey. *American Psychologist* 57(9): 705–717.

Locke, Edwin A., Karyll N. Shaw, Lise M. Saari, and Gary P. Latham. 1981. Goal setting and task performance: 1969–1980. *Psychological Bulletin* 90(1): 125–152.

Lockton, Daniel. 2013. Design with intent: A design pattern toolkit for environmental and social behaviour change. Thesis, Brunel University School of Engineering and Design PhD theses. http://dspace.brunel.ac.uk/handle/2438/7546

Lupkin, Sydney. 2014. You consented to Facebook's social experiment. *ABC News*, June 30. http://abcnews.go.com/Health/consented-facebooks-social-experiment/story?id=24368579

Maniago, Vince. 2015. Invisible steps: Behavioral economics driving design. http://www.slideshare.net/IntuitInc/invisible-steps-behavioral-economics-driving-design. Accessed 1 May 2015.

Meyer, Robinson. 2010. Everything we know about Facebook's secret mood manipulation experiment, June 28. http://www.theatlantic.com/technology/archive/2014/06/everything-we-know-about-facebooks-secret-mood-manipulation-experiment/373648/

Milkman, Katherine L., John Beshears, James J. Choi, David Laibson, and Brigitte C. Madrian. 2011. Using implementation intentions prompts to enhance influenza vaccination rates. *Proceedings of the National Academy of Sciences* 108(26): 10415–10420.

Miller, George. 1956. The magical number seven, plus or minus two: Some limits on our capacity for processing information. *The Psychological Review* 63: 81–97.

Morningstar. 2015. Morningstar behavioral science advisory board. http://corporate1.morningstar.com/Behavioral-Science-Advisory-Board/

Nodder, Chris. 2013. *Evil by design: Interaction design to lead us into temptation.* Indianapolis: Wiley. http://site.ebrary.com/id/10716209

Omada Health. 2014. *The prevent online Diabetes Prevention Program (DPP),* November. https://go.omadahealth.com

Optimizely. 2015. What is multivariate testing?. https://www.optimizely.com/resources/multivariate-testing/

Petakov, Artem. 2015. Interview with Artem Petakov. Phone, April 1.

Redström, Johan. 2006. Persuasive design: Fringes and foundations. In *Persuasive technology,* eds. Wijnand A. IJsselsteijn, Yvonne A. W. de Kort, Cees Midden, Berry Eggen, and Elise van den Hoven, 112–122. Lecture notes in computer science, vol. 3962. Springer: Berlin/Heidelberg. http://link.springer.com/chapter/10.1007/11755494_17

Richards, Tim. 2015. The big list of behavioral biases. http://www.psyfitec.com/p/the-big-list-of-behavioral-biases.html. Accessed 1 May 2015.

Ryan, Richard M., and Edward L. Deci. 2000. Self-determination theory and the facilitation of intrinsic motivation, social development, and well-being. *American Psychologist* 55(1): 68–78.

Smith, Kirsten P., and Nicholas A. Christakis. 2008. Social networks and health. *Annual Review of Sociology* 34(1): 405–429.

Stango, Victor, and Jonathan Zinman. 2011. Limited and varying consumer attention: Evidence from shocks to the salience of bank overdraft fees. NBER working paper. http://www.dartmouth.edu/~jzinman/Papers/SZ_LimitedAttention_Overdrafts_2011apr_wp.pdf

Steverman, Ben. 2014. Manipulate me: The booming business in behavioral finance. *Bloomberg.com,* April 7. http://www.bloomberg.com/news/articles/2014-04-07/manipulate-me-the-booming-business-in-behavioral-finance

SXSW Interactive. 2014. Session signup: How to design products for behavior change. http://sup.sxsw.com/presenters/stephen_wendel.html

Thaler, Richard H.. 2005. *Advances in behavioral finance. Volume II.* Illustrated edition. Princeton University Press.

Thaler, Richard H., and Cass R. Sunstein. 2008. *Nudge: Improving decisions about health, wealth, and happiness.* New Haven, CT: Yale University Press.

Tversky, Amos, and Daniel Kahneman. 1974. Judgment under uncertainty: Heuristics and biases. *Science.* http://link.springer.com/chapter/10.1007/978-94-010-1834-0_8

Volpp, Kevin G., George Loewenstein, Andrea B. Troxel, Jalpa Doshi, Maureen Price, Mitchell Laskin, and Stephen E. Kimmel. 2008. A test of financial incentives to improve warfarin adherence. *BMC Health Services Research* 8(1): 272.

Volpp, Kevin G., Andrea B. Troxel, Mark V. Pauly, Henry A. Glick, Andrea Puig, David A. Asch, Robert Galvin, et al. 2009. A randomized, controlled trial of financial incentives for smoking cessation. *New England Journal of Medicine* 360(7): 699–709.

Wansink, Brian. 2015a. Interview with Brian Wansink. Phone, April 1.

————. 2015b. *Slim by design*. Presented at the Action Design DC, March 23.

Wendel, Stephen. 2013. *Designing for behavior change: Applying psychology and behavioral economics*, 1st edn. Sebastopol, California: O'Reilly Media.

————. 2014. *Improving employee benefits: Why employees fail to use their benefits and how behavioral economics can help*. Washington, DC: Longfellow Press.

————. 2015. Workshop slides and booklet. *Action Design*. http://actiondesign. hellowallet.com/workshop-slides-booklet/. Accessed 9 Oct 2015.

Wilson, Timothy D. 2011. *Redirect: The surprising new science of psychological change*, 1st edn. New York: Little, Brown and Company.

Wood, Molly. 2014. OKCupid plays with love in user experiments. *The New York Times*, July 28, http://www.nytimes.com/2014/07/29/technology/okcupid-publishes-findings-of-user-experiments.html

Private-Sector Nudging: The Good, the Bad, and the Uncertain

Jodi N. Beggs

Behavioral economics has increased dramatically in popularity over the last decade. Not surprisingly, academic researchers have expressed significant interest in this (relatively) new line of inquiry, but behavioral economics has also received a disproportionate amount of attention from outside of the academic community. For example, policy makers have embraced behavioral economics as a way to understand how people's actions deviate from their long-term best interests and, as a result, how governments can mandate changes to consumers' choice architectures in order to "nudge" them toward greater long-term happiness. In addition, marketers have (knowingly or unknowingly) embraced behavioral economics as a way to exploit consumers' decision-making biases in order to increase profitability.

Anyone who has ever watched a typical late-night infomercial is familiar with this phenomenon—it's not a coincidence that the host asks if you would pay $200 for the new state-of-the-art whatchamajig and then proceeds to work his way down to the actual price of $19.99. Instead, the infomercial writers know that, by setting an initial high anchor price for the viewer to consider, the tactic causes viewers to be willing to pay more for the item than they would otherwise. Similarly, have you ever stopped

J.N. Beggs (✉)
Northeastern University, Boston, MA, USA

© The Editor(s) (if applicable) and The Author(s) 2016
S. Abdukadirov (ed.), *Nudge Theory in Action*,
DOI 10.1007/978-3-319-31319-1_6

125

to consider why so many companies offer free shipping when shipping is obviously not free to provide? Perhaps it's because people will buy far more than $5 of stuff that they wouldn't have bought otherwise in order to qualify for the irrationally attractive free shipping (known to behavioral economists, appropriately, as "FREE!" shipping[1]) rather than pay $5 for shipping.

As behavioral economists uncover and document more ways in which individuals are biased in their decision-making, both marketers and policy makers get more ways to nudge consumers in various directions. One common perception is that policy makers nudge consumers toward their long-term best interests and marketers nudge consumers away from their long-term best interests, usually by manipulating consumers into buying more than they would if they were being economically rational. In fact, nudge pioneers Richard Thaler and Cass Sunstein assert that "the key point here is that for all their virtues, markets often give companies a strong incentive to cater to (and profit from) human frailties, rather than try to eradicate them or to minimize their effects."[2] But is this always the case?

There is obviously a significant incentive for private producers (i.e. companies that sell goods and services to consumers) to implement nudges that improve their bottom lines. These nudges that are profitable for producers could, in turn, be either good or bad for consumers, or they could even be good for some consumers and bad for others. Furthermore, there is some opportunity for entrepreneurs to either "sell" nudges directly to consumers or to get into the business of helping producers implement effective nudges. That said, it's important to recognize that there are limitations on the ability (or, perhaps more accurately, willingness) of private markets to provide nudges that are helpful for consumers and, conversely, to refrain from providing nudges that are harmful to consumers. In some of these cases, policy makers have the incentive and ability to step in and implement nudges that are societally productive, but it should also be noted that governments face many of the same incentives and logistical limitations that prevent private enterprise from implementing nudges that increase consumers' long-term happiness.

NUDGING BY PRODUCERS

One of the main economic premises of private firms is that they operate so as to maximize profit.[3] Realistically, it's probably unreasonable to assume that firms are perfect profit maximizers in all cases, but the notion that firms are likely to undertake initiatives that add to a firm's profit and avoid initiatives that subtract from it is likely a pretty accurate general guide to firm behavior. As such, we can expect that the types of nudges that firms choose to implement are those that are profitable for the firm itself. Note, however, that we can't assume that firms will implement all nudges that may be profitable (or avoid all nudges that reduce profit), since a firm might not be aware that such a nudge exists or may have logistical considerations that prevent it from implementing an otherwise profitable nudge.

It's intuitively appealing to assume that nudges that are profitable for firms are bad for consumers, but this is not necessarily the case. "Beneficial nudges" (i.e. those that are in consumers' long-term best interests) are consistent with profit maximization when the company's incentives are aligned with the desires of the individuals' long-term selves—in other words, when companies want to sell more and consumers' long-term selves know that they should consume more, or when companies want consumers to use less of a product and consumers' long-term selves know that they should curb their consumption. In keeping with economic terminology, let's refer to a nudge that is both profit maximizing for producers and long-term utility maximizing for consumers as a "Pareto nudge."[4] (Note that Pareto nudges are a subset of beneficial nudges.) Again, in keeping with economic terminology, we can also refer to nudges that are bad for consumers' long-term utility but good for producers as "rent-seeking nudges."[5] Using these definitions, we can categorize nudges that are profitable for private producers as either Pareto nudges or rent-seeking nudges.

Pareto Nudges

Despite the popular conception that there is a universal tension between the incentives of marketers and the well-being of consumers, it's not actually that difficult to find examples where companies use the principles of behavioral economics to not only enhance their profitability but also better align consumers with their long-term best interests. Let's examine a few categories of such Pareto nudges in order to understand how they work and in what contexts they tend to appear.

Savings Nudges

Many households report not saving enough, whether it be for retirement, for large purchases, or to cover unexpected financial needs. While lack of financial resources does contribute to this situation in many cases, behavioral economists suggest that the tendency to procrastinate also plays a role—our desire for immediate gratification tends to tell us that it's optimal to start saving tomorrow rather than today, but our time-inconsistent preferences[6] suggest that the same is true when tomorrow becomes today!

It's therefore pretty clear that the long-term best interests of many consumers are well served by programs that encourage them to save more. What companies, then, have incentives that align with these consumers' best interests? Most likely not those organizations that are trying to get consumers to spend more (unless perhaps they sell products to retirees and take a very long-term view of their business). Instead, let's take a look at those organizations that benefit when consumers save more—financial institutions and, in some cases, employers.

Financial institutions benefit when consumers increase their saving because this saving is what creates demand for the products that the financial institutions offer. Employers benefit when employees save more when such saving takes place via higher 401(k) contributions. Why is this the case? Conventional wisdom suggests that participating in an employer-sponsored 401(k) program (as opposed to just being given cash compensation) makes employees feel more attached to their employer, thereby increasing productivity and reducing turnover. From a legal and taxation standpoint, however, the incentives are much more clear—in order to have a 401(k) program classified as "nondiscriminatory," which prevents higher-earning employees from having part of their contributions subject to taxation, companies must show that 401(k) contributions are not too skewed toward the higher-earning employees in the organization.[7] It is fairly typical for companies to make contributions on behalf of lower-earning employees in order to meet the nondiscriminatory requirement when necessary, so increasing overall participation in the employer's 401(k) program is often viewed as a cost-saving measure, even when an employer match is present.

"Keep the Change" Programs

Around 2005, in order to generate demand for savings accounts and debit card transactions, Bank of America introduced a program called "Keep the Change." This program rounds consumers' debit card transactions up to the next dollar, and then deposits the "change" into consumers' savings accounts. To sweeten the deal, Bank of America matches consumers' savings deposits 100 % for the first three months and then 5 % thereafter, up to $250 per year.[8] Since then, other banks have followed suit with similar programs.

In its first two years, Bank of America customers saved $400 million via the Keep the Change program.[9] (Note however, that some of this amount could have replaced other amounts that the consumers would have saved, but the figure most likely represents a net increase in saving.) This change in behavior can be explained by a number of behavioral economics principles:

- Narrow choice bracketing[10] and the "peanuts principle": Taken one at a time, none of the savings amounts generated by the program seem significant to the consumer, whereas a one-time savings amount of a more considerable sum would likely remind the consumer of what she was giving up in order to save. Therefore, by framing the saving as a bunch of small amounts that, individually, wouldn't have been able to purchase anything of note anyway, such a behavior is less painful to the consumer.
- Mental accounting[11]: Since customers can freely (and basically immediately nowadays) transfer funds between their checking and savings accounts, the money in these accounts is fungible from a rational standpoint. Many individuals, on the other hand, assign some psychological significance to money being in the savings account rather than the checking account and are therefore more likely to not spend the money when it's labeled as being in the savings account, even when this distinction is mostly artificial.

This market-based nudge appears to be pretty solidly in the best interests of consumers, especially since the program requires consumers to actively sign up for the program. (One drawback worth noting, however, is that some consumers have experienced issues with overdraft fees that they attribute to the program.) The downside of this active sign-up requirement, of course, is that consumers need to be self-aware regarding their need to be nudged (or have enough desire for the match incentive) in order to take the trouble to sign up, and the choice architecture of the decision of whether or not to enroll is biased in favor of not enrolling since that is the default option for the consumer. (This of course could be changed, and many consumers would likely benefit, but that doesn't mean that they won't complain in the short term.) Fortunately, the presence of the match incentive likely gets at least some consumers to sign up for non-nudge-related reasons.

401(k) Default Enrollment

Much has been made in academia, in the media, and in business of the effects of defaults on employee 401(k) participation. In one landmark field study, employee 401(k) participation was shown to increase from less than 50 % to almost 90 % as a result of simply switching from a system where employees had to actively opt in to the 401(k) program (via a short process that was not intended to be burdensome) to a system where employers were enrolled in the program by default but could opt out by completing a short form.[12] In another analysis, 401(k) participation rates were shown to be higher when employees are given fewer choices of plans to pick from.[13] (Note that this is technically more than a nudge if consumers' choices are forcibly limited, which is why some organizations present a few choices as the default but have more options available for those who want to consider all of them.) Behavioral economists are not shocked that such nudges work, since they are in line with fundamental principles in the field:

- Status-quo bias[14]: Experimental evidence suggests that people tend to view new options in comparison to their current situations—that is, the status quo. Furthermore, people tend to be loss averse, meaning that they dislike losses more than they like equivalent gains, and therefore weight losses in the decision-making process more than is rational. Because the downsides of moving away from the status quo are weighted more than the upsides, consumers are biased toward sticking with the scenario that they perceive as being the status quo. By setting a default option, the 401k plan managers are instilling a psychological (though somewhat arbitrary) status quo in the minds of consumers, and their ultimate choices are biased toward that initial status quo.
- Overchoice[15] (aka the Paradox of Choice): If consumers were rational computational robots, adding more options couldn't make them worse off—after all, the worst-case scenario would be that they don't like the new option and therefore don't choose it. In reality, however, consumers can get overwhelmed by too many choices (theoretically because they worry about making a suboptimal choice when the choice is difficult), and this frustration can prevent them from

making a decision at all. By limiting the number of available options, the plan designers decreased the amount of potential frustration and encouraged more people to make a choice rather than to balk at the program.

As a result of these initial studies, many companies have adopted policies for default 401(k) enrollment (often on the recommendation of human resources and retirement program consultants), and agencies such as the Department of Labor provide materials that advise businesses on how to implement automatic enrollment in their organizations. As a related nudge, human resources consulting firm Aon Hewitt offers a Quick Enrollment™ product that provides a simplified choice architecture for 401(k) enrollment, complete with a default contribution rate and asset allocation. Like automatic enrollment, Quick Enrollment™ has been shown to significantly increase 401(k) participation rates.[16]

Programs of this type appear to be both in the best interests of the companies offering them (as evidenced by their revealed preference for undertaking the expense and effort to implement them) and beneficial in the long term to consumers. Though we technically can't be entirely certain, it's fairly difficult to envision a common scenario where the default nudge leads to enrollment when it's actually optimal for a consumer to not enroll in a 401(k) program (mainly because it's pretty rare that people save "too much" for retirement!).

"Save More Tomorrow" Programs

Behavioral economists have also thought about how to help people overcome their time inconsistency and biases toward immediate gratification that lead to procrastination in saving decisions. For example, Shlomo Benartzi and Richard Thaler lay out a plan entitled "Save More Tomorrow" in which participants are encouraged not to put more money away today but instead to commit a portion of future pay increases to savings.[17] These plans, when implemented in pilot organizations, were accepted by almost 80 % of participants, and, of those participants, 80 % remained in the program after four pay-raise cycles. Behavioral economics can help explain why this is the case:

- Time inconsistency and biases toward immediate gratification[18]: Traditional economic models of intertemporal choice imply that individuals' preferences regarding a future decision will not change as the time to make the choice draws nearer—that is, individuals are "time consistent." Behavioral economists, on the other hand, incorporate the potential for time inconsistency into their choice models to explain why our preferences often change as potential costs and benefits become more immediately realized. (Hopefully we can all acknowledge that procrastination and biases toward immediate gratification have a plethora of empirical documentation in various forms.) By not asking for an immediate contribution, the program sidesteps consumers' bias toward immediate gratification and takes away a strong incentive to not join. Once enrolled, enrollment becomes the status quo and, as a result, status-quo bias serves to mitigate the time inconsistency that might otherwise cause individuals to unenroll when the time to start saving more rolls around.

- Loss aversion[19]: As mentioned earlier, people tend to be "loss averse" and overweight potential losses in the decision-making process. As a result, the framing of an outcome as a foregone gain rather than an explicit loss can make the outcome seem more favorable (or less unfavorable) to the individual. By only asking that portions of future raises rather than current compensation get committed to savings, the program designers turn what would in the moment feel like a loss into a foregone future gain and again lessen the incentive to not participate.

One of the interesting aspects of this program is that consumers could choose to implement this strategy themselves via strategically timed changes in contribution to a traditional retirement plan, so the increase in participation is likely either due to the power of suggestion or the fact that consumers hadn't thought of this strategy until it was presented to them.[20] Again, given that most consumers report wanting to save more than their short-term selves will allow, this nudge is most likely a Pareto nudge.

Usage Nudges
Many companies utilize business models that, rather than charge a fee for each use of a product, collect a time-based subscription fee. Therefore, companies whose products are not free to provide find themselves with an incentive to nudge customers toward lower usage of their products since such usage adds to cost but not revenue. Similarly, some companies have an incentive to nudge customers toward lower usage when the price charged to the consumer doesn't cover the marginal cost to the producer

at high levels of usage. Intuition suggests that this sort of nudge is not good for consumers, but is this always the case?

Online Streaming Nudges

Many people feel that they watch too much TV and that a "better" version of themselves would spend their time differently. Traditional cable television providers don't have an incentive to help these people be their better selves—cable programming is going to your television whether or not you are watching it,[21] and the providers want you to watch enough that you feel justified in continuing to subscribe to the service.

Some people who appear to want to cut back on their television consumption state that relying solely on streaming content is one way to help achieve this goal. So where do the incentives of streaming services lie? Are they going to nudge consumers in a productive way or are they, like the cable companies, going to encourage overconsumption? On one hand, streaming providers sometimes have to pay a licensing fee each time that a piece of content is viewed, which gives an incentive to nudge toward decreased consumption.[22] (In other words, marginal cost is not always effectively zero, even when bandwidth is cheap.) On the other hand, more content viewed means more opportunity to show revenue-generating advertisements, which gives an incentive to nudge toward increased consumption. In addition, increased viewing often gets pepole talking about shows, which drives subscriptions. This creates an ambiguous trade-off for services such as Hulu, which places ads in its programming content. Other services, such as Netflix and Amazon, don't place ads in their content and, as a result, have less of an incentive to encourage viewing above and beyond what is required to keep a consumer subscribing and what is helpful for word-of-mouth marketing. So what nudges do the streaming services provide?

The main way that streaming services nudge consumers is that they periodically require some action from the consumer in order to confirm that the consumer is still watching or listening. This is clearly in the company's best interests from a licensing fee perspective, and it might even be mandated from the advertisers' perspective (since they don't want to pay for things that the consumer isn't paying attention to). This is likely also in the interest of those consumers looking to cut back on their consumption, since they are essentially asked "Do you REALLY want to keep watching the shiny box?" and required to actively respond in the affirmative rather than just go with the default of the next episode or next series coming on. (Interestingly, Hulu's interface is more "user friendly" in terms of automatically playing the next episode or show once the current one is finished, which is entirely consistent with the incentives that the advertising model creates.) Again, this nudge is thought to be effective based on two behavioral principles:

- Status-quo bias[23]: As mentioned earlier, loss aversion causes individuals to be biased toward choices that are closer to an individual's current state, that is, the status quo. Because the status quo is similar to a default in that it is often the outcome that will persist if the consumer does nothing, consumers are biased toward the default option of continuing to watch if no "do you want to keep watching" question is asked. By introducing such a question and requiring the consumer to take explicit action in order to keep watching, the service is debiasing customers and perhaps even biasing them toward watching less, since that is technically the outcome that will occur if the consumer does nothing.
- Salience and decision-making[24]: Economic research suggests that consumers overweight more salient attributes of a product in their decision-making processes. By asking consumers if they want to continue watching, streaming services are making it salient that the consumer has already been watching for a while, thus encouraging them to overweight "time already spent" in the choice process and discouraging further consumption.

Note that the above considerations imply that even seemingly similar questions of "are you still watching?" and "do you want to keep watching?" may not have the same effect on consumers. In addition, consumers who feel that they are watching the right amount of content may get annoyed with the nudge, especially if they don't have a remote control nearby. Overall, however, this nudge is probably in line with what consumers would want in the long run—one only need to go online and compare the number of articles about how to watch less TV (or why people should watch less TV) to the number of articles about how to watch more TV to substantiate this generalization!

Utility Provider Nudges

If you are in charge of your household's utility bills, you have likely noticed a recent phenomenon where your utility bill now includes information on your energy usage as compared to that of your neighbors and then suggests some ways to conserve energy. Since conserving energy really means buying less of the product that the company is trying to sell you, these nudges may seem a little perplexing. Is it really the case that your utilities have the proper incentives to encourage energy conservation?

In many cases, the answer is yes, for two reasons. First, the government agencies that regulate the utilities often give either mandates or incentives to the companies in order to get them to encourage conservation.[25] Second, because the utilities are charged with serving what often seems to be an ever-expanding universe of energy demand, it is sometimes more cost effective intended encourage customers to use less energy than it is to either buy energy externally on wholesale markets in order to meet demand or incur the fixed costs of expanding one's own facilities. These two observations imply that it's pretty safe to conclude that the nudges put out by the utilities are intended to encourage less rather than more energy usage. What is less clear is whether consumers' long-term selves really care all that much about using less energy or whether the negative externalities generated by energy usage give society a reason to care even when individuals don't. (Economically speaking, both of these reasons give valid justification for putting a nudge in place, but it's important to recognize that the reasons are not one and the same and may affect the effectiveness of the nudge.) In either case, the nudge works because of a powerful principle of influence research:

- Descriptive social norms: People tend to want to behave in accordance with the behaviors of people like them. That said, "like them" has a number of different interpretations, but one interpretation that motivates behavior is "in a similar situation," and such a comparison is known as a descriptive social norm. In a seminal field experiment, for example, researchers increased hotel towel reuse by informing guests that most of the people who stayed in the same room decided to reuse their towels.[26] In the energy context, showing the energy usage of neighbors likely has the same effect in that it sends a message to large consumers of energy that "your neighbors are conserving, shouldn't you be conserving too?"

Field experiments specific to the energy industry have confirmed the effectiveness of social norm nudges in reducing consumption. For example, one study shows that receiving information about electricity usage in comparison to that of others in the neighborhood decreases usage by between 1 and 2 kWh per day for those households that were higher than average users.[27] Unfortunately, the study also suggests that the nudge slightly increases usage for those households that consume less than average, which somewhat mutes the overall effectiveness of the nudge unless the nudge is selectively applied. (This latter effect can be mitigated, however, with the inclusion of an injunctive message of approval or disapproval.) Similar energy reduction of 1–2 % as a result of peer comparison messages is found in studies conducted by energy providers themselves.[28]

Previous attempts at encouraging conservation have included the use of subsidies for energy-efficient light bulbs and other household products, but the nudge-based approaches appear to generate an effect at least as large at lower cost to the company (and, as a result in some cases, lower cost to the taxpayer). Does the nudge make consumers better off? After all, the descriptive norm by itself can cause some households to increase their energy consumption, and not everyone necessarily has energy conservation as a long-term goal. (In fact, the effects of such a nudge are much stronger for liberals than for conservatives, and conservatives disproportionately report not liking the messages and choose to opt out of such mailings.[29]) Narrowly speaking, it's unclear whether this nudge as typically enacted makes consumers better off, but it is possible to provide a more targeted nudge that will reach a largely receptive audience and mitigate perverse effects. From a broader societal perspective, the nudge is efficient because it reduces energy costs on average (eliminating some production that is sold at an inefficiently low price, particularly during peak usage) and reduces the externalities generated by energy consumption, which benefits consumers overall as a group.

Compliance Nudges

It's not difficult to acknowledge that, as long as the price charged for a product covers the producer's marginal cost of production, selling more of a product is beneficial to producers. Producers' nudging incentives are aligned with the incentives of consumers when the product is something that consumers' long-term selves wish that they would consume more of. With what types of products does this occur?

There are a number of markets that have such incentives—a quick thought exercise brings to mind pharmaceuticals, health food, and even auto maintenance. For example, drug treatment compliance is a big issue in the medical field, and it would be in patients' best interests to have a system that encourages proper and complete usage of the prescriptions that they are given. Similarly, it is in the interest of pharmaceutical companies for consumers to finish their prescriptions since it results in more product being purchased. (Insurance companies may also benefit if compliance in the short term decreases medical costs in the long run.) Therefore, understanding in what ways consumers can be nudged toward better drug compliance using behavioral principles is of paramount importance:

- Descriptive social norms[30]: It is likely the case that the same descriptive norm messages that have been shown to help consumers reduce their energy usage can get them to take their pills as well.
- Overweighting of small probabilities[31]: The notion of prospect theory, developed by Daniel Kahneman and Amos Tversky as an empirically supported alternative to expected utility theory, states that consumers tend to subjectively overweight small probabilities in the decision-making process (as long as the probabilities aren't so small that consumers round them to zero). This observation can help explain, for example, why people participate in state-sponsored lotteries, even though the odds are clearly not in their favor. It's not surprising, therefore, that similar logic suggests that small lottery incentives for drug compliance could be leveraged in a nudge-like manner.

In one study, stroke patients who were prescribed the drug warfarin were entered into a lottery that offered a 1 % chance of winning $100, with the payout being contingent on proper adherence to the drug regimen. The study was based on a small sample size, but it did show a compliance rate of 100 % as compared to 80 % in the control group that was not given the lottery.[32] While more of a financial incentive than a nudge in the strictest sense, this result is consistent with the nudge ideals of not forcing the consumer to do anything and to offer a small change that has a disproportionately large effect.

Similar opportunities may exist in other contexts to encourage compliance with agreed-upon rules and practices. For example, credit-card companies have largely shifted to offering auto-pay options for customers, and one has even implemented a rewards system that credits customers both when they make purchases and when they make payments. Such systems are clearly good for consumers as long as it is reasonable to believe that their long-run selves would want to pay down their debt rather than amassing fees, but they will most likely only be provided by companies that find encouraging timely payment to be more profitable than charging fees and risking future consumer default and collection costs.

It's interesting to note that the nudges studied here are profitable for the firms implementing them because they increase the profit that the firms earn from each consumer. It's important to keep in mind, however, that this is not necessary in order for a nudge to be profitable for a firm. Counterintuitively, it is possible for a nudge that is unprofitable on a per-customer basis to be profitable overall if it increases the number of consumers doing business with the nudge-providing producer. (Like some other cases that we analyze, this outcome requires consumers to be self-aware about their need for a nudge.) In addition, a nudge that is not directly profitable could still be beneficial to a firm if it improves brand image or loyalty in a general sense.

Rent-Seeking Nudges

It's probably not shocking that most academic research focuses on nudges that are at least perceived as being in consumers' best interests. Unfortunately, this doesn't mean that most of the nudges implemented by private firms actually benefit consumers—one need only think back to the infomercial and free shipping nudges described earlier to see that various forms of marketing fit pretty squarely into the category of rent-seeking nudges. Therefore, it's important to examine where else rent-seeking nudges tend to occur and how to spot them, especially since they often rely on the same tactics used to generate Pareto nudges in other contexts.

Choice Architecture Nudges
Just as the presence of a default can have strong effects on 401(k) participation, defaults can be chosen by marketers to increase adoption and sales of items that consumers' long-term selves may not necessarily want. This sort of choice architecture or "default" nudge has become so ubiquitous that we almost don't notice it any more—how many times do we encounter a default opt-in to an email newsletter, for example? Such default nudges also arise when a consumer installs Java and is presented with a default of installing a particular browser toolbar or antivirus software, or when the consumer has to actively opt out if she doesn't want the supplementary insurance on a car rental. Such nudges are particularly effective because they exploit not only status-quo bias as discussed earlier but also lack of salience, since the consumer may not even realize that she had a choice to make in the first place. (Note that salience in this context refers not only to the features of a consumer's options but also to the opportunity to make an active choice in the first place.) Given that car rental insurance

is both generally vastly overpriced and often redundant, a choice architecture nudge that results in consumption is pretty clearly a rent-seeking nudge. As for the email and toolbar defaults, one need only consider how many people set up a separate junk email account for such items and how many people have signed a change.org petition requesting that Oracle stop bundling the Ask toolbar with the Java Installer by default[33] to infer that such nudges are of the rent-seeking variety.

Usage Nudges

As noted earlier, there is a general incentive for firms that charge subscription fees to discourage actual use of their products. This is obviously bad for consumers when consumers get positive marginal utility from using the products and especially when consumers know that their long-term selves would want them to use the products more. This misalignment of incentives can give rise to rent-seeking nudges, whose effects are often compounded by nudges that discourage consumers from cancelling the service that they are underutilizing. In other words, for anyone who has ever tried and failed to "quit the gym,"[34] the next section is for you.

Gym Memberships

Many individuals report that their long-term selves would like their short-term selves to go to the gym more than they actually do. In contrast, many gyms operate via business models that depend on most people not actually going to the gym.[35] (This is particularly true for gyms with very low monthly fees.) Therefore, these gyms have incentives to nudge customers toward continuing to pay the monthly fees and away from actually using the facilities, which is somewhat of a delicate balance. Gyms achieve this balance using a number of behavioral economics principles:

- The Sunk-Cost Fallacy[36]: Research in behavioral economics shows that people are more likely to use a good or service if they pay a higher amount for it. (This stands in contrast to rational behavior because the amount paid is a nonrecoverable sunk cost and therefore shouldn't factor into the forward-looking decision-making process.) Therefore, some gyms will charge a low monthly fee that brings in revenue but doesn't make the consumer feel like she has to "get her money's worth."
- Lack of payment salience: Because payments are generally made via a debit or credit card, the customer doesn't go through the act of

writing a check or otherwise actively handing over the payment each month. This lack of salience makes customers less likely to reevaluate their membership decisions and more likely to stay enrolled. In fact, customers on month-to-month contracts are more likely than those on yearly commitment contracts to maintain their membership past the one-year mark, likely because they aren't faced with a salient renewal decision.[37]

- Hurdles to contract termination: The success of nudges rests on the observation that seemingly small hurdles or transaction costs can have irrationally large effects on behavior. By requiring that contracts be terminated in person or via registered mail, gyms create exactly these theoretically small hurdles that prevent people from cancelling. Whereas a long-run-oriented consumer realizes that the small action saves her from what is potentially a lifetime of future gym payments, the short-run-oriented consumer views the hassle of cancelling against the immediate small monthly payment and decides that the effort isn't worth it ... only to find that the effort is again not worth it the next month![38]
- Noncore utilization: Some gyms, both by setting low monthly fees and by showcasing nongym amenities (couches, juice bars, etc.), actively select for consumers who are predisposed to not use the gym. Furthermore, these gyms actually nudge customers away from using the actual gym part of the gym by hosting seemingly absurd pizza parties and movie nights. The logic is that these amenities will get people to keep paying their membership even when they realize that they are not going to actually use the gym, but there is an additional nudge in that these activities make people feel like they've used the gym (i.e. gotten their money's worth) and therefore decreases the desire for them to actually come back and use the gym part in order to "recoup" their sunk cost.

This scenario highlights the danger in trusting markets to provide productive nudges to consumers, since it's very clear that these nudges are not things that most consumers' long-term selves would approve of. Such policies are typically associated with the gym industry, but they can arise in a number of different contexts—just think of how many companies make it very easy to sign up for a service online and how few make it easy to cancel service in a similar manner.

I think WSJ is notorious for this (NYT too)

Rental Subscription Nudges

In 1997, Netflix debuted a novel business model when it offered customers the opportunity to pay a monthly fee for unlimited DVD rentals by mail, subject to the constraint that customers could only keep three DVDs out at a time. Under this system, customers do not pay an explicit late fee regardless of how long a DVD is kept, which was in stark contrast to the policies of traditional video rental stores at the time. (There is, of course, an implicit late fee in that if a consumer holds a DVD for a long time it reduces the capacity to receive other DVDs.) More recently, companies have introduced this model to other industries—nowadays, you can even pay $139 per month for unlimited fashion rentals![39]

Under this business model, companies have no direct way to increase revenue per customer, which leaves cost reduction as the most likely path to increased profits. Since the marginal cost of shipping out another DVD, outfit, or other item is not zero, companies that use rental subscription business models have a financial incentive to nudge consumers to keep items longer and exchange them less frequently. Interestingly enough, such companies also benefit from open-ended rental periods and longer (and more uncertain) holding periods because such behavior means that they don't have to stock as many items categorized as "new releases" in order to meet customer demand.[40]

Do rental-subscription companies nudge in this manner, and, if so, how? First and foremost, it's highly unlikely that such companies are going to increase the salience of the fact that you've had an item checked out for far longer than is probably rationally reasonable by emailing or otherwise contacting customers regarding such matters (or at all unless necessary), and this lack of action can be viewed as a passive nudge. Theoretically, a company could even nudge strategically in this way by only reminding customers regarding their rentals when they hold an item that is in high demand overall, but this behavior does not appear to be prevalent. Furthermore, rental subscription companies have an incentive to nudge consumers away from all wanting new products at the same time, and there is evidence that such companies passively implement such nudges. For example, Netflix made the decision a number of years ago to remove the "Releasing This Week" section of its site for its physical DVD rentals but kept other similar recommendation sections for older titles.

Overall, such nudges increase the effective price per item that consumers pay and reduce the value that they get from their purchases. While it is possible that consumers feel that they consume more movies than their long-term selves would want in the same way that they feel about streaming video, the lack of immediate gratification inherent in the mailing process makes it less likely that their behavior differs from rational utility maximization to the degree that it does with streaming video. As a result, such nudges that are good for the rental subscription services are not good for consumers—that is, they count as rent-seeking nudges. Luckily for consumers, Netflix hasn't yet decided to nudge consumers toward ordering documentaries rather than action thrillers, even though there is evidence that such a policy would help its bottom line via longer holding periods![41]

Honesty Nudges

There are many cases in the marketplace where the price of a service to the consumer (and, in most cases, the cost of providing the service) depends on the particular characteristics of each consumer. In some of these cases, logistics dictate that the most efficient way of documenting these characteristics is to have the consumer report them herself. For example, this approach is prevalent in a number of insurance markets, where potential customers are asked for information about their health, personal property, and so on without having this information verified by a third party. Getting customers to report data that results in higher prices is in the best interests of the producer (as long as the customer doesn't decide not to purchase), so how can they nudge consumers in a profitable direction?

One study suggests that the answer might be as simple as having customers sign the form (thus affirming that all information is accurate) at the beginning rather than at the end. In a sample of about 13,000 auto insurance customers who were asked to report their mileage driven, a "sign at beginning" policy resulted in almost 11 % more miles being reported than an otherwise equivalent "sign at end" form.[42] (In contrast, the "sign at end" approach doesn't result in behavior that is significantly different from not asking for a signature at all.) Granted, the categorization of this nudge as rent-seeking requires a bit of philosophical pondering—while it is true that many consumers' long-term selves would place a priority on being honest, it is nonetheless true that such nudges make consumers financially worse off in a way that is profitable for producers, thus fitting the definition (though perhaps not the spirit) of a rent-seeking nudge.

The above examples illustrate the "dark" side of private-sector nudging in that they show that what is best for firms' profits isn't always in line with what is in consumers' long-term best interests. As an educated onlooker, it's easy to spot rent-seeking nudges where the incentives of firms and consumers are not aligned, but there is no guarantee that consumers themselves will be aware that they are being nudged away from their long-term best interests. Furthermore, it is entirely possible that consumers are still susceptible to rent-seeking nudges (technically, to any nudge) even if they are aware that they are in fact being nudged.

Nudges and Market Heterogeneity

The nudges described so far have been fairly simple to analyze in that they were judged as (at least approximately) universally good for consumers or universally bad for consumers, and likewise for producers. If we were to take the definition of "universally" very literally, of course, we would realize that no nudge can be counted on to be either universally good or bad—for example, there's always going to be those idiosyncratic people who would want to be nudged to save less, go to the gym less frequently, or watch more streaming video. Overall, this sort of heterogeneity isn't worrisome for two reasons. First, given that a nudge can be argued to *(1)* benefit society overall if it helps more people than it hinders, a small idiosyncratic minority isn't enough to negate the overall wisdom of the nudge. Second, it is often not possible to create a truly neutral choice architecture, *(2)* which implies that a nudge of some sort is in place whether it is explicitly designed or not. It is somewhat nonsensical to see this somewhat random nudge as more valid simply because it's already there, especially since such a nudge also likely benefits some people and hinders others.

   That said, one can easily identify cases where the effect of a nudge on consumers is truly ambiguous due to heterogeneity in preferences and behavior. It's important to recognize when these situations occur, since this heterogeneity makes it difficult to classify a nudge as either Pareto or rent-seeking. In addition, it is possible to identify cases where further investigation is needed in order to determine whether a nudge is even profitable for a producer in the first place.

this is a big component of Rizzo's point

Savings Nudges

In the aggregate, it appears that automatic enrollment programs for 401(k) participation make employees better off (i.e. are Pareto nudges) because overall employee participation increases, and, as stated earlier, most people are well served by saving more. It should be noted, however, that the evidence also suggests that some employees are harmed by the program in that they would have chosen to save more if prompted with the need to opt in and actively choose a contribution amount, whereas the default allows them to just go with the flow and, as a result, go with a lower rate of saving.[43] An ideal program would try to correct for this and actively encourage people to engage on the contribution amount decision even if they are not engaging on the enrollment decision itself.

Nutrition Nudges

By now, just about everyone interested in the power of nudges has heard about former New York City mayor Michael Bloomberg's ill-fated attempt to nudge by banning all sugary drinks over a certain size.[44] (He argued that this counts as a nudge rather than an outright ban because people still had the option to purchase multiple smaller beverages.) This is obviously a government-sponsored nudge, but, as a related matter, do private companies in the food industry have the proper incentives to nudge consumers toward their long-term well-being, and, just as importantly, is there a universal direction in which it's "good" to nudge consumers?

The answer is unfortunately (at least from a public policy perspective) less clear than one would hope. On the pessimistic side, it is unlikely that a company selling mainly unhealthy products would voluntarily nudge consumers toward better long-term choices. On a brighter note, stores that sell both healthy and unhealthy products would likely be more than happy to nudge customers toward healthier alternatives—provided, of course, that the healthy alternatives are higher-margin products than the unhealthy ones! Stores that sell mainly healthy products seem like they might have an incentive to nudge consumers by providing calorie counts on menus and other informational nudges, but this isn't necessarily the case. Because many consumers know very little about the nutrition information in what they consume, it could be the case that even the nutrition information of healthy items looks intimidating or somehow bad compared to the blissful ignorance of the nonlabeled food at the less healthy store. If this is the prevailing mindset, then even the stores selling healthy items have an incentive to keep their nutrition information less visible. (This helps to explain why some restaurants welcome nutrition information mandates even when they wouldn't print the nutrition information on their menus voluntarily.)

One area where Pareto nudges may be available, however, is in the realm of voluntary downsizing. With such a nudge, rather than being asked "would you like to supersize that?", consumers would be asked if they would like to downsize their portion of an unhealthy item. In one study, up to one-third of consumers accepted the downsizing offer, even when no nontrivial price decrease was present.[45] If consumers accept a smaller portion without requiring a significant price decrease, such a nudge should be profitable for producers. In addition, since very few people cite "not eating enough unhealthy food" as keeping them from being their long-term best selves, this nudge also appears to generally be in the best interests of consumers. That said, such an approach must be applied carefully in order to be beneficial—since it appears that consumers are fairly susceptible to the power of suggestion in general, one could likely achieve a similar result by asking consumers to downsize a portion of a healthy item (and likely make up for it with a less healthy item later), which would be classified as a rent-seeking nudge.

The previous example notwithstanding, nutrition-based nudges are somewhat of a mixed bag overall. Whether nudges that promote healthy choices will be provided by private firms depends both on whether healthy foods are more profitable than unhealthy ones and whether healthy foods can be marketed as effectively as unhealthy foods. Whether such nudges will be helpful for consumers depends on their ability to properly interpret the information that such nudges convey and whether their goals are in line with the promoted definition of "healthy" in the first place. For example, calorie counts essentially tell consumers where to get the most energy per dollar spent, so it's not obvious that providing such information would result in lower-calorie choices or even choices that are beneficial in a long-term sense. In addition, calorie counts taken out of context could nudge people away from more nutrient-rich choices and trigger a form of availability bias[46] in decision-making.

Further complicating the implementation of beneficial nutrition nudges is the fact that companies may not even always realize when they are nudging their customers. For example, retailers have found that dedicated produce sections of shopping carts as well as the presence of mirrors encourage healthy choices,[47] but they might not be aware of the fact that consumers seem to choose more unhealthy items as a reward for the perceived effort of lugging a basket around the store.[48] In this sort of environment, whether nudges are good or bad for consumers likely depends on a number of factors both relating to the individual and to her particular purchasing experience, making such nudges difficult to implement and evaluate individually.

Salience Nudges

Many companies claim to help consumers by simplifying the buying process and thus making consumers' lives easier. Overall, can we tell whether such policies make consumers better off in the long run? Let's examine.

Auto-renewal Nudges

Anyone who has purchased typical household items on Amazon.com recently has likely noticed that the company now offers a discount for customers who are willing to sign up for a subscription to the item, in which case a recurring quantity of the item will be shipped automatically until the subscription is actively cancelled. This is obviously a nudge toward purchasing more of the item, and it is likely quite powerful in that it switches the default from not receiving the item to receiving the item.

Many services have had this model for a long time, and it's clearly in the best interest of those trying to increase sales. What is less clear is whether this nudge is good or bad for consumers. Some consumers—for example, those who rush around frantically looking for that last roll of toilet paper that they hid in case of emergency—are likely better off with this kind of nudge. Those customers who can plan for themselves and would use the flexibility wisely are probably worse off, especially in the condition where they find their stockpile of paper products growing without bound.

Automatic Payment Nudges

In the movie *Manhattan*, Woody Allen comments that his lady love looks so beautiful that he can barely keep his eyes on the taxi meter. The line is obviously included for comedic effect, but it also illustrates the behavioral principle that people don't like their costs to be numerous and salient. By this logic, consumers could be nudged to consume more by taking away the meter and making payment more automatic.

Lots of companies already do this by simply accepting credit cards. Credit cards, aside from relaxing consumers' liquidity constraints, nudge them toward more consumption by taking away the pain of paying—a single swipe of a card (especially because it doesn't feel like money) is less painful than the aggregation of handing over each individual bill, and, by extension, paying one credit card bill is less painful to many than the aggregation of each individual transaction. (In fact, economists Drazen Prelec and Duncan Simester find that consumers' willingness to pay can be increased significantly by instructing them to use credit cards rather than cash.[49]) Some companies, such as Uber, take this principle one step further by keeping your payment information on file and not even making consumers swipe a card at the time of purchase. This behavior nudges consumers further toward increased consumption, but is this in the best interests of consumers?

The answer is far from clear. If people objectively weigh costs and benefits when they are forced to look at the cash or the meter, then taking away these features of the decision will cause consumers to consume more than is in line with their long-term interests. On the other hand, if people are being irrationally stingy when they see the cash being handed over or the meter running, then the nudges that are in line with the companies' incentives could in fact be a good thing for consumers as well. Overall, it is difficult to judge the productivity of this nudge without first determining how many of each type of consumer exist in a market.

[handwritten margin note: but we rarely, if ever, know the distribution of consumers]

As the heterogeneity of the effect of a nudge increases, the social justification for implementing such a nudge decreases. This doesn't mean, however, that attempts to nudge in such ways should be immediately abandoned. Instead, companies could try to identify consumer groups that would benefit from the nudge (or would at least make the nudge profitable) and target accordingly, or they could rely on self-selection by having customers voluntarily subject themselves to the nudge (as we've already seen is done in a number of cases).

The preceding examples show that it is certainly possible, but in no way guaranteed, that marketers have incentives to nudge consumers toward rather than away from their long-term best interests. This suggests, at the very least, that not all Pareto nudges have to come from the government. That said, until the social pressure for corporate social responsibility becomes much greater than it is today, private companies can only be relied upon to provide nudges that are either in line with their profitability or are directly or indirectly mandated by the government (such as the 401(k) enrollment and the energy use incentives). This implies that markets will fail to provide Pareto nudges when at least one of the following conditions is met:

- The private incentives of the firms encourage marketers to nudge consumers away from rather than toward their long-term best interests.
- Consumers are heterogeneous in their preferences and behaviors to a degree that it's not obvious what a "good" versus "bad" nudge is.

In these situations, either private nudging firms or the government could step in to provide the appropriate nudges, though care must be taken in order to avoid the same difficulties often encountered by private producers when designing nudges.

Opportunities for Other Market Nudges

We've just seen that, while it's not impossible for companies to have incentives to provide Pareto nudges, these incentives don't exist in all organizations. One natural implication of this observation is that the government has an opportunity to step in and provide consumer-welfare-enhancing nudges itself. What is less often considered, but is potentially a powerful possibility, is that markets provide the incentives for entrepreneurs to create beneficial nudges even when companies trying to sell their wares to consumers don't have the incentives to provide such nudges themselves.

For example, after studying behavioral economics and consumer irrationality for a number of years, I have an entrepreneurial dream of opening a mall kiosk, preferably directly outside of a Best Buy, that sells advice to not, except perhaps in very extenuating circumstances, purchase any point-of-sale extended warranties that are offered. Unfortunately, I have yet to envision a satisfactory business model for such an endeavor that would both be acceptable to the consumer and compensate me for my time and ingenuity. The problem appears to lie in the fact that, if consumers knew that such advice was valuable and thus worth paying for, they likely would also know not to purchase the extended warranty without me having to advise them as such. (I hereby declare this the economics version of the Dunning – Kruger effect.) That said, let's examine some other business models that appear to make consumer-welfare-enhancing nudges profitable.

In 2007, Yale economics professor Dean Karlan, along with cofounders Ian Ayres and Jordan Goldberg, decided to create what he viewed as an online "commitment store." In this store, consumers can define a goal that they want to be nudged toward (weight loss, finishing a draft of that novel, etc.) and assign a monitor to confirm whether or not the goal has been achived. The consumer also assigns an amount of money to the goal, which, if the goal is not met, will be charged to the consumer's credit card and either given to a third-party individual or an "anti-charity"—that is, a charity for a cause that the consumer does not believe in. Karlan named this company stickk.com, to represent either "sticking" to one's goal or being prodded with the stick part of a carrot-and-stick incentive. (The additional k is an homage to the fact that K is legal jargon for a contract.)[50]

Stickk.com essentially acts as a soft commitment device for consumers—"soft" because, unlike Ulysses tying himself to his ship's mast to make him unable to succumb to the Sirens, consumers at stickk.com are still free to fail to achieve their goals, they just face an artificially constructed monetary penalty for doing so. Therefore, stickk.com's product fits within the definition of nudges or libertarian paternalism since it is focused on changing incentives rather than specifically constraining behavior. The company, registered as a for-profit LLC, earns its revenue via advertising and customized and cobranded enterprise solutions.

Once we start looking, it's not that hard to find commercial products that either purposefully or inadvertently serve a nudging function. A FitBit, for example, is a simple device that tracks how much physical activity an individual experiences throughout the day. A side effect of the device, however, is that it serves as a physical reminder to be active (since it's usually worn on the wrist) and a source of positive and negative reinforcement when the activity statistics are viewed.

These examples show that, in some cases at least, the free market provides sufficient incentives to bring helpful nudges to some groups of consumers. In addition, it is entirely possible that not-for-profit organizations could step in to provide societally beneficial nudges when a specific business model can't be developed, though such developments are often driven by ideology on a one-off basis and thus can't be guaranteed to occur. Endeavors such as stickk.com shouldn't be viewed as a panacea for all self-control problems and deviations from long-term well-being, however, since people must be self-aware to some degree to realize that they could benefit from using such tools, and such self-awareness is not likely to be universally present. In addition, people must be willing to be nudged in a good direction, whereas they might not even be aware that their status-quo environment is nudging them in a bad direction. The good news is that these companies have a profit motive to raise awareness regarding the need for and benefits of nudges!

One additional area where there appears to be significant opportunity is in the market for companies that sell nudge strategies to private firms and governments. For example, Allianz Global Investors has developed a "PlanSuccess" product that purports to use the principles of behavioral economics and finance to improve 401k plans,[51] and you may have noticed some brand names on the nudge strategies described earlier. Even

UK Prime Minister David Cameron's Behavioral Insights Team (aka the "nudge squad"), founded in 2010, is being spun off as a for-profit enterprise, replacing two-thirds of the government ownership with private investment and employee ownership.[52]

GOVERNMENT'S ROLE IN NUDGING

So far, we've seen not only that private enterprise has some incentives to provide nudges that are beneficial to consumers (either directly or indirectly) but also that it lacks incentives to provide some beneficial nudges and instead has incentives to provide some rent-seeking nudges. In an economic context, an inability of markets to self-organize to provide a good or service for which the benefits to society outweigh the costs to society (or, conversely, to refrain from producing a good for which the costs outweigh the benefits) is classified as a market failure, which enables the government to create rather than destroy market value via regulation or direct provision. Similarly, the failure of markets to provide nudges that are socially efficient and the incentives for markets to provide nudges that are socially inefficient provide justification for the government to implement its own beneficial nudges and outlaw rent-seeking nudges.

One appealing feature of government nudges is that they rely far less on voluntary participation than do many private-sector nudges. In addition, nudges coming from the government are often thought of as created solely with the direct well-being of citizens in mind. In reality, however, governments often face similar incentives as those of private businesses when it comes to revenue generation and budgeting, so it is entirely possible that a similar tension exists between governments and citizens as exists between marketers and consumers. In addition, even governments can't escape the existence of consumer heterogeneity and thus don't always have a logistical opportunity to improve upon market-provided nudges.

As the above caveat suggests, many initial official government nudges focused on increasing tax receipts, or, somewhat equivalently, decreasing the "pain" associated with paying taxes. As mentioned earlier, UK Prime Minister David Cameron created the cabinet office's Behavioral Insights Team, more affectionately (or at least colloquially) known as the "nudge squad," in 2010. The mandate of this group was to find ways to nudge people toward their long-term best interests in ways that, as a matter of course, also serve to benefit the government. In order to increase tax compliance, personalized letters were sent to those who owed taxes on their cars (including pictures of said delinquent cars); this nudge tripled the response rate to tax demands. Informing citizens that most of their neighbors had already paid their taxes caused tax payment rates to increase by 15 percentage points. Sending texts to those who owe court fines increased compliance by 28 percentage points.[53]

In addition, many states have seen the introduction of electronic transponders (EZPass in New York, for example) that are designed to simplify the process of paying highway tolls. Such devices are clearly a convenience for drivers, and it's easy to imagine how they also save governments money in the long run since they replace an ongoing cost of having to staff people at toll booths with a (mainly) fixed cost of automated system implementation. Behavioral economists see an additional reason why such ✓ *true* systems may be appealing to governments. Because the salience of paying a toll is decreased when a repeated cash outlay is replaced with a monthly line item on a credit card statement, the automated systems act as a nudge to get people to keep using toll roads when tolls (i.e. tax rates) increase. This nudge, in turn, makes it easier for governments to increase tax revenue by increasing tolls. To this end, economist Amy Finkelstein finds that implementation of such automated systems results in toll rates that are 20–40 % higher than what they would have been had the systems not been put in place.[54]

Are such nudges in the best interests of citizens? It depends, since such an assessment depends on one's perspective. In the short run, the policies do result in citizens paying more money to the government, resulting in rent-seeking nudges. In the longer term, however, it is likely that people would want to pay their taxes simply and on time rather than incur fines, interest, and hassle, and citizens in general benefit from the lower tax rates that prompt and effective tax collection enables. Nonetheless, it's worth noting that the long-term Pareto aspect of the nudges arises somewhat by coincidence rather than by design. This is not to say that governments never create nudges solely with citizen welfare in mind (in fact, that's supposed to be one of the main ways in which governments and private firms differ), but it's important to keep in mind that this sole priority is in no way a guarantee.

DISCUSSION

The examples in this essay show that both private firms (either directly or as a third party) and governments have incentives to provide both Pareto and rent-seeking nudges, depending on the market situation. For both types of entities, the incentive to provide nudges that are beneficial to consumers depends (hopefully to varying degrees) mainly on whether such nudges are also beneficial to the organization. In addition, the ability of both types of entities to provide nudges that make consumers better off is logistically constrained by whether consumers are similar enough to one another that a beneficial nudge can be identified. Furthermore, private firms are sometimes limited in their ability to unilaterally impose nudges (even Pareto nudges) and often have to rely on consumers being self-aware enough to voluntarily submit to a nudge.

Much discussion exists regarding the appropriate role for government in nudging consumers toward "good" long-run outcomes. To understand this topic, it's helpful to consider the economic role of government more generally. From an economist's standpoint, two efficiency-increasing roles of government are to provide public goods and to internalize market externalities. One feature of public goods, as defined by economists, is that they are not limited to paying customers.[55] With public goods, the incentives to not pay and instead free-ride off of the payments of others create a coordination failure whereby free markets can't profit by providing public goods even when such goods would be beneficial to society. Similarly, products that generate positive externalities are underproduced in a free market because the benefits to society generated by the products (as opposed to the benefits that go specifically to consumers of the products) aren't able to be captured by the producers as profit.

Nudges that are beneficial to consumers but not profitable to private firms can be viewed as a form of a public good. By this logic, government can help society not by providing all nudges but by implementing those nudges that markets don't have incentives to provide themselves (and potentially correcting for counterproductive nudges that markets do provide). In addition, as we've seen in several cases, governments have an opportunity to provide indirect incentives for private firms to implement nudges that are beneficial to consumers. Taken this way, government-provided nudges would, in part, serve a similar function as existing subsidies for activities that generate positive externalities, though likely at a much lower cost.

Put another way, government has a valuable role as the "nudger of last resort," especially when nudges can't or shouldn't be limited to self-aware or paying customers or when nudges replace more expensive and/or distortionary subsidies and taxes. This role is not without responsibilities, however—namely, to maintain a fiduciary duty to the consumer's long-term preferences rather than impart value judgments of what consumers' long-term preferences should be and to give the market a chance to nudge in a helpful manner before taking over to "fix" the situation.

One common criticism of using the findings of behavioral economics to design public policy is that there is no guarantee that policy makers don't suffer from the same biases and socially unproductive incentives as other players in the economy.[56] While this is certainly a reasonable concern, behavioral economists find in a number of contexts that people exhibit fewer behavioral biases when asked to make decisions on behalf of others,[57] which suggests that it is sometimes possible to identify a "good" outcome even when people can't act on the good outcome for themselves. (For example, it's not particularly controversial to say that most people would want to be nudged to be more active rather than less active, but people often choose to be less active.)

Other critics of government-sponsored nudging point out that many nudges will likely be ineffective (or inappropriate) because citizens behave more rationally than the government gives them credit for.[58] Nudge architects Thaler and Sunstein argue that ineffective nudges aren't harmful because of their noncoercive nature, and that the worst-case scenario is that a nudge gets ignored. While this is true in a narrow sense, the supposedly innocuous nature of nudges doesn't imply that they shouldn't be meted out judiciously. For one thing, it's important to note that political capital is expended each time that a nudge is put in place, and political capital certainly shouldn't be squandered on ineffective policies. Furthermore, ineffective nudges can be counterproductive in that they lower the perceived power of nudges and potentially weaken both the political support and the consumer willingness to be subjected to future nudges. At least some policy makers in both the US and the UK seem to realize this, since their "nudge squads" are focused on evidence-based decision-making and randomized trials in order to determine which nudges have significant impact before rolling them out to all citizens.

NOTES

1. Dan Ariely, *Predictably Irrational: The Hidden Forces That Shape Our Decisions* (New York: Harper Perennial, 2010).
2. Richard H. Thaler and Cass R. Sunstein, *Nudge: Improving Decisions About Health, Wealth, and Happiness* (New York: Penguin Books, 2009).

3. The definition of "private firm" in this context excludes nongovernmental nonprofit organizations, which generally are more similar to governments in terms of their incentives to nudge.
4. The use of this term refers to the concept of a Pareto improvement, which is a change that makes all parties involved (weakly) better off.
5. In economics, "rent seeking" refers to activity that merely benefits one party at the expense of another rather than creating new value or wealth.
6. Time inconsistency refers to a condition where individuals' preferences regarding a future activity or choice change as time moves forward and the point in the future gets closer.
7. For more, see "Highly Compensated Employee Rules Aim to Make 401k's Fair." 401khelpcenter.com. http://www.401khelpcenter.com/mpower/feature_030702.html#.Ve59KvlVhBc.
8. For more, see https://www.bankofamerica.com/deposits/manage/keep-the-change.go.
9. Jeremy M. Simon, "Bank of America Sued Over 'Keep the Change' Program." creditcards.com. http://www.creditcards.com/credit-card-news/bofa-lawsuit-keep-the-changer-program-1282.php, May 10, 2007.
10. Narrow choice bracketing refers to the tendency to consider decisions one at a time rather than in a more global context. For more, see Daniel Read, George Loewenstein, and Matthew Rabin, "Choice Bracketing," *Journal of Risk and Uncertainty* 19 (1999): 171–197.
11. For more on mental accounting, see Richard H. Thaler, "Mental Accounting Matters," *Journal of Behavioral Decision Making* 12 (1999): 183–206.
12. Brigitte C. Madrian and Dennis F. Shea, "The Power of Suggestion: Inertia in 401(k) Participation and Savings Behavior," *The Quarterly Journal of Economics* 116 (2001): 1149–87.
13. Sheena S. Iyengar, Wei Jiang, and Gur Huberman, "How Much Choice Is Too Much?: Contributions to 401(k) Retirement Plans," Pension Research Council Working Paper, 2003.
14. For more on status-quo bias, see Daniel Kahneman, Jack L. Knetsch, and Richard H. Thaler, "Anomalies: The Endowment Effect, Loss Aversion, and Status-Quo Bias," *The Journal of Economic Perspectives* 5 (1991): 193–206.
15. For more on overchoice, see Sheena Iyengar and Mark Lepper, "When Choice Is Demotivating: Can One Desire Too Much of a

Good Thing?" *Journal of Personality and Social Psychology* 79 (2000): 995–1006.

16. James Choi, David Laibson, and Brigitte Madrian, "Reducing the Complexity Costs of 401(k) Participation Through Quick Enrollment(TM)." NBER Working Paper, 2006.

17. Richard H. Thaler and Shlomo Benartzi, "Save More Tomorrow: Using Behavioral Economics to Increase Employee Saving," *Journal of Political Economy* 112 (2004): S164–S187.

18. For more on time inconsistency and procrastination, see Ted O'Donoghue and Matthew Rabin, "Doing It Now or Later," *The American Economic Review* 89 (1999): 103–124.

19. For more on loss aversion, see Daniel Kahneman, Jack L. Knetsch, and Richard H. Thaler, "Anomalies: The Endowment Effect, Loss Aversion, and Status-Quo Bias," *The Journal of Economic Perspectives* 5 (1991): 193–206.

20. It could also be the case that consumers require the automatic nature of the contribution changes in order to avoid reneging on their saving plans.

21. This is technically not true in the case of switched digital video (SDV), but SDV is not yet a mainstream technology.

22. This is largely not yet true for streaming music, however, since creator compensation in that industry takes the form of a revenue share.

23. For more on status-quo bias, see Daniel Kahneman, Jack L. Knetsch, and Richard H. Thaler, "Anomalies: The Endowment Effect, Loss Aversion, and Status-Quo Bias," *The Journal of Economic Perspectives* 5 (1991): 193–206.

24. For more on salience and decision-making, see Pedro Bordalo, Nicola Gennaioli, and Andrei Shleifer, "Salience and Consumer Choice," *Journal of Political Economy* 121 (2013): 803–843.

25. For example, see Stacey Paradis, "Good News: Mandated Energy Savings Making an Impact in Illinois." chicagobusiness.com. http://www.chicagobusiness.com/article/20131203/OPINION/131209979/good-news-mandated-energy-savings-making-an-impact-in-illinois, December 3, 2013.

26. Noah J. Goldstein, Robert B. Cialdini, and Vladas Griskevicius, "A Room with a Viewpoint: Using Social Norms to Motivate Environmental Conservation in Hotels," *Journal of Consumer Research* 35 (2008): 472–482.

27. P. Wesley Schultz, Jessica M. Nolan, Robert B. Cialdini, Noah J. Goldstein, and Vladas Griskevicius, "The Constructive, Destructive,

and Reconstructive Power of Social Norms," *Psychological Science* 18 (2007): 429–434.

28. Ian Ayres, Sophie Raseman, and Alice Shih, "Evidence from Two Large Field Experiments That Peer Comparison Feedback Can Reduce Residential Energy Usage," *Journal of Law, Economics, and Organization* 29 (2013): 992–1022.

29. Dora L. Costa and Matthew E. Kahn, "Energy Conservation 'Nudges' and Environmentalist Ideology: Evidence from a Randomized Residential Electricity Field Experiment," NBER Working Paper, revised January 2015.

30. For more, see Noah J. Goldstein, Robert B. Cialdini, and Vladas Griskevicius, "A Room with a Viewpoint: Using Social Norms to Motivate Environmental Conservation in Hotels," *Journal of Consumer Research* 35 (2008): 472–482.

31. For more, see Daniel Kahneman and Amos Tversky, "Prospect Theory: An Analysis of Decision under Risk," *Econometrica* 47 (1979): 263–292.

32. Kevin G. Volpp, George Loewenstein, Andrea B. Troxel, Jalpa Doshi, Maureen Price, Mitchell Laskin, and Stephen E. Kimmel, "A Test of Financial Incentives to Improve Wayfarin Adherence," *BMC Health Services Research* 8 (2008).

33. For more, see https://www.change.org/p/oracle-corporation-stop-bundling-ask-toolbar-with-the-java-installer.

34. For more on this reference, see the Season 4 Episode 4 of *Friends*— "The One with the Ballroom Dancing."

35. Laura Northrup, "Gym Business Models Depend on You Being Too Lazy to Work Out." consumerist.com. http://consumerist.com/2014/12/18/gym-business-models-depend-on-you-being-too-lazy-to-work-out/, December 18, 2014.

36. For more on sunk costs and subsequent consumption, see Richard H. Thaler, "Mental Accounting Matters," *Journal of Behavioral Decision Making* 12 (1999): 183–206.

37. Stefano DellaVigna and Ulrike Malmendier, "Paying Not to Go to the Gym," *The American Economic Review* 96 (2006): 694–719.

38. This can technically be explained either by a form of mental accounting or by irrationally high discounting of future benefits.

39. See www.renttherunway.com.

40. Achal Bassamboo, Sunil Kumar, and Ramandeep S. Randhawa, "Dynamics of New Product Introduction in Closed Rental Systems," *Operations Research* 57 (2009): 1347–1359.

41. See Katherine L. Milkman, Todd Rogers, and Max H. Bazerman, "Highbrow Films Gather Dust: Time-Inconsistent Preferences and Online DVD Rentals," *Management Science* 55 (2009): 1047–1059.

42. Lisa L. Shu, Nina Mazar, Francesca Gino, Dan Ariely, and Max Bazerman, "Signing at the Beginning Makes Ethics Salient and Decreases Dishonest Self-reports in Comparison to Signing at the End," *Proceedings of the National Academy of Sciences* 109 (2012): 15197–15200.

43. Brigitte C. Madrian and Dennis F. Shea, "The Power of Suggestion: Inertia in 401(k) Participation and Savings Behavior," *The Quarterly Journal of Economics* 116 (2001): 1149–87.

44. For background, see Chris Dolmetsch, "New York Big-Soda Ban Rejected by State's Highest Court." Bloomberg.com. http://www.bloomberg.com/news/articles/2014-06-26/new-york-big-soda-ban-rejected-by-n-y-top-court-as-overreach, June 26, 2014.

45. Janet Schwartz, Jason Riis, Brian Elbel, and Dan Ariely, "Inviting Consumers to Downsize Fast-Food Portions Significantly Reduces Calorie Consumption," *Health Affairs* 31 (2012): 399–407.

46. Technically, availability bias refers to bias arising from the use of a heuristic where people view more easily recalled or imagined events as being more likely to occur, but it also applies to situations where more recent or available information is overweighted in the decision-making process.

47. Michael Moss, "Nudged to the Produce Aisle by a Look in the Mirror," *The New York Times*, August 27, 2013.

48. Bram Van Den Bergh, Julien Schmitt, and Luk Warlop, "Embodied Myopia," *Journal of Marketing Research* 48 (2011): 1033–1044.

49. Drazen Prelec and Duncan Simester, "Always Leave Home Without It: A Further Investigation of the Credit-Card Effect on Willingness to Pay," *Marketing Letters* 12 (2001): 5–12.

50. For more, see www.stickk.com.

51. For more, see "Allianz Tool Gives Retirement Plans a Checkup." ThinkAdvisor.com.   http://www.thinkadvisor.com/2012/09/17/allianz-tool-gives-retirement-plans-a-checkup, September 17, 2012.

52. Patrick Wintour, "Government's Behaviour Insight Team to Become a Mutual and Sell Services." TheGuardian.com. http://www.theguardian.com/politics/2014/feb/05/government-behaviour-insight-nudge-mutual-nesta-funding, February 4, 2014.

53. *Behavioural Insights Team Annual Update 2010–11.* https://www.gov.uk/government/uploads/system/uploads/attachment_data/

file/60537/Behaviour-Change-Insight-Team-Annual-Update_acc.
pdf.

54. Amy Finkelstein, "E-ZTax: Tax Salience and Tax Rates," *The Quarterly Journal of Economics* 124 (2009): 969–1010.

55. That is, are not excludable, in economic terms.

56. For example, see http://thepsychreport.com/essays-discussion/nudge-review-cass-sunsteins-why-nudge/.

57. For example, see Brian J. Zikmnud-Fisher, Brianna Sarr, Angela Fagerlin, and Peter A. Ubel, "A Matter of Perspective: Choosing for Others Differs from Choosing for Yourself in Making Treatment Decisions," *Journal of General Internal Medicine* 21 (2006): 618–622.

58. For example, see http://blogs.lse.ac.uk/politicsandpolicy/the-richness-of-personal-interests-a-neglected-aspect-of-the-nudge-debate/.

Who Should Nudge?

Sherzod Abdukadirov

INTRODUCTION

In a follow-up to the highly influential *Nudge*,[1] one of the book's coauthors, Cass Sunstein, asks "*Why Nudge?*" in order make his case for the utility of nudges in solving many social problems.[2] In the new volume, he expands on the key ideas first mentioned in "*Nudge*" and takes an opportunity to respond to his critics. He argues, quite convincingly, that the insights of behavioral economics could be crucial if we are to address pressing social issues including health, safety, environment, and retirement savings.

There is, however, one question which Sunstein fails to address but which is crucial to his case for government nudge policy. The question is not "why" but "who" should nudge. As I will demonstrate in this chapter, the answer to this question has major implications for the government's role in developing nudges that would help consumers improve their health and well-being.

Throughout his works, Sunstein assumes that the primary responsibility for nudging consumers should fall on the government.[3] To the argument that markets already provide consumers with useful nudges,

S. Abdukadirov (✉)
Mercatus Center at George Mason University, Arlington, VA, USA

© The Editor(s) (if applicable) and The Author(s) 2016   159
S. Abdukadirov (ed.), *Nudge Theory in Action*,
DOI 10.1007/978-3-319-31319-1_7

[Handwritten margin notes:]
sounds like
a version
of welfare
economics

what does
public
choice have
to say abt
both
incentives
+
ability?

Sunstein replies that government nudges complement market efforts. He draws no distinction between government and private sector nudges and in fact asserts that in some cases markets may not have the right incentives to produce effective nudges.

Sunstein implicitly assumes that both governments and private firms can be equally efficient in producing nudges—he focuses exclusively on their incentives to create nudges and not on their ability to do so. In this chapter, I examine this assumption. In the second section, I describe the different processes that companies follow in creating new products and examine which process is more appropriate for designing nudges. In the third section, I describe the regulatory process and examine how well it fits the task of designing nudges. I analyze the challenges that federal and local governments face in designing effective nudges. In the fourth section, I contrast the regulatory process with the process used by the private sector. Finally in the fifth section, I argue that producing effective nudges requires a more flexible, iterative approach, which the regulatory process cannot accommodate. Consequently, the business of nudging should be left to the private sector.

Note that I focus only on the ability of private and public sectors to design effective nudges. While there are important ethical issues related to both regulatory and market nudges, they are outside the scope of this chapter.

DESIGNING NUDGES

Disagreements on the effectiveness or even desirability of nudges often hinge on the difference in what scholars or policymakers mean by nudges. For example, when some nudge critics pointed to New York City's ban on large size soda containers as an example of how nudges can go wrong,[4] Thaler replied that the ban was not a nudge.[5] In order to avoid the confusion, I will start the chapter by defining the terms regulatory nudge and market nudge the way I use them in this chapter.

Regulatory Nudges

Sunstein and Thaler popularized the term nudge to refer to the use of behavioral science insights in order to change people's behavior. Importantly, the authors insisted that nudges must be choice preserving—consumers should have the ability to opt out of the nudge and the cost of opting out should be trivial to consumers.

However, many proposed and implemented policies inspired by Sunstein and Thaler's work skirted the second condition. While the policies used behavioral insights to manipulate consumers' choice to change behavior, they frequently imposed nontrivial costs on those who wanted to opt out of the nudge. The term nudge came to be used to describe any policy that aims to change consumer behavior through behavioral economics, regardless of whether it is choice preserving or not.

In this chapter, I similarly use the term regulatory nudge in its broader sense in order to discuss any regulatory policies that use behavioral economics to change consumer behavior.

Market Nudges

Private companies have long used behavioral sciences in their product design and marketing to influence consumers.[6] These behavioral technologies can take a form similar to regulatory nudges and explicitly attempt to change consumer behavior. For example, energy data analytics company Opower teams up with utility companies to provide consumers feedback on their energy use on their utility bill.[7] In addition to consumers' own energy use, the bill includes the energy use of their neighbors. Thus, Opower uses social norms to get consumer to save energy.

Alternatively, behavioral technologies can help consumers simply by redesigning their products to limit human errors. For example, a medical device startup Vitality designed medicine bottles that begin to glow if a patient forgets to take the prescription medication.[8] The product does not exploit behavioral biases to counter consumers' other biases. Yet, it is informed by behavioral sciences, which point out that cognitive capacity is a limited resource.

In some cases, these behavioral technologies benefit both the companies and consumers; in others, they increase the companies' bottom line at consumers' expense.[9] For simplicity, I will use the term market nudge for all types of behavioral technologies.

Market Incentives

Sunstein assumes that markets do not have incentives to address certain problems caused by behavioral biases, and consequently, only governments are in a position to solve these problems.[10] While it is not spelled out, Sunstein's argument seems to rest on two assumptions. The first assumption is that consumers are unaware of their biases or the impact those biases have on their health or finances. Consequently, they do not demand solutions for these problems. The second assumption is that the interests of consumers and companies do not align. Thus, companies face strong incentives to nudge consumers away from choices that are better for consumers.

However, the conditions that must be met under Sunstein's assumptions for markets to respond to consumers' needs are unnecessarily strict. While consumers may not fully understand or be aware of the different biases that lead them astray, they can easily observe the outcomes—excess weight, low savings rate, high energy bill, and so on. For markets to work and supply the helpful nudges, consumers need not fully understand why and how their decisions are suboptimal; they need only to be aware that they have a problem. It is the nudge designers' task to figure out what behavioral biases lead to the problematic outcome and how to counter these biases.

Similarly, the assertion that private companies lack incentives to nudge consumers toward better choices focuses too narrowly on the companies where the "bad" choices happen. For example, retailers have strong incentives to get consumers to spend more money, which may conflict with the consumers' interest in increasing their savings. This is taken as evidence that markets are unlikely to nudge consumers to save.

However, the fact that some companies have incentives that conflict with consumers' best interest does not mean that all companies face the same conflict. Consumers who wish to save more can readily subscribe to a number of personal finance tools that will help them achieve their goal. Many of these tools explicitly use behavioral technologies to help consumers overcome biases. The same is true with obesity. While food companies and supermarkets may want consumers to purchase more food, numerous weight-loss companies work to help consumers eat healthier or exercise more.

As chapters in this volume demonstrate, there are numerous examples of market nudges competing with regulatory nudges to supply solutions. Thus, markets clearly provide incentives for companies to produce effective nudges helping consumers address their behavioral biases.

Models of Innovation

When designing nudges, both regulators and private firms attempt to take novel insights from behavioral economics and transform them into functional products or services for consumers. Yet, the process of going from ideas to functional products is rarely straightforward. In fact, only one out of six new ideas that companies decide to invest in ever becomes a successful commercial product; the rest are screened out at various stages of product development.[11] Even when a new product is launched commercially, there is no guarantee of success—approximately 40 % of new products fail.[12]

Depending on the complexity of the product and the amount of knowledge and information required to produce it, the innovation process follows either a linear or an interactive model.[13] The linear model is characterized by an orderly progression of information from research, to design, to manufacturing, and finally to marketing and distribution (see Fig. 1).[14] The process follows only in one direction with the outcomes of the earlier stage serving as inputs in the following stage. Each stage is neatly self-contained and separated from the others and actors at each stage have no need to interact with each other.

On the other side of the spectrum is the interactive model of innovation, which is characterized by frequent interactions between actors within different stages (see Fig. 2). In this model, information flows both ways with feedback from the later stages informing the earlier ones. In addition to intrafirm communication, many researchers and engineers frequently interact and share knowledge with their colleagues from rival firms.[15] Finally, end users are a crucial source of information and new ideas for many companies.[16]

Most importantly, the interactive model includes an additional stage between applied research and manufacturing—an iterative redesign and testing stage. Designers have to compensate for gaps in knowledge with continuous experimentation.[17] As they discover through trial and error some of the

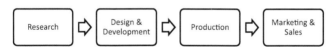

Fig. 1 Linear Model of Innovation

Fig. 2 Interactive Model of Innovation

information that they missed in the earlier iteration, they update their design based on new knowledge. Some companies go beyond experimenting with new ideas to actually experimenting with the very process of innovation.[18] They seek to increase the effectiveness of their experimentation process.

The state of knowledge determines whether the innovation process will follow a linear or interactive model. Some issues are well researched and experts can accurately predict the outcomes of innovations in these fields. In these cases, the innovation process is closer to the linear model. In contrast, some innovations occur in areas that are still poorly understood or where knowledge cannot be easily codified and transferred from one stage to another. These innovations follow the process that closely resembles the interactive model.

The linear model is more typical for the chemical and pharmaceutical industries.[19] For example, the concerns over the impact of chlorofluorocarbons (CFCs) on depletion of the ozone layer led the USA and many other countries to phase out their use in consumer products such as aerosols and refrigerants.[20] DuPont, one of the largest CFC producers, responded to the CFC ban by developing alternative compounds that would not interact with ozone. In this case, the basic science of chemical interactions was well researched. Building on the fundamental scientific knowledge, DuPont scientists conducted extensive applied research to identify a particular chemical compound that would have the same useful qualities of CFCs but without their harmful impact on ozone.[21] Once the scientists identified the alternatives, DuPont used its existing knowledge in chemical production in order to produce and distribute the CFC substitute.

In contrast, the interactive model is more typical for consumer products, especially in cases where consumers' preferences and environment can impact the product's success. In a famous example, Coca Cola decided to replace its classic drink with a new version in 1983—just in time for the iconic drink's 100th birthday.[22] The early consumer tests clearly indicated that consumers liked the new coke and preferred its taste to the original. What the company did not expect was the emotional attachment that many American's felt to the soda drink. After an uproar, the company backtracked and brought back the original version of coke. The newer version, rebranded as Coke II, languished for a while before it was discontinued. In this case, all upfront research pointed to the success of the new coke. Yet, the real-world test revealed its shortcomings—inability to engender the same emotional response as the original coke. Consumer feedback informed the decision to revert to the original coke.

Uncertainty in Designing Nudges

Whether designing effective nudges requires a linear or interactive model of innovation depends on the amount of uncertainty that designers face. When it comes to designing nudges, regulators face uncertainty at various stages of innovation.

First is our incomplete understanding of the basic science behind behav-ioral biases. While we do have evidence that people do not behave rationally, behavioral scientists have yet to develop a comprehensive theory that describes how people do behave.[23] For many decisions, there are often several different biases that could plausibly influence a person's decision. Some of these might push the person to make the decision too hastily, while others may cause her to procrastinate. Yet as the economist David K. Levine put it "The world doesn't need a thousand different theories to explain a thousand different facts. At some point there needs to be a discipline of trying to explain many facts with one theory."[24] Unfortunately, behavioral economists have yet to develop a cohesive theory that would tell us which if any biases are present and how they interact with each other. Thus, a regulator deciding which biases may be at work in a given context would necessarily base her decision on a set of assumptions, which may prove to be incorrect.

Energy and fuel efficiency regulations are one area where uncertainty regarding behavioral biases play out. Over the last decade, the Department of Energy has issued a series of regulations requiring higher energy efficiency standards on commercial and consumer appliances.[25] Similarly, the Department of Transportation and the Environmental Protection Agency issued a joint regulation to mandate higher fuel efficiency standards for cars and trucks.[26] In both cases, the federal agencies attempted to solve the so-called energy paradox. The energy paradox, also known as the energy efficiency gap, is a phenomenon identified in numerous studies, which show that consumers undervalue the future energy costs when they purchase new appliances.[27] Consequently, they opt for appliances that have a lower sticker price but are also less energy efficient, even though the appliances would cost consumers more in the long term due to higher operation costs. In behavioral terms, the consumers are essentially present biased. They overvalue the present, that is, lower appliance price, and undervalue the future, that is, energy costs of running the appliance.

Yet, not everyone is convinced by the present bias explanation of consumer choices. Economists Hunt Alcott and Michael Greenstone questioned whether the energy efficiency gap even exists.[28] The authors point out that the potential energy savings are based on engineering analyses, which can overstate potential savings by a substantial amount. In addition, appliances typically differ on more than just energy consumption. More energy-efficient appliances tend to be smaller and incorporate fewer amenities. Consumers who purchase less-efficient appliances might in fact be making a rational choice; they purchase the model that has the desired features that an energy-efficient model does not.

The point here is not to claim that one side or the other is mistaken. Rather, it is to show how difficult it can be to determine whether consumer choices are driven by behavioral biases. In the case of energy efficiency regulations, the federal agencies assumed that the observed reticence on the part of consumers to choose energy-efficient appliances was driven by behavioral biases rather than rational trade-offs or other unobserved variables. The evidence on this issue is still far from settled.

(2)   The <u>second</u> source of uncertainty enters at the design stage. For many proposed nudges, behavioral scientists test their impact in the lab. But lab settings rarely recreate the full decision-making environment; instead, they focus on a few key elements that researchers think are important to the experiment. Yet, if they miss a key variable that can influence consumers' decisions, the study's results could be misleading and not replicated in the real-world setting.

This is what innovation scholar Eric von Hippel calls the problem with "sticky" information.[29] Since people who will use nudges are not the same people who design them, the information about the environment in which the nudges will operate has to be transferred from users to designers. Yet, much of this information is difficult to transfer. In some cases, the relevant information is tacit and is hard to codify. Imagine, for example, if you had to explain to someone how to ride a bike. You clearly have that knowledge since you can ride bikes, but transferring that knowledge to someone would be difficult.

In other cases, the necessary information may be difficult to access, particularly when decisions are not entirely rational. What consumers say they will do and what they actually do can often differ substantially. This is what is known as hypothetical bias—the difference between the stated and revealed preferences.[30] In addition, the very process of eliciting preferences in a lab setting can change the way people respond to particular circumstances.[31]

The problem with sticky knowledge may be exacerbated in the behavioral context. One of the key insights of behavioral economics is that consumer decisions may be affected by seemingly irrelevant information.[32] This makes the job of identifying the information that needs to be included to develop a successful nudge much harder. Consequently, as Steve Wendel in this volume points out, behavioral nudges are often sensitive to precise implementation. For example, consumer responses to a selection menu may easily change due to changes in wording or in the preceding questions due to priming effects.

Finally, the users may omit some crucial information simply because there is so much information that is potentially relevant that transferring all of it would be cost prohibitive.[33] Predicting what information is actually important to the new product development is often difficult.

Take, for instance, the power of defaults often touted by Sunstein and Thaler as a powerful tool to unobtrusively change behavior.[34] In one well-publicized application, behavioral economists Richard Thaler and Shlomo Benarzi used the power of defaults to increase employees' retirement savings rate through the Save More Tomorrow (SMT) scheme.[35] They set up a simple plan that would automatically increase the retirement savings rate for employees by a small percentage each year until the overall savings rate reached a target level. The increase in the savings rate would coincide with pay raises to minimize the visible impact of the increase. Thus, for many employees, the take-home pay would remain roughly the same before and after the pay raise, with most of the pay raise going toward retirement savings. Throughout the program, employees could choose to opt out at any point; yet only a few dropped out. This simple plan, which the authors tested in several organizations, drastically improved employee retirement savings.

Encouraged by SMT's success, other researchers sought to use the power of defaults to increase the savings rate among low-income individuals.[36] In a field experiment, low-income tax filers were assigned into two groups. In the first group, tax filers could choose to invest some of their tax refund into US Savings Bonds. For the filers in the second group, a portion of the tax refund was automatically invested in the US Savings Bonds, but the filers could choose to opt out and receive the money in hand. Thus, the default for the second group was to save their refunds.

In contrast to the SMT scheme, the default saving scheme did not work for the low-income tax filers. Most filers in the default saving groups chose to opt out of the savings scheme, preferring to receive the entire amount in hand. Researchers hypothesized that, unlike SMT participants, low-income tax filers did not intend to save their tax refunds. In fact, many filers had specific plans to spend their refunds. Thus, default-based nudges may only work when they encourage actions that consumers intended but failed to take due to procrastination. The importance of intention as a key variable only became apparent in a specific setting. It would have been difficult to predict its importance based on the Thaler and Benartzi study alone.

(3)   The third source of uncertainty comes at the production or, in the case of government, rulemaking stage. With few exceptions, regulatory agencies do not actually nudge consumers. Instead, they require the private companies that sell products or otherwise interact with consumers to nudge their consumers. For example, if a financial regulator were to issue a rule mandating the SMT plan, it would be the human resource departments across the private sector that would change the procedures to set new retirement savings defaults. This means that regulators face the same "sticky" information problem with the numerous firms that would have to implement the nudges within their specific environments as they do with the end users of these nudges. While the rulemaking process offers these firms a chance to provide feedback to regulators, the sheer volume of information that could potentially be relevant makes it impossible to relate all of it.

This was the case with the overdraft protection regulation issued by the Federal Reserve Board (FRB).[37] When consumers either pay or take out cash from their checking account using debit cards, many banks honor the transaction even if consumers do not have sufficient funds left on their account to cover the purchase amount. Instead, they charge consumers a fee for overdrawing on their account. The fees can be quite steep—an average overdraft fee in 2006 was $27, by 2011 the fees increased to $35—and provide a substantial source of profits for banks.[38]

While one could easily imagine scenarios where paying high overdraft fees would be a rational choice (e.g., in case of emergencies), in most cases consumers have better alternatives. For example, they could open an overdraft line of credit or link their checking account to a saving account.[39] Both would result in considerably lower fees for overdrawing on the checking account. Alternatively, they could choose to forego the purchase by instructing their bank to deny transactions if they do not have sufficient funds to cover them. In a 2012 poll, 90 % of consumers who incurred overdraft fees reported that they overdrew their account by mistake.[40] Had they known about the potential fees at the time of purchase, they might have either postponed their purchase or chosen an alternative payment method.

The challenge facing the FRB was to help consumers avoid unnecessary overdraft fees while still allowing the transaction for consumers who truly need to overdraw on their account. The agency decided to use the power of defaults to address the situation. Prior to its 2010 regulation, most banks would allow consumers to overdraw their accounts but charge them an overdraft protection fee. Consumers would have to actively instruct their banks to deny overdraft transactions. In contrast, the FRB regulation required that by default banks deny all overdraft transactions. Consumers now have to actively sign up for overdraft protection. The agency reasoned that, by using defaults, it would allow those consumers who incurred overdraft fees by mistake to avoid the fees in the future, while the consumers who need the overdraft protection would still have that option available to them.

The regulation's outcomes were unexpected. Even though 75 % of consumers who reported overdrawing their accounts preferred to have their transactions denied rather than pay a $35 overdraft fee,[41] almost half of heavy overdraft users signed up for the overdraft protection.[42] The numbers were slightly lower for moderate and infrequent users. Incidentally, this is another example of the difficulties that nudge designers face in trying to elicit consumers' preferences.

The FRB failed to anticipate the environment in which the regulation would be enforced. By using defaults, the FRB intended to simplify consumers' choices; yet the regulation only added to confusion. The default to deny overdraft transactions applies only to debit card transactions; banks continue covering overdraft charges incurred through checks. Yet in a survey, nearly two-thirds of respondents who chose to change the default mistakenly believed that their checks would bounce for insufficient funds if they did not opt in for overdraft protection.[43] The fact that some banks refer to debit cards as "check cards" may have added to the confusion. In addition, 60 % of respondents mistakenly believed that they would be charged a fee for denied debit transactions.

Most importantly, the FRB failed to anticipate the steps that banks might take in order to subvert the impact of defaults. While not all banks pursued overdraft fees, those that did were quite effective in getting consumers, especially heavy overdraft users, to actively sign up for the overdraft protection. They did so by framing overdraft as a free perk.[44] Alternatively, they urged consumers to sign up or risk losing the protection that they currently enjoy, effectively framing the default option as a loss. They also made it extraordinarily easy for customers to opt in.

While it may be tempting to assert that the banks' reaction was predictable, it is important to note that not all banks acted in the same fashion. In fact, many banks chose not to pursue overdraft fee revenues and turned toward other services instead. In addition, the FRB did expect to see some attempts to subvert the regulation.[45] To that end, it required banks to get an explicit consumer request in order to sign them up for the service. It also required banks to offer consumers the same terms of service on checking accounts regardless of their overdraft protection choice. Yet, these safeguards proved insufficient. The goal here is not to fault the FRB for poor analysis; rather, it is to point out that it was extremely difficult to predict how banks would ultimately implement the regulation.

Nudging Through Regulation

Both private firms and government regulators face a great deal of uncertainty when designing nudges. Government attempts to create nudges through regulation have to follow an elaborate and rigid process. Both at the federal and local levels, the regulatory process has clearly defined sequential steps and involves numerous stakeholders—often wielding veto powers—who ultimately have little connection to the actual end users of the regulatory nudges. Effectively, the rulemaking process follows a strictly linear model of innovation. The problems that arise from applying this process on the federal and local level are described below.

Federal Nudges

The specific rulemaking requirements differ depending on the agency issuing the regulation, the statutory language authorizing the regulation, and the economic costs or significance of the regulation.[46] Broadly, rulemaking follows the following steps. First, every regulation starts in Congress with a statute authorizing a federal agency to issue a regulation. Regulations are laws and all legislative powers are vested in Congress. Agencies cannot issue regulations on their own; for every regulation, they must point to the authorizing congressional statute. Typically, congressional authorization is broad and leaves agencies considerable discretion in implementing the statute.

Upon receiving congressional authorization, agencies must interpret congressional intent and design the specific regulation. In designing the regulation, agencies draw on their subject matter expertise as well as research from academia and industry. In addition, they typically conduct an economic analysis to figure out the most practical and most efficient solutions to the problem. Once they have that analysis, they propose the regulation.

At first the proposed regulation goes to the White House Office of Information and Regulatory Affairs (OIRA) for review. At this stage, the proposed regulation undergoes presidential oversight. Once OIRA reviews the regulatory analysis, it returns the proposal with its comments and suggestions, which agencies generally implement.

At this point, the proposed regulation goes to the next stage—the commenting process. Agencies publish the proposed regulation in the Federal Register and open the regulation for public comments. The commenting period typically lasts several weeks. During this time, any interested party can transmit their support, reservations, or concerns with the regulation directly to the agency. Unsurprisingly, the process tends to be dominated by organized groups.[47] Once the commenting period closes, agencies comb through the comments they have received and decide how and if they should respond. They incorporate the suggestions and then issue the final regulation, which goes through another round of OIRA review.

Once it passes the OIRA review, the rule becomes final. In theory, Congress can invalidate the regulation through a joint resolution within a short time frame immediately after the rule becomes final. In practice, Congress used this procedure only once to disapprove a controversial ergonomics rule.[48] After this step, the rule goes into effect and agencies begin to enforce it.

However, some rules get challenged in court. If a party affected by the regulation believes that the agency did not follow all the procedural requirements of the rulemaking process or have proper congressional authorization, it can sue the agency. The courts can invalidate the regulation, forcing the agency to go back to the proposal stage and correct its shortcomings.

Finally, for some regulations, agencies go back and conduct a retrospective review, typically five or ten years after the regulation took effect. Retrospective review may be required by statute or initiated by agencies voluntarily. The review stage gives agencies an opportunity to correct potential mistakes or to fine-tune the regulation.

This is the process that the federal agencies have to follow in order to issue regulatory nudges. So how does it work out in practice? Let's start with an example of a nudge policy that came directly from Congress—the Vending Machine rule.[49] In addition to hotly debated provisions related to insurance coverage, the Affordable Care Act (ACA) contained a provision that required all vending machines to display a calorie count for each sold item next to the selection button.[50] The provision only applied to vending machines where the Nutrition Facts Panel was not clearly visible to consumers prior to purchase. In addition, the provision applied to businesses that owned 20 or more vending machines.

The statute itself provides few clues as to what motivated Congress to impose the calorie-posting requirement on vending machines, but the FDA's analysis clearly describes the regulation as an attempt to nudge consumers to make healthier food choices.[51] Importantly, the FDA explicitly states that it does not see information asymmetry, a traditional case of market failure, as the main cause for this regulation. The agency acknowledges that in a competitive vending machine market businesses would gladly post calorie counts if consumers wanted to see them. Thus, it is the fact that consumers do not care about calorie count information when purchasing snacks that the FDA sees as the problem. Consumers, the agency argues, are too present biased and fail to account for the long-term consequences of their snack purchases. Consequently, they need to be nudged toward a healthier choice through calorie posting.

First, consider the timeline for this relatively simple nudge. Congress passed the ACA in March 2010. Then it took the FDA over four years to weave its way through the regulatory process and issue a final regulation.[52] The rule will not take effect until May 2017. Thus, it will take the federal government almost seven years to implement the nudge.

Beyond implementation, the FDA is required to review the regulation since it impacts many small businesses. But the agency does not have to perform the review for at least ten years after the rule becomes final. Thus, the next time the FDA will revisit the rule to see if it made any difference may not happen until 2024.

As the rule is yet to take effect, there is no data to judge its effectiveness. However, there are several areas of concern that may jeopardize the rule's ability to nudge consumers toward healthier choices. First is the fact that the nudge was not supported by any research. While it would have been relatively easy for the FDA to test whether the proposed nudge would actually work, the agency chose not to conduct any research. In response to public comments questioning whether the rule will actually lead to healthier food choices, the FDA simply stated that it is statutorily required to issue the rule.[53]

Second, it remains unclear what goals the rule aims to accomplish. For example, it makes sense to give consumers nutrition information for different foods at the supermarket. There, consumers face a great variety of choices and can use the nutrition information to opt for more nutritious and less caloric foods. But it is not clear what would constitute a healthy choice for a consumer standing in front a soda or candy vending machine. The regulation does not explain whether it expects consumers to walk away without a purchase or to seek out a less unhealthy junk food. Crucially, the regulation does not explain why consumers who clearly express no interest in calorie counts at the vending machines would somehow change their behavior in response to posted calories.

Third, it is unclear why the rule should apply only to businesses with 20 or more vending machines and what impact this exception may have on the rule's effectiveness. The main goal for this condition is to avoid imposing the regulation on small businesses. From the political and economic perspective, the provision makes sense. Politicians generally do not like to impose regulations that may impact small businesses. Consequently, they tried to shield small businesses from regulation through regulatory statutes including the Regulatory Flexibility Act and the Small Business Regulatory Enforcement Fairness Act. Excluding the very small local businesses from the regulation's reach makes the regulation more palatable to policymakers. In addition, the exclusion reduces the cost of the regulation. Compliance for smaller vending machine owners could be prohibitively costly, driving many out of businesses. By focusing on the larger businesses, the regulation limits its negative impacts on the economy.

Notice, however, that neither political nor economic considerations reflect the interests of consumers. From the consumers' perspective, the size of the business that owns the vending machines is irrelevant. If the regulation were effective in nudging consumers to make better choices, the consumers would want to have these nudges available at every vending machine where they shop. I am not suggesting that political and economic considerations in the regulatory process are not important. I am only pointing out that the regulatory process is designed to reflect the interests of the various stakeholders and not necessarily those of the consumers.

Ultimately, the rule is unlikely to change consumers' behavior and improve their diet. The lack of evidence supporting the nudge, combined with its limited applicability, reduces the probability that the rule will achieve its goal. At the same time, it imposes considerable costs on vending machine owners who have to bear the burden of implementing the rule.

One could plausibly argue that the Vending Machine rule's shortcomings were specific to congressionally designed nudges—Congress may lack the expertise to design effective nudges.[54] Thus, a better approach would be for Congress to instruct the federal agencies to come up with nudges and leave the details to the agency experts. However, the FRB's overdraft protection regulation described earlier shows that federal agencies are not necessarily more effective nudge designers.

While the concerns over the impact of overdraft fees were building up for some time, the Board first began working on the overdraft regulation in 2008.[55] In the original form, the regulation would have required banks to allow customers an opportunity to opt out of the overdraft protection before enrolling them in the service. Based on the feedback it received, the Board decided to change the regulation in favor of making the opt-out a default choice. In the modified regulation issued in 2009, consumers had to actively sign up for overdraft protection. The rule took effect in 2010.

In contrast to the FDA, the Board conducted several consumer studies prior to issuing a final regulation. Yet, as the previous section describes, the agency faced considerable uncertainty with regard to the implementation and banks' responses to the regulation. As a result, the nudge had a smaller impact than originally anticipated.

In 2010, the newly formed Consumer Finance Protection Bureau (CFPB) took the issue over from the Federal Reserve.[56] In 2012, the CFPB launched an inquiry into the effectiveness of the regulation, publishing its findings in a 2013 report and in a 2014 follow-up report.[57] It found that for customers who stuck with the default option, the regulation drastically reduced fee payments. However, for customers who chose to sign up for the service, the total fees actually increased since the banks increased their overdraft fees in response to falling revenues. Five years after the rule took effect, the agency has yet to initiate any changes to the regulation despite the documented problems with its implementation. Note, however, that the CFPB launched the review at its own initiative; the agency is not required to review the regulation until 2020.

State and Local Nudges

Beyond the federal regulators, local governments tend to be most active in nudging consumers. State-level regulatory nudges are currently less common. Most state and municipal governments have a version of the rulemaking process that is modeled after the federal one, although considerable variations exist between states and municipalities.[58] Typically, the state or local processes are less stringent than the federal one. Let's consider two examples of local government nudges.

The New York City's Administrative Procedure Act outlines procedural requirements for municipal agencies issuing new rules.[59] Similar to the federal process, the NYC's process requires agencies to publish the rule in advance and allow ample time for public hearings and deliberations. But it has no provisions requiring agencies to provide analysis of the new rule's impact nor does it provide for external regulatory oversight similar to OIRA or congressional review. In addition, it lacks any provisions for retrospective analysis, which means that city regulators do not have to revisit their regulations to check if they could be improved. In general, the process involves fewer steps and is faster than federal rulemaking.

Under Mayor Bloomberg, New York City became the center of a very public but ultimately failed attempt to nudge consumers toward smaller size sodas. In June 2012, the city's Department of Health and Mental Hygiene proposed a Portion Cap rule, which would preclude restaurants from serving sugary drinks in cups larger than 16 fluid ounces.[60] After holding public hearings, the Health Department finalized the Portion Cap rule in September 2012 to go into effect in March of the next year. The rule was part of Mayor Bloomberg's broader strategy to combat obesity; yet it attracted the most attention.[61]

In justifying the rule, the Department pointed to behavioral studies, which showed that people tend to overeat when given large size portions.[62] Thus, the Department assumed that given the smaller size sodas New Yorkers would drink less soda. Though consumers could relatively easily go around the ban by purchasing two cups of soda, the Department predicted that the default option would be sticky enough that most consumers would not opt out of the Portion Cap rule.

While the rule had many supporters, especially among consumer groups and nutrition experts, it generated vocal opposition from food vendors and business groups. The opposition led business groups to successfully contest the rule in court.[63] In addition, the rule generated a nationwide public backlash as Mayor Bloomberg's administration was derided as a nanny-state.[64] The backlash itself may be an example of behavioral bias.[65] Studies show that people react negatively to rules or actions that restrict or eliminate their choices. While many regulations generate opposition from some interest groups, the degree of public anger at the rule was perhaps unexpected.

There are several areas of uncertainty that could impact the rule's effectiveness. First, there was uncertainty about the very evidence that the department was relying on to design its nudge. As the rule was proposed, the authors of one the referenced studies, Brian Wansink and David Just, wrote in the *Atlantic* that their work was misinterpreted and misused.[66] They pointed out that in their study consumers overate because they were unaware of the actual amount of food they were served. In their experiments, the soup cups were continuously refilled through a tube at the bottom of the cup unbeknownst to subjects. In contrast, consumers buying large size sodas know exactly how much soda they drink. On the other hand, there were other studies that linked portion size to consumption, which seemed to support the city's efforts.[67]

Second, there was uncertainty about the potential unintended effects. In some studies, people who used smaller size plates in a cafeteria made more trips to the buffet, thereby negating the impacts of the nudge.[68] In other studies, consumers making a "healthy" purchase would often combine it with an unhealthy snack.[69] They would feel that by buying a healthy food, they "earned" the right to indulge themselves with a tastier but high-calorie snack. Both biases could be active in the case of the large soda ban, which could potentially diminish the nudge's impact.

Ultimately, the courts struck down the rule before it took effect, finding that the Health Department had exceeded the authority delegated to it by the legislature.[70] Thus, it is unclear whether it would have had the intended effect. Some studies suggest that it may have backfired.[71]

Legal concerns and uncertainties are not unique to government actions; private innovations can face similar concerns. Yet, the rule's failure did not result from the substance of the action itself—had it been a voluntary private initiative to limit large sodas it would have raised few objections. It was the Health Department's failure to secure proper statutory authorization that led the court to invalidate the rule.

This points to a considerable limitation on the part of regulatory agencies in designing nudges. They can only nudge consumers in areas where they have explicit delegated authority to regulate. Regulators may have to resort to less-effective nudges simply because designing better nudges would require rulemaking powers that they currently do not have. In contrast, private firms do not face such rigid procedural requirements and have greater flexibility to experiment with different nudge designs.

Beyond regulations, government-produced behavior change policies often come in the form of taxes such as the tax on sugar-sweetened soda beverages in Berkeley, California.[72] Similar to the FDA's vending machine regulation, Berkeley's tax targeted sodas, which public health officials see as one of the leading causes of obesity in youth. But despite similar end goals, the measure followed a very different process.

Part of the rationale for the tax was based on the traditional economic model—increasing the price in order to reduce consumption. Yet, advocates of the soda tax had behavioral mechanisms in mind when they sought to use the tax to increase the salience of drink choice to consumers.[73] They hoped that the tax itself and the publicity that surrounded it would trigger consumers to think about their health goals and to choose healthier drinks.

In addition, tax proponents argued that attaching higher costs to unhealthy choices at the time of purchase would help undercut consumers' myopia. One of the reasons why sticking with healthy diets is so difficult is that the benefits of choosing a sugar-packed highly caloric beverage are immediate, while the costs of the resulting obesity emerge much later. Present-biased consumers heavily discount future costs and therefore decide that the immediate benefits of enjoying a soda outweigh the future health costs. A soda tax would help offset consumers' myopia by countering the immediate benefits of drinking soda with the immediate costs of the tax.

While tax proponents and many news outlets described the measure as a sales tax, the description is not accurate. California's constitution explicitly prohibits local governments from imposing sales taxes on food in addition to those already in the state law.[74] So while soda beverages are already taxed under the current state law among other products, Berkeley could not impose an additional tax on sugary drinks. Instead, Berkeley had to resort to indirect measures like taxing soda distributors.[75] In November 2014, citizens of Berkeley overwhelmingly approved the soda tax with over 76 % voting in favor.[76]

As with New York's Portion Cap rule, there is a considerable uncertainty with the underlying empirical evidence. The goal of the soda tax is to give consumers an additional incentive to choose healthier drinks. As Berkeley Councilmember Susan Wengraf put it "I don't want it to just be making people pay more for the poison, I want people to stop buying the poison."[77] But the obese already have incentives to choose a healthier diet as they face substantial medical and financial costs.[78] Their inability to make a rational healthy choice is the very reason for the public intervention. The very biases that lead consumers to overeat in the first place could similarly impact their reactions to soda taxes.

Empirical evidence on the health impact of sugar or similar fat taxes is mixed.[79] A preliminary survey indicates that Mexico's soda tax imposed in 2014 has led to some decreases in soda consumption.[80] However, in a field study, a soda tax led to an initial drop in consumption followed by a return to the original consumption levels.[81] Unexpectedly, the tax also led some consumers to switch to beer.

Another level of uncertainty relates to the implementation of the tax. Berkeley imposed the tax on the distributors of sugary drinks in the hope that the distributors would in turn pass the tax onto consumers. At the time, there was some debate on whether the distributors would actually pass the additional costs onto consumers.[82] It was equally plausible that they would choose to absorb the tax or increase prices across the board on all distributed items.

In addition, the soda tax sought to exclude small businesses from compliance. Thus, the soda tax would be levied only on soda distribution to stores that have more than $100,000 in annual revenues.[83] Similar to the FDA's vending machine regulation, Berkeley's decision to limit the tax's applicability was driven primarily by the political logic of taxation policy rather than consumers' interests.

The point here is not to argue for or against taxes as tools of behavior change; rather, it is to point out that numerous restrictions on taxation and the way taxation power is divided between different levels of government can prevent some jurisdictions from effectively crafting the policies that they want to produce. In addition, the use of taxes for behavioral change rarely comes with plans for retrospective analysis of their effectiveness. Thus, if Berkeley's soda tax fails to achieve its stated goals, it would require political action to revise or if necessary repeal the tax.

MARKET NUDGES

Unlike the regulatory process, where every step is clearly prescribed through congressional statutes, presidential executive orders, or federal court cases, new product development in the private sector does not have to follow any specific process. The process varies widely from one company to the next, making it impossible to compare the regulatory process to a specific private product development process.

However, most companies follow an interactive model of innovation for new product development; the linear process is used in limited cases.[84] Private firms deal with this uncertainty through trial and error. They normally try their ideas out with focus groups, beta testing, A/B testing, and other techniques that allow them to weed out good and bad ideas.[85] Even after releasing a product, firms continue to monitor the product's performance in the real-world setting and feed this information back to designers in order to fix the newly discovered issues or to improve the product based on consumer feedback.

An example of testing and experimenting with new ideas prior to implementation comes from Jawbone, a maker of fitness tracking wristbands. The company had an idea that it could nudge its customers to exercise more during Thanksgiving.[86] To do so, they sent 5 % of their customers a challenge to take more steps during the holiday season. Customers who accepted the challenge ended up taking an additional 1500 steps. Thus, Jawbone used the commitment principle, a common nudging technique, to help customers fight back against the extra pounds most people put on during Thanksgiving. At the same time, when it tested different wording for the challenge, the company found that it had no impact on the outcomes. The outcome of these tests was a new feature added to the product that helped customers stay on top of their exercise goals. Importantly, the company tested its idea for the new feature and experimented with different variations of the concept prior to rolling it out to all consumers.

In a different example, Opower modified its nudges in response to consumer feedback after market release. In addition to comparing a utility customer's energy use to his or her neighbors, Opower's Home Energy Report originally included an injunctive message—a smiley or a frowny face depending on whether the customer's consumption was above or below average.[87] Guided by a well-known study, Opower included the injunctive message to avoid a boomerang effect, where more efficient customers would view the report as an excuse to increase energy consumption.[88] However, after rollout, Opower received too many complaints from customers who received a frowny face.[89] Customers were incensed that a utility company would pass judgment on them. Consequently, Opower dropped the frowny face and now uses the absence of smiley face as a sign of disapproval for wasteful customers.

In addition to differences in the production process, there are two key elements that make market nudges more effective than regulatory ones: customization and competition.

Customization

A prominent behavioral scientist Sendhil Mullainathan identifies scalability as a major problem in designing effective nudges.[90] He notes that evidence for many nudges typically comes from small-scale research projects conducted in lab settings whose main goal is to test if and how behavioral biases impact subjects' behavior in a specified context. These findings may not hold up when applied on a large scale in real-world settings. Thus, they need to be tested and if necessary redesigned to ensure scalability.

Steve Wendel in this volume echoes Mullainathan's concern. In his work on behavioral technologies, Wendel found that population characteristics may impact the effectiveness of some nudges. Thus, nudges that change behavior of some test populations may have no impact on others. Consequently, testing nudges on different populations is crucial to ensure their effectiveness.

For regulatory nudges, this presents a problem. Since regulations apply to the entire population, implementing nudges that work only for some segment of a population entails unnecessary expenditure—many individuals would be exposed to nudges that do not impact their behavior. Furthermore, if different nudges work for different people, then to achieve a broad behavior change under the rulemaking process the regulators would have to impose all nudges on all people. The rulemaking process' inability to target specific populations leads to a considerable waste of resources.

In contrast, private companies have the ability to customize their nudges and target only the populations amenable to specific nudges. Consider Express Scripts, a pharmacy benefit management company that helps health insurance companies improve medication adherence of their patients.[91] Poor medication adherence is a major problem in health care.[92] Many chronic patients undergoing a lengthy course of medication, often lasting more than a year, fail to complete the treatment. This failure to complete the course often results in higher hospitalization rates and more expensive treatment at a later time, with estimated annual costs ranging between $100 billion and $300 billion.[93] Consequently, any measures that would nudge patients to take their medication could prevent future health problems for the patients and save health insurance companies from paying for more expensive treatment.

The problem with addressing poor medication adherence is that patients stop taking medication for different reasons.[94] Some may not fully understand the need to take medication due to low medical literacy levels. Thus, a helpful nudge would be to explain the treatment in simple accessible terms to the patients or their family members. Others may have financial concerns over the cost of medication, which can be addressed through lower copayments. Some patients may simply forget or have other behavioral reasons for not taking medications. In this case, timely reminders, calendarized packaging, or monitoring systems may be helpful.

In response to this demand, Express Scripts created a data analytics tool ScreenRX, which uses over 300 variables in order to identify patients at most risk for nonadherence.[95] This allows health insurers to focus only on patients that need intervention and not waste their nudges on patients that are likely to take the medication anyway. In addition, ScreenRX identifies the likely causes for nonadherence, which allows health insurers to tailor their interventions to the patient's needs and increase the effectiveness of each intervention.

In a similar example, Opower uses data analytics to identify the major causes for excessive energy consumption and provide tailored energy-saving recommendations to each customer.[96] Thus, if a customer's energy usage patterns point to an inefficient clothes dryer as a major energy hog, Opower's Home Energy Report would include a recommendation to upgrade the clothes dryer to a more efficient model.

By targeting and tailoring their nudges, private companies reduce the overall costs of nudging. First, they only nudge consumers that actually need to be nudged; they do not waste nudges on consumers who make better choices on their own. Second, companies improve the effectiveness of their nudges by identifying the underlying cause of biased behavior and using the nudges that specifically address the identified cause. They avoid imposing nudges that would not work for a particular consumer.

(2) Competition

Another advantage of market nudges is that typically there are competing firms working on similar nudges. Thus, market competition offers a way to test multiple version of the same nudge. The failure of any single company's process to produce an effective nudge does not doom the prospects of that nudge becoming available to consumers. Given the parallel experimentation by multiple companies, there is a greater chance that at least one of them will be successful and will produce an effective nudge.

For example, two personal finance software companies, Mint.com and Wesabe, competed to help consumers organize their personal finances and to work toward specific financial goals, for example, reduce spending or pay off debts.[97] As they developed their products, they both faced a choice: import customers' banking data automatically or ask customers to do it manually. Automatic import obviously offered a more convenient service to customers, but it came at a cost. To import data automatically, the company would have to contract with a third party, a company called Yodlee, which had the software capable of extracting necessary data from banking statements. However, at the time, Yodlee was experiencing financial and managerial difficulties and faced a risk of going under.

The two companies made different choices. Wesabe chose not to expose itself to Yodlee's risks; it judged that manual import would not pose a substantial burden on consumers. In contrast, Mint.com decided that offering the convenience of automatic import was worth the risk, so it paired up with Yodlee. In the end, Mint.com won over most of the customers, while Wesabe was forced to close down.

Note that both companies had good reasons for the different decisions they made and there was no way to know beforehand which decision would be better. It was market competition that allowed for both options to be tested and the better one to be chosen.

Another example of market competition is in medication adherence nudges. In addition to Express Scripts, FICO and RxAnte have developed their own data analytics tools to identify at-risk patients.[98] On the intervention side, a number of companies are experimenting with different designs for pill bottles that would track patients and nudge them to take the pill if they are missing a dose. For example, Vitality makes bottles that begin to glow and emit sounds if patients miss a dose.[99] It tracks whether the patient opened the bottle to identify missed doses. In contrast, AdhereTech's bottles track the actual contents and are even smart enough to track liquid medications, whereas Proteus Digital Health attached sensors to pills themselves to track when pills are actually taken.

Since the field of medication adherence is still in its infancy, it is too early to tell which of these behavioral technologies will be successful. However, the fact that companies are experimenting with a wide variety of technologies increases the chances that some of these pursuits will prove fruitful. Since health insurance companies are paying for interventions, they have strong incentives to increase their effectiveness and reduce their costs.

WHY REGULATORY NUDGES FAIL

Regulatory nudges fail because their proponents attempt to use a legislative process to develop consumer products. Regulations are laws and rule-making is essentially a legislative process. One would expect the process that lays out the rules of the game to require considerable deliberation and buy in from stakeholders as well as a certain degree of permanence.

For example, our views on the harm of companies making false claims to consumers are unlikely to change considerably over time. It would make sense to address such issues through the conservative rulemaking process.

Where regulations fail is on issues that require constant innovation. Given behavioral economics' relatively young age and the rapid pace of change in our understanding of its implications on human decision-making, the process of producing nudges must be nimble and flexible enough to respond and incorporate those changes. In addition, it must be able to deal with a high degree of uncertainty and limited knowledge. The rigid linear rulemaking process is simply not suited for the task of producing and constantly improving nudges.

Ultimately, the private sector is better equipped to produce effective nudges that would help consumers overcome their biases and improve their well-being. Private companies are better able to harness the power of big data to customize and target nudges to specific subpopulations or even individuals. In addition, market competition allows for parallel experimentation with variations of similar nudges, increasing the chances that an effective nudge would be discovered.

Regulators' attempts to complement the private sector's efforts, as suggested by Sunstein, are unlikely to be successful. While the utility of nudges is not in question, the government's resources may be better spent supporting private sector efforts rather than competing with them.

NOTES

1. Richard H. Thaler and Cass R. Sunstein, *Nudge: Improving Decisions About Health, Wealth, and Happiness* (New Haven: Yale University Press, 2008).
2. Cass R. Sunstein, *Why Nudge?* (New Haven: Yale University Press, 2014).
3. See e.g. Cass R. Sunstein and Richard H. Thaler, "Libertarian Paternalism Is Not an Oxymoron," *The University of Chicago Law Review* 70(4) (October 1, 2003): 1159–1202; Cass R. Sunstein, *Simpler: The Future of Government* (New York: Simon & Schuster, 2013); Sunstein, *Why Nudge?*
4. Oliver Burkeman, "How Bloomberg's Soda Ban Is a Classic Example of 'Choice Architecture,'" *The Guardian*, July 10, 2012, http://www.theguardian.com/commentisfree/oliver-burkemans-blog/2012/jul/10/bloomberg-soda-ban-new-york-freedom

5. Richard H. Thaler, "To State the Obvious: A BAN Is Not a NUDGE. The Opposite in Fact. So Don't Blame Bloomberg's Ban on Large Soda Cups on Us.," Twitter, @R_Thaler, May 31, 2012, https://twitter.com/R_Thaler/status/208273339507150849

6. See e.g. Robert B. Cialdini, *Influence: The Psychology of Persuasion*, Revised edition (New York: Harper Business, 2006).

7. Hunt Allcott, "Social Norms and Energy Conservation," *Journal of Public Economics*, Special Issue: The Role of Firms in Tax Systems 95(9–10) (October 2011): 1082–1095.

8. Arundhati Parmar, "Start-up Developing Smart Pill Bottle Targets HIV, Cancer, Transplant Meds & Speciality Pharmacies," *MedCity News*, January 2, 2013, http://medcitynews.com/2013/01/start-up-developing-smart-pill-bottle-targets-hiv-cancer-transplant-drugs-and-speciality-pharmacies/

9. For a more detailed discussion on company incentives see the chapter by Jody Beggs in this volume.

10. Sunstein, *Why Nudge?*, 113–114.

11. Gloria Barczak, Abbie Griffin, and Kenneth B. Kahn, "Trends and Drivers of Success in NPD Practices: Results of the 2003 PDMA Best Practices Study," *Journal of Product Innovation Management* 26(1) (January 1, 2009): 6.

12. George Castellion and Stephen K. Markham, "New Product Failure Rates: Influence of Argumentum Ad Populum and Self-Interest," *Journal of Product Innovation Management* 30(5) (September 1, 2013): 976–979.

13. Stephen J. Kline and Nathan Rosenberg, "An Overview of Innovation," in *The Positive Sum Strategy: Harnessing Technology for Economic Growth*, ed. Ralph Landau and Nathan Rosenberg, 1986, 275–305.

14. See Dora Marinova and John Phillimore, "Models of Innovation," in *The International Handbook on Innovation*, ed. Larisa V. Shavinina, 2003, 44–53; Kline and Rosenberg, "An Overview of Innovation"; Roy Rothwell, "Towards the Fifth-generation Innovation Process," *International Marketing Review* 11(1) (February 1994): 7–31.

15. Eric von Hippel, *The Sources of Innovation* (Oxford University Press, 1988).

16. Eric von Hippel, *Democratizing Innovation* (MIT Press, 2006).

17. Kline and Rosenberg, "An Overview of Innovation."

18. Stefan Thomke, Eric von Hippel, and Roland Franke, "Modes of Experimentation: An Innovation Process – and Competitive – Variable," *Research Policy* 27(3) (July 1998): 315–332.
19. Margherita Balconi, Stefano Brusoni, and Luigi Orsenigo, "In Defence of the Linear Model: An Essay," *Research Policy* 39(1) (February 2010): 1–13.
20. James Maxwell and Forrest Briscoe, "There's Money in the Air: The CFC Ban and DuPont's Regulatory Strategy," *Business Strategy and the Environment* 6(5) (November 1, 1997): 276–286.
21. DuPont, "Backgrounder: DuPont and the CFC/Ozone Depletion Issue," *DuPont*, February 9, 2007, http://www2.dupont.com/Media_Center/en_US/assets/downloads/pdf/Backgrounder_CFCs.pdf
22. Betsy D. Gelb and Gabriel M. Gelb, "New Coke's Fizzle: Lessons for the Rest of Us," *Sloan Management Review* 28(1) (Fall 1986): 71–77.
23. David K. Levine, *Is Behavioral Economics Doomed? The Ordinary versus the Extraordinary* (Cambridge, UK: Open Book Publishers, 2012).
24. Tim Harford, "Nudge or Fudge?," *Financial Times*, March 22, 2014, sec. Life&Arts.
25. Department of Energy, "Energy Conservation Program: Energy Conservation Standards for General Service Fluorescent Lamps and Incandescent Reflector Lamps," *Federal Register* 74(69) (April 13, 2009): 16920–17027; e.g. Department of Energy, "Energy Conservation Program: Energy Conservation Standards for Certain Consumer Products (Dishwashers, Dehumidifiers, Microwave Ovens, and Electric and Gas Kitchen Ranges and Ovens) and for Certain Commercial and Industrial Equipment (Commercial Clothes Washers)," *Federal Register* 74(215) (November 9, 2009): 57738–57802.
26. Environmental Protection Agency and Department of Transportation, "Proposed Rulemaking to Establish Light-Duty Vehicle Greenhouse Gas Emission Standards and Corporate Average Fuel Economy Standards," *Federal Register* 74(186) (September 28, 2009): 49454–49789; Environmental Protection Agency and Department of Transportation, "Greenhouse Gas Emissions Standards and Fuel Efficiency Standards for Medium- and Heavy-Duty Engines and Vehicles," *Federal Register* 75(229) (November 30, 2010): 74152–74456.

27. Adam B. Jaffe and Robert N. Stavins, "The Energy Paradox and the Diffusion of Conservation Technology," *Resource and Energy Economics* 16(2) (May 1994): 91–122; Eric Hirst and Marilyn Brown, "Closing the Efficiency Gap: Barriers to the Efficient Use of Energy," *Resources, Conservation and Recycling* 3(4) (June 1990): 267–281.

28. Hunt Allcott and Michael Greenstone, *Is There an Energy Efficiency Gap?*, NBER Working Paper 17766 (Cambridge, MA, January 2012), Cambridge, MA, http://www.nber.org/papers/w17766

29. Hippel, *Democratizing Innovation*, 66–70.

30. Glenn W. Harrison and E. Elisabet Rutström, "Experimental Evidence on the Existence of Hypothetical Bias in Value Elicitation Methods," in *Handbook of Experimental Economics Results*, ed. Charles R. Plott and Vernon L. Smith, Volume 1 (New York: North Holland, 2008), 752–767, http://www.sciencedirect.com/science/article/pii/S1574072207000819

31. Steven D. Levitt and John A. List, "What Do Laboratory Experiments Measuring Social Preferences Reveal About the Real World?," *Journal of Economic Perspectives* 21(2) (2007): 153–174.

32. E.g. priming, anchoring, and information bias. See Daniel Kahneman, *Thinking, Fast and Slow* (New York: Farrar, Straus and Giroux, 2013).

33. Hippel, *Democratizing Innovation*, 68–69.

34. Thaler and Sunstein, *Nudge*.

35. Richard H. Thaler and Shlomo Benartzi, "Save More Tomorrow™: Using Behavioral Economics to Increase Employee Saving," *Journal of Political Economy* 112(S1) (February 1, 2004): S164–S187.

36. Erin Todd Bronchetti et al. *When a Nudge Isn't Enough: Defaults and Saving Among Low-Income Tax Filers*, NBER Working Paper 16887 (Cambridge, MA, March 2011), Cambridge, MA, http://www.nber.org/papers/w16887

37. Board of Governors of the Federal Reserve System, "Electronic Fund Transfers," *Federal Register* 74(220) (November 17, 2009): 59033–59056.

38. Lauren E. Willis, "When Nudges Fail: Slippery Defaults," *University of Chicago Law Review* 80(3) (2013): 1185.

39. Board of Governors of the Federal Reserve System, "Electronic Fund Transfers," 59047.

40. Pew Center on the States, *Overdraft America: Confusion and Concerns About Bank Practices* (Washington, DC, n.d.), 4, Washington, DC,

http://www.pewtrusts.org/~/media/legacy/uploadedfiles/pcs_
assets/2012/SCIBOverdraft20America1pdf.pdf

41. Ibid., 5.
42. Consumer Financial Protection Bureau, *CFPB Study of Overdraft Programs: A White Paper of Initial Findings* (Washington, DC, June 2013), 30–31, Washington, DC, http://files.consumerfinance. gov/f/201306_cfpb_whitepaper_overdraft-practices.pdf
43. Willis, "When Nudges Fail," 1189.
44. Willis, "When Nudges Fail."
45. Board of Governors of the Federal Reserve System, "Electronic Fund Transfers."
46. Susan E Dudley and Jerry Brito, *Regulation: A Primer* (Arlington: Mercatus Center at George Mason University, 2012).
47. Marissa Martino Golden, "Interest Groups in the Rule-Making Process: Who Participates? Whose Voices Get Heard?," *Journal of Public Administration Research and Theory* 8(2) (1998): 245–270; Jason Webb Yackee and Susan Webb Yackee, "A Bias Towards Business? Assessing Interest Group Influence on the U.S. Bureaucracy," *Journal of Politics* 68(1) (2006): 128–139.
48. Morton Rosenberg, *Congressional Review of Agency Rulemaking: An Update and Assessment of the Congressional Review Act after a Decade*, CRS Reports (Washington, DC, May 8, 2008), Washington, DC.
49. Food and Drug Administration, "Food Labeling; Calorie Labeling of Articles of Food in Vending Machines," *Federal Register* 76(66) (April 6, 2011): 19238–19255.
50. *Patient Protection and Affordable Care Act, Pub. L. No 111-148, 124 Stat. 119,* 2010, sec. 4205.
51. Food and Drug Administration, "Calorie Labeling of Articles of Food in Vending Machines," 19245–19246.
52. Food and Drug Administration, "Food Labeling; Calorie Labeling of Articles of Food in Vending Machines," *Federal Register* 79(230) (December 1, 2014): 71259–71293.
53. Ibid., 71261 (see comment 2 and FDA's response).
54. See e.g. David Epstein and Sharyn O'Halloran, *Delegating Powers: A Transaction Cost Politics Approach to Policy Making Under Separate Powers,* First Edition (New York: Cambridge University Press, 1999); John D. Huber and Charles Shipan, "Politics, Delegation, and Bureaucracy," in *The Oxford Handbook of Political Economy,* ed. Barry

R. Weingast and Donald A. Wittman (New York: Oxford University Press, 2008), 256–272.

55. Board of Governors of the Federal Reserve System, "Electronic Fund Transfers," 59034–59035.

56. Consumer Financial Protection Bureau, *CFPB Consumer Laws and Regulations: Electronic Fund Transfer Act* (Washington, DC, October 2013), Washington, DC, http://files.consumerfinance. gov/f/201310_cfpb_updated-regulation-e-examination-procedures_including-remittances.pdf

57. Consumer Financial Protection Bureau, *CFPB Study of Overdraft Programs*; Consumer Financial Protection Bureau, *Data Point: Checking Account Overdraft* (Washington, DC, July 2014), Washington, DC, http://files.consumerfinance.gov/f/201407_cfpb_report_data-point_overdrafts.pdf

58. *Revised Model State Administrative Procedure Act*, 2010, http:// www.uniformlaws.org/shared/docs/state%20administrative%20procedure/msapa_final_10.pdf

59. *New York City Administrative Procedure Act. NYC Charter ch. 45*, 2004, http://www.nyc.gov/html/records/pdf/section%201133_citycharter.pdf

60. Department of Health and Mental Hygiene, *Notice of Adoption of an Amendment (§81.53) to Article 81 of the New York City Health Code* (New York, NY, September 13, 2012), New York, NY, http://www.nyc.gov/html/doh/downloads/pdf/notice/2012/notice-adoption-amend-article81.pdf

61. The New York City Obesity Task Force, *Reversing the Epidemic: The New York City Obesity Task Force Plan to Prevent and Control Obesity* (New York, NY, May 31, 2012), New York, NY, http://www.nyc.gov/html/om/pdf/2012/otf_report.pdf

62. Department of Health and Mental Hygiene, *Notice of Adoption*.

63. *N.Y. Statewide Coalition of Hispanic Chambers of Commerce v. N.Y.C. Department of Health and Mental Hygiene*, 23 n.y.3d 681 (New York State, Court of Appeals 2014).

64. Karen Harned, "The Michael Bloomberg Nanny State In New York: A Cautionary Tale," *Forbes*, May 10, 2013, http://www.forbes.com/sites/realspin/2013/05/10/the-michael-bloomberg-nanny-state-in-new-york-a-cautionary-tale/

65. Melissa Healy, "Proposed Soda Ban Likely to Backfire, Study Finds," *Los Angeles Times*, April 11, 2013, http://articles.latimes.com/2013/apr/11/science/la-sci-small-sodas-20130411

66. Brian Wansink and David Just, "How Bloomberg's Soft Drink Ban Will Backfire on NYC Public Health," *The Atlantic*, June 14, 2012, http://www.theatlantic.com/health/archive/2012/06/ how-bloombergs-soft-drink-ban-will-backfire-on-nyc-public-health/258501/

67. e.g. Julie E. Flood, Liane S. Roe, and Barbara J. Rolls, "The Effect of Increased Beverage Portion Size on Energy Intake at a Meal," *Journal of the American Dietetic Association* 106(12) (December 2006): 1984–1990 (cited in the Notice of Adoption).

68. Barbara J. Rolls et al. "Using a Smaller Plate Did Not Reduce Energy Intake at Meals," *Appetite* 49(3) (November 2007): 652–660.

69. Keith Wilcox et al. "Vicarious Goal Fulfillment: When the Mere Presence of a Healthy Option Leads to an Ironically Indulgent Decision," *Journal of Consumer Research* 36(3) (October 1, 2009): 380–393.

70. *N.Y. Statewide Coalition of Hispanic Chambers of Commerce v. N.Y.C. Department of Health and Mental Hygiene*, 23 n.y.3d.:

71. Brent M. Wilson, Stephanie Stolarz-Fantino, and Edmund Fantino, "Regulating the Way to Obesity: Unintended Consequences of Limiting Sugary Drink Sizes," *PloS One* 8(4) (2013): e61081.

72. City of Berkeley, "Measure D – Impose a General Tax on Distributors of Sugar-Sweetened Beverages," *Election Information: 2014 Ballot Measures*, September 2, 2014, http://www.cityofberkeley.info/ Clerk/Elections/Election__2014_Ballot_Measure_Page.aspx

73. Maddie Oatman, "Soda: Ban It? Nah. Tax It? Yep," *Mother Jones*, June 18, 2012, http://www.motherjones.com/environment/2012/ 06/soda-sugar-tax-richmond

74. California Constitution, article XIII, sec. 34.

75. Public Health Law & Policy, *Local Taxes on Sugar-Sweetened Beverages in California: Legal Considerations and Procedural Requirements.*

76. Alameda County Registrar of Voters, "General Election – Unofficial – November 04, 2014," *Alameda County Registrar of Voters*, November 12, 2014, http://www.acgov.org/rov/current_elec-tion/226/index.htm

77. Berkeleyside, "Will Berkeley Be First in Nation to Impose Soda Tax?," *Berkeleyside*, February 12, 2014, http://www.berkeleyside.com/2014/ 02/12/will-berkeley-be-first-in-nation-to-impose-sugar-tax/

78. Michael L. Marlow and Sherzod Abdukadirov, "Can Behavioral Economics Combat Obesity?," *Regulation* 35(2) (July 9, 2012); see also Marlow's chapter in this volume.

79. Oliver Mytton, Dushy Clarke, and Mike Rayner, "Taxing Unhealthy Food and Drinks to Improve Health," *BMJ* 344 (May 15, 2012): e2931.
80. Amy Guthrie, "Survey Shows Mexicans Drinking Less Soda After Tax," *Wall Street Journal*, October 13, 2014, sec. Business, http://www.wsj.com/articles/survey-shows-mexicans-drinking-less-soda-after-tax-1413226009
81. Brian Wansink et al. *From Coke to Coors: A Field Study of a Fat Tax and Its Unintended Consequences*, SSRN Scholarly Paper (Rochester, NY, July 29, 2014), Rochester, NY, http://papers.ssrn.com/abstract=2473623
82. Jennifer Brockett and Loring Rose, "Berkeley's Measure D: What Distributors, Restaurants and Retailers Need to Know about the Berkeley 'Sugar Tax,'" *Hospitality Law Blog*, November 21, 2014, http://www.dwthospitalitylaw.com/2014/11/articles/food-beverage/berkeleys-measure-d-what-distributors-restaurants-and-retailers-need-to-know-about-the-berkeley-sugar-tax/
83. City of Berkeley, "Measure D."
84. Kline and Rosenberg, "An Overview of Innovation."
85. See Wendel's chapter in this volume.
86. Parmy Olson, "The Guinea Pig Economy: A Massive Social Experiment on You Is Under Way, and You Will Love It," *Forbes*, February 9, 2015.
87. Mark Joseph Stern, "A Little Guilt, a Lot of Energy Savings," *Slate*, March 1, 2013, http://www.slate.com/articles/technology/the_efficient_planet/2013/03/opower_using_smiley_faces_and_peer_pressure_to_save_the_planet.html
88. See P. Wesley Schultz et al. "The Constructive, Destructive, and Reconstructive Power of Social Norms," *Psychological Science* 18(5) (May 1, 2007): 429–434.
89. Stern, "A Little Guilt, a Lot of Energy Savings."
90. Hunt Allcott and Sendhil Mullainathan, "Behavior and Energy Policy," *Science* 327(5970) (March 5, 2010): 1204–1205; Saugato Datta and Sendhil Mullainathan, "Behavioral Design: A New Approach to Development Policy," *Review of Income and Wealth* 60(1) (2014): 7–35.
91. Express Scripts, "Healthier Outcomes Require Better Decisions," *Express Scripts Lab*, 2013, http://lab.express-scripts.com/insights/adherence/infographic-predicting-rx-nonadherence

92. Hayden B. Bosworth et al. "Medication Adherence: A Call for Action," *American Heart Journal* 162(3) (September 1, 2011): 412–424.
93. Meera Viswanathan et al. "Interventions to Improve Adherence to Self-Administered Medications for Chronic Diseases in the United States: A Systematic Review," *Annals of Internal Medicine* 157(11) (December 4, 2012): 785–795.
94. Bosworth et al. "Medication Adherence."
95. Express Scripts, "INFOGRAPHIC: Predicting Rx Nonadherence," *Express Scripts Lab*, April 23, 2013, http://lab.express-scripts.com/insights/adherence/infographic-predicting-rx-nonadherence
96. Allcott, "Social Norms and Energy Conservation."
97. Victor Lombardi, *Why We Fail: Learning from Experience Design Failures* (Brooklyn: Rosenfeld Media, 2013), 73–86.
98. Deanna Pogorelc, "Can Data Analysis Predict Who Will Adhere to Medications, Which Interventions Would Help?," *MedCity News*, September 28, 2012, http://medcitynews.com/2012/09/can-data-analysis-predict-who-will-adhere-to-medications-which-interventions-would-help/
99. Parmar, "Start-up Developing Smart Pill Bottle Targets HIV, Cancer, Transplant Meds & Speciality Pharmacies."

PART II

Case Studies

Weight-Loss Nudges: Market Test or Government Guess?

Michael Marlow

> *When self-control problems and mindless choosing are combined, the result is a series of bad outcomes for real people…. Nearly two-thirds of Americans are overweight or obese…. Together, these facts suggest that significant numbers of people could benefit from a nudge.*
> — Richard H. Thaler and Cass R. Sunstein,
> *Nudge: Improving Decisions about Health, Wealth, and Happiness.*

INTRODUCTION

Rising obesity in the USA has led public health experts to propose solutions to what is frequently called an obesity epidemic. Obesity rates have doubled during the past three decades and, as of 2009, more than one-third of adults were obese.[1] A recent study predicts that, by 2030, 42 % of Americans will be obese and 11 % will be severely obese.[2] Obesity is a major health concern, given its association with chronic conditions that include diabetes, hypertension, high cholesterol, stroke, heart disease, certain cancers, and arthritis.[3]

M. Marlow (✉)
California Polytechnic State University, San Luis Obispo, CA, USA

© The Editor(s) (if applicable) and The Author(s) 2016
S. Abdukadirov (ed.), *Nudge Theory in Action*,
DOI 10.1007/978-3-319-31319-1_8

195

Many behavioral economists believe that undesired weight gain is the result of unconscious and irrational decisions that result from psychological, social, cognitive, and emotional factors. In their book *Nudge: Improving Decisions about Health, Wealth, and Happiness*, Richard H. Thaler and Cass R. Sunstein espouse the behavioral economics view that well-designed nudges devised by "choice architects" can steer individuals toward wiser decisions that enhance their welfare.[4] They argue that the most important applications of nudge theory often lie with governments rather than markets, as the following statement makes clear: "The key point here is that for all their virtues, markets often give companies a strong incentive to cater to (and profit from) human frailties, rather than try to eradicate them or to minimize their effects."[5]

This chapter examines the effectiveness of nudges designed to steer us toward better food and beverage consumption behaviors as a means of lowering population weight. It first discusses our state of knowledge on obesity causes and prevention. Next, it presents the basics of nudge theory followed by criticisms of that theory. It then discusses various imperfections that all choice architects—whether in governments or markets—must face, which suggest that nudges are a blunt instrument for reducing population weight. Finally, the paper discusses how nudging by governments differs from nudging by markets, and concludes that market nudging is the more promising avenue for helping citizens lose weight.

THE STATE OF OUR KNOWLEDGE ON OBESITY CAUSES AND PREVENTION

Historical BMI data show that Americans started gaining weight in the 1920s, but only in the 1980s did a large number of Americans begin crossing the body mass index (BMI) threshold of 30 that defines obesity.[6] To calculate BMI, individuals divide their weight by the square of their height, with values given in units of kg/m^2. A six-foot-tall male, for example, is obese if he weighs at least 221 pounds.

The timing of the "obesity epidemic" is sensitive to the measures of fatness used.[7] BMI, for instance, does not distinguish fat from lean mass, thus leading to greater misclassification in men due to larger variation in muscularity. BMI misclassifies substantial percentages of individuals as obese and nonobese when compared with more accurate measures such as percentage of body fat.[8] Measures using skinfold thickness indicate that obesity rates started rising 10–20 years earlier than the 1980s, thus suggesting that gradual influences on weight are more important than commonly thought.

Despite decades of research into the causes of the obesity epidemic, a clear understanding of obesity has proven elusive.[9] A short list of potential causes for rising obesity prevalence includes increased consumption of sugar-sweetened beverages,[10] falling food prices,[11] urban sprawl,[12] increases in calories consumed away from home,[13] sedentary lifestyles fostered by technology,[14] and agricultural policies that encourage production of unhealthy foods[15].

Obstacles believed to impede a better understanding of the obesity epidemic include problems in defining obesity, lax application of scientific standards, tenuous assumption making, flawed measurement, and limited examination of alternative explanations of cause.[16] A team of obesity researchers recently argued that, while energy intake and physical activity energy expenditure are key modifiable determinants of energy balance, self-reports of these measures are so poor that they are wholly unacceptable for scientific research on obesity.[17] A major concern is that past use of self-reported data for studies has led to misguided health care policies, research, and clinical judgment.

A recent study in the *New England Journal of Medicine* argues that scientifically unsupported beliefs about obesity are pervasive in both the scientific literature and the popular press.[18] The authors identify myths, presumptions, and facts based on the current state of scientific knowledge. They consider propositions to be true only when supported by confirmatory randomized studies. The following "myths," "presumptions," and "facts" are most relevant to the present paper.

The authors define "myths" as beliefs that persist despite clear contradicting evidence:

- Small, sustained changes in energy intake or expenditure will produce large, long-term weight changes.
- Setting realistic goals in obesity treatment is important because otherwise patients will become frustrated and lose less weight.
- Large, rapid weight loss is associated with poorer long-term weight outcomes than is slow, gradual weight loss.

The authors define "presumptions" as beliefs about obesity that persist in the absence of supporting scientific evidence:

- Regularly eating (vs. skipping) breakfast protects against obesity.

- Eating more fruits and vegetables will result in weight loss or less weight gain regardless of whether one intentionally makes any other behavioral or environmental changes.
- Snacking contributes to weight gain and obesity.

"Facts" are <u>beliefs consistent with the evidence</u>:

- Diets very effectively reduce weight, but trying to go on a diet or recommending that someone go on a diet generally does not work well in the long term.
- Exercise helps mitigate the health-damaging effects of obesity, even without weight loss.
- Physical activity in a sufficient dose aids long-term weight maintenance.
- Involving parents promotes greater weight loss or maintenance in overweight children.
- Provision of meals by an outside source and use of meal-replacement products promote greater weight loss.

A recent study finding no support for the common belief that eating more fruits and vegetables promotes weight loss is consistent with the view that many popular myths persist regarding obesity.[19] Such recommendations are included in the Department of Agriculture's "Choose My Plate," for example.[20] Fruit and vegetable consumption has demonstrable health benefits, but apparently weight loss is not one of them as long as individuals do not also reduce intake of other foods.

The current state of knowledge is thus far from complete. Researchers have yet to reach consensus on what causes for excessive weight gain are most important in explaining our rising obesity rates. Unfortunately, there are also relatively few facts about how to successfully lose weight, and the evidence does not fully support many widely held beliefs.

THE OBESE MAY UNDERSTAND THE HEALTH AND ECONOMIC CONSEQUENCES OF THEIR CHOICES

A critical assumption of nudge theory is that individuals are acting out of sync with their long-term interests. The obese, for example, often want to lose weight, but nonetheless frequently fail in their weight-reduction efforts. The evidence, however, on whether the obese are truly misinformed or simply irrational is less than complete.

One study of 1130 adults examined whether overweight and obese individuals believed they were at greater risk of obesity-related diseases and premature mortality.[21] Obese and overweight adults forecasted life expectancies that were 3.9 and 2.4 years, respectively, shorter than those of normal-weight adults. Excess weight was associated with greater self-perceived risk of developing diabetes, cancer, heart disease, and stroke. Mortality predictions were reasonably close to those from actual life tables. These results are consistent with another study of 9035 individuals that found that overweight and obese adults aged 51–61 predicted that their weight will reduce their life expectancy by an average of 2.5 and 4 years, respectively.[22]

The obese also face penalties for being overweight in the labor market.[23] Economists Charles L. Baum II and William F. Ford find that both men and women experience a persistent obesity wage penalty during the first two decades of their careers.[24] Another study finds that obese white females earn 11.2 % less than their nonobese counterparts, with a difference in weight of roughly 65 pounds associated with a 9 % difference in wages.[25] Another study finds that obese workers who receive employer-sponsored health insurance pay for their higher medical costs by receiving lower cash wages than nonobese workers.[26]

One possibility is that the obese may be putting less effort into controlling their weight in response to advances in medical technology that lessen the health consequences of being obese. Economists Eric A. Finkelstein and Kiersten L. Strombotne argue that recent drug and surgical treatments for high cholesterol, blood pressure, and other risk factors that obesity promotes are important reasons why obese adults exhibit better blood pressure and cholesterol concentrations than normal-weight individuals did a few decades ago.[27] The obese may therefore be less likely to make an effort to decrease their weight because they have processed information on reduced health consequences.

Whether the obese are unaware that they are penalized in the labor market, that they live shorter lives, or that they experience improved health prospects because of advances in medical technology remain open issues that merit further study. But even if the obese are well informed, many would surely prefer to weigh less.

NUDGE THEORY BASICS

Individuals are not always rational when it comes to eating, according to behavioral economists.[28] Irrational decisions are believed to contribute to undesired weight gain when individuals do not realize how much food they actually eat. One study by eating-behavior researchers Brian Wansink and Jeffery Sobal concludes that test subjects underestimated the number of daily food-related decisions by an average of more than 221 decisions in what the authors refer to as "mindless eating."[29]

Behavioral economists frequently propose setting default options that nudge people toward healthier eating. Plate shapes and sizes, lighting, color, and convenience are a few of the hidden environmental factors believed to increase consumption norms and decrease consumption monitoring.[30] Eating-behavior researcher Brian Wansink suggests the following default option changes aimed at lessening temptations to overeat[31]:

- Store tempting foods in less-convenient locations (such as basements or top cupboards).
- Do not leave serving bowls and platters on the dinner table.
- Reduce the convenience of stockpiled foods by boxing them up or freezing them.
- Replace short, wide glasses with tall, narrow ones.
- Reduce serving sizes and consumption by using smaller bowls and plates.
- Use smaller spoons rather than larger ones.

The following passage from *Nudge* demonstrates that Wansink's experimental research on "mindless eating" has heavily influenced nudge theory[32]:

> In another Wansink (2006) masterpiece, people sat down to a large bowl of Campbell's tomato soup and were told to eat as much as they wanted. Unbeknownst to them, the soup bowls were designed to refill themselves (with empty bottoms connected to machinery beneath the table). No matter how much soup subjects ate, the bowl never emptied. Many people just kept eating, not paying attention to the fact that they were really eating a great deal of soup, until the experiment was (mercifully) ended. Large plates and large packages mean more eating; they are a form of choice architecture, and they work as major nudges. (Hint: if you would like to lose weight, get smaller plates, buy little packages of what you like, and don't keep tempting food in the refrigerator).[33]

Other experiments have also found that altering choice architecture influences eating. One study by a team of psychologists found that slight changes in the accessibility of foods in a cafeteria salad bar reduced intake by 8–16 %.[34] Making food slightly more difficult to reach (varying proximity by 10 inches) and changing sizes and accessibility of serving utensils were two such changes. A team of eating-behavior researchers also found that moving healthier foods to the convenience line in a high school lunchroom, where unhealthy foods were usually placed, increased sales of healthy foods by 18 %, but decreased sales of unhealthy foods by 28 %.[35]

Limiting the hours during which restaurants may be open or operate drive-up windows and forbidding placement of candy near cash registers at stores are examples of changing choice architecture by imposing search or travel costs. Former New York City Mayor Michael Bloomberg's proposal to ban sugary beverages in portions over 16 ounces also attempted to steer consumers away from excessive soda consumption. These changes are not nudges, however, even though they are based on paternalism and attempt to steer consumers toward healthier food choices. Instead, they are tools of hard paternalism as they raise costs for consumers or ban certain food choices outright.

CRITICISMS OF GOVERNMENT NUDGE THEORY

Nudge theory draws both praise and criticism. This section summarizes criticism that focuses on nudges aimed at steering individuals toward weight loss.

The Evidence Is Far from Settled

Empirical evidence on nudges indicates that they do not always work out as planned. One study by a group of nutritionists found that altering plate sizes had no significant effect on energy intake at meals eaten in three laboratory experiments.[36] Participants made significantly more trips to the buffet when they were given the smallest plate in one of these experiments.

Nutrition researchers recently reviewed studies that experimentally manipulated the dishware size to determine if such a change in choice architecture lowered subsequent food intake.[37] Nine experiments from eight publications were eligible for inclusion. The majority of experiments found no significant difference in food intake, leading authors to conclude that evidence to date does not show that dishware size has a consistent effect on food intake.

Adding "healthy" options to "unhealthy" meals is also problematic. One study authored by marketing professors finds that the mere presence of a healthy food option vicariously fulfills nutrition goals and provides consumers with a license to indulge, thus exerting ambiguous effects on overall diets.[38] Psychologists also report "negative calorie illusion," whereby adding a healthy option to weight-conscious individuals' unhealthy meals decreases their perception of the meals' calorie content. For example, weight-conscious participants estimated that a hamburger alone contains 734 calories but only 619 calories when accompanied by celery sticks.[39] Studies also suggest that restaurants claiming to serve "healthy" foods may cause diners to underestimate the caloric density of their foods and that diners are more likely to purchase higher-calorie side dishes at restaurants that claim to offer "healthy" foods when compared with those not making such claims.[40]

Nutrition researchers have recently suggested that a simple and inexpensive strategy to increase vegetable consumption is to use large plates—a recommendation clearly opposed to the conventional wisdom of behavioral economics.[41] Their controlled laboratory experiment investigated whether a standard (27 cm) plate vs. large (32 cm) size influenced the composition of a meal and the total meal energy of 83 participants invited to serve themselves lunch from a buffet containing 55 items. Plate size had no significant effect on the total energy of the meal, but participants using a large plate served themselves significantly more vegetables.

Labeling requirements are designed to help individuals who routinely underestimate calories, fats, and other attributes of foods.[42] Studies have found that labeling improves calorie estimates, but evidence so far does not clearly demonstrate that required labels result in healthier eating[43]. A study of New York City's 2008 law requiring restaurant chains to post calorie counts finds no change in calories purchased after the law was passed.[44] A similar conclusion was reached in a study of menu-labeling regulation in King County, Washington.[45] A study of mandatory calorie posting on purchase decisions at Starbucks finds virtually no change in purchases of beverage calories.[46] Providing daily, per-meal, or no calorie recommendations to randomized subsets of adult customers entering two McDonald's restaurants had no effect on purchases in another study.[47] Calorie labeling did not influence what patrons of a large chain bakery café ordered for lunch in still another study.[48]

Obesity researchers recently examined the effect of menu labeling with both caloric information and exercise equivalents on food selection.[49]

Exercise equivalents define how much time doing particular physical activities is needed to burn off calories in foods. For example, a 300-calorie hamburger requires about 75 minutes of walking. Calories ordered by a sample of 62 females, ages 18–34, who ordered fast food meals were not altered by this approach.

Conflicting evidence on nudge efficacy may stem from the fact that nudges are often based on laboratory experiments. There are well-known problems in extrapolating results from laboratory experiments to the real world.[50] Participants' choices in experiments are influenced by factors that include financial incentives, how choices are framed, the nature of others' scrutiny, and participant selection. Real-world decisions are made under circumstances not easily mimicked in laboratories. A recent review of the evidence on the effectiveness of calorie labeling examines 31 studies published from January 1, 2007 through July 19, 2013.[51] Of the 31 studies reviewed, 18 were conducted in "real world" settings and focused on actual food purchases. "Real world" studies found that calorie labels do not reduce total calories ordered. Additionally, a review of 12 studies altering choice architecture found that studies were generally of short duration, had questionable methodology, and were not conducted in "real world" environments.[52]

Overconfidence in nudge efficacy probably explains some rather ambitious claims. One study by psychologists claims that very small but cumulative decreases in food intake from modest changes in accessibility and sizes of serving utensils may be sufficient to "erase obesity" over a period of years.[53] Eating-behavior researcher Brian Wansink argues that small changes in choice architecture allow people to "effortlessly control their consumption and lose weight in a way that does not necessitate the discipline of dieting."[54] Thaler and Sunstein appear to overstate as well: "Consider the issue of obesity.... There is overwhelming evidence that obesity increases risks of heart disease and diabetes, frequently leading to premature death. It would be quite fantastic to suggest that everyone is choosing the right diet, or a diet that is preferable to what might be produced with a few nudges."[55]

In sum, the empirical evidence suggests that nudges are a particularly blunt and possibly ineffective tool for addressing obesity.

Choice Architects Are Also Human

Behavioral economists rarely question why choice architects themselves are not subject to the same decision-making flaws as other people. It is often assumed that choice architects, for example, mostly escape the irrational decision-making that behavioral economists believe affects so many individuals, and they know all relevant information about individuals' true preferences.[56] Economist Niclas Berggren examined behavioral economics articles in ten highly ranked economics journals from 2000 through 2009 to determine whether the authors had addressed the rationality or cognitive ability of policymakers.[57] Berggren found that 20.7 % of all articles contained a policy recommendation and that 95.5 % of these did not contain any analysis of the rationality or cognitive ability of policymakers. Only two of the 67 articles with a policy recommendation contained an assumption or analysis of policymakers of the same kind as that applied to economic decision makers.

Choice architects are also implicitly assumed to not fall victim to the many presumptions and myths surrounding obesity, as previously discussed. These are (1) small sustained changes in energy intake or expenditure will produce large, long-term weight changes; (2) setting realistic goals in obesity treatment is important because otherwise patients will become frustrated and lose less weight; and (3) large, rapid weight loss is associated with poorer long-term weight outcomes than is slow, gradual weight loss. The previous discussion includes various examples of overstated promises that a few small nudges can significantly dent population weight. These would appear to be based more on myths regarding "small changes" than on factual evidence.

Past Government Nudges May Have Promoted Obesity

Investigative journalist Nina Teicholz argues that the US government fostered dietary changes that contributed to our growing weight problem and diabetes prevalence through its emphasis on limiting consumption of eggs, butter, milk, and meat, while bulking up on carbohydrate-rich foods like pasta, bread, fruit, and potatoes.[58] Such guidelines are contained in the Dietary Guidelines for Americans jointly published by the US Department of Agriculture (USDA) and the Department of Health and Human Services (HHS) every five years. Teicholz believes that the low-fat nutrition advice of the past 60 years has harmed public health by espousing the myth that low-fat (especially low saturated fat) is the best diet.

Government promoted the notion that obesity and heart disease are linked to the consumption of fats when, in 1992, the USDA introduced the "Food Guide Pyramid." This pyramid-shaped diagram represents the "optimal" number of servings to be eaten each day from each of the basic food groups. This pyramid recommended that the majority of calories (up to 11 servings per day) should come from complex carbohydrates—primarily breads, cereals, rice, pasta, potatoes, and other starches—while relegating meats, fish, eggs, and other protein sources to 2–3 servings per day. Fats were also to be used sparingly. The Food Guide Pyramid was last updated in 2005 and then replaced by MyPlate in 2011, which slightly downplayed grains as the most important dietary ingredient by making vegetables the largest "slice."

Despite a lack of evidence supporting low-fat diets, only in 2010 did the Dietary Guidelines committee stop recommending limits on total fat. A meta-analysis of all available evidence recently published in the *Annals of Internal Medicine* concludes that current evidence does not clearly support high consumption of polyunsaturated fatty acids and low consumption of total saturated fats.[59] The authors note that, while saturated fats moderately raise "bad" LDL cholesterol, this does not apparently lead to adverse health outcomes such as heart attacks and death.

Ironically, obesity prevalence began rising noticeably around 1980, the year in which the Dietary Guidelines were introduced, leading to questions surrounding the unintended role of government in promoting obesity in the USA through its nudges on dietary choices. Meanwhile, recent Gallup polls demonstrate that most citizens remain committed to avoiding fat in their diets, with nearly twice as many Americans saying that they actively avoid fat in their diet (56 %) as say they actively avoid carbohydrates (29 %).[60]

MARKET NUDGING THEORY

It's no secret that many of us are concerned with our weight. A recent Gallup poll found that 51 % of adult Americans want to lose weight, although only 25 % are seriously working toward that goal.[61] People were undoubtedly eating on smaller plates, avoiding buffets, and skipping desserts for many years before behavioral economics came to light. Apparently, Americans are lowering caloric intakes. The USDA reports that average daily caloric intake declined by 118 calories (about 5 %) between 2006 and 2009 among working-age adults.[62]

Markets nudge all the time, as Thaler and Sunstein acknowledge. Thaler and Sunstein, however, appear to strongly favor government nudges rather than market nudges when they argue, "Markets provide strong incentives for firms to cater to the demands of consumers, and firms will compete to meet those demands, whether or not those demands represent the wisest choices."[63] Moreover, they state, "The key point here is that for all their virtues, markets often give companies a strong incentive to cater to (and profit from) human frailties, rather than to try to eradicate them or to minimize their effects."[64]

Thaler and Sunstein (2008) use the term "planner" to describe a far-sighted nudger with the ability to identify welfare-enhancing choices for individuals who suffer from various decision-making flaws. The following passage provides an interesting take on market nudging:

> Even when we're on our way to making good choices, competitive markets find ways to get us to overcome our last shred of resistance to bad ones. At O'Hare Airport in Chicago, two food vendors compete across the aisle from each other. One sells fruit, yogurt, and other healthy foods. The other sells Cinnabons, sinful cinnamon buns that have a whopping 730 calories and 24 grams of fat. Your Planner may have set the course for the yogurt and fruit stand, but the Cinnabon outlet blasts the aromas from their ovens directly into the walkway in front of the store. Care to guess which of the two stores always has the longer line?[65]

This view suggests that sellers that provide "unhealthy" products are the most profitable, thus placing blame squarely on sellers who exploit consumers' faulty decision-making. This view, however, appears out of sync with the views of the general public. Economists Jayson Lusk and Brenna Ellison conducted a nationwide study of 800 individuals in the USA in order to assess blame given to seven different entities (food manufacturers, grocery stores, restaurants, government policies, farmers, individuals, and parents).[66] Eighty percent said individuals were primarily to blame for the rise in obesity, followed by 59 % placing blame on parents. Apparently, people believe they themselves are mostly responsible for weight gain.

An alternative view is that sellers can systematically profit when marketing "healthier" products to customers interested in controlling their weight. The finding that 51 % of adult Americans want to lose weight indicates that many potential customers are looking for products that will help them do this. Food and restaurant businesses have been increasingly experimenting with smaller plates and packages to meet growing consumer demand for products that help them control their weight. Research indicates that the number of small plates and smaller-portion items at restaurants has grown 32 % since 2009.[67] Of course, few customers would single out calories as the only attribute of interest. Calories are one attribute along with price, taste, convenience, appearance, size, storage, and others.

Eating-behavior researcher Brian Wansink and former Arkansas Governor Mike Huckabee describe the importance of sellers:

> Food companies are not focused on making people fat, but on making money. If they are not profitable, their shareholders will abandon their stocks, fire their executives, put their employees out of work, bankrupt their suppliers, and collapse their pension funds. The first steps toward an obesity solution do not involve increased government regulation; they involve market-based changes that help consumers develop a new appetite for healthy foods.[68]

"Stealth health" is the tactic that food and restaurant businesses employ to make products healthier when they don't want to directly inform customers they are cutting fat or salt.[69] A concern is that customers sometimes connect healthy with less taste, especially when foods are considered indulgences, such as mashed potatoes, gravy, stuffing, and other items typically loaded with sodium and fat. Otherwise, companies are quick to tout nutritional improvements for foods aimed at health-conscious consumers.

Public health researchers Sara N. Bleich, Julia A. Wolfson, and Marian P. Jarlenski examined menu items in 66 of the 100 largest US restaurant chains in 2012 and 2013.[70] Mean calories among items on menus in both 2012 and 2013 did not change, but there were overall declines in calories (average of 56 calories, 12 % decline) in newly introduced menu items. Declines were concentrated mainly in new main course items (−67 calories, 10 % decline), although new beverage (−26 calories, 8 % decline) and children's (−46 calories, 20 % decline) items also had fewer mean calories.

Evidence on Market Nudges

Huge market for weight control. Products and services designed to help people change their behavior are part of the large and growing market in "behavioral technologies." They represent the market equivalent of nudges.

Marketdata Enterprises (2013) estimates that the weight-loss market was $60.5 billion in 2013 and almost evenly split in dollar terms between weight-loss products and services.[71] The breakdown is:

- Diet soft drinks ($20.64B)
- Artificial sweeteners ($2.53B)
- Diet dinner entrees ($2.16B)
- Prescription diet drugs ($0.54B)
- Meal replacements and OTC diet pills ($2.8B)
- Diet books and exercise DVDs ($1.13B)
- Commercial chains (e.g., Weight Watchers, Jenny Craig) ($3.34B)
- Health clubs ($22.6B)
- Weight-loss surgery ($2.85B) and
- Medical programs ($1.87B)

Industry promotion of health food. A widely reported study concludes that 16 of the nation's leading food and beverage companies collectively sold 6.4 trillion fewer calories in 2012 than they did in 2007.[72] These companies had pledged to lower calories and have so far exceeded their 2015 goal by more than 400 %. However, it remains unclear what effect this reduction in calories sold exerts on population weight. Consumers may substitute other products and alter their behaviors in other ways that make predictions ambiguous at best.

Clearer evidence comes from a USDA study conducted by economist Steve W. Martinez showing rapid growth of new products appealing to weight-conscious consumers.[73] Displaying health claims is considered evidence of growing awareness of obesity-related issues. Health- and nutrition-related claims (HNR) per product increased from 2.2 in 2001 to 2.6 in 2010, which the author interprets as competition fostering a more complete representation of products' health and nutritional attributes. Claims related to gluten, antioxidants, and omega-3s ranked among the leading HNR claims. The study suggests that growing demand for food products that contribute to overall health beyond basic nutrition provided incentives to manufacturers to supply and promote these products. The largest increase in HNR claims from 2001 to 2010 was for "no gluten," followed by "no trans fats."[74]

The same study finds that voluntary use of HNR claims on new food products was an important component of food companies' marketing strategies. The percentage of new food products carrying HNR claims grew from 25 % in 2001 to 43 % in 2010. Claims related to calories, whole grains, fiber, sugar, and vitamins and minerals were important contributors to the growth in HNR claims on new products after 2001. Sales of new products introduced in 2009 and 2010 with nutrient content claims exceeded those of all new food products with a range from 8 % higher to 28 % higher. Again, there is no direct evidence that population weight has changed as a result.

A study of Nielsen sales data from 2007 through 2011 from grocery stores, drug stores, and mass merchandisers reports similar results.[75] Food products by 15 of the largest food and beverage manufacturers were classified into traditional and "better-for-you" (BFY) categories. BFY products included those designated as diet, lite, fewer calorie, or zero calorie (e.g., Lean Cuisine, Coca-Cola Zero, Tropicana 50) as well as "good" foods, including whole-grain products and healthier traditional product formulations such as Cheerios, Dannon yogurt, and Nabisco Wheat Thins. Traditional products (i.e., not BFY items, such as Pepsi, Kellogg's Frosted Flakes, and Hellmann's Mayonnaise) accounted for 61.4 % of sales, while "lite" and "good" products each accounted for 19.3 % of sales. BFY products accounted for less than 40 % of sales but accounted for more than 70 % of sales growth. Again, there is no direct evidence that population weight has changed as a result.

Not all health claims are based on solid evidence that such products are "healthier" or even support weight loss. It has been reported that almost one-third of Americans are trying to avoid gluten, a protein found in grain.[76] This behavior has led to a market of gluten-free products estimated at $23.3 billion in 2013. Yet many health experts believe there is little to no benefit from gluten-free products for most Americans because few people cannot process the protein. Ironically, some supposedly healthier gluten-free foods contain more sugar, less fiber, and fewer vitamins than their counterparts with gluten. In other words, growth in gluten-free products might promote weight gain for some people.

The expanding market for "healthier" products is evidence that consumers and producers are responding to growing concerns regarding population weight. But evidence so far is more suggestive than conclusive that these trends have resulted in population weight loss.

Employer interest in weight reduction. Employers have incentives to nudge overweight employees toward weight loss to the extent that excess weight harms productivity and increases health costs. Numerous experiments are ongoing by businesses dedicated to designing nudges that work well.

A team of economists examined whether 1868 employees in 17 community colleges and 12 universities in North Carolina who achieved clinically significant weight loss of at least 5 % had reduced medical expenditures and lowered absenteeism.[77] The authors find some evidence of productivity gains, but no reduction in medical expenditures, but the authors suggest anticipated reductions may occur over longer periods.

Another study finds no evidence that "lifestyle management or wellness" nudging at PepsiCo lowered employer health costs, but nudges aimed at helping people with chronic diseases to stay healthy apparently do.[78] Disease-management nudges (e.g., text message reminders for taking medicine) lowered health care costs by $136 per member per month, driven by a 29 % reduction in hospital admissions. Workplace wellness programs did not show a similar reduction in costs.

Offering overweight individuals financial incentives is another approach. Economists John Cawley and J.A. Price report modest results from their examination of workplace wellness programs (2635 workers across 24 worksites) that offered financial rewards and deposit contracts for weight loss.[79] This study examines various deposit contracts where participants put their own money at risk if they failed to achieve weight-loss goals. This method attempts to increase motivation to reach goals when individuals suffer from "loss aversion bias," whereby people feel the pain of a loss more than the pleasure of a gain. Workers offered financial rewards did not exhibit higher year-end weight loss than those in the control group, but those who made deposit contracts had year-end weight loss that was two pounds greater than that of the control group. Cawley and Price suggest rewarding loss of fat and gain of muscle or even rewarding behavior change rather than weight loss as means of improving incentives.

A recent article in the *Wall Street Journal* describes other efforts by employers to nudge workers toward better health.[80] Johnson & Johnson employees receive a $500 credit toward their annual medical premium if they participate in a health assessment. Workers at CVS Health Corp. who don't complete an annual health screening pay $600 more per year for their insurance premiums. JetBlue Airways Corp. contributes up to $400 a year into employees' health savings accounts for about 45 different activities such as participating in smoking-cessation programs and completing Ironman races. Businesses navigate concerns that range between sowing discontent among workers and inviting legal complaints when they attempt to steer worker health. The article, for example, suggests that workers are wary of anything that smacks of coercion as indicated by a survey that found that 62 % of respondents said it is inappropriate to require workers to pay more for their health insurance if they don't participate in wellness programs.

Apps and weight-loss firms. A survey of more than 6000 people in six countries (Australia, Canada, India, South Africa, the UK, and the USA) found that more than half of consumers are interested in buying wearable technologies such as fitness monitors for tracking physical activity and managing their personal health.[81] There are more than 40,000 health, fitness, and medical apps currently available that focus on healthy eating, weight management, fitness, healthy living, smoking cessation, stress management, and sleep.[82] They display information, show preloaded instructions for diet and fitness, record and display user-entered data, and track weight measurements over time. Social networks such as Facebook, Twitter, and LinkedIn are increasingly used as platforms for healthcare marketing of new behavioral technologies, with recommendations from friends being particularly effective in promoting sales of weight-loss products.[83]

One market test of apps is whether they encroach on the turf of more traditional businesses. Falling share prices of several widely recognized weight-loss companies suggest their businesses are being undermined by mobile technology.[84] Jenny Craig has performed poorly with its plan of prepackaged meals with nutritional counseling. Nutrisystem has struggled with its model providing home-delivered meal plans and nutritional counseling. Weight Watchers, too, has struggled with attracting new customers.[85] Weight Watchers in 2012 added a mobile app for tracking food and activity, but this feature was an add-on to its paid subscription. Many apps, however, are free and do not require monthly payments for a base subscription bundled with services such as menus and counseling.

StickK.com creates precommitment contracts, an approach advocated by behavioral economists to help people with self-control problems. StickK.com is designed to promote healthier lifestyles by allowing users to create contracts that nudge them into achieving personal goals that include losing weight, exercising regularly, quitting smoking, and maintaining weight. Individuals sign legally binding contracts that send their money to third parties, including either individuals or a number of organizations and charities, in the event they fail to stick to their contracts. As of December 15, 2014, there were 271,514 commitment contracts with $19,028,336 in deposits by users of StickK.com. Users had created a total of 300,659 workouts and refrained from smoking 2,502,250 cigarettes. Use of StickK.com is free.

Rapid expansion of weight-loss and health apps provides strong evidence that consumers are sampling the growing number of behavioral technologies offered by markets for weight-loss and health apps. Markets are, in effect, the choice architects of these behavioral technologies, and businesses have financial incentives to meet this growing demand. The evidence on whether these nudges are effective is more promising than certain at this point.

MARKET NUDGING IS MORE PROMISING THAN GOVERNMENT NUDGING

Nudge theory can play a role in helping us lose weight, despite the previous discussion indicating that all choice architects—government or market—are imperfect. Experimentation is the key to overcoming choice architects' imperfections, including flawed decision-making, basing nudges on pervasive myths regarding weight loss, and the inability to know individual preferences. Any of these imperfections could be fatal, but market choice architects hold significant advantages over those in governments.

Businesses face "market tests" in a world where consumers may reject products that fail to deliver value. Consumers eventually understand whether marketing claims are real or not, with poorly designed products being improved or simply removed from markets. Evidence is imperfect so far on whether currently available products result in weight loss, but ongoing feedback from consumers helps to weed out poor designs. All product attributes, including calories, size, packaging, taste, simplicity, and pricing, receive market scrutiny.

Government choice architects do not face comparable "market tests" and thus face greater problems overcoming their imperfections. Poor products do not directly jeopardize the financial solvency of governments because they do not face profit constraints. Businesses that provide nudges that do not enhance consumer welfare are not profitable for long in competitive environments such as those aimed at weight-conscious consumers.

Thaler and Sunstein argue we should not be too concerned about imperfect or ineffective nudges.[86] They argue that the noncoercive nature of government nudges allows easy exiting by those wishing to avoid them. But this argument simply acknowledges that poorly designed nudges can easily be avoided. This view suggests that there is little harm in designing numerous nudges because some government nudges might help people meet their weight-loss goals. This is not an approach, however, that allows researchers to easily parse out effective from ineffective nudges or discern what interrelationships might exist among the many nudges. It is also possible that nudges that turn out to be harmful might never be discarded.

The fact that it took decades for the USDA to stop encouraging low-fat diets demonstrates that regulators do not face strong incentives to correct themselves. That many consumers continue to avoid fat indicates that incorrect nudges may not be so harmless. Unfortunately, there appears to be little interest in examining how attempts to alter behavior in one area may lead to unanticipated changes in other areas that are potentially harmful.[87]

[handwritten margin note: general insights for reg policy too]

This view that ineffective but easily avoided nudges are not harmful fails to recognize the superiority of markets in helping choice architects overcome their various imperfections. Consumers directly signal to market choice architects which products are ineffective or detrimental. They simply stop buying them, thus leaving little doubt that product attributes do not meet their approval. Harmful products might yield costly lawsuits directly aimed at businesses. Businesses read these signals routinely because they threaten their financial health. Market nudges face not only market tests but also competitive pressures from other firms thus providing strong incentives to continuously improve the effectiveness of their nudges.

Government nudging suffers from higher hurdles in getting nudges "right." Their nudges do not have to withstand "market tests." Government revenues do not rise or fall to signal the good from the bad. Government employees typically are not fearful that failed products place their jobs in jeopardy. Effective feedback becomes even more problematic when governments supply many nudges based on the view that they pose little harm since citizens can easily avoid them. Feedback is limited at best for government choice architects in an environment where ineffective nudges do not directly jeopardize their jobs or financial viability. In effect, government nudges represent "government guesses" that are not constrained by "market tests."

Markets are also superior at being true to the noncoercive spirit of nudging theory. Businesses do not have incentives to keep nudging those unwilling to change their behavior. They may try to educate customers unwilling to buy their products, but financial incentives are a clear limit facing businesses that continue nudging consumers toward products they do not purchase. Low-calorie snacks, for example, may sit on the shelves no matter where the grocer locates them or how many advertising dollars are invested. Markets will eventually get the message and either alter product attributes or drop products altogether.

Governments have considerably more latitude to repeatedly nudge people toward behavior that choice architects believe improves their lives. It can be difficult to determine when changes in choice architecture cross the line into coercion, especially when government choice architects believe people exhibit decision-making flaws or are resistant to educational nudges. A slippery slope problem may arise. Noncoercive but ineffective nudges may also engender coercive policies (e.g., taxes and subsidies) as government choice architects remain convinced that people's behavior should change. Government choice architects therefore must exercise considerable restraint in resisting urges to "ramp up" the pressure on citizens that resist their nudges.

ROLE FOR GOVERNMENT

An appropriate role for government is to facilitate market correction of fraudulent practices and claims that may undermine consumer trust in the whole weight-loss industry and lead them away from potentially helpful solutions. Most consumers do not have the expertise to judge claims and government can speed up the process by which deceptive products are taken off the market.

For instance, the Federal Trade Commission (FTC) recently fined several weight-loss businesses $34 million after it concluded that they made deceptive advertising claims that their products would help people lose weight with little effort.[88] The $34 million included a $26.5 million settlement against Sensa Products LLC, which markets a dietary supplement called Sensa that weight-conscious consumers may sprinkle on foods. One Sensa advertisement stated that "whether you need to lose 10 pounds, 50 pounds or more, now you can without dieting. Simply sprinkle Sensa on, eat all the foods you love and watch the pounds come off."

Economists at the FTC argue that advertising from the weight-loss industry is frequently misleading, confusing and even deceptive.[89] In one study the authors found evidence of consumer deception in 65 % of all weight-loss ads that employed unproven testimonials and before/after photos. More than 57 % promised rapid weight loss beyond realistic expectations, and, more than 41 % falsely stated that diet aids result in long-term weight loss.

Examples provided by the FTC include:

- "awesome attack on bulging fatty deposits … has virtually eliminated the need to diet." (Konjac root pill)
- "They said it was impossible, but tests prove [that] my astounding diet-free discovery melts away…5, 6, even 7 pounds of fat a day." (ingredients not disclosed)

- "The most powerful diet pill ever discovered! No diet or workout required. The secret weight-loss pill behind Fitness models, Show Biz and Entertainment professionals! No prescription required to order." (ingredients not disclosed)
- "lose up to 30lbs... No impossible exercise! No missed meals! No boring foods or small portions!" (plant extract fucusvesiculosus)
- "lose up to 8 to 10 pounds per week... [n]o dieting, no strenuous exercise." (elixir purportedly containing 16 plant extracts)
- "my 52lbs of unwanted fat relaxed away without dieting or grueling exercise." (hypnosis seminar)
- "no exercise...[a]nd eat as much as you want – the more you eat, the more you lose, we'll show you how." (meal replacement)

Policies that penalize or remove fraudulent claims help consumers receive accurate information about the products they purchase.

CONCLUSION

Obesity remains a serious health problem, and it is no secret that many people want to lose weight. Behavioral economists typically argue that nudges help individuals with various decision-making flaws live longer, healthier, and better lives. This paper has also argued that even if the obese are not subject to these flaws, many are still interested in products that help them lose weight.

Nudges remain well-intentioned but blunt tools for lowering population weight. This conclusion is not surprising given the current state of knowledge. Researchers have yet to reach a consensus on what specific causes for excessive weight gain are most important in explaining rising obesity rates. There are also relatively few facts about how to successfully lose weight, and the evidence does not fully support many widely held beliefs. The empirical evidence also indicates that nudges do not always work as planned.

Market nudges play a potentially important role in helping citizens control their weight. The evolving markets in apps, weight-loss programs, and "healthy" products indicate that many consumers are willing to purchase products that help them with their weight-loss goals. Worksite programs aimed at enhancing worker productivity and reducing health costs indicate that businesses are also interested in products that work well. The evidence so far is more promising than conclusive that markets have been effective in nudging people to lose weight.

Experimentation is the key to overcoming choice architects' imperfections, including flawed decision-making, basing nudges on various myths regarding weight loss, and the inability to know individual preferences. Choice architects in markets hold significant advantages over those in governments; however, in their efforts to overcome these shortcomings. Unlike governments, businesses face "market tests" in a world where consumers reject products that fail to deliver value. Government nudges represent "government guesses" that are not constrained by "market tests." Markets also hold an advantage in sticking to the noncoercive spirit of nudging theory.

Past experience with government recommendations supporting low-fat diets suggests caution when it comes to government nudging since promoting diets rich in complex carbohydrates such as breads, cereals, rice, pasta, potatoes, and other starches may have unintentionally promoted obesity. Caution would also be prudent before recommending that governments experiment with market-based nudges on their own workforces or perhaps experiment with social programs whose costs are influenced by obesity. Governments can be expected to resist utilizing nudges that yield cost savings because governments do not face profit motives. Government choice architects may also prefer to design their own nudges, even though they face higher hurdles in designing effective nudges than market choice architects do.

NOTES

1. Katherine M. Flegal, Margaret D. Carroll, Brian K. Kit, and Cynthia L. Ogden, "Prevalence of Obesity and Trends in the Distribution of Body Mass Index Among U.S. Adults, 1999–2010," *Journal of the American Medical Association* 307(5) (2012): E1–E7. The authors also note that the rise in obesity prevalence appears to have leveled off in recent years.

2. Eric A. Finkelstein, Olga A. Khavjou, Hope Thompson, Justin G. Trogdon, Liping Pajn, Bettylou Sherry, and William Dietz, "Obesity and Severe Obesity Forecasts Through 2030," *American Journal of Preventive Medicine* 42(6) (2012): 563–70. Severely obese is defined [by who??] as being 100 or more pounds overweight.

3. John B. Dixon, "The Effect of Obesity on Health Outcomes," *Molecular and Cellular Endocrinology* 316 (2010): 104–8.

4. Thaler and Sunstein, *Nudge: Improving Decisions About Health, Wealth, and Happiness.*
5. Thaler and Sunstein, *Nudge: Improving Decisions About Health, Wealth, and Happiness,* 74.
6. John Komlos and Marek Brabec, "The Trend of Mean BMI Values of US Adults, Birth Cohorts 1882–1986 Indicates that the Obesity Epidemic Began Earlier than Hitherto Thought," *American Journal of Human Biology* 22(5) (2010): 631–38.
7. Richard V. Burkhauser, John Cawley, and Maximilian D. Schmeiser, "Differences in the U.S. Trends in the Prevalence of Obesity Based on Body Mass Index and Skinfold Thickness," *Economics and Human Biology* 7(3) (2009): 207–18.
8. John Cawley and Richard V. Burkhauser, "Beyond BMI: The Value of More Accurate Measures of Fatness and Obesity in Social Science Research," *Journal of Health Economics* 27 (2008): 519–29.
9. James R. Hebert, David B. Allison, Edward Archer, Carl J. Lavie, and Steven N. Blair, "Scientific Decision Making, Policy Decisions, and the Obesity Pandemic," *Mayo Clinic Proceedings* 88(6) (2013): 593–604.
10. Sara N. Bleich, Y. Claire Wang, Youfa Wang, and Steven L. Gormaker, "Increasing Consumption of Sugar-sweetened Beverages Among US Adults: 1988–1994 to 1999–2004," *American Journal of Clinical Nutrition* 89(1) (2009): 372–81.
11. John Cawley," The Economics of Childhood Obesity," *Health Affairs* 29(3) (2010): 364–71.
12. Zhenxiang Zhao and Robert Kaestner, "Effects of Urban Sprawl on Obesity," *Journal of Health Economics* 29(6) (2010): 779–87.
13. Nicole I. Larson, Mary T. Storey, and Melissa C. Nelson, "Neighborhood Environments: Disparities in Access to Healthy Foods in the U.S.," *American Journal of Preventive Medicine* 36(1) (2009): 74–81.
14. Darius Lakdawalla and Tomas Philipson, "The Growth of Obesity and Technological Change," *Economics and Human Biology* 7(3) (2009): 283–93.
15. David Wallinga, "Agricultural Policy and Childhood Obesity: A Food Systems and Public Health Commentary," *Health Affairs* 29(3) (2010): 405–10.
16. Hebert, Allison, Archer, Lavie, and Blair, "Scientific Decision Making, Policy Decisions, and the Obesity Pandemic."

17. N. V. Dhurandhar, D. Schoeller, A. W. Brown, S. B. Heymsfield, D. Thomas, T. I. A. Sørensen, J. R. Speakman, M. Jeansonne, D. B. Allison, "Energy Balance Measurement: When Something Is Not Better Than Nothing," *International Journal of Obesity* 13, November 2014 (early online).

18. Krista Casazza, Kevin R. Fontaine, Arne Astrup, Leann L. Birch, Andrew W. Brown, Michelle M. Bohan Brown, Nefertiti Durant, Gareth Dutton, E. Michael Foster, Steven B. Heymsfield, Kerry McIver, Tapan Mehta, Nir Menachemi, P. K. Newby, Russell Pate, Barbara J. Rolls, Bisakha Sen, Daniel L. Smith, Diana M. Thomas, and David B. Allison, "Myths, Presumptions, and Facts About Obesity," *New England Journal of Medicine* 368(13) (2013): 446–54.

19. Kathryn A. Kaiser, Andrew W. Brown, Michelle M. Bohan Brown, James M. Shikany, Richard D. Mattes, and David B. Allison, "Increased Fruit and Vegetable Intake Has No Discernible Effect on Weight Loss: A Systematic Review and Meta-analysis," *American Journal of Clinical Nutrition*, published online on June 25, 2014.

20. United States Department of Agriculture. 2013. Choose My Plate. Available at: http://www.choosemyplate.gov/ (cited December 17, 2014).

21. Eric A. Finkelstein, Derek S. Brown, and W. Douglas Eva, "Do Obese Persons Comprehend Their Personal Health Risks?" *American Journal of Health Behavior* 32(5) (2008): 508–16.

22. Tracy A. Falba and Susan H. Busch, "Survival Expectations of the Obese: Is Excess Mortality Reflected in Perceptions?" *Obesity Research* 13(4) (2005): 754–761.

23. There do not appear to be empirical studies examining whether obese individuals understand this penalty, however.

24. Charles L. Baum II and William F. Ford, "The Wage Effects of Obesity: A Longitudinal Study," *Health Economics* 13(9) (2004): 885–99.

25. John Cawley, "The Impact of Obesity on Wages," *Journal of Human Resources* 39(2) (2004): 451–74.

26. Jay Bhattacharya and M. Kate Bundorf, "The Incidence of the Healthcare Costs of Obesity," *Journal of Health Economics* 28(3) (2009): 649–58.

27. Eric A. Finkelstein and Kiersten L. Strombotne, "The Economics of Obesity," *American Journal of Clinical Nutrition*, 91(supp.), (2010): 1520S–4S.

28. David R. Just and Collin R. Payne, "Obesity: Can Behavioral Economics Help?" *Annals of Behavioral Medicine* 38(1) (2009): 47–55.
29. Brian Wansink and Jeffery Sobal, "Mindless Eating: The 200 Daily Food Decisions We Overlook," *Environment and Behavior* 39(1) (2007): 106–23.
30. Brian Wansink, "From Mindless Eating to Mindlessly Eating Better," *Physiology & Behavior* 100(5) (2010): 454–63.
31. Brian Wansink, "Environmental Factors That Increase the Food Intake and Consumption Volume of Unknowing Consumers," *Annual Review of Nutrition* 24 (2004): 455–79.
32. It should be noted, however, that Wansink does not directly argue for government nudges as he uses his experimental findings to argue that consumers can use his results to make better decisions.
33. Thaler and Sunstein, *Nudge: Improving Decisions about Health, Wealth, and Happiness,* 44.
34. Paul Rozin, Sydney Scott, Megan Dingley, Joanna K. Urbanek, Hong Jiang and Mark Kaltenbach, "Nudge to Nobesity I: Minor Changes in Accessibility Decrease Food Intake," *Judgment and Decision Making* 6 (2011): 323–32.
35. Andrew S. Hanks, David R. Just, Laura E. Smith, and Brian Wansink, "Healthy Convenience: Nudging Students Toward Healthier Choices in the Lunchroom," *Journal of Public Health* 34(3) (2012): 370–76.
36. Barbara J. Rolls, Liane S. Roe, Kitti H. Halverson, and Jennifer S. Meengs, "Using a Smaller Plate Did Not Reduce Energy Intake at Meals," *Appetite* 49 (2007), 652–60.
37. E. Robinson, S. Nolan, C. Tudur-Smith, E. J. Boyland, J. A. Harrold, C. A. Hardman, and J. C. G. Halford, "Will Smaller Plates Lead to Smaller Waists? A Systematic Review and Meta-Analysis of the Effect that Experimental Manipulation of Dishware Size Has on Energy Consumption," *Obesity Reviews* 15(10) (2014): 812–821.
38. Karen Wilcox, Beth Vallen, Lauren Block and Gavan J. Fitzsimons, "Vicarious Goal Fulfillment: When the Mere Presence of a Healthy Option Leads to an Ironically Indulgent Decision," *Journal of Consumer Research* 36(3) (2009): 380–93.
39. Alexander Chernev, "The Dieter's Paradox," *Journal of Consumer Psychology* 21(2) (2011): 178–83.

40. Pierre Chandon and Brian Wansink, "The Biasing Health Halos of Fast-Food Restaurant Health Claims: Lower Calorie Estimates and Higher Side-Dish Consumption Intentions," *Journal of Consumer Research* 34(3) (2007): 301–14.

41. E. Libotte, M. Siegrist, and T. Bucher, "The Influence of Plate Size on Meal Composition. Literature Review and Experiment," *Appetite* 82 (2014): 91–96

42. It should be understood that labeling requirements can also be justified on the basis of neoclassical economic theory when they lower search costs and alleviate asymmetric information problems.

43. Brian Elbel, "Consumer Estimation of Recommended and Actual Calories at Fast Food Restaurants," *Obesity* 19(10) (2011): 1971–78.

44. Brian Elbel, Rogan Kersh, Victoria L. Brescoll, and L. Beth Dixon, "Calorie Labeling and Food Choices: A First Look at the Effects on Low-Income People in New York City," *Health Affairs* 28(6) (2009): 1110–21.

45. Eric A. Finkelstein, Kiersten L. Strombotne, Nadine L. Chan, and James Krieger, "Mandatory Menu Labeling in One Fast-Food Chain in King County, Washington," *American Journal of Preventive Medicine* 40(2) (2011): 122–27.

46. Brian Bollinger, Phillip Leslie, and Alan Sorensen, "Calorie Posting in Chain Restaurants," *American Economic Journal: Economic Policy* 3(1) (2011): 91–128.

47. Julie S. Downs, Jessica Wisdom, Brian Wansink, and George Loewenstein, "Supplementing Menu Labeling with Calorie Recommendations to Test for Facilitation Effects," *American Journal of Public Health* 103(9) (2013): 1604–9.

48. Sarah L. Rendell and Charles Swencionis, "Point-of-Purchase Calorie Labeling Has Little Influence on Calories Ordered Regardless of Body Mass Index," *Current Obesity Reports*, published online June 26, 2014.

49. Charles Platkin, Ming-Chin Yeh, Kimberly Hirsch, Ellen Weiss Wiewel, Chang-Yun Lin, Ho-Jui Tung, and Victoria H Castellanos, "The Effect of Menu Labeling with Calories and Exercise Equivalents on Food Selection and Consumption," *BMC Obesity* 1 (2014): 21.

50. Glenn W. Harrison and John A. List, "Field Experiments," *Journal of Economic Literature* 42(4) (2004): 1009–55; Steven D. Levitt and John A. List, "What Do Laboratory Experiments Measuring Social

Preferences Reveal About the Real World?" *The Journal of Economic Perspectives* 21(2) (2007): 153–74.

51. Kamila M. Kiszko, Olivia D. Martinez, Courtney Abrams, and Brian Elbel, "The Influence of Calorie Labeling on Food Orders and Consumption: A Review of the Literature," *Journal of Community Health* 39 (2014): 1248–1269.

52. L. R. Skov, S. Lourenço, G. L. Hansen, B. E. Mikkelsen, and C. Schofield, "Choice Architecture as a Means to Change Eating Behaviour in Self-Service Settings: A Systematic Review," *Obesity Reviews* 14(3) (2013): 187–96.

53. Rozin, Scott, Dingley, Urbanek, Jiang and Kaltenbach, "Nudge to Nobesity I: Minor Changes in Accessibility Decrease Food Intake."

54. Wansink, "Environmental Factors That Increase the Food Intake and Consumption Volume of Unknowing Consumers," 472–3.

55. Thaler and Sunstein, *Nudge: Improving Decisions about Health, Wealth, and Happiness*, 7.

56. Edward L. Glaeser, "Psychology and the Market," *American Economic Review* 94(2) (2004): 408–13; Mario J. Rizzo and Douglas G. Whitman, "The Knowledge Problem of New Paternalism," *Brigham Young University Law Review* 4 (2009): 905–68.

57. Niclas Berggren, "Time for Behavioral Political Economy? An Analysis of Articles in Behavioral Economics," *The Review of Austrian Economics* 25(3) (2012): 199–221. The ten journals are *American Economic Review, Journal of Finance, Quarterly Journal of Economics, Econometrica, Journal of Financial Economics, Journal of Political Economy, Review of Financial Studies, Journal of Economic Theory, Review of Economic Studies*, and *Journal of Econometrics*.

58. Nina Teicholz, *The Big Fat Surprise: Why Butter, Meat, and Cheese Belong in a Healthy Diet* (New York: Simon & Schuster, 2014).

59. Rajiv Chowdhury, Samantha Warnakula, Setor Kunutsor, Francesca Crowe, Heather A. Ward, Laura Johnson, Oscar H. Franco, Adam S. Butterworth, Nita G. Forouhi, Simon G. Thompson, Kay-Tee Khaw, Dariush Mozaffarian, John Danesh, and Emanuele Di Angelantonio, "Association of Dietary, Circulating, and Supplement Fatty Acids with Coronary Risk. A Systematic Review and Meta-analysis," *Annals of Internal Medicine* 160(6) (2014): 398–407

60. Andrew Dugan, "Americans Still Avoid Fat More Than Carbs," Gallup, July 29, 2014. http://www.gallup.com/poll/174176/americans-avoid-fat-carbs.aspx?version=print

61. Allyssa Brown, "Americans' Desire to Shed Pounds Outweighs Effort," Gallup, November 29, 2013. http://www.gallup.com/poll/166082/americans-desire-shed-pounds-outweighs-effort.aspx?version=print

62. Jessica E. Todd, "Changes in Eating Patterns and Diet Quality Among Working-Age Adults, 2005–2010," Economic Research Report, Number 161, U.S. Department of Agriculture, January 2014.

63. Thaler and Sunstein, *Nudge: Improving Decisions About Health, Wealth, and Happiness*, 49.

64. Thaler and Sunstein, *Nudge: Improving Decisions About Health, Wealth, and Happiness*, 74.

65. Thaler and Sunstein, *Nudge: Improving Decisions About Health, Wealth, and Happiness*, 40.

66. Jayson L. Lusk and Brenna Ellison, "Who Is to Blame for the Rise in Obesity?" *Appetite* 68 (2013): 14–20.

67. Annie Gasparro and Julie Jargon, "The Problem with Portions: Cheesecake Factory, Applebee's, McDonald's Struggle to Find the Size That Sells," *Wall Street Journal*, June 24, 2014.

68. Brian Wansink and Mike Huckabee, "De-marketing Obesity," *California Management Review* 47(4) (2005): 6–18, pages 16–17.

69. Julie Jargon, "Less Salt, Same Taste? Food Companies Quietly Change Recipes. McDonald's, Boston Market, Kraft Are under Pressure to Alter Formulas, but Consumers Don't Always Like Them," *Wall Street Journal*, June 23, 2014.

70. Sara N. Bleich, Julia A. Wolfson, and Marian P. Jarlenski, "Calorie Changes in Chain Restaurant Menu Items. Implications for Obesity and Evaluations of Menu Labeling," *American Journal of Preventive Medicine* (online 2014).

71. Marketdata Enterprises, Inc., "The U.S. Weight Loss & Diet Control Market (12th Edition: March 2013)," Tampa, Florida.

72. The companies, acting together as part of the Healthy Weight Commitment Foundation (HWCF), pledged to remove 1 trillion calories from the marketplace by 2012, and 1.5 trillion by 2015. See Healthy Weight Commitment Foundation, "Major Food, Beverage Companies Remove 6.4 Trillion Calories from U.S. Marketplace," January 8, 2014, http://www.healthyweightcommit.org/news/major_food_beverage_companies_remove_6.4_trillion_calories_from_u.s._market/

73. Steve W. Martinez, "Introduction of New Food Products with Voluntary Health- and Nutrition-Related Claims, 1989–2010," EIB-108 Economic Research Service/USDA, February 2013.

74. Growth in "no trans fats" claims was partly caused by new labeling requiring disclosures of the trans fat content.

75. Hudson Institute, "Better-for-You Foods: It's Just Good Business," Obesity Solutions Initiative, Washington, DC, October 2011.

76. Julie Jargon, "The Gluten-Free Craze: Is It Healthy? Experts Question Benefits of Gluten-Free for All but a Small Minority," *Wall Street Journal,* June 22, 2014.

77. Marcel Bilger, Eric A. Finkelstein, Eliza Kruger, Deborah F. Tate, and Laura A. Linnan, "The Effect of Weight Loss on Health, Productivity, and Medical Expenditures Among Overweight Employees," *Medical Care* 51(6) (2013): 471–77.

78. John P. Caloyeras, Hangsheng Liu, Ellen Exum, Megan Broderick, and Soeren Mattke, "Managing Manifest Diseases, but Not Health Risks, Saved PepsiCo Money over Seven Years," *Health Affairs* 33(1) (2014): 124–31.

79. John Cawley and J. A. Price, "A Case Study of a Workplace Wellness Program That Offers Financial Incentives for Weight Loss," *Journal of Health Economics* 32(5) (2013): 794–803.

80. Lauren Weber, "Wellness Programs Get a Health Check," *Wall Street Journal,* October 7, 2014.

81. Leventhal, Rajiv, "Survey: Consumers Want to Track Health Data with Wearable Technologies," January 6, 2014; see http://www.healthcare-informatics.com/news-item/survey-consumers-want-track-health-data-wearable-technologies

82. Adam C. Powell, Adam B. Landman, and David W. Bates, "In Search of a Few Good Apps," *Journal of the American Medical Association* 311(18) (2014): 1851–52.

83. Viju Raghupathi and Joshua Fogel, "Facebook Advertisements and Purchase of Weight-Loss Products," *Journal of Medical Marketing* 13(4) (2013): 201–11.

84. Rachel Landen, "Obesity Rises, but Weight-Management Firms See Revenue Slimming," November 21, 2013; see http://www.modern-healthcare.com/article/20131121/NEWS/311219948; accessed December 14, 2014.

85. Tess Stynes, "Weight-Loss Firm's Shares Plummet on Forecast," *Wall Street Journal,* February 14, 2014.

86. Thaler and Sunstein, *Nudge: Improving Decisions about Health, Wealth, and Happiness*: 240.
87. Paul Dolan and Matteo M. Galizzi, "Like Ripples on a Pond: Behavioral Spillovers and Their Implications for Research and Policy," *Journal of Economic Psychology* (2015): 1–16.
88. Jennifer C. Dooren, "FTC Cracks Down on Weight-Loss Product Marketers: Companies Ordered to Pay $34 Million to Settle Deceptive Advertising Claims," *Wall Street Journal*, January 7, 2014.
89. Richard L. Cleland, Walter C. Gross, Laura D. Koss, Matthew Daynard, and Karen M. Muoio, "Weight Loss Advertising: An Analysis of Current Trends," Federal Trade Commission, Washington, DC, September 2002.

Nudging in an Evolving Marketplace: How Markets Improve Their Own Choice Architecture

Adam C. Smith and Todd J. Zywicki

INTRODUCTION

Behavioral economics (BE) and its applied counterpart, behavioral law and economics, are concerned with the nature of choice and how rational a person's decision-making really is. From loss aversion to confirmation bias, behavioral economists assert that people often act in ways that are at odds with what other economists assert to be rational behavior. To counter our supposedly biased predilections, behavioral theorists have urged policy experiments that would consciously alter individuals' "choice architecture"—that is how choices are structured and presented to the consumer—found in the marketplace. By, for example, changing the default choice option, people can be nudged into making different choices that behavioral planners believe will improve their welfare.

To date, BE remains plagued by methodological difficulties that cast doubt upon the validity of many biases. For example, the so-called "endowment effect," which had stood as supposedly one of the most well

A.C. Smith (✉)
Johnson & Wales University, Charlotte, NC, USA

T.J. Zywicki
GMU Law School, Arlington, VA, USA

© The Editor(s) (if applicable) and The Author(s) 2016
S. Abdukadirov (ed.), *Nudge Theory in Action*,
DOI 10.1007/978-3-319-31319-1_9

225

confirmed of supposed biases, has been demonstrated to be little more than the artifact of experimental design and other flaws.[1] The existence or prevalence of numerous other purported biases remains open to doubt as a result of the highly context-dependent nature in which they are found and the resulting difficulty in replicating those results in a robust fashion.[2] Multiple supposed biases can simultaneously apply to any given choice, and in many situations they predict inconsistent results with no means to reconcile those inconsistencies. In short, responsible policymakers should move with caution before designing behavioral-based policy experiments for human subjects.[3]

Although the verifiability of much of BE thus remains an open question, that the approach has nevertheless found extensive application in the policy realm is not. In areas like consumer finance[4] and environmental regulation,[5] behaviorally influenced ideas are having a notable impact. Not all of this seems to be aimed at improving choices for consumers, but much of it is. And we can expect this trend to continue and expand into new regulatory fronts as policymakers find further merit in the behavioral approach.

Despite this recent trend, improving choice architecture to help consumers make better decisions is not a novel concept. Indeed, it is reasonable to assume that improving how we make our choices is at least as old as choices themselves. If people act to better their condition, then we can assume that there is an inherent desire to make their choices align with their long-term well-being. Even when people do not act in their own interest, there is still a desire to make better choices in the future.[6] This is particularly true when the externalities of choosing are relatively high such as when our choices affect others; that is, when additional people bear the cost of our choice, then the consequences of a biased decision become greater.

This brings us to the context of the market and how its choice architecture develops through a spontaneous process organized by dispersed persons and their limited knowledge of local conditions. Markets can only become sustainable when those wanting to exchange are satisfied with their choices. Happy customers are repeat customers. Thus businesses crucially care about helping consumers make good decisions that will make them happy. "Money back guarantees" long ago replaced *caveat emptor* as the prevailing ethic of consumer retailing. Competition between different firms ensures that customer dissatisfaction is unlikely to emerge as a long-run equilibrium outcome. Instead, those that fail to satisfy their customer's preferences will be driven out of the market.

To reiterate, the self-interest of profit-maximizing businesses, urged on by competition, is the most powerful force yet invented to help consumers make satisfying choices. A firm whose customers constantly feel under-served is begging for a competitor to come in and take their business. And in a real-life, dynamic, evolving economy, this is just what happens. For example, Netflix arose in part as a market solution to the excessive number of late fees charged by the then-dominant firm Blockbuster. Blockbuster relied on these late fees to generate sufficient revenue for the firm and its "profits were highly dependent on penalizing its patrons."[7] Focusing on whether the practice was unfair or exploitive of underlying consumer bias misses the larger point of the market's ability to improve its own choice architecture. By providing a service that eschewed these fees, Netflix has replaced Blockbuster as the dominant firm with the latter company exiting the market altogether in 2010.

Simply put, markets demonstrate a tendency toward improving choice architecture in order to increase consumer satisfaction. The reason this isn't recognized is that the process for this is complex, often unintended, and not confined to the choices of one or even a handful of people. It is instead the product of countless choices by both firms and consumers to improve their well-being. Furthermore, this process is unplanned, so it is only in hindsight that we can see which market innovations have led to better choices. This may not seem as blatant as government-imposed nudgemaking but is in fact a more durable, naturally occurring process. It may be true that firms would like to systematically exploit consumer biases if they could; it is also true that McDonald's would like to charge $20 for a hamburger if they could. The reason why they generally do not isn't because of the paternalistic beneficence of the seller but rather the ruthless forces of competition that forces them to help, not exploit, their custom-ers to make choices that will make them happy.

BE, by contrast, rests on a contrary view of market competition. Rather than a competition to satisfy consumer demand, BE frequently views mar-ket processes as a competition to see which business can best exploit the alleged biases of their customers.[8] From hidden fees to low-quality goods, consumers are seen as little more than lambs to the slaughter to be "used by more sophisticated parties to take consumers' money without giving value in return."[9] In this model there would seem to be little room for firms to take actions that improve consumer decision-making.

Despite its novelty in the policy realm, however, the intervention-ist arguments of behavioral economists are not fundamentally different from earlier generations of paternalistic arguments for intervention based on alleged market failures that harmed consumers. Concerns over market power, asymmetric information, and consumer impulsivity have long motivated arguments for regulation. But others have recognized that many of these supposed market "failures" have also produced a demand for market "solutions"—such as disruptive technology, advertising, repeat dealing, and branding to name a few—that ameliorate or eliminate these theoretical market failures in the real world. Treating consumers fairly, it turns out, usually makes good business sense.

Essential to this approach, however, is the understanding of markets as a dynamic process of discovery, a fluid process of experimentation and search in a world of uncertainty and creativity. Consumers are not passive—even if they make mistakes, they tend to correct those mistakes over time. Moreover, many supposed choices that are deemed mistakes by BE theorists may in fact be rational, given a consumer's particular preferences and constraints. Before arrogating power to steer consumer decisions by manipulating their choice architecture, the new generation of policymakers must make sure that they are actually making consumers better off in the short run and not shutting down a beneficial process of discovery over the long run.

To illustrate how markets improve their own choice architecture, we will provide examples of various consumer financial products that already incorporate some form of unrecognized private nudging. Credit cards, mortgages, and other basic banking services like overdraft protection are particularly rife with examples of this. Our framework helps organize and provide clarity to numerous consumer financial products in a way that challenges current regulatory practices by illuminating the beneficial order already provided by markets. We will also examine some examples of efforts by government regulators to create regulatory nudges that have displaced the existing choice architecture to determine whether central planning of nudges tends to produce better results for consumers than those evolved by the marketplace.

BEHAVIORAL BIAS IN AN EVOLVING, ECOLOGICALLY RATIONAL LANDSCAPE

The beneficence of markets is something that has and likely always will be a topic of dispute. For many decades arguments against the free market have been levied on the grounds of market failure.[10] Characteristics like asymmetric information, externalities, and non-excludability have all been invoked to question whether markets truly allocate effectively. Taken to the extreme, any market not displaying conditions of perfect competition is susceptible to failure. After all, it is always possible to advance a strong claim by assuming the conclusion. The difficulty with this position, of course, is that it posits markets as working only when conditions are unrealistic, thus ruling out effectiveness by assumption, not by demonstrated empirical relevance.

BE makes much the same critique of markets but from a different angle. Rather than challenge institutions, the behavioral approach challenges the individual's rationality. Put another way, if perfect competition is an unrealistic assumption, so surely is that of perfect rationality on the part of consumers. So, much like the market failure argument, behavioralists utilize a neoclassical characterization of markets as a foil for its critique. Invoking biases like loss aversion, confirmation bias, and anchoring effects, this approach shows that consumers are likely to err in their decision-making in ways that markets may not correct for; indeed they may even exploit them.

The policy conclusions that emerge from this perspective are largely interventionist, though not always as heavy-handed as the older market failure perspective. For example, soft paternalism as presented in the popular book *Nudge* claims that biases can be rectified with simple solutions like changing default choices, contextualizing information for consumers, and providing fewer though more pointed choices.[11] Other theorists support stronger forms of intervention, however, that eliminate certain services altogether.[12] This hard paternalism is more reminiscent of the broader market failure approach. In addition, the coherence of the "soft paternalism" of nudging has been called into question—if central planners supposedly know enough to create efficient "nudges" for consumers, it seems like a slippery slope to compulsion if consumers nevertheless persist in "erroneous" decision-making.[13] So while BE claims to recommend lighter-touch interventionism than traditional regulation, this is not necessarily clear in practice.

Although market failure and behavioral arguments share some differences, at root they share an important similarity: a belief that profit-maximizing firms operating in a competitive market will be unable to address these problems (or might even exploit them), therefore requiring government intervention. But at least with respect to traditional market failure arguments like asymmetric information, economists have long recognized that profit-maximizing firms operating in a competitive market

[handwritten margin notes: "again look", "to mkt", "for lemons"]

have incentives to voluntarily provide information that will improve consumer decision-making, and thereby, consumer welfare. Common market practices like advertising, investments in name brands, money-back guarantees, and the constraints of repeat dealing and reputation all serve, at least in part, to benefit the consumer.[14]

For all these reasons, the benefits of maintaining a good reputation typically outweigh any advantage that a seller can receive from ripping off consumers in the short run. So, for example, when a recent Consumer Financial Protection Bureau (CFPB) survey of consumers asked what they would do if they felt that their credit card issuer had mistreated them, the majority (57 %) said that they would simply cancel their card.[15] Given the implicit power that consumers hold to take their business elsewhere, it is little wonder that according to the data of one mid-sized bank, some two-thirds of complaints by consumers about bank fees are resolved in the consumers' favor, resulting in the refunding of millions of dollars every year to customers.[16] Competition and the threat of loss of repeat business are powerful forces for treating customers fairly irrespective of the seller's purported greater sophistication.

Furthermore, markets can improve choice architecture in ways that government cannot. For example, as discussed below, private advertising was much more effective at educating the public regarding the health benefits of dietary fiber than years of government public service announcements and other educational efforts.[17] Moreover, credible third parties, such as *Consumer Reports* magazine or Underwriter's Laboratory accreditation, can provide still further information to consumers regarding product quality.[18] The fact that many consumers voluntarily pay attention to and are willing to pay for those third-party certification services illustrates that they are aware of their limited knowledge and act to try to correct it before making purchase decisions.

So while the behavioral approach provides insight into the difficulties of making strictly rational choices, its characterization of the market is just as wrongheaded as the older market failure approach it so closely resembles. Left to these approaches, the market would seem to be a fragile edifice on which exchange totters back and forth between sophisticated sellers and exploited consumers. Such an ineffective mechanism would seem to ill-serve its billions of everyday users. What this approach fails to address, though, is how markets have survived for so long as tools of human enterprise if they are in fact ineffective at getting people what they need. Discovering just how humans make their choices does nothing to diminish the fact that markets have been—and likely always will be—utilized to coordinate those who wish to truck, barter, and exchange.

We believe the challenges made against markets have more to do with the background assumptions of the behavioralist, who sees any erring from perfection as an opportunity to tinker with highly complex market institutions.[19] We contend that such a notion only recognizes order when in a controllable form. In this way, behavioralists are no better than their neoclassical counterparts. Finding people coordinating all by themselves— "in the wild" no less, as one prominent behavioral law and economics article put it[20]—only confirms the prior assumption that people left to their own devices are incapable of making beneficial choices, and hence is prima facie evidence of being ripe for tinkering. If instead the market is the product of an evolutionary, unguided process, then it's not surprising that it little resembles the telltale fantasies of neoclassical theory. And though it is unplanned, the market is far from ineffective in getting people what they want. It coordinates among agents in a way that not only allows for but relies on people's underlying biases. After all, it has grown up around them for thousands of years, long before behavioralists made the scene.

What we must distinguish is the difference between what is known by the behavioralist and what is known by those engaging in trade. Nobel prize winner and prominent experimentalist, Vernon Smith, provides an insightful comparison between these two perspectives of organizing human behavior: Constructive and Ecological Rationality.[21] As has been noted elsewhere, constructive rationality in effect limits itself by not allowing for greater complexity than can be achieved by human design.[22] Put another way, this perspective demands the same market conditions as would be necessary for someone to understand the market environment in its totality. But we know from simple introspection that such knowledge is not just elusive but impossible to acquire. Leonard Read's classic essay *I, Pencil* demonstrates that no single person or organization even has the knowledge required to construct something as simple as a pencil from scratch, much less a comprehensive understanding of the market structure needed to create and deliver this product.[23]

So how do markets function then? As our examples above demonstrate, the information market participants need is far more manageable than what is needed to understand them in their totality. Far from complete, information is instead localized to what Friedrich Hayek termed the "man on the spot."[24] Each person in their own limited capacity contributes to the operation of the market by lending his or her knowledge and abilities by, for example, knowing the market price of certain economics textbooks. While any one individual contribution is not likely to matter much, the total contribution matters quite a bit. Furthermore, individual actions lead to dispersed knowledge moving through the marketplace like electricity through a network. So what one person understands about a particular product helps in part to inform the market as a whole.

Economists, Pauline Ippolito and Alan Mathios, studied the role of advertising in educating consumers about the health benefits of dietary fiber.[25] It was known for several years that a diet high in fiber generated substantial health benefits. Yet it wasn't until Quaker Oats began an advertising campaign aimed at persuading consumers to purchase its oatmeal that general awareness of the health benefits of dietary fiber spread. Not only did this advertising campaign lead to an increase in the amount of fiber in American's diets, it increased the general public awareness of the benefits of dietary fiber. Moreover, Quaker Oats advertising campaign was particularly effective at reaching and improving the knowledge among lower-income families regarding the health benefits of fiber.

To summarize our framework, rather than a fixed strategy environment among perfectly (or imperfectly) rational agents as depicted from the constructive perspective, we argue the market instead resembles more what Vernon Smith labels an ecologically rational environment among locally informed persons that allows for multiple strategies (indeed an endless amount) played out among these different individuals over time. Few businesses can prosper by making one-time sales to consumers; most successful businesses rely on repeat dealing with consumers to thrive over the long run. Moreover, the effects of repeat dealing are magnified through the consideration of reputational constraints, as consumers who have good or bad experiences share those experiences with others, thereby persuading others to purchase or not purchase the products. What survives in this environment is likely to enhance, not hinder, choice. Obstacles that prohibit individuals from engaging in meaningful exchange, such as constant exploitation of the consumer's underlying bias, would lead to suboptimal outcomes over time. How this would survive in a dynamic environment largely defined by the individuals themselves is a challenge that behavioralists need to meet on an empirical level.

We provide our own view on why consumer products have survived below, by first examining a number of market nudges in the area of consumer finance that serve to prod individuals in their preferred direction (the good). What makes these features so remarkable is that they are rarely even noticed. This is part of their advantage. If noticed, they would likely not serve well as nudges. In fact, many of the features of the market that behavioralists lament (the bad) actually serve as useful nudges to market participants. With that said, a number of market nudges are not the product of firms competing to retain customers but instead represent policies imposed at the insistence of government policy (the ugly). These distort market outcomes in ways that are not likely to be in the consumer's best interest.

To be clear, we are not making the claim that all government nudges are faulty, only that many that have been designed to improve consumer welfare have instead reduced it for a number of incentive-related reasons we have detailed elsewhere.[26] In contrast, we show by example how profit-seeking firms act as if they are seeking to improve the consumer's choice architecture in a manner that enables consumers to improve their own welfare. In particular, we will argue that not only do markets often provide "nudges" that tend to improve consumer decision-making, but that in general market nudges are more likely to be effective at improving consumer welfare than nudges designed by policymakers. Or, to put the point more accurately, the decentralized, dynamic, discovery process of the market is more likely to generate welfare-improving nudges than the static, central-planning mindset of government bureaucrats seeking to construct nudges. Through a process of trial and error, consumer learning, and dynamic competition, markets tend to converge on the mix of products, services, and prices that maximize consumer welfare. And—crucially—as part of that process, sellers as well as consumers have incentives to seek to minimize the frequency and costs of the errors that they make.

MARKET NUDGES: THE GOOD, THE BAD, AND THE UGLY

Market nudges would seem almost a misnomer given how often behavioralists link nudging with market intervention. Nevertheless, the concept itself—that is, manipulating choice architecture to improve consumer outcomes—is something the market does every day. Better-served customers translate into greater profit opportunities. As a consequence, there are countless untold examples of these features.   We will focus on examples that vividly illustrate the market nudge concept in the domain of consumer finance, an area that has attracted a great deal of attention from behavioralists.

The chief outlet for behavioral interventions in this area is the CFPB which was established in reaction to the 2008–2010 financial crisis. The CFPB is formally advised by a group of behavioralists, including *Nudge* co-author Richard Thaler.[27] It has intervened in a wide variety of consumer credit markets including credit card services, bank mortgages, student loans, auto lending, and payday loans among others.[28] The CFPB ostensibly seeks to redress underlying behavioral biases by changing choice architecture in the marketplace. According to their website, "The Consumer Financial Protection Bureau (CFPB) is a 21st century agency that helps consumer finance markets work by making rules more effective, by consistently and fairly enforcing those rules, and by empowering consumers to take more control over their economic lives."[29]

As we will show, the CFPB intervenes in a market already filled with nudges. There are those created by private forces ("the Good"), those vilified by behavioralists ("the Bad"), and those created by government interventions ("the Ugly"). By comparing these categories of nudges, we hope to shed light on how choice architecture is improved by markets already and why public nudging is more problematic than behavioralists believe.

is this characterization fair ?

"The Good"

You may have noticed when withdrawing your money at an ATM that the machine releases your card before giving you your cash. This would seem out of order. Wouldn't it make more sense to give you your card back once the transaction is complete? It can even be a nuisance as you may want to make another transaction after withdrawing money which means you have to put your card in all over again. Before deciding "there ought to be a nudge!" to improve this clear market imperfection, consider just what sort of behavioral bias is common among bank customers. Customers withdrawing cash are often in a hurry and the most salient part of the exchange is receiving the money, not reclaiming the card. But leaving the card behind means at the very least ordering a new one and, at worst, possible identity theft by the next customer in line.

So how have banks responded? By nudging customers to take their card before releasing their cash, banks ensure that customers in a rush are not inconvenienced by a lost card. While this may cause frustration for those who wish to engage in additional transactions after withdrawing their cash, customers as a whole are better off. This example may seem simple and not very impressive in its scope but consider that the market is filled with helpful nudges like this. Do banks do this out of a paternalistic concern for their customers? It seems unlikely. Instead, the likely explanation is that consumer errors (such as forgetting an ATM card) are expensive for both the consumer *and* the bank. When a consumer forgets his or her ATM card, the bank must take steps to retrieve the card and reissue it to consumers, as well as any additional security issues that may arise from a missing ATM card. Out of self-interest, a profit-maximizing bank has adopted practices that appear to be a consumer-centered nudge.

Consumer use of debit cards provides another example of what some behavioralists might consider a pro-consumer nudge. The existence of debit cards—much less their extraordinary popularity—is inexplicable to orthodox behavioral law and economics scholars. For example, writing in 2006, Professor Oren Bar-Gill predicted that because of the comparative advantage of credit cards in exploiting consumer behavioral biases (such as the so-called optimism bias), "without regulatory help [issuers of debit cards could] expect only limited success vis-à-vis the credit card."[30] This prediction that debit cards would never become a major market presence, which was compelled by the logic of BE, has proven spectacularly wrong. Indeed, even at the time that Bar-Gill made the statement in 2006, debit cards had already overtaken credit cards in terms of transaction volume and have only continued their explosive growth in the decade since.[31]

The growth in debit cards came about with no regulatory interventions designed to subsidize them. Instead, they came about because of competition and consumer choice. There are myriad theories why consumers use debit cards instead of credit cards. In some instances, it appears explicable by rational choice theory—thus, those who revolve credit card balances are more likely to use debit cards than those who pay off their credit card balances every month.[32] Others have argued that it is best explained by various mental accounting models of consumers who distinguish between transactions that they prefer to make out of current funds via a debit card (such as gasoline and groceries) versus those that they see appropriate to finance with credit (such as purchasing consumer durables or vacation travel). Regardless, far from refusing to offer debit cards to consumers, banks have eagerly put debit cards in consumers' hands, even creating rewards programs comparable to credit card rewards programs in order to induce greater use.[33] This widespread enthusiasm for banks to spur debit card use for consumers, especially by offering rewards and the like, has "nudged" some consumers toward greater use of debit cards.

One area in which the market is particularly good at nudging is with information retrieval. People are notoriously bad at filtering large amounts of information and are alleged by behavioral scholars to be susceptible to numerous biases due to framing effects, short attention spans, and confirmation of their prior beliefs.[34] So it would make sense that firms would put certain fail-safes in place to avoid negative outcomes, both with their customers and employees. An example that nudges the former group involves the use of credit scores. Firms regularly draw on credit score information of their customers even when it's not entirely clear why a score is needed. One possibility for this practice is that a credit score serves to undermine any confirmatory bias the lending agent may have in approving services. Dealing with a personal account can create favorable impressions that mask underlying issues with the customer's true reliability. Relying on outside objective measurements can offset this bias and thereby reduce losses for the financial institution by not making unsafe loans.[35]

And of course outside measurement tools are not just for firms. Think of all the rating websites available to consumers such as Amazon, Carfax, Angie's List, Rotten Tomatoes, yelp, and so on. By aggregating and distributing an enormous quantity of information in a simple, accessible form, these firms provide greater choice architecture for everyone. We should note that even the CFPB has gotten in on the act with their own database of consumer complaints, though whether its purpose is to inform consumers or simply a way to hold leverage over financial firms remains an open question.

"The Bad"

We next examine market practices that behavioralists point to as examples of nudges gone awry. We offer reasons why even some of the most vilified practices are more likely to offset the customer's prior behavioral bias than take advantage of it. One category of products behavioralists are particularly hostile to is so-called "shrouded fees," which encompass any and all products that serve as add-ons to primary products like car purchases, credit cards, and so on. An example of an add-on product that has been challenged by behavioralists is credit life insurance.[36] The way this service works is if the customer dies before finishing payment on a loan, the insurance company will pay the remaining balance. Behavioralists claim that much like overdraft protection, this service is inordinately expensive relative to alternatives like general life insurance, which would cover any and all liabilities at the time of death.

Once again, however, we must think about the nature of the program, given that people are behaviorally biased, and not just ignorant of more attractive alternatives. While it's true that an insurance product like this would benefit sellers, the service can still be quite beneficial for buyers. In fact, this is what a randomly controlled survey of households conducted by the Federal Reserve demonstrated. The Fed authors report, "It seems that the marketplace offers consumers a choice concerning the purchase of debt protection products and consumers exercise that choice as part of their financial decisions about borrowing. While there may be abusive practices among some lenders who operate outside the realm of ethical behavior with respect to the sale of debt protection products, survey evidence suggests that, in the views of consumers, such behavior is not the norm."[37]

Purchasing add-on insurance products is also a relatively low-cost means of signaling risk aversion to the insurance firm and can generate reduced insurance premiums as firms are able to estimate costs, and to some extent, minimize their liability in the event of casualty. Furthermore, it represents a specific obvious benefit to the consumer. While comprehensive life insurance could potentially take care of this liability and in some cases at lower cost, we cannot simply assume that consumers have access to or can afford these alternatives.

Now let's turn to the much-vilified banking service, overdraft protection. When a person overdrafts her account, the bank will supply the necessary funds to cover the transaction, but for a fixed fee. Customers can utilize this overdraft service or if they prefer (and if available) link their checking account to an additional savings account or credit line. Some customers use this service quite often. In fact, heavy users, which we will define as those using the service ten times or more in a year, provided about two-thirds of the overall revenue collected by banks for this service.[38]

Some critics feel these users are being exploited by the overdraft system and demand that banks reduce fees. In recognition of this, in 2010 the Federal Reserve required that all banks change the default option to no overdraft protection, forcing those who wish to use the service to explicitly say so. The result, unsurprisingly, was that three times the number of heavy users explicitly signed up for the service compared to normal users.[39] Put another way, it should come as no surprise to the rest of us that those who more heavily rely on the service would want to utilize it. The behavioral response has been a call for hard paternalism by prohibiting banks from providing customers with this service.[40]

The BE criticism of default rules regarding overdraft protection demonstrates the dangers of displacing the ecologically rational, market-evolved rule (opt-out from overdraft protection) with the constructively rational, centrally planned rule (opt-in for point-of-sale debit card transactions and ATM transactions and opt out for checks and recurring debit card payments). The fact is that most consumers effectively "opt out" of overdraft protection by simply not overdrawing their account—the overwhelming majority of bank consumers never or rarely overdraft their accounts, including a majority of low-balance accounts.[41] In addition, we should note that the transaction costs of banks trying to contact consumers to get them to opt-in are much more difficult than for consumers to opt-out. When the rules were changed, banks had to make multiple phone calls and contacts to consumers to gain their consent to opt-in to overdraft protection. Even if a majority of consumers were to opt-out, it would still be much less expensive in total terms to retain the market rule of opt-out than the much more expensive opt-in regime.

More generally, the reality of overdraft protection shows the dangers of setting rules by the intuitions of government central planners rather than decentralized market processes. In particular, although the Federal Reserve conducted consumer research in establishing the default rules for overdraft protection, the answers to questions depend very heavily on the phrasing of the question. For example, according to one survey of consumers, when consumers were asked whether they would ever want access to overdraft protection, a small majority said "yes."[42] But when they were asked whether they would want access to overdraft protection *in an emergency*, an overwhelming majority said yes. In short, faced with the non-contextual question of overdraft protection generally, consumers had difficulty anticipating the circumstances under which they might want access to overdraft protection. But when prompted by an unusual situation that they might not have considered, consumers overwhelmingly recognized the value of access to the product. By making overdraft protection opt-out instead of opt-in, banks appeared to be nudging consumers toward the decision that they would make if they were fully informed and could anticipate all of the possible scenarios under which they might overdraw their accounts but might not make if they had limited information and attention at the time of opening their account.[43]

The trouble with all this is that in making it more difficult for consumers to gain access to overdraft protection, regulators can impose disproportionately large costs on certain groups of consumers. Those who use overdraft protection frequently do so because they have limited credit options and overdraft protection is frequently the least-expensive and most-convenient source of short-term liquidity available. Many consumers rely on overdraft protection to be able to afford products that are arguably necessities, such as groceries, fuel, and insurance payments.[44] These are hardly superfluous expenditures by uninformed persons. Those who want to "nudge" consumers away from overdraft protection—or still worse prohibit the product altogether—have focused only on the costs of overdraft protection and entirely ignored the benefits, that is, the ability to put food on the table and gas in the car without resorting to less preferred sources of credit. For many heavy users of overdraft protection, the next-best alternative available is a payday loan, bounced check, or late payment, all of which can be more expensive, especially in the long run. Moreover, the government's preferred nudge rule seemed to have little basis in the real world. For example, according to the experience of one bank, when it was forced to adopt the rule of "opt-in" for ATM transactions, some 95 % of customers who were confronted with an insufficient funds notice when they sought to make an ATM transaction consented to opt in.[45] The bank's default rule again appeared to be more consistent with expressed consumer preferences than the government's mandated default rule.

Another recent credit practice condemned by the CFPB is Marketing Services Agreements (MSAs), which establish a preexisting relationship between realtors and certain credit institutions. The idea is that upon processing a real estate sale, the broker would identify the credit institution as a preferred lender and encourage the buyer to work with this particular lender in financing the home. The CFPB has described this practice as an underhanded means of generating kickbacks to realtors. The claim is that realtors make deals with credit institutions that may not be the best fit for the future homeowner but promote them anyway based on the preexisting MSA.[46]

Note first of course that "best" is not a quality that can be defined by the CFPB. It can only be defined by the consumer. Furthermore, in the case of mortgage loans, the typical consumer is unlikely to have the prior knowledge necessary to discern between different loan agreements, much less different mortgage companies altogether. Government reporting requirements have been used to make these comparisons more easily. Further, household names like Bank of America can help provide certain reputational information. Still, boundedly rational consumers are surely at a disadvantage. This means that realtors have an opportunity to provide additional support to their clients in the form of credit referrals. It's possible that these recommendations could occur without the underlying MSAs. But then how would the realtor identify which institutions are optimal for their clients? They could simply do the research themselves and charge the client accordingly. But this of course entails additional costs on top of the home purchase. Plus, even a proactive realtor can only know so much about the real competency of an outside firm.

Although it is conceivably possible that MSA relationships between realtors and lenders are merely sophisticated schemes to cheat consumers, a more-beneficent alternative explanation is readily available: MSAs are a service provided by the realtor to reduce the costs to the home purchaser of finding a mortgage at a competitive rate and with high-quality service. In exchange for the stream of referrals provided by the realtor to the lender, the lender essentially promises to provide high-quality service and a good price. If the lender does not do so, the reputational damage will effect not just the lender but the realtor as well. Thus, the realtor has a strong incentive to ensure that the lender is providing quality service to its customers. In return, the stream of referrals provides a form of credible commitment from the broker to the realtor that high-quality service will be forthcoming.[47] Whereas the malign scenario rests on the idea that the realtor and broker can conspire to fleece consumers over and over again, the beneficent scenario proposes the arrangement as a value-increasing mechanism for reducing the cost and hassle to consumers of finding home financing at a competitive rate and with minimal search costs. An incompetent firm could conceivably pay for the service as well. But then what would happen once they failed to provide for the realtor's customers? This could potentially damage the realtor's reputation, resulting in a termination of the MSA and a loss of any goodwill engendered by the agreement. Knowing this, only a lender serious in gaining clients would contract with the realtor, as a charlatan business would only meet with rejection once the realtor found out their customers were being ill-treated.

"The Ugly"

Not all nudges are the result of private enterprise. While the application of BE to the policy realm is in its infancy, the CFPB has been aggressive in taking action in consumer credit markets. Furthermore, we should note that historical policies aimed at behavioral change offer insight into what can emerge from public nudging, even if these policymakers were unaware of the later contributions from BE.

One of the earliest examples of government-induced market nudges occurred in response to the Great Depression, when a number of federal subsidies and programs were created to extend the payment period for long-term mortgages. Prior to this period, long-term mortgages were typically paid within a 10- to –15-year period with a large upfront deposit and balloon payment at the end. Policymakers felt at the time that reducing the monthly burden of payments would help generate much-needed growth.[48] Moreover, fixed-rate mortgages create waves of refinancing activity as interest rates adjust, creating mortgage market instability and increasing the prepayment risks for banks.

Regardless of its short-term effects on increasing home ownership,[49] the long-term result of this policy was to create the standard 30-year, fixed-rate mortgage that dominates the US mortgage market. This effort to nudge consumers toward the 30-year fixed-rate mortgage has proven quite problematic for consumers and the economy. The persistence of the 30-year fixed-rate mortgage is especially inexplicable given the pivotal role it played in precipitating the savings and loan (S & L) crisis of the 1980s. Forced to raise capital through short-term consumer deposit accounts and lend for long-term 30-year fixed-rate mortgages, the interest rate mismatch that precipitated the S & L catastrophe was virtually inevitable. And eventually, the high-inflation period of the 1970s precipitated the savings and loan crisis on precisely this factor.[50]

Yet despite this catastrophe caused by the dominance of the 30-year fixed-rate mortgage, policymakers persisted in artificially maintaining its privileged position in the US mortgage market through the intervention of Fannie Mae and Freddie Mac. Yet it is hard to see how consumers in general benefit from being nudged into this product. After all, consumers must pay a premium—frequently a large premium of over 100 basis points—in order to obtain a fixed-rate mortgage.[51] This is because the consumer must compensate the financial institution for holding the risk of a fixed-rate asset for a full 30 years, an exceedingly long period for a financial instrument. Yet the average American owns his or her home (and hence mortgage) only about five years on average. Thus, the consumer is being nudged to buy 30 years of interest rate insurance, when it is likely that for the average consumer a five- or ten-year fixed-rate period (and hence a lower risk premium) would be optimal. For many consumers, the cost of this government nudge can amount to hundreds of dollars per month in higher monthly mortgage payments. Moreover, empirical evidence indicates that consumers typically choose wisely in deciding between fixed- and adjustable-rate mortgages, based on their individual level of risk tolerance and expected duration of holding the mortgage.[52]

As the last financial crisis demonstrated, the dependence on the 30-year fixed-rate mortgage not only harms many consumers who pay an implicit premium for unnecessary long-term interest rate insurance, it also increases economic instability during periods of falling housing prices. When the Federal Reserve pushed down interest rates to record-low levels, only those consumers with equity in their homes were able to refinance. Those who were underwater (owed more than the home was worth) were trapped in higher interest rates and unable to take advantage of the Fed's intervention. At the peak of the housing bust it was estimated that over 20 % of home-owners were underwater, often by tens of thousands of dollars—and hence unable to refinance if they held fixed-rate mortgages because refinancing would have required them to bring the difference to the closing table. In addition, even if they could refinance these distressed homeowners would have been required to come up with thousands of dollars of liquid funds to refinance. As a result, the Federal Reserve's extraordinary interventions did little to stabilize the housing market because of the limited ability of homeowners to act. By contrast, although many countries in Europe suffered housing bubbles comparable to that in the USA, their foreclosure rates were typically a fraction of those here, due in some part to the greater ability that banks had to push down mortgage interest rates as a result of the dominance of adjustable-rate mortgages in Europe. Nudging American consumers toward 30-year self-amortizing, mortgages with an unlimited right to prepay not only harmed many consumers by pushing them into higher interest rate loans than appropriate but also contributed to the depth of the mortgage crisis in the USA.

A similar outcome emerges when policymakers close off services that cater to low-income consumers. A perpetual adversary of supposed consumer advocates is payday lending. With its high interest rates and potential for revolving service periods, the efficacy of this service is constantly called into question. Consumer advocates believe that, rather than providing a service, payday lending really just captures the poor in a never-ending cycle of debt and hardship due to the terms of the loan. Based on this logic, in Spring 2015 the CFPB suggested that it was going to begin a new rule making on payday lending that would require lenders paternalistically to establish the borrower's "ability to repay" the payday advance before making the loan. It is estimated that if the rule is eventually adopted it would reduce the revenues of the payday lenders by over 80 % on average.[53] Moreover, by reducing access to payday loans, the rule will force many payday loan customers into greater use of bank overdraft protection, installment loans that require them to borrow larger principal amounts for longer periods of time, or late bill payments. Rather than attempt to nudge consumers, policymakers believe that removing the service altogether is in the consumer's best interest.

This exposes the dark side of public nudging. Once a product or service is considered *non gratis*, policymakers quickly move from subtly changing choice architecture to outright elimination of the service, as suggested by the rapid rush to impose prohibitions on overdraft protection. After all, if the service can only do harm, wouldn't removing it completely be the most effective means of increasing consumer benefits? This would be accurate if true. Unfortunately, policymakers rarely, if ever, conduct the kinds of empirical investigation needed to meet the evidentiary burden of determining that a service is in most cases ineffective and harmful to consumers.

Surveys of payday loan customers show that they, on average, are capable of accurately anticipating whether they will roll over their balances or not and how long it will take them to pay off their loan.[54] Payday loan customers also are acutely aware of the cost of payday loans, as one survey found that approximately 98 % of payday loan customers knew the finance charge of their most recent payday loan.[55] Finally, those who use payday loans do so because, despite their cost, they are often less-expensive than available alternatives such as overdraft protection, bounced checks, and pawn shops. Coupled with the fact that most customers report being satisfied with the service as a source of short-term credit[56], it's unclear *ex ante* why the service is obviously harmful. It's true that more attractive credit products are available to some consumers, especially to those who engage in academic scholarship or government service. But the alternatives open to payday lending customers are few.[57]

Credit cards have also been the subject of behaviorally inspired government nudges that have backfired. For example, in 2009 Congress enacted the Credit CARD Act, which imposed new limits on the pricing of credit card terms (such as certain fees) and restricted the ability of credit card issuers to adjust interest rates and other terms when a borrower's risk profile changed. The law largely codified existing Federal Reserve regulations that had been proposed and then become final the year before. Behavioral scholars have endorsed the law, claiming that it eliminated so-called hidden, "non-salient," or "shrouded" fees that credit card issuers used to exploit consumers.[58] Empirical studies of the effects of the Federal Reserve rules and the CARD Act, however, have found that their combined effects have proved disastrous for consumers.[59] Interest rates for all cardholders rose and the cost of other fees increased. In addition, credit card ownership decreased, especially for lower-income families, and credit lines were reduced for many cardholders. In short, by intervening to regulate certain terms, the CFPB made credit cards more expensive and less available, forcing many lower-income consumers to rely on payday lending to make ends meet.

PUBLIC VERSUS PRIVATE NUDGES

We have showcased a number of nudges from different variations of private and public influence. Not everyone will agree with our choice of nudges or in how we present them. Surely there are some government nudges that can lead to better outcomes. For example, the Behavioral Insights Team (or Nudge Unit) within the UK cabinet has provided valuable insight into issues like collecting late court fees and how people respond to government documents.[60] And can we really say that all market nudges are beneficial? Even the strongest market proponent would wince at the actuarial terms of certain extended warranties.[61] Clearly we should not rule either of these scenarios out.

At the same time, we wish to highlight the most likely scenarios given the institutional differences between market and political mechanisms. A firm that tries to exploit its customers with private nudges on an ongoing basis can only afford to do so under a very narrow set of market conditions. At a minimum, such firms would need market power to ward off competitive pressures. Competing companies will undermine any such effort in the long run by either providing better quality services or gaining market share by pointing out the exploitive efforts of its rival, as happened with our introductory example of Netflix running Blockbuster out of business.

Furthermore, market actors are more likely to be on the lookout for and adhere to feedback from consumers than their government counterparts. What reason does a bureaucrat have to acknowledge potential pitfalls of a nudge gone awry or alternatives that better utilize market forces when given a mandate from higher authority? By comparison, market nudges that harm consumers generate direct, negative feedback to firms who bear the cost of their choices. Firms that do not use nudges appropriately are likely to lose market share to those who do.

We showed above how government nudgers that do listen to negative feedback are likely to utilize stronger tactics in response. After all, negative feedback does not necessarily mean that the original goal is mistaken, and again policymakers have less incentive to reexamine their given mandate than their market counterparts. As a consequence, "the ugly" turns uglier. We see this with calls to ban overdraft services for certain consumers or the removal of payday lending services in some states. We also see this with add-on products as the CFPB has vilified a number of practices regarding mortgage services, credit card products, and banking fees.

Finally, market participants engage in iterated exchanges with one another at a far greater rate than do consumers and government. An agency may only engage in a policy review twice a year. Markets have the advantage of gathering feedback on a daily basis. Nudges or other strategies can be evaluated and altered according to this feedback much more often than can government policy. As we noted above, the nudges that work the best won't even be observed by consumers. This is much more likely to happen with the receipt of constant feedback and adaptation, two qualities in which markets excel over government.

More important than comparisons of private and public changes to choice architecture, however, is the recognition of how the market functions. Construing the market as a planned and plannable landscape distorts the reality that none of us is capable of fully comprehending such a complex social order. We at best can make marginal changes that may or may not improve the overall landscape. Therefore, we are best served when recognizing the natural limits of our action and what mechanisms will be most effective in generating greater consumer well-being.

As we have explained, this is most likely to occur when market participants have repeated exchanges that allow for lots of feedback and adaptation that ensure only the most competent firms will continue to serve consumers. Any attempts to alter this natural landscape from policymaking risks distorting outcomes in unintended and unappreciated ways. Removing whole credit services from the marketplace rarely affects the person or persons responsible for their removal. But consumers of the products can face devastating consequences with little recourse to changing policy goals.

Indeed, by not allowing for alternative explanations of behavior, policymakers render themselves impotent in dealing with consumer feedback. Any information that comes from "in the wild" will only be placed within the policymaker's prior beliefs on consumer rationality and the efficacy of markets. New information only serves then to confirm the goals already in place with the only change being how best to meet these goals, when instead policymakers should be evaluating the desirability and/or feasibility of the goals themselves.

To summarize, the marketplace is an ecological landscape in which complex, multifaceted strategies play out among imperfect persons. What emerges is a social order composed of plenty of rational and irrational elements. When we examine it as it is, rather than as we wish it would be, we can see plenty of evidence in its favor along with opportunities for positive change. To be most effective, though, these opportunities should be pursued in a way that accounts for the limits of human cognition, both by consumers and those who would instigate positive change. Only when working within the logical parameters of this social order can we hope to make it better.

NOTES

1. Kathryn Zeiler and Charles R. Plott, "The Willingness to Pay/ Willingness to Accept Gap, the Endowment Effect, Subject Misconceptions and Experimental Procedures for Eliciting Valuations," *American Economic Review* (2004).
2. *See* Joshua D. Wright and Douglas H. Ginsburg, "Behavioral Law and Economics: Its Origins, Fatal Flaws, and Implications for Liberty." *Northwestern University Law Review* 106 (2012): 1033.
3. Todd Zywicki, "The Behavioral Law and Economics of Fixed-Rate Mortgages (and Other Just-So Stories)," *Supreme Court Economic Review* 21(1) (2013): 157–214.
4. Adam Christopher Smith and Todd J. Zywicki, "Behavior, Paternalism, and Policy: Evaluating Consumer Financial Protection," *George Mason Law & Economics Research Paper* 14–05 (2014).
5. Ted Gayer and W. Kip Viscusi. "Overriding Consumer Preferences with Energy Regulations," *Journal of Regulatory Economics* 43(3) (2013): 248–264.
6. James M. Buchanan, "Natural and Artifactual Man," *What Should Economists Do* (1979): 93–112.
7. Greg Satell, "A Look Back At Why Blockbuster Really Failed and Why It Didn't Have To." *Forbes.com* (2014) http://www.forbes.com/sites/gregsatell/2014/09/05/a-look-back-at-why-blockbuster-really-failed-and-why-it-didnt-have-to/
8. Geoffrey A. Manne and Todd J. Zywicki, "Uncertainty, Evolution and Behavioral Economic Theory," *Journal of Law, Economics, and Policy* 10 (2013): 555.
9. Oren Bar-Gill and Elizabeth Warren, "Making Credit Safer," *University of Pennsylvania Law Review* (2008): 1–101, p. 7.

10. Joshua D. Wright, "The Antitrust/Consumer Protection Paradox: Two Policies at War with Each Other," *Yale Law Journal, Forthcoming* (2012): 12–45.
11. Richard H. Thaler and Cass R. Sunstein, *Nudge* (Yale University Press, 2008).
12. Ryan Bubb and Richard H. Pildes, "How Behavioral Economics Trims Its Sails and Why," *Harvard Law Review* 127 (2014): 13–29.
13. Mario J. Rizzo and Douglas Glen Whitman, "Little Brother Is Watching You: New Paternalism on the Slippery Slopes," *Arizona Law Review* 51 (2009): 685.
14. *See* Benjamin Klein and Keith B. Leffler, "The Role of Market Forces in Assuring Contractual Performance," *Journal of Political Economy* 89 (1981): 615.
15. "Arbitration Study: Report to Congress." Consumer Financial Protection Bureau (2015): http://www.consumerfinance.gov/reports/arbitration-study-report-to-congress-2015/
16. *See* Jason Scott Johnston and Todd Zywicki, "The Consumer Financial Protection Bureau's Arbitration Study: A Summary and Critique" at p. 32. Mercatus Working Paper (August 2015), available at http://mercatus.org/publication/consumer-financial-protection-bureau-arbitration-study-summary-critique
17. *See* discussion *infra* at note 23, and accompanying text.
18. *See* Daniel B. Klein (ed.), Reputation: Studies in the Voluntary Elicitation of Good Conduct (1997).
19. Vernon L. Smith, "Method in Experiment: Rhetoric and Reality," *Experimental Economics* 5(2) (2002): 91–110.
20. Ryan Bubb and Richard H. Pildes, "How Behavioral Economics Trims Its Sails and Why," *Harvard Law Review* 127 (2014): 13–29.
21. Vernon L. Smith, "Constructivist and Ecological Rationality in Economics," *American Economic Review* (2003): 465–508.
22. Peter J. Boettke, W. Zachary Caceres, and Adam G. Martin, "Error Is Obvious, Coordination Is the Puzzle," in Roger Frantz and Robert Leeson (eds.), *Hayek and Behavioral Economics* (Palgrave-MacMillan, Forthcoming, 2012), 12–23.
23. Leonard E. Read, "I Pencil: My Family Tree, as Told to Leonard E. Read" (1958), available at http://www.econlib.org/library/Essays/rdPncl1.html
24. Friedrich August Hayek, "The Use of Knowledge in Society," *The American Economic Review* (1945): 519–530.

25. P. M. Ippolito and A. D. Mathios, "Information, Advertising, and Health Choices: A Study of the Cereal Market." in *Economics of Food Safety* (Springer Netherlands, 1991), 211–246.

26. Adam Christopher Smith and Todd J. Zywicki, "Behavior, Paternalism, and Policy: Evaluating Consumer Financial Protection," *George Mason Law & Economics Research Paper* 14-05 (2014).

27. *Treasury Department Announces Senior Leadership Hires for CFPB Implementation Team*, U.S. Dep't of the Treasury (December 15, 2010), available at skaddenpractices.skadden.com/cfs/attach.php?documentID=1750

28. Adam Christopher Smith and Todd J. Zywicki, "Behavior, Paternalism, and Policy: Evaluating Consumer Financial Protection," *New York University Journal of Law & Liberty* (2015).

29. Consumer Financial Protection Bureau, "About Us," http://www.consumerfinance.gov/the-bureau/

30. Oren Bar-Gill, "Seduction by Plastic," *Northwestern University Law Review* 98 (2003): 1373.

31. T. A. Durkin, G. Elliehausen, and T. J. Zywicki, "An Assessment of Behavioral Law and Economics Contentions and What We Know Empirically About Credit Card Use by Consumers," *Supreme Court Economic Review* 22 (January 2014): 1–54.

32. T. A. Durkin, G. Elliehausen, and T. J. Zywicki, "An Assessment of Behavioral Law and Economics Contentions and What We Know Empirically About Credit Card Use by Consumers," *George Mason Law & Economics Research Paper* (2014): 14–46.

33. Debit card reward programs, however, have largely disappeared in the wake of the Dodd-Frank financial reform legislation and particularly the so-called Durbin Amendment, which placed priced controls on debit card interchange fees. *See* Zywicki, Manne, and Morris, *Price Controls on Debit Card Interchange Fees: The U.S. Experience* cite.

34. Daniel Kahneman, *Thinking, Fast and Slow* (Macmillan, 2011).

35. See Geoffrey A. Manne and Todd J. Zywicki, "Uncertainty, Evolution, and Behavioral Economic Theory," *Journal of Law, Economics and Policy, Forthcoming* (2014): 14–04.

36. Tom Baker and Peter Siegelman, "'You Want Insurance with That?' Using Behavioral Economics to Protect Consumers from Add-on Insurance Products," *Connecticut Insurance Law Journal* 20 (2013): 13–1.

37. T. Durkin and G. Elliehausen, "Consumers and Debt Protection Products: Results of a New Consumer Survey," *Federal Reserve*

Bulletin 98(9) (2012). http://www.federalreserve.gov/pubs/bulletin/2012/pdf/consumer_debt_products_20121227.pdf

38. Ryan Bubb and Richard H. Pildes, "How Behavioral Economics Trims Its Sails and Why," *Harvard Law Review* 127 (2014): 13–29.

39. Ryan Bubb and Richard H. Pildes, "How Behavioral Economics Trims Its Sails and Why," *Harvard Law Review* 127 (2014): 13–29.

40. Lauren E. Willis, "When Nudges Fail: Slippery Defaults," *The University of Chicago Law Review* (2013): 1155–1229.

41. Todd J. Zywicki, "The Economics and Regulation of Bank Overdraft Protection," *Washington and Lee Law Review* 69 (2012): 1141.

42. "Design and Testing of Overdraft Disclosures: Phase Two." ICF Marco International, Inc. (2009). http://www.federalreserve.gov/newsevents/press/bcreg/bcreg20091112a4.pdf

43. As noted above, banks frequently grant refunds of assessed fees such as for occasional or inadvertent use of overdraft protection, which a consumer might also not be aware of at the time of opening the account. Again, the bank may have greater knowledge of its willingness to waive overdraft fees in the future than the consumer at the time of opening the account. More specifically, the bank refunded assessed overdraft fees in 63% of cases in which consumers requested a refund.

44. G. Michael Flores and Todd J. Zywicki, "Commentary: CFPB Study of Overdraft Programs," *George Mason Law & Economics Research Paper* 13–60 (2013).

45. Todd J. Zywicki, "The Economics and Regulation of Bank Overdraft Protection," *Washington and Lee Law Review* 69 (2012): 1141.

46. Mark Greene, "Play by the Rules of the CFPB Is Coming for You," *Forbes.com* (2015): http://www.forbes.com/sites/markgreene/2015/01/30/play-by-the-rules-or-the-cfpb-is-coming-for-you/

47. Oliver E. Williamson, "Credible Commitments: Using Hostages to Support Exchange," *The American Economic Review* (1983): 519–540.

48. See Todd Zywicki, "The Behavioral Law and Economics of Fixed-Rate Mortgages (and Other Just-So Stories)," *Supreme Court Economic Review* 21(1) (2013): 157–214.

49. Any effects from the policy were short term and transitional, of course, as the tax benefit from home ownership eventually became capitalized into the relative prices of owning and renting housing, so the long-term impact on home ownership was negligible. In fact, equilibrium home ownership rates in the USA do not differ significantly from those in similar countries elsewhere in the world.

50. Michael Lea and Anthony B. Sanders, "Government Policy and the Fixed-Rate Mortgage," *Annual Review of Financial Economics* 3(1) (2011): 223–234.
51. Todd Zywicki, "The Behavioral Law and Economics of Fixed-Rate Mortgages (and Other Just-So Stories)," *Supreme Court Economic Review* 21(1) (2013): 157–214.
52. Todd Zywicki, "The Behavioral Law and Economics of Fixed-Rate Mortgages (and Other Just-So Stories)," *Supreme Court Economic Review* 21(1) (2013): 157–214.
53. *See* Arthur Baines, Marsha Courchane, and Steli Stoianovici, "Economic Impact on Small Lenders of the Payday Lending Rules Under Consideration by the CFPB " (Prepared for: Community Financial Services Association of America Prepared by Charles River Associates), available at http://www.crai.com/sites/default/files/publications/ Economic-Impact-on-Small-Lenders-of-the-Payday-Lending-Rules- under-Consideration-by-the-CFPB.pdf (May 12, 2015).
54. Ronald Mann, "Assessing the Optimism of Payday Loan Borrowers," *Supreme Court Economic Review* 21(1) (2013): 105–132.
55. Gregory Elliehausen, An Analysis of Consumers' Use of Payday Loans 43 (Fin. Servs. Research Program, Monograph No. 41, 2009), available at http://www.cfsaa.com/portals/0/RelatedContent/Attachments/ GWUAnalysis_01-2009.pdf
56. Robert L. Clarke and Todd J. Zywicki, "Payday Lending, Bank Overdraft Protection, and Fair Competition at the Consumer Financial Protection Bureau," *Review of Banking & Financial Law* 33(1) (2013): 235–281.
57. Todd J. Zywicki, "The Economics and Regulation of Bank Overdraft Protection," *Washington and Lee Law Review* 69 (2012): 1141.
58. Oren Bar-Gill and Ryan Bubb, "Credit Card Pricing: The CARD Act and Beyond," *Cornell Law Review* 97 (2012): 967; Sumit Agarwal, Souphala Chomsisengphet, Neale Mahoney, and Johannes Stroebel, "*Regulating Consumer Financial Products: Evidence from Credit Cards,*" *Quarterly Journal of Economics* 130 (2014): 111–64.
59. *See* Durkin, Elliehausen, and Zywicki, *supra* note 31.
60. Cass R. Sunstein, "Nudging: A Very Short Guide," *Journal of Consumer Policy* 37(4) (2014): 583–588.
61. Tom Baker and Peter Siegelman, "'You Want Insurance with That?' Using Behavioral Economics to Protect Consumers from Add-on Insurance Products." *Connecticut Insurance Law Journal* 20 (2013): 13–1.

One Standard to Rule Them All:
The Disparate Impact of Energy Efficiency Regulations

Sofie E. Miller and Brian F. Mannix

INTRODUCTION

Regulations establishing energy efficiency and fuel economy standards are intended to conserve energy by getting consumers to choose more energy-efficient products. Federal regulations restrict how much energy dozens of everyday products can use, for everything from the car you drive to the microwave in your house. While these rules impose significant costs on consumers—especially low-income consumers—the benefits are harder to identify.

Agencies claim that restricting consumers' choices provides consumers with enormous net benefits, but this reasoning is hard to reconcile with the fact that consumers have many legitimate reasons to have heterogeneous preferences for the appliances they buy and the cars they drive. In addition to disregarding consumer preferences, these rules may not conserve as much energy as advertised due to unintended behavioral consequences. This chapter explores the reasoning behind energy efficiency

S.E. Miller (✉) • B.F. Mannix
The George Washington University Regulatory Studies Center, Washington, DC, USA

© The Editor(s) (if applicable) and The Author(s) 2016   251
S. Abdukadirov (ed.), *Nudge Theory in Action*,
DOI 10.1007/978-3-319-31319-1_10

regulations and why these reasons are insufficient support for the large costs they impose on consumers, especially low-income consumers.

THE BEHAVIORAL ECONOMICS OF ENERGY EFFICIENCY

Regulations establishing energy efficiency standards provide useful case studies of the application of behavioral economics insights to set policy. In the past decade especially, federal regulators have cited behavioral economics and "consumer irrationality" to justify standards that limit the amount of fuel, electricity, and water that vehicles and appliances can use.[1,2] In 2014, federal regulations setting energy efficiency standards accounted for $153 billion in claimed regulatory benefits.[3] Because they comprise such a large proportion of overall regulatory benefits—and because they affect all households—these rules merit a closer look.

Household energy consumption is closely linked to behavior, so that energy consumption might be reduced either through technological mandates that set energy consumption maximums for appliances, or through changes in the behavior of energy-consuming individuals. Despite this interplay, federal policies intended to reduce energy consumption rely almost entirely on technological mandates to do so.[4] The role of behavior in energy consumption is pervasive, so behavioral economics should provide insights for reducing consumption.

First, this chapter examines the policy tools used by regulators to reduce energy consumption. While many government regulations are concerned with reducing energy consumption, this chapter will focus in particular on energy efficiency standards promulgated by the Department of Energy (DOE) and fuel efficiency standards promulgated by the Environmental Protection Agency (EPA) in conjunction with the Department of Transportation (DOT). In both of these cases, instead of presenting consumers with the information to make the best possible choice, regulators ban a subset of products from the marketplace. While this strategy has the potential to reduce energy consumption, it may also pose large costs to consumers in the form of lost consumer surplus.

In contrast, some private companies have developed technologies that are designed to change the behavior of energy consumers. Unlike the approaches used by regulators, private behavioral technologies attempt to cause changes in consumer behavior by providing timely information and tools to improve energy use. While these technologies may in some ways pose an alternative to regulating energy efficiency, some federal and state regulatory programs are beginning to blur the lines between public and private nudges, making it difficult to clearly delineate between the two.

REGULATING ENERGY EFFICIENCY

The Energy Policy and Conservation Act of 1975 (EPCA) authorizes the DOE to establish energy conservation standards for consumer appliances that are both technologically feasible and economically justified, while also resulting in a "significant conservation of energy."[5] EPCA requires DOE to establish energy and water efficiency standards for 20 different categories of covered consumer products, including refrigerators, freezers, furnaces, dishwashers, clothes dryers, televisions, faucets, and lamps.[6]

In addition to this wide range of covered appliances, EPCA also gives DOE the authority to establish energy conservation standards for "Any other type of consumer product which the Secretary classifies as a covered product under subsection (b)."[7] This subsection of the Act allows the Secretary broad discretion in classifying consumer products as a "covered product" if she determines that:

(A) classifying products of such type as covered products is necessary or appropriate to carry out the purposes of this Act, and
(B) average annual per-household energy use by products of such type is likely to exceed 100 kilowatt-hours (or its Btu equivalent) per year.[8]

Since energy use is a function of water use in many appliances (e.g., clothes or dish washers), the statute gives the Department authority to regulate energy and water usage of a wide swath of products used every day in nearly every American household.

The EPCA also delegates authority to DOE to establish energy conservation standards for 12 classes of commercial appliances, including commercial ice machines, air conditioners, heating equipment, walk-in coolers and freezers, and commercial clothes washers.[9] Beyond these explicitly covered products, DOE also has authority to regulate "Any other type of industrial equipment which the Secretary classifies as covered equipment under section 341(b)."

The number of energy efficiency standards promulgated by the federal government has increased rapidly since passage of the Energy Independence and Security Act of 2007 (EISA), which amended the EPCA to increase Corporate Average Fuel Economy (CAFE) standards and efficiency standards for energy-using durables. The semiannual Unified Agenda, published by the Office of Management and Budget (OMB), lists ongoing and upcoming regulations planned by agencies for the year ahead. The Spring 2016 Unified Agenda listed 3 energy efficiency standards from DOE in the prerule stage, 12 standards in the proposed rule stage, and 13 in the final rule stage,[10] indicating that federal regulators do not plan to slow the promulgation of energy efficiency rules any time soon.

Energy Efficiency Standards for Residential Appliances

DOE has recently finalized energy conservation standards for residential dishwashers,[11] microwaves,[12] clothes washers,[13] furnaces, and air conditioners,[14] appliances that most households rely on for everyday tasks. Each of these regulations increases the price of appliances in return for reducing long-term energy usage and energy bills.[15] These standards affect nearly all American households, so it is important to examine the rationale that regulators use to promulgate them.

Government regulation is primarily intended to correct market failures,[16] and Executive Order 12866 requires executive branch agencies to identify the problem that they are attempting to solve via regulation. The language of E.O. 12866 clearly indicates that an agency should not promulgate a regulation that is not made necessary by a failure of the private market or other compelling public need unless it is statutorily required.[17] The types of market failure that typically are used to justify government intervention fall into one of the following categories: externalities, monopoly power, and asymmetric information.

As directed by E.O. 12866, DOE identifies three problems that its rules are intended to address: externalities from carbon dioxide emissions as a result of inefficient appliances, asymmetric information about the potential savings yielded by efficient appliances, and a lack of consumer information/processing capability about energy efficiency.[18] DOE's claim is that two types of market failure could potentially be addressed by setting energy efficiency standards for commercial and residential equipment.

First, energy used to power appliances results in some greenhouse gas emissions. Because the social cost of greenhouse gas emissions may not be fully represented in the price of energy, these emissions are externalities which regulatory policies could address. Second, consumers are currently purchasing appliances with higher long-term energy costs, which may indicate that they do not have sufficient information about the energy cost savings that higher-efficiency products make possible. This asymmetric information, if it exists, could be remedied by improved labeling or other types of consumer education campaigns.

While it doesn't fall into the category of a traditional market failure, the Department also intends for its rules to address a third problem: consumers' lack of "information processing capability."[19] It is clear from the text of DOE's rules that the Department believes consumers aren't adequately equipped to trade off upfront price increases against long-term energy savings. Overcoming this presumed consumer cognitive failure is the primary focus of DOE's energy conservation standards, rather than reducing information asymmetry or pollution externalities.[20,21]

However, DOE's energy efficiency standards don't ultimately address either of these market failures. The environmental benefits of these rules are so small relative to the private benefits, and relative to the upfront costs, that reduced externalities alone don't justify the standards.[22] While reducing carbon emissions may be a worthwhile goal for regulation, these rules only tangentially reduce carbon emissions, and primarily focus on reduced energy expenditures by consumers.[23]

In addition, these rules don't address information asymmetry in the marketplace by promoting labeling requirements or other standards that could improve the quality of information available to consumers, even though EPCA grants the federal government broad authority to require labeling of energy-using products.[24] Despite this authority, and the relatively low cost of implementing labeling requirements, regulators don't rely heavily on labeling or other disclosures that would communicate potential energy savings to consumers. Instead, DOE rules ban products from the marketplace, which restricts choice rather than improving information.

The following sections explore how the Department justifies its energy efficiency standards, the massive regulatory benefits that DOE calculates as a result, and the assumptions on which those regulatory benefits are based. We find that the assumptions that DOE uses to formulate its analyses are not representative of the real-world tradeoffs faced by consumers, and modeling techniques that better represent consumer preferences and tradeoffs instead suggest consumers will bear large net costs.

Regulatory Benefits

To justify most of its regulations, DOE relies almost entirely on one type of regulatory benefit: the cost savings consumers are estimated to enjoy over the life of a more energy-efficient appliance. For example, Miller finds that between 2007 and 2014 private benefits constituted 88 % of all benefits from energy efficiency standards.[25] Because this cost saving is a benefit felt exclusively by the private consumer, rather than society at large, the benefits that justify DOE's energy efficiency rules are "private benefits" rather than public benefits.

This differentiates efficiency rules from the majority of federal regulations, which have historically relied on public benefits—such as reduced externalities—for justification. However, the private benefits of DOE's efficiency rules dwarf the anticipated public benefits, such that most of these rules would not pass a benefit-cost test if relying on externality benefits alone.[26]

In many cases, consumers already had the option to purchase more efficient, higher-priced appliances prior to regulation, indicating that a lack of energy-efficient appliances in the market is not the impetus for these standards. However, regulators draw on the behavioral economics literature to argue that consumers fail to purchase these high-efficiency appliances due to inadequate information processing capability. In doing so, regulators overlook the possibility that consumers may have legitimate preferences for less-efficient appliances based on household characteristics or other observable product qualities (such as size, durability, reliability, speed, or noise level).[27] By regulating away the option for consumers to purchase less-efficient appliances, DOE is ostensibly improving consumers' choice structure by removing choices.

Instead of taking these revealed preferences as indications of legitimate consumer preferences, DOE argues that they reveal behavioral biases that could be resolved through regulation. In a recent final rule establishing efficiency standards for furnace fans, DOE provided a review of the behavioral economics literature on how consumers trade off upfront costs and long-term energy savings, which largely attempts to explain why consumers consistently "undervalue" improvements in energy efficiency. DOE draws on this literature to conclude that consumers are unaware of potential savings, have insufficient savings to make efficiency improvements, place an excessive focus on the short term, or struggle with an inability to calculate long-term energy savings benefits. Without specifying which explanation it finds most compelling, DOE concludes that "This undervaluation suggests that regulation that promotes energy efficiency can produce significant net private gains (as well as producing social gains by, for example, reducing pollution)."[28]

DOE presumes that its own valuation for energy efficiency is the correct one and that consumers should make product choices based on energy savings as DOE projects and values them. The fact that consumers do not currently choose to buy efficient appliances, instead of revealing consumers' preferences for other product attributes, reveals to the Department only that consumers must undervalue efficiency. However, efficiency is just one attribute of an appliance, and consumers may be making a correct valuation if they are weighing increased efficiency against other product attributes that they value more highly.[29] Ultimately, the Department cannot know enough about consumer households and constraints to be able to optimize consumer welfare across all of the considerations consumers ought to be able to take into account when making purchases of energy-using durables.

By eliminating the option to purchase low efficiency appliances, DOE believes that its energy conservation standards create significant private benefits. But this claim is difficult to reconcile with the standard economic definition of regulatory benefits: the surplus "willingness to pay" remaining after the regulation's winners fully compensate all of the losers.[30] How much is the average consumer willing to pay in order to be prohibited from buying, for example, an incandescent light bulb? After all, prior to the regulation, not buying the incandescent bulb is free. Why would anyone pay to have that choice imposed on them?[31] As one recent paper noted:

> How can it be that consumers are leaving billions of potential economic gains on the table by not buying the most energy-efficient cars, clothes dryers, air conditioners, and light bulbs? … If the savings are this great, why is it that a very basic informational approach cannot remedy this seemingly stunning example of completely irrational behavior? It should be quite simple to rectify decisions that are this flawed. Rather than accept the implications that consumers and firms are acting so starkly against their economic interest, a more plausible explanation is that there is something incorrect in the assumptions being made in the regulatory impact analyses.[32]

There are a number of reasons why the assumptions made by regulators do not accurately portray the tradeoffs faced by consumers. We expand on some of these problems in the sections below.

Consumer Heterogeneity

To justify its conclusion that consumers will be better served by a more limited array of product choices, regulators assume an unrealistic degree of consumer homogeneity when setting efficiency standards. However, we know that this assumption is far from the truth: markets respond to consumer preferences, and products differ because consumer preferences differ. As Gayer and Viscusi observe:

> The principal impetus for respecting consumer decisions can be traced to the fundamental role of heterogeneity in undermining the desirability of mandating uniformity. Differences in preferences and income generate different consumer demand for products. Even for products all consumers might find attractive, there will be differences in preferences; some consumers are willing to pay more for the product than others, giving rise to the usual downward-sloping demand for the product.[33]

People are influenced by a number of factors when they make an appliance purchase, not just energy efficiency. For example, consumers in Maine are more likely to buy efficient furnaces, but not air conditioners, while consumers in Texas are more likely to do the reverse.[34] This is, in fact, the *economically* efficient outcome. Valuing one product attribute (e.g., price, size, reliability) over another (e.g., energy efficiency) does not indicate information processing deficiencies, it just reinforces that consumers have heterogeneous preferences due to location, climate, household size, and income, among other reasons.

Moreover, a furnace or water heater in a beach house may be used rarely; a window air conditioner in the guest room may be used only a tiny fraction of the time that the one in the master bedroom is used.[35] While the same consumer will adapt her or his choices to particular locations and circumstances, regulators do not take the same approach. Because regulators cannot access, let alone process, all of this relevant information, one-size-fits-all technological mandates lead to lost consumer surplus by reducing the ability of consumers to optimize their choices in the marketplace.

A recent example of one-size-fits-all standards gone awry is the Department's furnace efficiency rule, which mandates that 30 northern states use furnaces with 90 % efficiency or greater. However, these high-efficiency furnaces require a vent to outside air, making them difficult (and costly) to install in households with a furnace located in interior rooms—such as townhouses and condominiums.[36] In this case, it's reasonable to assume that these households didn't use high efficiency appliances because they didn't fit, not that households were acting irrationally against their own long-term interests. By requiring use of a furnace that did not fit actual household space constraints, DOE illustrates its inability to make better decisions for consumers than they could make for themselves.

In its final rules for residential appliances, DOE briefly mentions the concept of heterogeneous consumer preferences. However, the Department does not account for this variation in its analyses of energy efficiency rules:

> DOE's current analysis does not explicitly control for heterogeneity in consumer preferences, preferences across subcategories of products or specific features, or consumer price sensitivity variation according to household income.[37]

Failure to account for diverse consumer preferences and constraints misrepresents the true effects of energy efficiency standards, and results in analyses showing consistently high net benefits from efficiency rules that do not reflect actual household experience. Consumer preferences and household characteristics vary in a number of ways that determine whether investing in energy-efficient equipment is cost-beneficial. Ignoring this basic truth results in one-size-fits-all standards that reduce choices and consumer welfare.

Heterogeneous Time Preferences

Because consumers receive the benefit of reduced energy or water bills over the entire estimated lifetimes of their appliances, DOE must discount these benefits to make them comparable with the upfront costs resulting from the standards. Benefits expected in the future are diminished in this calculation because people generally prefer present consumption to future consumption; that is, they have positive time preferences.[38] Discounting benefits and costs allows comparison between values occurring in different time periods by converting values to a common unit of measurement.[39] In its analyses, DOE compares discounted benefits to discounted costs to calculate the net present value of its standards.

A very low discount rate implies that present consumption is not valued much more than future consumption, whereas a very high discount rate implies that future consumption has little value relative to present consumption. The appropriate rate by which to discount future benefits is not certain, and assuming a discount rate that is too high or too low can mischaracterize consumption preferences over time. This further complicates the calculation because a rule's future expected costs and benefits can vary dramatically depending on the discount rate used to compare them to present costs and benefits. Using an inaccurate discount rate could jeopardize the economic justification of DOE's energy conservation standards.

Furthermore, consumer time preferences are far from homogenous and can differ to such an extent that DOE's analyses may not reflect actual household effects. For example, a recent working paper from the National Bureau of Economic Research (NBER) finds that different consumer groups have vastly different discount rates for purchases of energy-efficient appliances. Richard Newell and Juha Siikamäki find that race, education, and other household characteristics can significantly influence consumer discount rates. This is crucial because "the profitability of EE [energy efficient] investments depends fundamentally on the rate at which individuals discount future energy savings relative to the required upfront investment."[40]

In Circular A-94, the OMB recommends that agencies use default real discount rates of 3 % and 7 % when measuring the benefits of public investments and regulations. These discount rates approximate the "social rate of time preference" and the opportunity cost of capital,[41] respectively.

When benefits for DOE's efficiency rules are discounted at 3 % and 7 %, its rules result in large net private benefits for consumers. For example, using discount rates of 3 % and 7 % puts the annualized benefits of its recent furnace fans rule at $2.17 billion and $1.45 billion, respectively, a range of $720 million. This large range indicates that the discount rate used in DOE's assessment is critically important in calculating the anticipated benefits of the regulation and in determining whether the regulation is economically justified, as required by the statute.[42]

OMB's guidance on discounting may be appropriate when evaluating government expenditures, where the typical practice is to use a low, risk-free, discount rate because no single expenditure is likely to be more than a small part of the government's budget. But this is not true of automobiles and appliances purchased by consumers, who have budget constraints and an aversion to risks, and thus, experience real costs that do not get captured by an artificially low discount rate.[43,44] Consumers' actual discount rates are not homogenous, either across the population or across purchase types, and the estimate of a regulation's benefits is reduced when using actual consumer discount rates for home appliance purchases.

Many studies of implicit consumer discount rates use the purchase of energy-using durables (such as air conditioners, dishwashers, and refrigerators) to measure consumer time preferences. This is because these appliances have upfront costs that can potentially be offset by long-term energy savings,[45] and there are often many available options with varying costs and levels of energy efficiency among which consumers may choose.

Based on field studies in the literature, Frederick et al. find implicit discount rates of between 17 % and 300 % for energy-using durables.[46] The variance is so wide that DOE's use (and OMB's recommendation) of 3 % and 7 % seems to be an inaccurate measure of actual consumer benefits from energy efficiency standards. The advantage of using field studies to measure discount rates is that they examine actual marketplace behavior and are therefore more applicable to consumer behavior for energy-using durables.

This is in contrast to OMB's approach, which uses the real rate of return on long-term government debt, such as ten-year Treasury notes, to approximate consumer discount rates. While a ten-year Treasury note's interest rate is useful for analysis, it is not directly useful for understanding the tradeoffs that consumers make when purchasing durable energy-using goods. In their regression analysis, Newell and Siikamäki find that

> individual discount rates exhibit considerable heterogeneity and systematically influence household willingness to pay (WTP) for EE [energy efficiency], as measured through product choices, required payback periods, and EE tax credit claims. The relationship is statistically significant, empirically robust, and not confounded by the characteristics of the homeowner, household, and their home.[47]

DOE tallies the benefits of its energy efficiency standards by treating consumers as a homogenous group, but this doesn't reflect reality. If consumers don't value the appliance attributes that DOE is mandating, these rules impose huge net costs on consumers rather than benefits. Using a low discount rate to set standards effectively forces consumers to accept a very low rate of return on their investments in appliances and vehicles.

There are a number of reasons why reasonable consumers might use discount rates higher than those assumed by DOE. Capital markets are not completely frictionless, and so it is not realistic to assume that everyone is able to borrow and lend until their discount rates come into equilibrium. Low-income consumers, in particular, are likely to have a higher discount rate that accurately reflects their opportunity cost for capital.[48] For example, average interest rates on consumer credit cards are closer to 15 % than the 3 % return on a Treasury bill.

Moreover, the returns on energy efficiency investments may be extremely risky (due, e.g., to the variability of gasoline prices in recent years); so a risk-free discount rate is inappropriate for risk-averse consumers. Many consumers, for a variety of reasons, may be in a position to earn much higher returns on other investments—such as education, or even meals, for their children. It is not a benefit to deprive them of those superior investments.

Distributional Effects

But consumer discount rates don't just vary widely: they also correlate with other household characteristics, such as income, education, and race.[49] For example, high-income households are more likely to use low implicit discount rates, because they have more certain future streams of income and can afford to make higher-priced upfront investments. Low-income households, on the other hand, do not benefit from the same certainty and are more likely to have much higher discount rates. This disparity means that "a result of [energy efficiency] standards is to place an implicit tax on those individuals who are thought to have the highest discount rates: the less well off. Thus efficiency standards can have an adverse income distribution effect."[50]

As Hausman observes in his early field study of implicit consumer discount rates, the only individuals with actual discount rates that are approximate to the prevailing interest rates in credit markets are high-income households. This implies that only high-income households are adequately represented by the discount rates DOE uses to calculate the benefits of energy efficiency standards. Even median-income US households have significantly higher discount rates of 27 % for the purchase of energy-using durables.[51]

Other studies relying on elicitation and experiments also find higher median individual discount rates. For example, Andersen et al find that individual discount rates have a mean of 25.3 % and a median of 18.7 %, with a standard deviation of 14.1 %.[52] These rates are similar to those found by Harrison et al, who estimate mean and median discount rates of 24.2 % and 24.5 %, respectively, and a standard deviation of 15.7 %.[53] While these studies determine general discount rates rather than rates used by individuals purchasing energy-using durables, they still serve to reinforce that individuals have differing time preferences and that typical discount rates are much higher than those used in DOE's analysis.

Recent research by Miller finds that DOE's efficiency rule for furnace fans results in large net costs for consumers with discount rates higher than 12 %, which is most consumers.[54] These costs are especially high for low-income households and individuals with high discount rates, indicating that DOE's efficiency standards are highly regressive, burdening low-income households with net costs rather than net benefits.[55]

Energy Efficiency Standards for Commercial Appliances

DOE also issues energy conservation standards for commercial appliances, such as walk-in coolers and freezers, air conditioners, and commercial refrigerators. According to DOE, the energy conservation program covers more than 60 products, representing 60 % of commercial building energy use, and approximately 30 % of industrial energy use.[56]

Despite the fact that commercial entities are profit-motivated and have access to more resources for planning upfront capital costs and long-term savings than households, DOE applies the same logic to commercial appliances as it does to residential appliances. DOE does not seem fazed by the logical difficulties of applying shortcomings in consumer processing capabilities to commercial entities. Interestingly enough, following this logic implies that federal employees are somehow mysteriously better than private businesses at making business investment decisions.

In 2013, DOE proposed a rule establishing energy efficiency standards for commercial refrigerators. DOE noted that while its analysis predicted large financial benefits from higher-efficiency standards, users of commercial refrigeration were not already demanding the production of high-efficiency equipment. Instead of evaluating whether its modeling assumptions accurately reflected real world conditions and tradeoffs, DOE relied on several theories as to why commercial customer preferences might be incorrect (without distinguishing the large, repeat purchases of profit-motivated commercial entities from individual household decisions).[57] However, because commercial entities are primarily profit-motivated, have access to greater information, and can forecast future costs with greater precision than households, it is difficult to explain how DOE can defend applying the same behavioral economics arguments to commercial actors as it does to residential consumers.

Particularly in these cases, where the "consumers" in question are cost-conscious purchasers of commercial equipment, DOE should consider alternative explanations for the difference between its estimates of costs and savings and the revealed calculations of purchasers. Rather than assuming the equipment purchasers are wrong, DOE should consider the alternative hypothesis that its analysis does not reflect real world conditions and tradeoffs.[58]

For example, DOE discounts future energy savings at a discount rate of 3 % for its primary benefit estimates, whereas the cost of equity for private firms is much higher. New York University's Stern School of Business estimates that the cost of capital for restaurants is 8.48 %, nearly three times the discount rate of future energy savings used by DOE. NYU Stern puts Wal-Mart's cost of capital at above 7 %, more than twice the rate used in DOE's calculation. This difference between the discount rate DOE uses and the rates firms actually face appears to be a more likely explanation for the difference in how DOE and commercial purchasers of refrigeration equipment value future energy savings than DOE's explanation that purchasers lack "information," "sufficient salience of the long-term or aggregate benefits," or the proper "incentives."[59]

DOE's analyses do not seem to consider that commercial customers may value attributes other than energy efficiency when making equipment purchases. Commercial customers have vast amounts of information, unavailable to DOE, that is relevant to their investment decisions; yet it is difficult to think of any bit of information that DOE might possess that is not also readily available to the businesses. Despite the fact that cost-conscious commercial consumers are not demanding access to higher-efficiency appliances, DOE implausibly concludes that reducing commercial consumers' options will make them better off.

Fuel Economy Standards

The EPCA of 1975, as amended by the EISA, authorizes DOT to issue fuel economy standards for passenger vehicles and trucks. The DOT issues CAFE standards in conjunction with the EPA, pursuant to its authority under the Clean Air Act. According to DOT:

The CAFE standards are fleet-wide averages that must be achieved by each automaker for its car and truck fleet, each year, since 1978. When these standards are raised, automakers respond by creating a more fuel-efficient fleet, which improves our nation's energy security and saves consumers money at the pump, while also reducing greenhouse gas (GHG) emissions.[60]

In its most recent iteration of the CAFE standards, EPA estimated that total fuel savings for consumers comprised about 79 % of the rule's total anticipated benefits.[61] In the text of their rule, the agencies explain that, while the standards will increase the price of a new vehicle by $1,800 on average, consumers who drive the vehicle for its entire lifetime will recoup a net savings of between $3,400 and $5,000.[62]

However, consumers already have the option not to buy the less fuel-efficient car (although certainly not all consumers exercise that option). To reiterate the question asked previously in this chapter, how much are consumers willing to pay to be prohibited from buying the vehicle that they prefer?[63]

Behavioral Arguments
EPA and DOT make the foundation of their reasoning explicit: the only reason that consumers buy less efficient vehicles is due to insufficient reasoning capacity to understand the value of high-efficiency vehicles. The agencies posit that consumers might be myopic, may lack sufficient information about future fuel savings, or may lack the ability to process information about future fuel savings.[64]

In their final rule setting CAFE standards for light-duty vehicles, EPA and DOT draw on the behavioral economics literature to explain why consumers may not adequately value long-term fuel savings.[65] In doing so, the agencies question whether consumers internalize the potential private benefits of fuel-efficient vehicles when making purchasing decisions.[66]

> Other potential sources of market failure include phenomena highlighted by the field of behavioral economics, including loss aversion, inadequate consumer attention to long-term effects of their decisions, or a lack of salience of benefits such as fuel savings to consumers at the time they make purchasing decisions.[67]

However, as we examine in the next section, the agencies do not explore the possibility that consumers may prefer other vehicle attributes over fuel economy. This omission leads the agencies to conclude that failure to make purchase decisions based on the agencies' own valuation of fuel economy indicates consumers' inability to rationally choose an optimal product.

Another potential argument to justify CAFE standards is not that consumers don't understand the value of fuel economy, but they aren't able to accurately predict gas prices.[68] This uncertainty would lead consumers to undervalue the potential savings available through increased fuel efficiency. In his 1985 piece in *Regulation Magazine*, David R. Henderson notes:

> The problem [with this argument] is, no one can predict future gasoline prices accurately; consumers, in fact, do as well as or better than the government experts. Based on prices of used cars, Daly and Mayor found, for example, that consumers expected real gasoline prices to fall after 1980. The Department of Energy (DOE) on the other hand, together with most energy experts, predicted in 1980 that the real price of unleaded gasoline would reach about $1.80 a gallon in 1984 (in [1985] dollars). Consumers—not the experts—were right; DOE was off by a staggering 34 %.[69]

After all, Henderson remarks, consumers themselves make millions of purchase decisions every year, which gives them the opportunity to adjust their actions to new information if market conditions (such as fuel prices) change. Government, on the other hand, is much less flexible. In fact, by establishing fuel economy standards that do not respond to changes in the price of gasoline, "CAFE is a case in point" of failure to adjust policy to actual marketplace conditions.[70]

Consumer Preferences: One Size Fits All?

Importantly, the agencies also list among these cognitive shortcomings that consumers "may consider fuel economy after other vehicle attributes and, as such, not optimize the level of this attribute."[71] That is, consumers err by giving more weight to product attributes other than fuel economy.

According to the agencies' reasoning, fuel economy should not be subordinated to other product attributes that consumers consider in the car and light truck market. Failure to make purchase decisions based on the agencies' own valuation of fuel economy indicates consumers' inability to rationally choose an optimal product. In their final rule setting CAFE standards for light-duty vehicles, EPA and DOT contend that "Even if consumers have relevant knowledge, selecting a vehicle is a highly complex undertaking, involving many vehicle characteristics. In the face of such a complicated choice, consumers may use simplified decision rules."[72] The agencies seem not to recognize that they themselves, rather than consumers, are guilty of using limited information and of oversimplifying a complex purchase decision.

It should be no surprise that the agencies' myopia harms consumers:

> Consumer harm is a central consideration in the analysis of CAFE standards. Cars have many attributes that consumers care about, including mileage, price, safety, reliability, performance, and so forth. By constraining the corporate average mpg, CAFE standards "put a thumb on the scale," tipping the balance more in favor of mileage and away from other desirable attributes. In order to comply with the CAFE standards, manufacturers must redesign their product line, and must price cars so that consumers will buy a mix that meets the required standard. The result is that consumers are worse off. That is the tradeoff the government makes for pursuing gasoline savings beyond the point that consumers want to pursue it.[73]

The agencies' approach treats diverse preferences as a problem to be fixed, rather than a fact of the marketplace. After all, no one can know a household's own characteristics and constraints better than the household itself, although DOT and EPA may disagree. So long as agencies treat consumers' preferences for other attributes as illegitimate, consumers bear the costs in the form of higher prices and fewer choices.[74]

Behavioral Consequences

While fuel economy and appliance efficiency standards set technological mandates for energy use, they don't address the other driver of energy consumption: behavior. As it turns out, efficiency standards change behavior in a number of ways that can counteract the intended purposes of these rules.

A prime example of how technological mandates change behavior is the rebound effect, which describes how consumers increase product usage as their energy costs decrease. Counterintuitively, an effect of EPA and DOE's efficiency standards may be increased energy use, because it becomes cheaper to drive one more mile or run the dishwasher one more time.[75] The extent of a rebound effect can be measured by using elasticity of demand, which quantifies in percent terms how much demand for (or in this case, usage of) a product increases with each 1 % decrease in price.

In 1980, the Regulatory Analysis Review Group (RARG) within the Council of Wage and Price Stability issued a report on DOE's proposed energy efficiency standards for appliances, which found that:

> efficiency standards for appliances with a high usage elasticity will tend to be ineffective in saving energy. If this elasticity is as great as −1, any increase in the efficiency of individual appliances will be offset by an equal increase in usage. If it is more elastic, efficiency standards will actually cause total energy consumption of individual appliances to increase: Thus the assumption of constant usage could obscure a very serious flaw in the proposed standards.[76]

RARG concluded that increases in appliance efficiency will lead to proportional reductions in energy consumption only if demand for services is completely inelastic and will lead to increased total energy consumption if usage elasticity is more elastic than −1.[77] In this way, rational consumer behavior in response to regulation could partially counter the intended effects of energy efficiency rules.[78,79]

While RARG used rebound effect as an argument against energy efficiency standards, others have argued that the rebound effect is actually "a measure of the benefit of appliance standards to the consumer."[80] Though DOE generally doesn't account for rebound effects when estimating the costs and benefit of its appliance efficiency rules, EPA and DOT do count additional rebound-effect driving as a benefit of their CAFE standards,[81] which they calculate using an elasticity of 10 %.[82] However, EPA and DOT also note that the effect of their standards on emissions is dependent on the size of the accompanying rebound effect, concluding that "the net effect of stricter CAFE standards on emissions of each pollutant depends on the relative magnitudes of its reduced emissions in fuel refining and distribution, and increases in its emissions from vehicle use."[83]

However, if people's product usage is more sensitive to price than the agencies assume, efficiency standards will be less successful than expected. For example, the agencies admit that the elasticity used above "is on the low end of the range reported in previous research,"[84] which finds elasticities as high as 75 % and with a median around 23 %.[85] Although the studies examined by the agencies find a wide range of estimates, they "generally conclude that a significant rebound effect occurs when the cost per mile of driving decreases."[86] In a comprehensive estimate of the rebound effect for all domestic household vehicles, Greene et al. find a rebound effect of about 20 %, based on the Residential Transportation Energy Consumption Surveys.[87]

The rebound effect is not limited to vehicles: some research has quantified the rebound effect for household appliances, as well. For example, Fouquet and Pearson use vector error-correction models to estimate a long-run uncompensated demand elasticity for lighting of –0.6 (or 60 %).[88] While it appears that "backfire"—or, rebound large enough to offset 100 % of efficiency savings—is unlikely, rebound for fuel economy and household appliances "is a substantial factor which, if ignored, would lead to significant overstatement of energy savings."[89] If this is the case, then the rebound effect from these fuel-economy rules will partly erase the gain in fuel savings, carbon emissions, and emissions of other pollutants.

Another unintended result from increased efficiency could be delays in market penetration for efficient products. If new, efficient products have higher prices and fewer desirable attributes, consumers may delay new vehicle and appliance purchases longer than they otherwise would have.[90,91] For example, a family with a less-efficient 15-year-old minivan may choose to keep the van for longer than they otherwise would rather than buy a new, more efficient vehicle. They may make this decision because the price of new vans with similar features has increased—along with their fuel efficiency—or because they prefer the attributes of their old van, and can't find similar features in new, fuel-efficient models. Either way, the result is that fuel-inefficient models are on the road for longer, postponing the savings in carbon emissions that the agencies envisioned when finalizing their regulations.[92,93]

Another unfortunate effect of fuel economy standards is increased risk for car occupants. As CAFE standards have increased, companies have been incentivized to make smaller, lighter cars in order to reach overall fleet fuel economy standards. These smaller, lighter cars provide less protection for passengers, increasing both risk and fatalities.[94]

The agencies are cognizant of this unintended consequence. In the preamble of their 2012 final CAFE rule, EPA and DOT devoted a significant amount a space to safety concerns[95] and will continue to monitor the effects of fuel economy standards on societal fatalities.[96] However, EPA and DOT are unable to provide exact estimates of the fatality effects because there are multiple options available to manufacturers for meeting the CAFE standards, and the agencies cannot foresee to what extent manufacturers will rely on reduced vehicle size and weight versus other options.[97] Beginning in 2011, the CAFE standards have incorporated a "footprint" adjustment that accounts for vehicle size. While this may help reduce the degree to which manufacturers rely on vehicle downsizing to meet the standards, it is likely to encourage tradeoffs in other attributes of the vehicle, with additional unintended consequences.

In 2011, Jacobsen used a fixed effects model to measure the effects of vehicle class, engineering risk, and exposure on fatal accidents to find that each incremental increase in the CAFE mpg requirements results in an additional 150 annual fatalities.[98] An earlier report from the National Research Council relying on engineering studies of vehicle weight found that the CAFE standards in 2002 were responsible for 2,000 additional fatalities annually.[99] Using the prevailing value of statistical life used by the DOT, these additional fatalities add up to approximately $18 billion in annual costs from lives lost.[100]

BEHAVIORAL TECHNOLOGIES

As mentioned at the beginning of this chapter, energy consumption can be reduced either through technological mandates that set energy consumption maximums for appliances or through changing the behaviors of energy-consuming individuals. Despite this interplay, policies intended to reduce energy consumption—such as the CAFE standards and appliance efficiency standards—rely almost entirely on technological mandates to do so.[101] While federal regulators also use labeling programs to motivate energy-efficient purchases, their primary mechanism for reducing energy consumption remains technological mandates and product bans.

Despite federal agencies' track record, technological mandates are not the only way to effectively reduce residential energy consumption. Because the role of behavior in energy consumption is pervasive, the role of behavioral economics as a tool to reduce energy consumption will continue to grow. But technological mandates aren't the only policy tools that rely on behavioral economics. More recently, private firms have employed a variety of behavioral technologies to incentivize consumers to reduce energy consumption. In their report for the American Council for an Energy-Efficient Economy, Mazur-Stommen and Farley examine the prevalence of behavioral technologies being employed by energy providers:

> The majority of utility-based energy efficiency programs focus on physical energy efficiency improvements. But all demand-side and energy efficiency programs involve human activity and decision making. Programs can achieve greater impact and deeper savings by incorporating insights from

social and behavioral sciences. Many utilities have undertaken behavior-based programs to help meet savings targets set by regulators and their own business needs.[102]

In their study, Mazur-Stommen and Farley find 281 behavior-based energy conservation programs were offered between 2008 and 2013, with participation from 104 energy providers and third parties.[103] The potential energy savings from such behavior-based programs could be as large as 88 million metric tons of carbon emissions.[104] For these reasons, voluntary technologies for reducing energy usage could act as a "behavioral wedge" to provide immediate emissions reductions:

> This potential "behavioral wedge" can reduce emissions much more quickly than other kinds of changes and deserves explicit consideration as part of climate policy. It can potentially help avoid "overshoot" of greenhouse gas concentration targets; provide a demonstration effect; reduce emissions at low cost; and buy time to develop new technologies, policies, and institutions to reach longer-term greenhouse gas emissions targets and to develop adaptation strategies.[105]

Rather than relying on technological mandates, these programs function by relying on social norms to incentivize home energy conservation. Using social norms can help motivate "good" behavior and discourage "bad" behavior "by correcting targets' misperceptions regarding the behaviors' prevalence."[106]

That is, those who consume lots of energy at the household level may not realize that their neighbors are consuming less energy. Introducing households to this information can change household behavior enough to have a significant effect on energy usage. For example, Dietz calculates that simple no-cost behavioral changes, such as adjusting the default water heater temperature and changing thermostat settings, have the potential to reduce carbon dioxide emissions by 88 million metric tons over ten years,[107] which represents a 10 % reduction in residential energy use.[108]

These reductions are accomplished without technological mandates and their accompanying price increases and loss of consumer welfare, and without the rebound effect and other counterproductive side effects. Using norms to motivate energy consumption reduces "[c]osts to the household budget and harm to the environment... without reducing the well-being provided by energy services."[109] This is in contrast to the one-size-fits-all efficiency standards promulgated by the DOE, DOT, and EPA, which have the potential to reduce households' well-being from energy-using durables.

According to Mazur-Stommen and Farley, there are three different ways that programs use the insights from behavioral science to reduce energy consumption:

1. *Cognition programs* focus on delivering information to consumers. Categories include general and targeted communication efforts, social media, classroom education, and training.
2. *Calculus programs* rely on consumers making economically rational decisions. Categories include feedback, games, incentives, home energy audits, and installation.
3. *Social interaction programs* rely on interaction among people for their effectiveness. Categories include social marketing, person-to person efforts, eco-teams, peer champions, online forums, and gifts.[110]

The following sections explain how private companies are using behavioral technologies, such as social norms and information availability, to reduce energy consumption.

Opower

> Simply providing people with smart meter data in real time in a form that helps them understand how much power they're using and how much it's costing them could inspire many behavioral changes that could add up to big energy savings—and big emissions cuts.—*Washington Post*, *"We could keep a huge amount of carbon out of the atmosphere just by changing people's behavior,"* 2/27/2015

Opower is making great use of behavioral technologies to reduce energy consumption. Opower, a publicly held software-as-service company, achieves these reductions in energy use not through mandates or bans, but by providing customers with information about their energy usage compared to their neighbors'. Opower partners with over half of the 50 largest electric utilities in the USA to provide their customers with household-specific energy usage data. In addition to ranking households on their energy usage relative to neighbors, these reports also provide customers with tips for reducing energy consumption. On average, sending out these home energy reports (HERs) reduces energy consumption by 2 %.[111]

Alcott notes that this approach is "a remarkable departure from traditional energy efficiency programs in that it is a non-price intervention designed with direct insight from behavioral science that is evaluated using randomized controlled trials."[112] In contrast to technological mandates from the federal government, Opower is not a one-size-fits-all solution— and its effects on energy consumption can be directly measured through meter readings.

Because Opower's approach doesn't rely on price signals to change behavior, it instead has to draw on another resource to motivate behavior change: social norms. In their experiments on reducing litter, Cialdini et al. find that both injunctive and descriptive norms significantly change behavior.[113] In the case of household energy consumption, an *injunctive* norm could be "it's good to conserve energy," whereas a *descriptive* norm might be "you use more energy than your neighbors." In a later article, Schultz et al. built on this research to demonstrate that communicating social norms to the relevant households caused them to reduce energy consumption.[114]

While Opower doesn't rely on price signals, its technique may have a large effect on energy use and emissions. In his evaluation of Opower's HERs, Alcott finds that "the effects of sending Home Energy Reports are equivalent to a 11 to 20 % short-run price increase or a 5 % long-run price increase. Taken as a whole, these effects are remarkable: simply sending letters can significantly and cost-effectively affect energy use behaviors."[115]

These approaches are promising because they leave consumers with the option to use or conserve energy based on their household needs and constraints. Because this is the case, any resulting behavioral changes will result in actual private benefits for consumers. These non-price signals direct households toward energy savings without reducing the choices available to them.

Nest

Another example of a behavioral technology for reducing energy consumption is the Nest Thermostat, which programs itself to adjust temperature settings based on observed household preferences. The Nest Thermostat can also sense when households are unoccupied and adjust temperature settings accordingly to save energy. Because temperature control comprises almost half of household energy use,[116] even minor adjustments have the potential to conserve measureable amounts of energy.

While many households already have the option to program thermostats, not many take advantage of this option. For consumers who value these savings but are not ambitious enough to do the legwork, Nest removes the burden of thermostat programming by automating settings based on observed consumer schedules and preferences after only a week of use. In addition to adjusting to consumer schedules, Nest can also adjust to seasonal changes to enhance consumer savings on utility bills. To the extent that households fail to choose optimal temperature settings at home due to procrastination or absent mindedness, these built-in features can provide households with savings without limiting their appliance options or reducing their choices.

BLURRING THE LINE: WHOSE NUDGE IS IT, ANYWAY?

While is seems simple to distinguish between technological mandates from the federal government and behavioral technologies, the lines between public and private nudges are starting to blur. In 2013, the idea that regulators would use behavioral technologies as a tool to reduce energy consumption was a bit far-fetched. As Mazur-Stommen and Farley commented in 2013:

> Since many behavior initiatives are still in the pilot phase, regulators do not have sufficient evidence to justify treating such programs as energy efficiency resources. In many states, regulatory language either fails to recognize the programs or defines them too narrowly. In states where behavior programs may be counted toward an energy efficiency resource standards (EERS) plan, utilities may miss this opportunity by labeling their programs as marketing initiatives rather than as energy savings mechanisms.[117]

However, this dynamic is beginning to change. As the *Washington Post* noted in 2015, the success of current behavioral programs suggests that these technologies will become more popular with federal regulators who are seeking to reduce energy consumption.[118] Private nudges, including those provided by companies like Opower, are being incorporated due to federal and state policies, rather than business motivations or altruism. For example, in 2011, Hunt Alcott noted the importance of incentives from federal and state governments for behavioral technologies:

Regulated utilities typically have the incentive to increase instead of decrease their customers' energy use. Why are utilities working with OPOWER? The company's partners are typically either non-profit municipal utilities whose goals include energy conservation or regulated investor-owned utilities in one of 24 states where policymakers have enacted energy conservation mandates called Energy Efficiency Resource Standards (EERS). These regulations require that electricity and natural gas retailers run energy conservation programs that reduce the quantity of energy demanded in their service territory by some amount relative to counterfactual, typically a few percent over several years. For example, under Minnesota's New Generation Energy Act of 2007, utilities in that state are required to run conservation programs that reduce energy demand by 1.5 % each year.[119]

In addition, EPA's recently proposed clean power rule initially included provisions attempting to codify behavioral technologies for reducing energy consumption by including demand-side energy efficiency as one of the "building blocks" available to state governments for carbon dioxide emissions.[120] While this building block was removed from EPA's final clean power plan rule, EPA expects that demand-side energy efficiency "will be a significant component of state plans under the Clean Power Plan" due to low costs of implementation and potential for energy savings.[121]

These examples illustrate that behavioral technologies are not being developed in a political vacuum—in many cases, they're not really "private nudges" at all, but another tool for federal regulators to govern private behavior. When that's the case, it is worth bearing in mind that the greatest benefit of behavioral technologies in the energy efficiency sphere is when they're used to provide information and choices that consumers otherwise lack. Once governments begin to employ behavioral technologies as mandates rather than as frameworks, consumers will be no better off than they were under the old one-size-fits-all regulations.

CONCLUSION

In issuing energy efficiency and fuel economy standards, federal regulators draw on the behavioral economics literature to argue that consumers fail to purchase these high-efficiency appliances and fuel-efficient cars due to an inadequate ability to process information about future energy savings. In doing so, regulators overlook the possibility that consumers may have legitimate preferences for less-efficient products based on household characteristics or other observable product qualities (such as size, durability, safety, or reliability).[122] By regulating away the option for consumers to purchase the products that best suit their needs, the agencies are ostensibly improving consumers' choice structure by removing choices.

However, this approach ignores the fact that consumers—and their preferences—differ widely, and the best product for one household may not be well suited to the next household. Removing choice from the marketplace saddles consumers with large net costs, rather than net benefits. In the cases where the "consumers" in question are cost-conscious purchasers of commercial equipment, DOE should consider alternative explanations for the difference between its estimates of costs and savings and the revealed calculations of purchasers. Rather than assuming the equipment purchasers are wrong, DOE should consider the alternative hypothesis that its analysis does not reflect real-world conditions and tradeoffs.[123]

While fuel economy and appliance efficiency standards set technological mandates for energy use, they don't address the other driver of energy consumption: behavior. As it turns out, efficiency standards change behavior in a number of ways that can counteract the intended purposes of these rules. Behavioral technologies, on the other hand, allow households the option to buy whatever products best suit their needs, and alter energy use through behavioral changes rather than through technological ones. This provides households with the potential to reduce energy expenditures (and carbon emissions) without constraining their choices or resulting in unintended consequences.

NOTES

1. Ted Gayer and Kip Viscusi, "Overriding Consumer Preferences with Energy Regulations," *Journal of Regulatory Economics* 43 (2013): 248–264.
2. Brian F. Mannix and Susan E. Dudley, "The Limits of Irrationality as a Rationale for Regulation," *Journal of Policy Analysis and Management* 34(3) (2015): 705–712.
3. Authors' own calculations from agency total benefits reported at the 3% discount rate for the seven efficiency rules finalized in 2014. To reproduce these data, use rules corresponding to the following

RINs: 1904-AC00, 1904-AB57, 1904-AC19, 1904-AC28, 1904-AB86, 1904-AC22, 1904-AC77.

4. Susan Mazur-Stommen and Kate Farley, *ACEEE Field Guide to Utility-Run Behavior Programs* (Washington, DC: American Council for an Energy-Efficient Economy, December 2013). Report Number B132: (http://www.iseif.org/wp-content/uploads/2014/01/ACEEE-Report.pdf).

5. 42 U.S.C. 6295(o)(3)(B) and 6313(d)(4) (http://www.gpo.gov/fdsys/pkg/USCODE-2013-title42/html/USCODE-2013-title42-chap77-subchapIII-partA-sec6295.htm).

6. Energy Policy and Conservation Act, as amended, §322 (http://legcounsel.house.gov/Comps/EPCA.pdf).

7. Energy Policy and Conservation Act, as amended, §322(a) (http://legcounsel.house.gov/Comps/EPCA.pdf).

8. Energy Policy and Conservation Act, as amended, §322(b) (http://legcounsel.house.gov/Comps/EPCA.pdf).

9. Energy Policy and Conservation Act, as amended, §340 (http://legcounsel.house.gov/Comps/EPCA.pdf).

10. These counts do not include test procedures or determinations of coverage which, while integral to the promulgation of energy efficiency rules, do not in themselves establish energy conservation standards.

11. 77 F.R. 31917.

12. 78 F.R. 36315.

13. 77 F.R. 32307.

14. 76 F.R. 37407.

15. Kenneth Gillingham, Richard G. Newell, and Karen Palmer, *Energy Efficiency Economics and Policy* (Washington, DC: Resources for the Future, April 2009). RFF DP 09-13.

16. Susan E. Dudley and Jerry Brito, *Regulation: A Primer*, 2nd Edition (Washington, DC: The Mercatus Center at George Mason University and the George Washington University Regulatory Studies Center, 2012), 12.

17. Exec. Order No. 12866, *Regulatory Planning and Review*, §1(a).

18. For examples of rules that rely on these justifications, see 78 F.R. 64132, 77 F.R. 31959, 78 F.R. 36365, 77 F.R. 32375, 76 F.R. 37540, and 79 F.R. 38203.

19. See, for example, 78 F.R. 64132, 77 F.R. 31959, 78 F.R. 36365, 77 F.R. 32375, 76 F.R. 37540, and 79 F.R. 38203.

20. Ted Gayer and Kip Viscusi, "Overriding Consumer Preferences with Energy Regulations," *Journal of Regulatory Economics* 43 (2013): 263.

21. Sofie E. Miller, *Whose Benefits Are They, Anyway? Examining the Benefits of Energy Efficiency Rules 2007—2014* (Washington, DC: The George Washington University Regulatory Studies Center, September 2015). http://regulatorystudies.columbian.gwu.edu/sites/regulatorystudies.columbian.gwu.edu/files/downloads/Examining-Energy-Efficiency-Standards_SMiller-9-2015.pdf.

22. Sofie E. Miller, *Whose Benefits Are They, Anyway? Examining the Benefits of Energy Efficiency Rules 2007—2014* (Washington, DC: The George Washington University Regulatory Studies Center, September 2015). (http://regulatorystudies.columbian.gwu.edu/sites/regulatorystudies.columbian.gwu.edu/files/downloads/Examining-Energy-Efficiency-Standards_SMiller-9-2015.pdf).

23. Sofie E. Miller, "One Discount Rate Fits All? The Regressive Effects of DOE's Energy Efficiency Rule," *Policy Perspectives* 22 (2015): 40–54. http://www.policy-perspectives.org/article/view/15110/pdf_21.

24. Energy Policy and Conservation Act, as amended, §324 (http://legcounsel.house.gov/Comps/EPCA.pdf).

25. Sofie E. Miller, *Whose Benefits Are They, Anyway? Examining the Benefits of Energy Efficiency Rules 2007–2014* (Washington, DC: The George Washington University Regulatory Studies Center, September 2015). http://regulatorystudies.columbian.gwu.edu/sites/regulatorystudies.columbian.gwu.edu/files/downloads/Examining-Energy-Efficiency-Standards_SMiller-9-2015.pdf.

26. Sofie E. Miller, "One Discount Rate Fits All? The Regressive Effects of DOE's Energy Efficiency Rule," *Policy Perspectives* 22 (2015): 40–54. http://www.policy-perspectives.org/article/view/15110/pdf_21.

27. *Addendum to Public Interest Comment on the Department of Energy's Proposed Clothes Washer Efficiency Standards.* Docket No. EE-RM-94-403. Arlington: Mercatus Center at George Mason University. 2000. (http://mercatus.org/sites/default/files/publication/Clothes_Washer_Standards.pdf).

28. 79 F.R. 38198.

29. *Addendum to Public Interest Comment on the Department of Energy's Proposed Clothes Washer Efficiency Standards.* Docket No. EE-RM-94-403. Arlington: Mercatus Center at George Mason University 2000.

(http://mercatus.org/sites/default/files/publication/Clothes_ Washer_Standards.pdf).

30. Brian F. Mannix and Susan E. Dudley, "The Limits of Irrationality as a Rationale for Regulation," *Journal of Policy Analysis and Management* 34(3) (2015): 707.

31. Brian F. Mannix and Susan E. Dudley, "The Limits of Irrationality as a Rationale for Regulation," *Journal of Policy Analysis and Management* 34(3) (2015): 707.

32. Ted Gayer and Kip Viscusi, "Overriding Consumer Preferences with Energy Regulations," *Journal of Regulatory Economics* 43 (2013): 263.

33. Ted Gayer and Kip Viscusi, "Overriding Consumer Preferences with Energy Regulations," *Journal of Regulatory Economics* 43 (2013): 248–264.

34. And, in fact, websites for homeowners considering high-efficiency furnaces suggest they do just that. See below.
    Don Vandervort. "Buying a High-Efficiency Furnace." HomeTips. Published April 23, 2015. http://www.hometips.com/ buying-guides/high-efficiency-furnaces.html.

35. Kenneth Gillingham, Richard G. Newell, and Karen Palmer, *Energy Efficiency Economics and Policy* (Washington, DC: Resources for the Future, April 2009). RFF DP 09-13. §5.4.

36. John Ewoldt, "New Furnace Is about to Get More Expensive," *Star Tribune*, October 4, 2012.

37. 78 F.R. 64126. See also 78 F.R. 36361.

38. Office of Management and Budget (OMB), "Circular A-4: Regulatory Analysis" (2003), 32.

39. Office of Management and Budget (OMB), "Circular A-94: Guidelines and Discount Rates for Benefit-Cost Analysis of Federal Programs"(1992), 4.

40. Richard G. Newell and Juha V. Siikamäki, "Individual Time Preferences and Energy Efficiency." National Bureau of Economic Research Working Paper No. 20969 (February 2015).

41. Office of Management and Budget (OMB), "Circular A-4: Regulatory Analysis" (2003).

42. Sofie E. Miller, "One Discount Rate Fits All? The Regressive Effects of DOE's Energy Efficiency Rule," *Policy Perspectives* 22 (2015): 40–54. http://www.policy-perspectives.org/article/view/15110/ pdf_21.

43. Brian F. Mannix and Susan E. Dudley, "The Limits of Irrationality as a Rationale for Regulation," *Journal of Policy Analysis and Management* 34(3) (2015): 708.

44. Sofie E. Miller, "One Discount Rate Fits All? The Regressive Effects of DOE's Energy Efficiency Rule," *Policy Perspectives* 22 (2015): 40–54. http://www.policy-perspectives.org/article/view/15110/pdf_21.

45. Kenneth Gillingham, Richard G. Newell, and Karen Palmer. *Energy Efficiency Economics and Policy* (Washington, DC: Resources for the Future, April 2009). RFF DP 09-13.

46. Shane Frederick, George Loewenstein, and Ted O'Donoghue, "Time Discounting and Time Preference: A Critical Review," *Journal of Economic Literature* 40(2) (2002): 384.

47. Richard G. Newell and Juha V. Siikamäki, "Individual Time Preferences and Energy Efficiency," National Bureau of Economic Research Working Paper No. 20969 (February 2015).

48. Kenneth Gillingham, Richard G. Newell, and Karen Palmer. *Energy Efficiency Economics and Policy* (Washington, DC: Resources for the Future, April 2009). RFF DP 09-13. §4.3.

49. Richard G. Newell, and Juha V. Siikamäki, "Individual Time Preferences and Energy Efficiency," National Bureau of Economic Research Working Paper No. 20969 (February 2015).

50. Jerry A. Hausman, "Individual Discount Rates and the Purchase and Utilization of Energy-Using Durables," *The Bell Journal of Economics* 10(1) (1979): 52.

51. Jerry A. Hausman, "Individual Discount Rates and the Purchase and Utilization of Energy-Using Durables," *The Bell Journal of Economics* 10(1) (1979): 53.
    This was also calculated by adjusting the 2013 median US income for inflation to find that $51,017 in 2013 dollars is closest to Hausman's figure of $15,000 in 1979 dollars.

52. Steffen Andersen, Glenn W. Harrison, Morton I. Lau, and Elisabet E. Rustrom, "Elicitation Using Multiple Price List Formats," *Experimental Economics* 9 (2006): 394.

53. Glenn W. Harrison, Morten Igel Lau, E. Elisabet Rutström, and Melonie B. Sullivan, "Eliciting Risk and Time Preferences Using Field Experiments: Some Methodological Issues," in *Field Experiments in Economics*, edited by J. Carpenter, G.W. Harrison,

and J.A. List (Greenwich: JAI Press, Research in Experimental Economics, Volume 10, 2005).

54. Sofie E. Miller, "One Discount Rate Fits All? The Regressive Effects of DOE's Energy Efficiency Rule," *Policy Perspectives* 22 (2015): 40–54. http://www.policy-perspectives.org/article/view/15110/pdf_21.

55. Sofie E. Miller, "One Discount Rate Fits All? The Regressive Effects of DOE's Energy Efficiency Rule," *Policy Perspectives* 22 (2015): 40–54. http://www.policy-perspectives.org/article/view/15110/pdf_21.

56. U.S. Department of Energy Fact Sheet, "Saving Energy and Money with Appliance and Equipment Standards in the United States." Published February 2015. http://energy.gov/sites/prod/files/2015/02/f19/equipment_standards_factsheet_updated_Feb_11_2015.pdf.

57. Energy Conservation Program: Energy Conservation Standards for Commercial Refrigeration Equipment. 78 FR 55980.

58. Sofie E. Miller, *Public Interest Comment on the Department of Energy's Proposed Rule Energy Conservation Program: Energy Conservation Standards for Commercial Refrigeration Equipment* (Washington, DC: The George Washington University Regulatory Studies Center, November 2013). http://regulatorystudies.columbian.gwu.edu/sites/regulatorystudies.columbian.gwu.edu/files/downloads/DOE_EERE-2010-BT-STD-0003.pdf.

59. 78 F.R. 55980.

60. U.S. Department of Transportation, "Corporate Average Fuel Economy (CAFE) Standards." Last modified August 27, 2014. (http://www.transportation.gov/mission/sustainability/corporate-average-fuel-economy-cafe-standards).

61. 77 F.R. 62629, author calculation based on Table I-19, *EPA's Estimated 2017–2025 Model Year Lifetime Discounted Costs, Benefits, and Net Benefits Assuming the 3% Discount Rate SCC Value (Billions of 2010 Dollars)*.

62. 77 F.R. 62627.

63. Brian F. Mannix and Susan E. Dudley, "The Limits of Irrationality as a Rationale for Regulation," *Journal of Policy Analysis and Management* 34(3) (2015): 707.

64. 77 F.R. 62914.

65. 77 F.R. 62914.

66. 77 F.R. 62914.
67. 77 F.R. 63114.
68. David R. Henderson, "The Economics of Fuel Economy Standards," *Regulation Magazine* (1985): 47. http://object.cato.org/sites/cato.org/files/serials/files/regulation/1985/1/v9n1-6.pdf.
69. David R. Henderson, "The Economics of Fuel Economy Standards," *Regulation Magazine* (1985): 47. http://object.cato.org/sites/cato.org/files/serials/files/regulation/1985/1/v9n1-6.pdf.
70. David R. Henderson, "The Economics of Fuel Economy Standards," *Regulation Magazine* (1985): 47. http://object.cato.org/sites/cato.org/files/serials/files/regulation/1985/1/v9n1-6.pdf.
71. 77 F.R. 62914.
72. 77 F.R. 62914.
73. Brian F. Mannix, "Bringing JAVA to the CAFÉ," *Regulation Magazine* (2001): 10. http://object.cato.org/sites/cato.org/files/serials/files/regulation/2001/10/mercatusreports.pdf.
74. J. Hayden Boyd and Robert E. Mellman, "The Effect of Fuel Economy Standards on the U.S. Automotive Market: An Hedonic Demand Analysis," *Transportation Research Part A: Policy and Practice* 14(5–6) (1980): 367–378.
75. Paul R. Portney, Ian W. H. Parry, Howard K. Gruenspecht, and Winston Harrington. *The Economics of Fuel Economy Standards* (Washington, DC: Resources for the Future, November 2003). RFF DP 03-44, 8.
76. *Department of Energy's Proposed Energy Efficiency Standards for Consumer Appliances.* Washington, DC: Executive Office of the President, Regulatory Analysis Review Group, Council on Wage and Price Stability, 1980, 20.
77. *Department of Energy's Proposed Energy Efficiency Standards for Consumer Appliances.* Washington, DC: Executive Office of the President, Regulatory Analysis Review Group, Council on Wage and Price Stability, 1980, A-2.
78. Severin Borenstein, "A Microeconomic Framework for Evaluating Energy Efficiency Rebound and Some Implications." E2e Working Paper 005. http://e2e.haas.berkeley.edu/pdf/workingpapers/WP005.pdf.
79. Paul R. Portney, Ian W. H. Parry, Howard K. Gruenspecht, and Winston Harrington. *The Economics of Fuel Economy Standards*

(Washington, DC: Resources for the Future, November 2003). RFF DP 03-44.

80. Henry Ruderman, *Do Appliance Efficiency Standards Really Save Energy?* (Applied Science Division, Lawrence Berkeley Laboratory, 1988). 9.152.

81. 77 F.R. 63118, 77 F.R. 62629.

82. *Joint Technical Support Document: Final Rulemaking for 2017–2025 Light-Duty Vehicle Greenhouse Gas Emission Standards and Corporate Average Fuel Economy Standards.* Washington, DC: U.S. Environmental Protection Agency and U.S. National Highway Traffic Safety Administration, August 2012. Chapter 4: "Economic and Other Assumptions Used in the Agencies' Analysis," 4–15.

83. 77 F.R. 62669.

84. *Joint Technical Support Document: Final Rulemaking for 2017–2025 Light-Duty Vehicle Greenhouse Gas Emission Standards and Corporate Average Fuel Economy Standards.* Washington, DC: U.S. Environmental Protection Agency and U.S. National Highway Traffic Safety Administration, August 2012. Chapter 4: "Economic and Other Assumptions Used in the Agencies' Analysis," 4–25.

85. *Joint Technical Support Document: Final Rulemaking for 2017–2025 Light-Duty Vehicle Greenhouse Gas Emission Standards and Corporate Average Fuel Economy Standards.* Washington, DC: U.S. Environmental Protection Agency and U.S. National Highway Traffic Safety Administration, August 2012. Chapter 4: "Economic and Other Assumptions Used in the Agencies' Analysis," page 4-22–4-23.

86. *Joint Technical Support Document: Final Rulemaking for 2017–2025 Light-Duty Vehicle Greenhouse Gas Emission Standards and Corporate Average Fuel Economy Standards.* Washington, DC: U.S. Environmental Protection Agency and U.S. National Highway Traffic Safety Administration, August 2012. Chapter 4: "Economic and Other Assumptions Used in the Agencies' Analysis," 4–19.

87. David L. Greene, James R. Kahn, and Robert C. Gibson, "Fuel Economy Rebound Effect for U.S. Household Vehicles," *The Energy Journal* 20(3) (1999): 1–31.

88. Roger Fouquet and Peter J. G. Pearson, *The Long Run Demand for Lighting: Elasticities and Rebound Effects in Different Phases of*

Economic Development (Basque Country: Basque Centre for Climate Change (BC3), July 2011). BC3 Working Paper Series 2011–06.

89. Severin Borenstein, "A Microeconomic Framework for Evaluating Energy Efficiency Rebound and Some Implications." E2e Working Paper 005. http://e2e.haas.berkeley.edu/pdf/workingpapers/WP005.pdf, 26.

90. Mark R. Jacobsen, "Evaluating US Fuel Economy Standards in a Model with Producer and Household Heterogeneity," *American Economic Journal: Economic Policy*, 5(2) (2013): 148–87.

91. Virginial McConnell, *The New CAFE Standards: Are They Enough on Their Own?* (Washington, DC: Resources for the Future, May 2013). RFF DP 13-14, 2.

92. Winston Harrington and Alan Krupnick. *Improving Fuel Economy in Heavy-Duty Vehicles* (Washington, DC: Resources for the Future, March 2012). Issue Brief 12–01.

93. Howard K. Gruenspecht, "Differentiated Regulation: The Case of Auto Emissions Standards," *The American Economic Review* 72(2) (1982): 328–331.

94. David R. Henderson, "The Economics of Fuel Economy Standards," *Regulation Magazine* (1985): 47. http://object.cato.org/sites/cato.org/files/serials/files/regulation/1985/1/v9n1-6.pdf.

95. See Section II.G, "Safety Considerations in Establishing CAFE/GHG Standards," at 77 F.R. 62740-68.

96. 77 F.R. 62767.

97. From the agencies' final rule: "Additionally, we note that the total amount of mass reduction used in the agencies' analysis for this rulemaking was chosen based on our assumptions about how much is technologically feasible without compromising safety. Again, while we are confident that manufacturers are motivated to build safe vehicles, we cannot predict with certainty that they will choose to reduce mass in exactly the ways or amounts that the agencies have analyzed in response to the standards." 77 F.R. 62767.

98. Mark R. Jacobsen, "Fuel Economy, Car Class Mix, and Safety," *American Economic Review* 101(3) (2011): 105–09.

99. National Research Council, *Effectiveness and Impact of Corporate Average Fuel Economy (CAFE) Standards* (Washington, DC: National Academy Press, 2002). Chapter 2: "The CAFE Standards: An Assessment." For another perspective, read Appendix A of the report: "Dissent on Safety Issues: Fuel Economy and Highway Safety" by David L. Greene and Maryann Keller (117–124).

100. The prevailing value of statistical life used by the Department of Transportation is currently monetized at $9.1 million.
Read more: Memorandum from Polly Trottenberg and Robert S. Rivkin to Secretarial Officers & Modal Administrators, 2013, U.S. Department of Transportation, Washington, DC. *Guidance on Treatment of the Economic Value of a Statistical Life in U.S. Department of Transportation Analyses.* Page 2.

101. Susan Mazur-Stommen and Kate Farley, *ACEEE Field Guide to Utility-Run Behavior Programs* (Washington, DC: American Council for an Energy-Efficient Economy, December 2013). Report http://www.iseif.org/wp-content/uploads/2014/01/ACEEE-Report.pdf

102. Susan Mazur-Stommen and Kate Farley, *ACEEE Field Guide to Utility-Run Behavior Programs* (Washington, DC: American Council for an Energy-Efficient Economy, December 2013). Report Number B132: http://www.iseif.org/wp-content/uploads/2014/01/ACEEE-Report.pdf

103. Susan Mazur-Stommen and Kate Farley, *ACEEE Field Guide to Utility-Run Behavior Programs* (Washington, DC: American Council for an Energy-Efficient Economy, December 2013). Report Number B132: http://www.iseif.org/wp-content/uploads/2014/01/ACEEE-Report.pdf

104. Thomas Dietz, Gerald T. Gardnerb, Jonathan Gilliganc, Paul C. Sternd, and Michael P. Vandenbergh, "Household Actions Can Provide a Behavioral Wedge to Rapidly Reduce US Carbon Emissions," *Proceedings of the National Academy of Sciences of the United States of America* 106(44) (2009): 18453, Table 1, "Achievable carbon emissions from household actions." Table 1 includes savings from both voluntary and non-voluntary household actions. Because the topic of this chapter is voluntary behavioral changes, the value of 88 million metric tons was tallied using emissions reductions from what Dietz et al. term *A actions* and *D actions*, or voluntary behavior changes that require no cost or new equipment to implement.

105. Thomas Dietz, Gerald T. Gardnerb, Jonathan Gilliganc, Paul C. Sternd, and Michael P. Vandenbergh, "Household Actions Can Provide a Behavioral Wedge to Rapidly Reduce US Carbon Emissions," *Proceedings of the National Academy of Sciences of the United States of America* 106(44) (2009): 18452.

106. P. Wesley Schultz, Jessica M. Nolan, Robert B. Cialdini, Noah J. Goldstein, and Vladas Griskevicius, "The Constructive, Deconstructive, and Reconstructive Power of Social Norms," *Psychological Science* 18(5) (2007): 429.

107. Thomas Dietz, Gerald T. Gardnerb, Jonathan Gilliganc, Paul C. Sternd, and Michael P. Vandenbergh, "Household Actions Can Provide a Behavioral Wedge to Rapidly Reduce US Carbon Emissions," *Proceedings of the National Academy of Sciences of the United States of America* 106(44) (2009): 18453, Table 1, "Achievable carbon emissions from household actions." See end-note 70 for more information on how this value was calculated.

108. *Emissions of Greenhouse Gases in the U.S.: U.S. carbon dioxide emission from residential sector energy consumption, 1990–2009.* Washington, DC: U.S. Energy Information Administration, March 31, 2011. (Download data here: http://www.eia.gov/environment/emissions/ghg_report/tables_ghg.cfm).

109. Thomas Dietz, "Altruism, Self-Interest, and Energy Consumption," *Proceedings of the National Academy of Sciences of the United States of America* 112(6) (2015): 1654.

110. Susan Mazur-Stommen and Kate Farley, *ACEEE Field Guide to Utility-Run Behavior Programs* (Washington, DC: American Council for an Energy-Efficient Economy, December 2013). Report Number B132: http://www.iseif.org/wp-content/uploads/2014/01/ACEEE-Report.pdf

111. Chris Mooney, "We Could Keep a Huge Amount of Carbon Out of the Atmosphere Just by Changing People's Behavior," *Washington Post*, February 27, 2015. http://www.washingtonpost.com/news/energy-environment/wp/2015/02/27/we-could-be-reaping-much-bigger-carbon-cuts-by-changing-peoples-behavior/.

112. Hunt Allcott, "Social Norms and Energy Conservation," *Journal of Public Economics* 95(2011): 1082–1095.

113. Robert B. Cialdini, Paymond R. Reno, and Carl A. Kallgren, "A Focus Theory of Normative Conduct: Recycling the Concept of Norms to Reduce Littering in Public Places," *Journal of Personality and Social Psychology* 58(6) (1990): 1015–1026.

114. P. Wesley Schultz, Jessica M. Nolan, Robert B. Cialdini, Noah J. Goldstein, and Vladas Griskevicius, "The Constructive, Deconstructive, and Reconstructive Power of Social Norms," *Psychological Science* 18(5) (2007): 429–434.

115. Hunt Allcott, "Social Norms and Energy Conservation," *Journal of Public Economics* 95 (2011): 1083.

116. *Residential Energy Consumption Survey 2009: Spreadsheet: CE3.1 End-Use Consumption Totals and Averages*, U.S. homes. Washington, DC: U.S. Energy Information Administration. (Download data here: http://www.eia.gov/consumption/residential/data/2009/index.cfm?view=consumption).

117. Susan Mazur-Stommen and Kate Farley, *ACEEE Field Guide to Utility-Run Behavior Programs* (Washington, DC: American Council for an Energy-Efficient Economy, December 2013). Report Number B132: http://www.iseif.org/wp-content/uploads/2014/01/ACEEE-Report.pdf

118. Chris Mooney, "We Could Keep a Huge Amount of Carbon Out of the Atmosphere Just by Changing People's Behavior," *Washington Post*, February 27, 2015. http://www.washingtonpost.com/news/energy-environment/wp/2015/02/27/we-could-be-reaping-much-bigger-carbon-cuts-by-changing-peoples-behavior/.

119. Hunt Allcott, "Social Norms and Energy Conservation," *Journal of Public Economics* 95 (2011): 1084–5.

120. Amanda R. Carrico, Michael P. Vandenbergh, Paul C. Stern, and Thomas Dietz, "US Climate Policy Needs Behavioural Science," *Nature Climate Change* 5 (2015): 177–179.

121. *EPA Factsheet: The Clean Power Plan. Key Changes and Improvements from Proposal to Final*. Washington, DC: The U.S. Environmental Protection Agency. August 2015. (http://www.epa.gov/airquality/cpp/fs-cpp-key-changes.pdf).

122. *Addendum to Public Interest Comment on the Department of Energy's Proposed Clothes Washer Efficiency Standards*. Docket No. EE-RM-94-403. Arlington: Mercatus Center Regulatory Studies Program. 2000. (http://mercatus.org/sites/default/files/publication/Clothes_Washer_Standards.pdf).

123. Sofie E. Miller. *Public Interest Comment on the Department of Energy's Proposed Rule Energy Conservation Program: Energy Conservation Standards for Commercial Refrigeration Equipment*. Washington, DC: The George Washington University Regulatory Studies Center, November 2013. (http://regulatorystudies.columbian.gwu.edu/sites/regulatorystudies.columbian.gwu.edu/files/downloads/DOE_EERE-2010-BT-STD-0003.pdf).

Nudges in Health Care

Robert Graboyes and Jessica Carges

INTRODUCTION: SLAYING DRAGONS, SWATTING BUGS

Nudges are a difficult topic to broach. Compared to other health care topics, they are small and, by nature, non-coercive (or only partially coercive). Almost any nudge, taken in isolation, can seem either reasonable or innocuous or both to those of varying ideological persuasions. It is in the aggregate, or in their secondary effects, where nudges may become expensive and disruptive.

It is an altogether different matter to write about, say, the Food and Drug Administration's (FDA) approval process for life-saving pharmaceuticals. There, the issues are stark. FDA regulations impose the full police powers of the state. People are forbidden to sell, give away, or use certain chemical substances the FDA has not approved.[1] Violators can be fined, arrested, or denied the right to practice their professions. Assuming a drug has been correctly judged unsafe by the FDA, people who used it might suffer grave illness or death.[2] If the FDA has correctly judged another drug to be safe but ineffective, a patient may suffer for using the unapproved drug, rather than an approved (and, presumably safe and effective) drug.[3] On the other hand, patients may suffer or die for lack of a safe, effective drug that the FDA has wrongly

R. Graboyes (✉) • J. Carges
Mercatus Center at George Mason University, Arlington, VA, USA

© The Editor(s) (if applicable) and The Author(s) 2016
S. Abdukadirov (ed.), *Nudge Theory in Action*,
DOI 10.1007/978-3-319-31319-1_11

289

disapproved or (at least) not yet approved.[4] In a blog comment, Alex Tabarrok wrote:

> Amazing that even after 50 years Thalidomide still scares. The basic fact is that dangerous drugs will sometimes be approved. That is a fact. But you also have to look at the costs of not approving drugs. Drugs that are *not* permitted by the FDA also kill. There is an invisible graveyard filled with the bodies of people who would have lived if more new drugs had been available and sooner.[5]

FDA issues are bold and stark—big, and painted in primary colors. The questions are clear-cut. The implications, financial and human, are massive. We could write similarly about other great issues of health care policy: hospital cartelization, Medicare reimbursement, the provision of care under Medicaid, the Affordable Care Act (ACA), medical licensure, the structure of medical school curriculum, international trade in medical goods and services, and mandatory vaccination.[6] If one wishes to arouse a reader's emotions, it is not difficult with big issues. If one wishes to do analytical work, it is helpful that the effects be large and easily measureable. With "big" issues, both the promises and the pitfalls are sizable.

Not so much with nudges. They are more difficult to pin down because their individual, immediate effects generally seem small and have a degree of voluntarism. They are evolutionary, not revolutionary. Erosive, not avulsive.

To criticize nudges is to swat bugs, not slay dragons. The swatting is all the more difficult because most would agree that some of the bugs are beneficial.

So the effects are small and may be difficult to measure, if they are measured at all. And, in a world in which there are many nudges, interactions among them may mean that the combined effects of multiple nudges may differ significantly from the sum of their individual effects. In attempting to measure nudges, we may run afoul of Lord Kelvin's dictum:

> [W]hen you cannot express it in numbers, your knowledge is of a meager and unsatisfactory kind; it may be the beginning of knowledge, but you have scarcely on your thoughts advanced to the state of Science.[7]

This chapter will first discuss the streams of thought that contribute to the creation and use of nudges with specific examples of where they exist in health care policy. Following this overview is a series of questions that looks at the validity of using nudges in policy.

Nudges: Confluence of Literatures

The idea of a health care nudge is that wise, benevolent experts can devise institutions that subtly induce us to make better health choices than we would make on our own—according to our own preferences. Nudges in health care draw on at least three streams of thought from, respectively, science, ethics, and politics:

1. *Behavioral Economics*: Attempts to increase the explanatory and predictive power of economic theory by providing it with more psychologically plausible foundations.[8] In health care, evolutionary psychology and prospect theory are the subsets of behavioral economics that most give rise to calls for nudges.
2. *Medical paternalism*: A notion, dating from antiquity, which holds that laypeople are unprepared to make choices with respect to their own health, whereas medical professionals can make rational choices on our behalf. This view holds that such paternalism is in the patient's own interest.
3. *Progressivism:* A political ideology that still underpins our modern view of government. Associated with Woodrow Wilson and other early progressives, progressivism created the belief that the state is best suited to amass expertise and design social institutions to better the rest of us.

Combining all three into a simple example:

- *Behavioral economics*: Politicians like New York's Mayor Michael Bloomberg have effectively argued that our carbohydrate-craving DNA urges us to drink larger quantities of sugary soft drinks than our health-conscious preferences would wish us to do.
- *Medical paternalism:* Limiting the size of soft-drink cups will diminish our consumption, which medical experts insist will result in increased health and therefore, happiness.
- *Progressivism:* The government, therefore, should outlaw the larger cups, thereby nudging people into lower carbohydrate intake.

This intersection of science, ethics, and politics produces a strong normative component melding into advocacy for behaviorist choice architectures to better our health. Each literature takes aim (in different ways) at the central assumption of neoclassical economics—namely, that people are rational or behave as if they were.

The classic statement of the rationality assumption comes from Milton Friedman, who argued that we need not believe in the literal truth of human rationality to find it a useful construct. Friedman argues the assumption is valuable as long as it yields useful predictions about human behavior.[9]

[science] *Behavioral Economics I (Evolutionary Psychology)*

Behavioral economists have searched for systematic, predictable deviations from rationality, and they often use evolutionary psychology to illustrate deviations that can be explained in terms of genetic survival strategies. Among other things, evolutionary psychologists suggest that altruism has an evolutionary rationale and that our genes drive us to do things that conflict with our preferences (e.g., eating too many cashews at a sitting);

> Economics has long found itself in the dock, accused of being the imperial discipline conquering all other social sciences. The profession must now face having the tables turned and being taken over by a new science that will include standard economics as a special subsection. Just as Einstein's theory of relativity turned Newton's theory of gravity into a special case, so evolutionary psychology contains utility theory as one very useful but limited paradigm.[10]

The challenge to by-the-book rationality was captured in Alan Greenspan's memorable assertion that financial markets were exhibiting "irrational exuberance". According to this body of theory, the traditional neoclassical economist's view of rationality is that humans are purely self-interested calculating machines. But often times, many examples prove difficult to explain with this definition.

Pinker provides the following example:

> More puzzling is discounting: the tendency in all of us to prefer a large late reward to a small early one, but then to flip our preference as time passes and both rewards draw nearer. A familiar example is deciding before dinner to skip dessert (a small early reward) in order to lose weight (a large late one), but succumbing to temptation when the waiter takes the dessert orders. ... The weakness of the will is an unsolved problem in economics and psychology alike.[11]

Pinker then notes that economist Thomas Schelling ponders the "rational consumer" construct by wading through a series of examples: smokers who wish to quit; a high-calorie diner who wishes to slim down; a television viewer with work to do.[12]

Evolutionary psychology suggests that we are adapted not to the world we live in now, but to the environment in which our species spent most of its history. Agriculture is considered a relatively recent development, and therefore, humans would be designed to produce success in the environment of small hunter-gatherer bands.[13] Discounting is therefore explained as a systematic deviation from neoclassical economists' definition of rationality due to evolutionary biases. As the above examples have shown, most people appear to have a very high discount rate for choices in the near future, and a much lower discount rate for alternative goals that are more distant. In a hunter-gatherer environment, nothing in the future is guaranteed or certain. It makes logical sense to value things that are assured immediately, even if today those assumptions do not necessarily still hold. Our evolutionary biases make us more susceptible to immediate, smaller rewards than future, larger ones.[14]

Continuing with Pinker:

> Schelling notes the strange ways in which we defeat our self-defeating behavior: putting the alarm clock across the room so we won't turn it off and fall back to sleep, authorizing our employers to put part of each paycheck away for retirement, placing tempting snacks out of reach, setting our watches five minutes ahead. Odysseus had his crewmates plug their ears with wax and tie him to the mast so he could hear the Sirens' alluring song and not steer the ship toward them and onto the rocks.[15]

Schelling, Pinker notes, sees a modularity of the mind. That "people behave sometimes as if they had two selves. ... The two are in continual contest for control." Pinker says "When the spirit is willing but the flesh is weak, such as in pondering a diet-busting dessert, we can feel two very different kinds of motives fighting within us, one responding to sights and smells, the other to doctors' advice."[16]

Our distant hunter-gatherer relatives can enlighten us on current health care trends as well. Genetic selection reveals that tendencies to eat too much salt or fat were adapted from an environment where such foods were rarer and labor more physical. Robin Hanson points out that among hunter-gatherers:

> Aid for injury is treated similarly to other forms of aid, such as sharing meat from [a] hunt, participating in a work party to build a hut, or joining in an

attempt to avenge the killing of an associate. Failing to help is interpreted as being less loyal to a group, coalition, or partner.[17]

We still use health care to signal loyalty today, whether it's buying lots of health care for our families or employees or pushing lots of care onto dying parents. By this argument, it is less concerning whether or not the health care is actually effective, just as long as it appears that we care sufficiently about others. Humans still cannot stand to be thought of as uncaring or unhelpful, since it is still interpreted as being less loyal to the group.

What can we conclude from all of this? Across cultures and time and ideologies, there is near-consensus that people are internally conflicted—that in each of us, a rational, well-informed being battles our animalistic, evolutionary nature. This duality appears especially strong in matters related to health. We engage in strategies to steer our actions more towards well-informed conclusions instead of evolutionary desires and sometimes, as with Odysseus, we delegate those actions to others.

[science] *Behavioral Economics II (Prospect Theory)*

Evolutionary biology tells us that our DNA can steer us away from rationality, particularly in matters related to health, and that we can engage in strategies to tack back toward rationality. Prospect Theory is the systematic study of those steering mechanisms.

Prospect Theory holds that our choices depend strongly on how the choices are presented to us. This school of thought began with two Israeli psychologists, Daniel Kahneman[18] and Amos Tversky, who illustrated deviations from rationality through a large set of simple anomalies. Kahneman provides an excellent survey of this literature.[19] Graboyes provides examples[20]:

> Why will a homeowner cut his own lawn to save $10, but will not mow his neighbor's lawn to earn $10? In a simple economic model, the two acts appear to be identical opportunities to choose between income and leisure, but the homeowner's choices seem inconsistent.
>
> Economics generally presumes that people prefer more choices to fewer choices. Why, then, will rational people thank you for removing a bowl of tempting, fat-rich cashews from their sight—thereby depriving them of a consumption choice?
>
> Why will people travel across town to save $10 on a clock radio or sweater but not to save $10 on a wide-screen TV or a car?

The rational-actor model underlying modern economics implicitly assumes that people act as if they were powerful, accurate calculating engines. According to Kahneman:

> Are people good intuitive statisticians? We already know that people are good intuitive grammarians: at age four a child effortlessly conforms to the rules of grammar as she speaks, although she has no idea that such rules exist. Do people have a similar intuitive feel for the basic principles of statistics? Amos reported that the answer was a qualified yes. We had a lively debate in the seminar and ultimately concluded that a qualified no was a better answer.[21]

Kahneman says:

> The assumption that agents are rational provides the intellectual foundation for the libertarian approach to public policy: do not interfere with the individual's right to choose, unless the choices harm others.[22]

Kahneman says he heard Gary Becker, partly in jest and partly not, say that the rise in obesity might result from people anticipating that a cure for diabetes is nigh upon us. Says Kahneman, "He was making a valuable point: when we observe people acting in ways that seem odd, we should first examine the possibility that they have a good reason to do what they do."[23] It is suggested that psychology should only enter when economic reasoning becomes implausible—which Kahneman thinks Becker's reasoning is. Kahneman then frames the dispute as one "between the Chicago school and the behavioral economists, who reject the extreme form of the rational-agent model."[24] Prospect Theory offers, in effect, a how-to guide on dealing with the internal conflicts that evolutionary biologists describe.

How a reference point is determined and framed in the decision-making process has large impacts in health care. The work of Rothman, Salovey, and colleagues on message framing has tested prospect theory predictions of how the description of test outcomes as gains or losses (as well as the conceptualization of the purpose of the test as preventative vs. diagnostic and the consequent perception of whether the test is "safe" or "risky") can affect test rates in health care.[25]

Alan Schwartz, Julie Goldberg, and Gordon Hazen illustrate that:

> Specifically, message framing theories predict that when a procedure is perceived as risky (e.g., cancer screening tests may cause a patient to find out

that they have cancer), loss-framed messages will promote testing more strongly than gain-framed messages, because people favor risky prospects over sure prospects in the domain of losses. On the other hand, when a procedure is perceived as safe (e.g., sunscreen prevents sunburn and skin cancer), gain-framed messages are predicted to be more effective because people prefer sure prospects to risky prospects in the domain of gains.[26]

There are a number of other studies that offer similar predictions, showing the true power of Prospect Theory in designing health care nudges.[27]

[ethics] *Medical Paternalism*

Eric Topol, cardiologist and editor of Medscape, reviews the history of medical paternalism from Hippocrates on.[28] He quotes Richard Gordon's comic novel: "doctors consider themselves the most evolved of the human species."[29]

Topol says of Hippocrates, "if he was the father of medicine, he was also the father of medical paternalism."[30] Among other things, Hippocrates urged physicians to conceal most things from patients, including present condition, prognosis, and medicinal formulas. Topol documents other physicians who thought it advantageous to avoid honesty with patients. But beyond matters of honesty and dishonesty (which may not be relevant to the nudge discussion), Topol offers the following:

> Dr. Benjamin Rush, who is regarded as both a founding father of the United States and the father of American psychiatry, wrote that doctors should "avoid sacrificing too much to the taste of (their) patients. ... Yield to them in matters of little consequence, but maintain an inflexible authority over them in matters essential to life."[31]

Topol says "what has been called the Age of Paternalism lasted for thousands of years." He quotes Siegler:

> This model of medicine—the "doctor knows best" model—was premised on trust in the physician's technical skills and moral stature, was buttressed by an attribution of magical powers to the healer, and was characterized by patient dependency and physician control.[32]

The symbol of the medical professions is the Rod of Asclepius—the Greek god of medicine and son of Apollo,[33] hinting at the divine nature of

medicine. (The American version has generally been the two-snake cadu-
ceus borne by Hermes).

Paternalism has persisted into the twenty-first century. Topol says he
became involved in a dispute with the American Medical Association
(AMA) over his call for relaxing medical paternalism. The dispute arose
from an interview with the *Wall Street Journal*:

> But what has really gotten me stirred up is the issue of whether patients
> should have access to their own health data. The AMA [...] was lobby-
> ing the government that consumers should not have access directly to their
> DNA data; that it has to be mediated through a doctor. The AMA did a
> survey of 10,000 doctors, and 90 % said they have no comfort using genom-
> ics in their clinical practice. So how could they be the ultimate mediator by
> which the public gets access to their DNA data? That really speaks to medi-
> cal paternalism.[34]

There is a long list of provisions from the AMA's 1847 *Code of Ethics*.[35]
Physicians, it says, pursue a "noble task." Later, "The obedience of a
patient to the prescriptions of his physician should be prompt and implicit.
He should never permit his own crude opinions as to their fitness, to
influence his attention to them," and "A patient should never send for
a consulting physician without the express consent of his own medical
attendant." And "A patient should, after his recovery, entertain a just and
enduring sense of the value of the services rendered to him by his physicians, for these are of such a character, that no mere pecuniary acknowl-
edgement can repay or cancel them."

No revisions occurred until 1903. Informed consent does not enter the
AMA's lexicon until 1957. There are many examples suggesting that the
ethic of paternalism persists in medicine to this day.

Ronald M. Epstein, MD, professor of family medicine, psychiatry,
and oncology, and director, Center for Communication and Disparities
Research, University of Rochester (NY) Medical Center, insists "most of
us do act paternalistically in ways that we often don't realize, [...] for
example, even the tone of voice you use to describe each option, or order
in which you present a choice to a patient, may influence a patient's decision. [...] And so, I think we are unwittingly paternalistic some of the
time... If you favor a certain option, you'll present it and frame it a bit
differently."[36]

There is a supreme irony in the paternalism of the past two centu-
ries. The AMA has appeared a decade or two into the period of medicine

known as "therapeutic nihilism." In the early nineteenth century, Western medicine arrived at the conclusion that it was doing more harm to patients than good. For the next century or so, physicians largely restricted themselves to diagnosis and prognosis, rather than therapeutics.[37]

Professor Lawrence Henderson of Harvard described 1910–1912 as "the Great Divide" when, for the first time ever, "a random patient with a random disease consulting a doctor chosen at random stands a better than 50/50 chance of benefiting from the encounter."[38] But Lewis Thomas wrote that even in the mid-1930s, Harvard's Medical School largely trained physicians "not to meddle" with the course of disease.[39] Therapeutic medicine began to advance in earnest with the widespread use of penicillin in the late 1930s.

The correctness of medical paternalism reached a high plateau in 1963, with the publication of Arrow's "Uncertainty and the Welfare Economics of Health Care."[40] Arrow enumerated the differences between health care and other areas of the economy: domination by nonprofits, insurers as intermediaries, consumer ignorance, and so forth. For the next half-century, this paper became the founding document for the notion that "health care is different"—that human rationality fails at the borders of medicine.[41]

Behavioral economics suggests an internal conflict between the rational and non-rational, and that the deviations are predictable and remediable. A body of tradition and literature adds that these circumstances are especially acute in the area of health and health care.

[politics] *Progressivism*

Woodrow Wilson entered the White House 12 years after the first Progressive Era president, Theodore Roosevelt. But the intellectual underpinnings of the expansive, activist modern state derive from the scholarly writings of Wilson years before the onset of the Progressive Era. Though progressivism advocated for many reforms, the central idea was that the government should lead efforts to change society's ills.[42]

Perhaps the first and most important piece of Progressive Era legislation was the Pure Food and Drug Act of 1906. Its main purpose was to ban foreign and interstate traffic in adulterated or mislabeled food and drug products, and it directed the government to inspect products and refer offenders to prosecutors. The act required that active ingredients be placed on the label of a drug's packaging and that drugs could not fall below purity levels established by the United States Pharmacopeia or the National Formulary.[43] For the first time, the federal government took responsibility for the safety of food and drugs in the USA.

Calls for broader federal involvement in health care began around the same time. The Socialist Party called for national unemployment, old age, and sickness insurance in its election platforms.[44] The ideas reached mainstream political circles in 1912, when Roosevelt's Progressive Party adopted a platform that "called for industrial health and safety standards, the prohibition of child labor, a minimum wage for women, compensation for industrial accidents, injuries, and occupational diseases, and 'the protection of home life against the hazards of sickness, irregular employment and old age through the adoption of a system of social insurance.'"[45]

The twentieth century saw a steady increase in federal and state intervention in health care. The federal government expanded its regulation of food and drugs in several big steps over the century, adding efficacy as a standard for approval and adding medical devices to drugs.[46]

Milton and Rose Friedman argued that through the twentieth century, the AMA acted as an anti-competitive guild, pushing for federal and state legislation to restrict who could practice medicine and how.[47]

NUDGE THEORY

To reiterate, we have three strains of thought converging: Humans exhibit systematic deviations from rationality and we can predictably steer their behavior. We ought to steer health-related behavior. And the state is well-suited for the task. Combining these notions, we arrive at the modern day use of behavioral economics and the idea of nudges. Food consumption is often the point of departure.

In *Nudge: Improving Decisions about Health, Wealth and Happiness*, Richard Thaler and Cass Sunstein present the notion of a nudge by way of a familiar, pedestrian example—the placement of food in a grocery store or cafeteria.[48] Any shopper knows instinctively that one is especially prone to purchase items placed at eye level in the aisles or placed anywhere in the checkout line. Food vendors pour large sums into market research on shelf placement and negotiate fiercely on this dimension, suggesting the truth of the proposition. It is doubtful that many would disagree with this point. Disagreements arise as to what to do with such knowledge.

Behavioral economics takes aim at a *homo economicus*—economic man. This notion from neoclassical economics is one of rational individuals who observe an array of options, evaluate them with perfection, and then choose optimally (according to their preferences).[49] *Homo economicus* is by design an artificial construct—an exaggeration, a simplification dreamed up by economists to clarify their analyses. In the simplest form of this construct, the presentation of options, indeed, has no impact on choices. People rationally choose among the options, irrespective of the presentation.

This discussion thus far has involved positive analysis, not normative. The behavioralist economists are correct in arguing that *homo economicus* is an unrealistic simplification of human behavior. Neoclassical economists may protest that they are perfectly aware of the caricatured nature of *homo economicus*, adding that, despite its unrealistic assumptions, it yields useful analysis. Behavioral economists argue that non-behavioralists take it too literally, and, in that respect, they are probably correct.

Thaler and Sunstein, however, venture forth from these positive propositions and into normative behavioral economics. Their argument is that: (1) choices are necessarily sensitive to how they are presented; (2) there is no such thing as a neutral presentation; and (3) public policy should therefore focus on steering individual choices by suggesting or mandating the initial presentations.

In health, Thaler and Sunstein single out three areas for nudges: Medicare prescription choices, organ donations, and environmental protection.[50] Other behavioral economists focus their efforts on areas such as obesity, alcoholism, drug use, sexually transmitted diseases, tobacco, exercise, driving, and prescription drug compliance.[51]

Thaler and Sunstein describe themselves as "libertarian paternalists," though that self-designation is controversial. They describe the libertarian aspect of their position as follows:

> The libertarian aspect of our strategies lies in the straightforward insistence that, in general, people should be free to do what they like—and opt out of undesirable arrangements if they want to do so. To borrow a phrase from the late Milton Friedman, libertarian paternalists urge that people should be "free to choose."[52]

They describe their paternalism as follows:

> The paternalistic aspect lies in the claim that it is legitimate for choice architects to try to influence people's behavior in order to make their lives longer,

healthier, and better. In other words, we argue for self-conscious efforts, by institutions in the private sector and also by the government, to steer people's choices in directions that will improve their lives. In our understanding policy is "paternalistic" if it tries to influence choices in a way that will make choosers better off, *as judged by themselves*.[53]

The authors' "libertarian paternalism" is, we would argue, clearly paternalistic. The libertarian aspect, we would continue, is much more debatable.

NUDGES: POLICY QUESTIONS

This section illustrates a series of ideas relevant to nudge-related public policy. Thaler and Sunstein recognize many of these problems in their book.

Are Fully Voluntary Nudges Objectionable?

Groceries and (as described by Thaler and Sunstein) cafeterias routinely practice nudging through placement of foods. Placing candy bars in the check-out lines where children often linger while parents await cashiers is presumably to nudge shoppers into a last-minute impulse purchase. Nutrition activists argue that removing the candy will nudge people away from purchasing the unhealthy candy bars. Some stores removed candies from those locations. Others didn't.

These actions nudge people into healthier choices without limiting their options. Most people won't argue against nudges in this context, but in other contexts it is more clearly seen as manipulation. Even fully voluntary, private-sector nudges draw some opposition.

Facebook has been something of a factory for nudges. Periodically, the company alters the default settings for, say, privacy, to nudge users into making certain decisions. These changes often draw vociferous criticism. Facebook also engaged in an experiment to determine whether the order of posts on a user's screen could nudge the user toward a particular mood. The experiment was successful, but the public outcry over perceived manipulation of users was significant.[54]

Nudges do not have to involve taxpayer funds, the power of the state, or mandatory usage of the venue. And yet there can still be sizable opposition to what is perceived of by some as manipulation.

Are Voluntary Nudges Voluntary?

It is also relevant to ask whether voluntary nudges are truly voluntary. Consider the case of New York City Mayor Michael Bloomberg's policy of nudging consumers away from soft-drink over-consumption. The policy banned the 32-ounce "Big Gulp"-sized drinks that are popular purchase items at convenience stores. As Oliver Burkeman in *The Guardian* opined:

> Ridiculous as all this is, it's worth briefly recapping why it makes no sense to see Bloomberg's policy as an incursion on anyone's liberty. The proposal is a classic example of a "nudge", as defined by Cass Sunstein and Richard Thaler in their famous book of that name. It doesn't stop you guzzling as much Coke as you like, but it modifies your "choice architecture"—the context in which you decide how much Coke to guzzle—so as to guide you towards the healthier option. Likewise, as Sunstein and Thaler explain, you can transform the dietary choices of school pupils by making salads slightly easier to reach for than fries; nobody's deprived of their right to fries. You can transform savings habits with bank accounts that move a portion of wages into a separate account unless the user opts out.[55]

Burkeman later appended an update to his *Guardian* article noting that Thaler himself had distanced himself from Bloomberg's large-soda ban, arguing on Twitter that, "To state the obvious: a BAN is not a NUDGE. The opposite in fact. So don't blame Bloomberg's ban on large soda cups on us."[56]

So we have a curious juxtaposition. Burkeman argues that the large-soda ban is a nudge because the consumer's diminished convenience does not constitute a reduction in anyone's liberty. Thaler does not consider this a nudge because it is a "ban" whose inconvenience, apparently, reduces consumers' liberty.

We are tempted to argue that the soda ban is both a nudge and a reduction in liberty—that the two concepts are not mutually exclusive. Bloomberg's law did not prohibit a consumer from purchasing 32 ounces of soda, but only made doing so slightly less convenient. We might ask whether this is qualitatively different from, say, limiting candy bars to inconvenient-to-reach grocery shelves—something Thaler does cite as a nudge. The real lesson here is that the difference between nudge and coercion is subjective. And add to this our earlier comment: "Almost any nudge, taken in isolation, can seem either reasonable or innocuous or both."

But the 32-ounce cup ban is not voluntary on the part of the vendors. And that ban entails real costs and diverts public funds from other uses. Consider a city deciding whether to impose vendor mandates in order to nudge customers in a desired direction. The government must expend resources to determine which nudges, if any, are desirable. The soft drink size is, after all, not the only nudge on the table. Let's say there are simultaneous drives to ban or limit trans fats, to require various forms of nutritional labeling, to have fresh fruit available, and so on. Each possible mandate requires its own cost-benefit analysis. The government, the wholesaler, and the retailers will engage in rent-seeking activities. For those mandates to be adopted, the government must establish an inspection and enforcement capability. With choices limited, profit margins (already razor-thin in these establishments) will be thinned even more. Depending on the bottom-line, the added regulatory burden can be the straw that breaks the camel's back, leading the most marginal establishments to close. Thus, there are potential labor market implications, and so forth.

Are Nudges Efficacious?

Then there is the question of whether the government actually gets nudges right.[57] Policymakers, like everyday people, are not fully rational and are also not fully knowledgeable on every subject. This leads to policy recommendations that can be wrong, which can harm the very people they are intended to help. For example, in the 1970s USDA Dietary Guidelines encouraged Americans to consume low-fat diets in order to decrease the risk of heart disease and obesity.[58] Despite the lack of evidence on these claims, it took until 2010 for the Dietary Guidelines committee to stop recommending limits on total fat. An article in the *Annals of Internal Medicine* conducted a meta-analysis of all available evidence and concluded that limits on fats should be lifted.[59] Despite the reversal, the American public still is more prone to actively avoid fats compared to carbohydrates.[60]

A large nudge for Americans was the 1990 Nutrition Labeling and Education Act, which required packaged food companies to apply nutritional labels by mid-1994.[61] In 1990, no state had an obese population exceeding 14 % of the total population. By 1994, the highest percentage was 19 %. In 2013, no state had fewer than 20 %, and 2 states were over 35 %.[62] There have been a number of local studies done to examine the effects of nutrition labeling. These include calorie labels at McDonald's fast food chains in New York, 15 restaurant chains in King County, Washington, and Starbucks. Evidence is overwhelming that posting of caloric information has little effect on the purchasing behavior of consumers.[63] The Age of Labeling became the Age of Obesity.

At this stage, the source of the obesity epidemic is unknown. Burn more calories than you consume and you'll lose weight. But cutting calories doesn't automatically mean weight loss. If cutting out 300 calories a day induces lethargy, maybe you'll spend more time on the couch, burn 300 fewer calories, and lose no weight; maybe you'll burn 500 calories fewer and actually gain weight. If you think the answers are easy, explain this: as we've grown heavier since the 1980s, so have animals, including pets, wildlife, and even laboratory animals on controlled diets.[64] No one really knows why.

Consider, also, that obesity is a serious problem in the one segment of American society where mandates and nudges ought to be at their most potent—the military. In many circumstances, the military services have a considerable degree of control over service personnel's diet and exercise. And yet, obesity is an increasing problem for the military.[65]

Are Nudges Inherently Political?

Lee Harris raises the prospect that nudges will transmogrify into shoves. In other words, the paternalism will rise and the libertarianism will fade.[66] Harris minimizes the differences between hard paternalism and the softer idea of nudges:

> The old metaphor of social engineering has been replaced with a new metaphor: the central planners are now architects of choice, to use Thaler and Sunstein's image, though they speak only of choice architecture, as if a piece of architecture could come about without an architect to design it.[67]

Both demand a cognitive elite, making decisions on behalf of the rest of us; and the cognitive elite is composed of fallible, self-interested, irrational human beings, much like the rest of us. Harris describes the ACA this way:

> Obamacare was the first large-scale attempt to implement the principles of libertarian paternalism that, as its architects assured us, would make us all healthier, wealthier, and happier. Prior to the rollout, Obamacare's architects were only able to present their designs in the form of abstract

blueprints—blueprints which looked just as beautiful and elegant on paper as the collective farm movement had looked to its Soviet designers.[68]

Harris adds that like earlier, more overt social planning schemes, this one, too, "was strikingly like one of the bizarrely complicated machines imagined by the great cartoonist Rube Goldberg." The nudges bundled together as the ACA often failed or spun off unintended consequences.[69]

The offer of federal funds was supposed to nudge states into expanding Medicaid and establishing health insurance exchanges. Only a few more than half expanded Medicaid, while just over one-third established exchanges. Matthew Baum quotes David Hyman as saying it isn't even clear in this case what constitutes a successful nudge or a failed one.[70] It is fair to say that the number of states expanding Medicaid and establishing exchanges is less than ACA backers had hoped.

At the individual level, the ACA mandated nutrition labeling to nudge consumers to maintain healthier weights. But Baum[71] quotes Andrea Freeman as noting that governments have conflicting goals and simultaneously nudge consumers in opposite directions. The USDA, Freeman says, can nudge consumers toward healthier food via nutrition guidelines while nudging them in the opposite direction by subsidizing unhealthy foods.

Casey Mulligan[72] details how the ACA's employer and individual mandates depress both wages and employment. ACA supporters have argued that neither feature is literally a mandate. Employers are not required to provide employees with health insurance; instead, they can pay penalties. The individual mandate was similarly structured in the law, and the Supreme Court, ruling in *NFIB v Sebelius*, recrafted the choice as purchase insurance or pay a tax. [We will add that, as with the large-soda ban described above, some would call these provisions nudges, while others would view them as coercive. As with the sodas, the delineation is ultimately subjective.]

Abdukadirov notes that encouragement can turn to coercion. Writing of New York City's ban on large sodas:

> nudges can easily turn to shoves. With nudges, policymakers suggest better choices but ultimately leave the decision up to the individuals. Yet, some policymakers do not stop there. They argue that if people are irrational, it is the government's responsibility to constrain individual choices. New York City Mayor Bloomberg's decision to ban large soda drinks, since declared unconstitutional by the state Supreme Court's Appellate Division, is a prime example.[73]

There were a good many reasons to be skeptical of centralized regulation during the twentieth century. Hayek's classic statement was that central planners could never absorb and process the myriad bits of knowledge spread across millions of individuals.[74] Hayek's logic underlay much of what became the public choice literature.[75] It also influenced some on the political left. An example is Steven Johnson, a "peer progressive" suspicious of central planning, who cites Hayek as an inspiration.[76] Johnson believes that networks of people ("peers") are better at collective decision-making than are centralized experts. This view is reflected also in Surowiecki, who catalogs the triumphs of networked laymen over credentialed experts. Surowiecki acknowledges the positive role of government and corporate command-and-control innovation, but notes: "in the history of science and technology, top-down organization has always been more of an anomaly than the ordinary way of doing business."[77]

But Graboyes notes that the capacity of centralized planners may have dimmed considerably in the Internet Age. Hayek described the difficulty central planners have in absorbing information that is dispersed among millions of individuals. But he was writing in an era when information was (compared with now) scarce. Today, information is super-abundant; it travels peer-to-peer across the Web and other conduits; and much of it never passes through the planner's central hub. Discussing regulation, Graboyes makes the following analogy:

> imagine an early 20th century market town, with multiple roads feeding all traffic through the center of town. This works quite well as long as the number of horse-drawn wagons and slow-moving automobiles are few and far-between. But deep into the Automobile Age, this perfectly well-designed traffic pattern clogs into maddening jams. And when an emergency occurs, traffic draws to a standstill. … With the market town, the answer is to reconfigure the hub-and-spoke roads into a more flexible grid of alternative nodes and routes, with commerce dispersed across the landscape.[78]

But the nudge does the opposite. It assumes that the necessary information will flow through the central hub—whether for mandates or nudges. But in the twenty-first century, medical data, goods, and services increasingly flow through decentralized networks. The Internet, low-cost health care technologies, and inexpensive travel make it far more difficult for central authorities to monitor and influence health care.

Some examples are:

23andMe.[79] For $99, this California company analyzes an individual's DNA and provides information on roughly 250 genetic conditions and familial connections with other 23andMe users. The FDA barred 23andMe from providing consumers with genetic information other than genealogical data. In contrast, the UK[80] allowed the company to sell its full range of products. Can one get the forbidden scan while traveling in the UK? Can one get the results in the USA by mailing the sample to a friend in Great Britain? (Note: 23andMe has tentatively resumed sale of genetic information in the USA, but only on low-risk conditions).[81]

PatientsLikeMe.[82] This is a crowdsourcing website that allows individuals to share information about their symptoms, illnesses, treatments, and other experiences. The site has been used to organize research trials.

FitBit[83] *and more.* Wearable health care telemetry is now inexpensive, light, and largely beyond the purview of medical professionals and governments. Recently, parents have programmed smartphones to monitor their children's insulin pumps[84] from afar.

3D-printed prosthetic hands. The e-NABLE consortium[85] uses social media to connect individuals needing prosthetic hands with individuals wishing to manufacture such hands. The hands are manufactured for $50 or less and distributed peer to peer.

WebMD.[86] Medical consultation sites are proliferating across the web.

Medical tourism.[87] Increasingly, Americans are going to other countries to receive medical care.

Telemedicine. Companies like Doctor on Demand[88] can provide medical examinations via smartphone and tablet, though state laws in the USA restrict the use of such services. Telemedicine companies are active in other countries, and it remains to be seen whether it is possible to control cross-border use of such services.

3D-printed drugs. The FDA recently approved[89] the first 3D-printed drugs. The possibility exists that 3D printers, the Internet, and open-source software will make it relatively inexpensive and private to produce elaborate pharmaceuticals in garage labs.

Biohacking. At the radical end of health care, "biohackers" conduct procedures unintermediated by medical professionals. These include surgical procedures and other alterations of human bodies. *Nature* recently reported in the possibility of amateurs performing gene splicing.[90]

The common thread in these and myriad other cutting-edge procedures is that they remove significant chunks of health care from the purview of centralized experts. In such an environment, it is difficult for the central hub (e.g., FDA) to monitor behavior, estimate individual reactions, and track results. In such an environment, can the central authorities estimate how nudges will affect populations or, retrospectively, determine whether or not they worked?

A particular challenge is that much information is now partitioned into micro-demographics. A generation ago, most of us communicated and obtained information through the same routes. Today, islets of communication are largely isolated within groups divided by age, gender, ethnicity, tastes, geography, and so forth. Paradoxically, the vastly increased amount of information available to all individuals has tended to compartmentalize our sources by demographic group.

Finkelstein and Zuckerman document the extent to which obesity is correlated with ethnicity.[91] If one designs nudges to combat obesity, does one design separate nudges for each ethnic community and other socio-economic communities? It is worth noting that nudges which impact ethnicities differently may come to be perceived as discriminatory. People are inherently different and will therefore respond to nudges in different manners. Should nudges be allowed to persist if their effectiveness can differ widely based on who encounters it?

The central fact that joins all of these developments is this: The IT revolution has changed the fundamental nature of specialized information in society. Google CEO Eric Schmidt said in 2010, "Every two days now we create as much information as we did from the dawn of civilization up until 2003." Schmidt noted that the sources of this information are highly decentralized—user-generated data. He added, "I spend most of my time assuming the world is not ready for the technology revolution that will be happening to them soon."[92]

From the FDA's inception until the late twentieth century, the agency was mostly concerned with regulating technologies that were big, heavy, expensive, visible, traceable, complex to operate, and produced by people in the FDA's Rolodex. An archetypical device of this era would be an MRI unit made by, say, Philips; there were no hobbyist MRIs built in garages. In contrast, the dominant twenty-first century technologies may be more like the smartphone-based insulin pump monitor mentioned above. In that case, a layman unknown to the FDA rigged up a powerful device at little cost, operated it himself, and in doing so, created no visible financial trail. With little difficulty, he could pass it along to friends (or customers) outside of the purview of regulators.

Furthermore, the cost of life-changing technologies is plummeting. In the early 2000s, sequencing a human genome cost around $3 billion. A little over a decade later, the cost had dropped to under $1,000.[93] With Moore's Law proceeding apace, the cost of a full sequence may drop in a few years to a few dollars. That, plus low-cost, omnipresent statistical software vastly expands the potential for decentralized discovery of connections between genes and health. With data and devices flowing peer to peer, Moore's Law becomes amplified by Metcalfe's Law (the value of a network is proportional to the square of the number of connected participants). If that is the case, consumers and producers will have a much greater incentive to ignore or defy the incentives that government planners seek to implement.

If 23andMe and e-NABLE and their successors can radically improve consumers' lives for small costs, will centrally planned regulations and nudges have the impacts their authors desire? Can the FDA effectively regulate (or even nudge) a world where massive volumes of data flow through a shifting mosaic of micro-demographics?

CONCLUSION

We have argued that health care nudges blend components of behavioral economics, medical paternalism, and Progressivism.

We raise questions of whether the ostensibly voluntaristic nature of nudges separates them from more coercive actions of the state: whether nudges are truly voluntary, efficacious, or inherently political.

We reiterate that the small effects of individual nudges makes them harder targets for analysis than big, sweeping social institutions—but the nudges still matter.

We'll close with Lee Harris's eloquent critique of nudges and the philosophy behind them:

Perhaps Daniel Kahneman should add another cognitive bias to his list—a bias that doesn't affect ordinary individuals very much, but which has always had a profoundly distorting effect on the judgments and decisions made by intellectuals, namely, an irrational infatuation with abstract theories and utopian ideals, despite the demonstrable fact that such theories and ideals, when put into practice, have inevitably failed to improve the human lot and in many cases have led to complete disaster. The small irrationalities of our daily individual lives, so well documented by Kahneman, can never damage society as much as the grandiose rationality of centralized planners—a vital truth that our generation seems to have forgotten, but of which Obamacare is rapidly reminding us.[94]

Notes

1. "U.S. Food and Drug Administration." U S Food and Drug Administration Home Page. 2002. Accessed August 31, 2015.
2. The most infamous case in history was the thalidomide disaster of the late 1950s and early 1960s, see Jack Botting, "The History of Thalidomide," *Drug News & Perspectives* (Impact Factor: 3.13) 15(9) (12/2002): 604–611.
3. Efficacy was added as an approval standard in 1962: US Food and Drug Administration. FDA, "Significant dates in US food and drug law history." (2014).
4. Milton Friedman and Rose D. Friedman, "Who Protects the Consumers?" in *Free to Choose: A Personal Statement*. Harvest. ed. (Harvest House, 1980), 203–210.
5. Alex Tabarrok, "The FDA and International Reciprocity," *Marginal REVOLUTION* November 19, 2013. Accessed August 31, 2015.
6. Robert Graboyes, "Island Hoping and Leapfrogging," in *Fortress and Frontier in American Health Care* (Arlington: Mercatus Center at George Mason University, 2014).
7. Baron William Thomas, Lecture, London, May 3, 1883.
8. Erik Angner, *A Course in Behavioral Economics* (Houndmills: Palgrave Macmillan, 2012).
9. Milton Friedman, *Essays in Positive Economics* (Chicago: University of Chicago Press, 1970), 3–43.
10. Thomas Gale Moore, "Reformulation of Microecon," Reformulation of Microecon.2014. http://web.stanford.edu/~moore/Evolution-aryEconomics.html. Additional literature description can be found here: Robert Graboyes, *Why We Want What We Want* (2012). http://www.robertgraboyes.com/writings_files/WWWWWW.pdf

11. Steven Pinker, *How the Mind Works*. Kindle edition (New York: Norton, 1997), 395.
12. Schelling cited in Pinker, ibid, p. 395.
13. Owen Jones uses the term "time shifted rationality" to express this idea.
14. David Friedman, *Economics and Evolutionary Psychology* (na, 2004).
15. Steven Pinker, *How the Mind Works*. Kindle edtion (New York: Norton, 1997), 395.
16. Schelling cited in Pinker, ibid, p. 395.
17. Robin Hanson, "Showing That You Care: The Evolution of Health Altruism," *Medical Hypotheses* 70(4) (2008): 724–742.
18. Kahneman, a psychologist and sharp critic of neoclassical economics, won the Nobel Memorial Prize in Economic Sciences for his work.
19. Daniel Kahneman, *Thinking, Fast and Slow* (Macmillan Kindle Edition, 2011).
20. Robert Graboyes, "...And Why What We Want Bugs Economists," Federal Reserve Bank of Richmond Equilibria #7. 2001/02. http://www.robertgraboyes.com/writings_files/Bugs%20Economists.pdf
21. Kahneman, op cit, p. 5.
22. Ibid, p. 411.
23. Ibid, p. 412.
24. Ibid.
25. Rothman, A. J., Bartels, R. D., Wlaschin, J., & Salovey, P. (2006). The strategic use of gain- and loss-framed messages to promote healthy behavior: How theory can inform practice. *Journal of Communication, 56*, S202–S220; Rothman, A. J., & Salovey, P. (1997). Shaping perceptions to motivate healthy behavior: The role of message framing. *Psychological Bulletin, 121(1)*, 3–19.
26. Alan Schwartz, Julie Goldberg, and Gordon Hazen, "Prospect Theory, Reference Points, and Health Decisions," Judgment and Decision Making 3(2) (2008): 174–180.
27. A. M. Apanovitch, D. McCarthy, and P. Salovey, "Using Message Framing to Motivate HIV Testing Among Low-Income, Ethnic Minority Women," *Health Psychology-Hillsdale-*, 22 (2003): 60–67. doi: 10.1037/0278-6133.22.1.60; A. Moxey, D. O'Connell, P. McGettigan, D. Henry. "Describing Treatment Effects to Patients: How They Are Expressed Makes a Difference," *Journal of General Internal Medicine* 18(11) (2003): 948–959.; S. E. Rivers, P. Salovey, D. A. Pizarro, J. Pizarro, and T. R. Schneider, Message Framing and Pap Test Utilization Among Women Attending a Community Health Clinic," *Journal of Health Psychology* 10 (2005): 65–77. doi: 10.1177/1359105305048556.

28. Eric Topol. *The Patient Will See You Now: The Future of Medicine Is in Your Hands* (Basic Books Kindle Edition, 2015).
29. Richard Gordon, *Doctor in the House* (Penguin, 1961).
30. Topol, op cit, p. 18.
31. Ibid, p. 21.
32. Ibid, p. 21.
33. Ibid.
34. Ibid, p. 22.
35. Ibid, 22ff.
36. "Paternalism: Does It Still Have a Place in Modern Medical Practice?" AHC Media Continuing Medical Education Publishing RSS. August 1, 2010. http://www.ahcmedia.com/articles/19883-paternalism-does-it-still-have-a-place-in-modern-medical-practice
37. Lewis Thomas, *Fragile Species* (Simon and Schuster, 1996).
38. Herman L. Blumgart, "Caring for the Patient," *The New England Journal of Medicine* 270 (1964): 449–456.
39. Thomas, op cit.
40. Kenneth J. Arrow, "Uncertainty and the Welfare Economics of Medical Care," *The American Economic Review* (1963): 941–973.
41. Avik Roy, "The Gospel According to Ken Arrow," *National Review Online*, August 30, 2010.
42. "Teddy Roosevelt and Progressivism." Slavery by another Name. PBS. http://www.pbs.org/tpt/slavery-by-another-name/themes/progressivism/
43. US Food and Drug Administration, " Federal Food and Drugs Act of 1906," *US Department of Health and Human Services* 20 (2009).
44. Anne-Emanuelle Birn, Theodore M. Brown, Elizabeth Fee, and Walter J. Lear, "Struggles for National Health Reform in the United States," *American Journal of Public Health* 93(1) (2003): 86–91.
45. Ibid.
46. Op cit., Efficacy was added as an approval standard in 1962: US Food and Drug Administration. FDA, "Significant dates in US food and drug law history." (2014), http://www.fda.gov/AboutFDA/WhatWeDo/History/Milestones/ucm128305.htm
47. Milton Friedman and Rose Friedman, *Free to Choose: A Personal Statement* (Houghton Mifflin Harcourt, 1990), 240.
48. Richard H. Thaler and Cass R. Sunstein, *Nudge: Improving Decisions About Health, Wealth, and Happiness* (New Haven: Yale University Press, 2008).

49. "Homo Economicus Definition | Investopedia." Investopedia. November 20, 2003.
50. Thaler and Sunstein, op cit, Part III
51. These and other topics are covered in: Christina A. Roberto and Ichiro Kawachi (eds.) *Behavioral Economics and Public Health* (Oxford University Press, 2015).
52. Milton Friedman, Rose Friedman, and Free To Choose, *A Personal Statement* (Secker and Warburg, 1980).
53. Thaler and Sunstein, op cit, p. 5.
54. Kashmir Hill, "Facebook Manipulated 689,003 Users' Emotions For Science," *Forbes*, June 28, 2014.
55. Oliver Burkeman, "How Bloomberg's Soda Ban Is a Classic Example of 'Choice Architecture'," *The Guardian*, July 12, 2012.
56. Richard Thaler, Twitter Post. May 31, 2012, 4:06 PM. https://twitter.com/R_Thaler/status/208273339507150849
57. "Food Pyramids and Plates: What Should You Really Eat?" The Nutrition Source. http://www.hsph.harvard.edu/nutritionsource/pyramid-full-story/
58. Paul R. Marantz, Elizabeth D. Bird, and Michael H. Alderman, "A Call for Higher Standards of Evidence for Dietary Guidelines," *American Journal of Preventive Medicine* 34(3) (2008): 234–240.
59. Rajiv Chowdhury, Samantha Warnakula, Setor Kunutsor, Francesca Crowe, Heather A. Ward, Laura Johnson, Oscar H. Franco, Adam S. Butterworth, Nita G. Forouhi, Simon G. Thompson, Kay-Tee Khaw, Dariush Mozaffarian, John Danesh, and Emanuele Di Angelantonio, "Association of Dietary, Circulating, and Supplement Fatty Acids with Coronary Risk. A Systematic Review and Meta-analysis," *Annals of Internal Medicine* 160(6) (2014): 398–407.
60. Andrew Dugan, "Americans Still Avoid Fat More Than Carbs." Gallup.com. July 29, 2014.
61. "H.R. 3562—101st Congress (1989–1990): Nutrition Labeling and Education Act of 1990." Accessed November 2, 2015.
62. See maps at "Obesity Prevalence Maps." Centers for Disease Control and Prevention. September 11, 2015.
63. Eric A. Finkelstein, Kiersten L. Strombot, Nadine L. Chan, and James Krieger, "Mandatory Menu Labeling in One Fast-Food Chain in King County, Washington," *American Journal of Preventive Medicine* 40(2) (2011): 122–7. Brian Elbel, Rogan Kersh, Victoria L. Brescoll, and L. Beth Dixon, "Calorie Labeling and Food Choices: A First Look at the

Effects on Low-Income People in New York City," *Health Affairs* 28(6) (2009): w1110–w1121. And Bryan Bollinger, Phillip Leslie, and Alan Sorensen. *Calorie Posting in Chain Restaurants.* No. w15648. National Bureau of Economic Research, 2010.

64. Alla Katsnelson, "Lab Animals and Pets Face Obesity Epidemic." Nature.com. November 24, 2010.

65. See, for example, Stew Smith, "U.S. Troops Too Fat to Fight?" Military.com.

66. Lee Harris, "When Nudge Comes to Shove." AEI. November 13, 2013.

67. Ibid.

68. Ibid.

69. Ibid.

70. Matthew Baum, "Potential Problems and Limits of Nudges in Health Care," *Bill of Health*, May 2, 2014.

71. Ibid.

72. Casey Mulligan, "The ACA's Unintended Consequences," *City Journal*, May 14, 2015.

73. Sherzod Abdukadirov, "When 'Nudge' Comes to Shove," *US News*, August 12, 2013.

74. Friedrich August Hayek, "The Use of Knowledge in Society." (1945).

75. For example, James M. Buchanan, *The Limits of Liberty: Between Anarchy and Leviathan.* No. 714. University of Chicago Press, 1975.

76. Steven Johnson, *Future Perfect: The Case for Progress in a Networked Age* (Penguin UK, 2012).

77. James Surowiecki, *The Wisdom of Crowds* (New York: Anchor, 2005), 163.

78. Robert Graboyes, "Why We Need to Liberate America's Health Care," *PBS*, January 9, 2015.

79. "23andMe—Genetic Testing for Ancestry." 23andMe. 2015. https://www.23andme.com/

80. Ronald Bailey, "23andMe Gene Test Banned by FDA Is Now Available in the U.K." Reason.com. December 4, 2014.

81. http://www.medscape.com/viewarticle/853481

82. https://www.patientslikeme.com/

83. "There's a Fitbit Product for Everyone." Fitbit Official Site for Activity Trackers & More. 2015. https://www.fitbit.com/

84. Dan Hurley, "Diabetes Patients Are Hacking Their Way Toward a Bionic Pancreas." Wired.com. December 24, 2014.

85. Jen Owen, "Enabling The Future." Enabling The Future, September 12, 2015. http://enablingthefuture.org/
86. "WebMD—Better Information. Better Health." WebMD. http://www.webmd.com/
87. "Medical Tourism Association—Medical Travel & Health Tourism: Medical Tourism Association." http://www.medicaltourismassociation.com/en/index.html
88. "Urgent Care Doctors & Psychologists—Doctor On Demand." Doctor On Demand. http://doctorondemand.com
89. Robinson Meyer, "3-D Printed Drugs Are Here," *The Atlantic*, August 19, 2015.
90. Heidi Ledford, "Biohackers Gear Up for Genome Editing." Nature.com. August 26, 2015.
91. Eric A. Finkelstein and Laurie Zuckerman, *The Fattening of America: How the Economy Makes Us Fat, If It Matters, and What To Do About It* (John Wiley & Sons, 2010).
92. M. G. Siegler, "Eric Schmidt: Every 2 Days We Create As Much Information As We Did Up To 2003," *TechCrunch.com*, August 4, 2010, accessed November 6, 2015. http://techcrunch.com/2010/08/04/schmidt-data/
93. Antonio Regalado, "EmTech: Illumina Says 228,000 Human Genomes Will Be Sequenced This Year," *TechnologyReview.com*, September 24, 2014, accessed November 6, 2015. http://www.technologyreview.com/news/531091/emtech-illumina-says-228000-human-genomes-will-be-sequenced-this-year/
94. Harris, op cit.

Conclusion: Behavioral Economics and Policy Interventions

Richard Williams

The purpose of this book is to demonstrate that there is a strong private sector that helps people's decision making and that stringent criteria ought to be met before governments attempt to improve on private decision making, whether through structuring information to "nudge" people into making the government-preferred decision or using more stringent measures to achieve the same thing. Where people have difficulty matching their inherent preferences into real life decisions that satisfy those preferences, a private market will almost always arise that can help to match decisions with preferences.

There are two issues related to the use of behavioral economics in policy discussed in this book and they are used without always distinguishing them. The first is how the findings of behavioral economics are used to justify a new policy. One primary justification for government policies, particularly government regulation, has been required by an Executive Order going back nearly two decades that regulations are needed "to interpret the law, or are made necessary by compelling public need, such as material failures of private markets to protect or improve the health and safety of the public, the environment, or the well-being of the American

R. Williams (✉)
Mercatus Center at George Mason University, Arlington, VA, USA

S. Abdukadirov (ed.), *Nudge Theory in Action*,
DOI 10.1007/978-3-319-31319-1_12

people."[1] The economic rationale contained in that order (still in force) suggests that a rule is needed to correct failures of private *markets*, not *personal* failures. Even if other parts of the order might be construed to suggest correcting personal failures, they should be of such magnitude as to be a "compelling public need."

The second use of behavioral economics in policy, as originally construed in the book *Nudge* by Thaler and Sunstein, is to construct less onerous remedies when there is a compelling public need.[2] The idea is to choose a policy option that provides people with well-ordered information that helps them match their inherent preferences with their actual choices. Rather than mandating reallocation of resources through product bans or mandated expenditures, the same goals might be accomplished by simply helping people to make choices aligned with what they might choose if they were perfectly rational. But when more stringent measures are chosen based on rationales using behavioral economic findings, these are no longer informational nudges but rather the older form of paternalism.

So there are several possibilities for the use of behavioral economics in policy. A finding of personal decision failures can be a rationale for policy, and we can either have a structured information remedy or a more stringent, paternalistic policy to remedy those failures. For example, suppose the decision failure is determined to be that consumers are shortsighted and do not choose cars that get high enough gas mileage. The remedy could be to structure the information that they receive about gas mileage in a way that nudges them toward higher mileage cars or the issue could be forced by ordering car manufacturers to make more fuel efficient cars. Identification of the problem uses behavioral economics and providing structured information would also use behavioral economics. The remedy to order changes in how cars are produced is just paternalistic.

Finally, there are some issues associated with the relatively new science of behavioral economics itself. Much of the research has been generated in laboratory experiments, and it is not always clear that these findings manifest themselves in real world situations. And, as will be discussed further on, there is the misguided notion that somehow behavioral economics repairs what is wrong with the simplistic assumptions associated with neoclassical economics that assumes perfectly rational participants. This assumption is made in neoclassical economics to predict population behavior; it is neither a prediction nor a prescription for individuals.

Several authors in this volume take on the charge that behavioral economics remedies an inherent weakness in neoclassical economics where the supposed weakness is the assumption that consumers and producers make perfectly rational and fully informed decisions always and everywhere. Mario Rizzo argues that the so-called assumptions of neoclassical theories were not prescriptions for how people ought to behave or even assumptions that they did behave that way, they were used to construct a theory that would have some predictive power. Adam Smith and Todd Zywicki point out that anyone that does believe in perfect rationality doesn't truly understand how markets work as they (markets) are "the product of an evolutionary, unguided process (and) it's not surprising that it little resembles the telltale fantasies of neoclassical theory."

Given the issues associated with the new science of behavioral economics and the enthusiasm that seems to be building to use it as a justification for new policies, there is an urgent need to consider when and where it is appropriate. The use of benefit-cost analysis dates back at least to 1978 (President Carter's Executive Order 12044) and attempts to set guidelines on where the federal government should use economic analysis to determine when regulations are necessary and what form they should take. These orders have been reinforced by every president since. To date, there has been no guidance with respect to the use of behavioral economics for government policies. Contrasting this failure is the fact that the Carter order, and every subsequent order has been informed by the century long theory associated with neoclassical economics.

For example, the case is made that we must take control of the dietary habits of overweight people because we have assumed collective responsibility for their health. That, of course, is a government choice, not a market choice so it is hard to argue that this represents a market failure, only personal failures. Given the exhaustive list of personal failures that the behavioral psychologists have identified there is no doubt much more work envisioned beyond making us thinner. So far we have apparently failed at choosing the correct cars, air conditioners, heat pumps, microwave ovens, refrigerators, and mortgages. What are the limits to government involvement using this theory? For example, given that over half of all marriages end in divorce, is a nudge in our future towards choosing a perfect match as seen by the Bureau of Marital Bliss within the Department of Health and Human Services?

On the other hand, if there are insufficient market incentives to help us make better decisions about problems that lead to irreversible effects (like fatal mistakes or failing to save enough for retirement) and there are poor market mechanisms that are not working, then there are good reasons to use this theory to fashion remedies. For example, the Social Security

Administration has used behavioral economics to help frame the decision as to when to start taking benefits.[3]

From the 1950s on, market failure was supposed to be the economic justification for intervening in markets.[4] That rationale has been side-stepped in many cases as agencies either ignore the requirement or just hypothesize about the existence of a market failure without data to back it up.[5]

Mario Rizzo argues in this volume that there are four conditions, all of which must be satisfied, in order to use behavioral economics to justify policy:

1. There must be some agreed-upon criteria for what would be welfare enhancing behavior.
2. We can observe real life examples where people (presumably a lot of people) are violating that behavior.
3. Policymakers can correct that behavior toward the right behavior.
4. We cannot do so without high costs of resources or liberty.

Professor Rizzo argues that it is extremely unlikely that all of these can be satisfied for most real world situations.

Many factors cast doubt on the ability of behavioral economics to solve a large variety of policy problems. These include: (1) the importance of decision errors as a learning mechanism; (2) the heterogeneous nature of public policy decisions; (3) unintended consequences of nudge policies; and (4) the fact that private markets generally perform better than government nudges. Each of these issues will be examined in turn.

DECISION ERRORS AS A LEARNING MECHANISM

One of the first things a government regulator should do when beginning to design a regulation is "identify the desired outcome."[6] Suppose we imagine that we are just beginning the entire enterprise of intervening in markets using behavioral economics. The desired outcome could be construed as preventing people from making mistakes–that is, ensuring that outcomes of individual actions are consistent with their underlying preferences. Given the enormous number of categories of mistakes people make (well over 100),[7] it's not too hard to imagine that the program might include all mistakes humans make. If they are successful, what will success look like?

In the *Time Machine*, the great science fiction book written by H.G. Wells in 1895, the world is divided into two classes of people in the distant future. The first group encountered are the Eloi, who live above ground and have all of their needs met, including shelter, food, and clothing. Their needs are provided by the second group, the underground dwellers known as the Morlocks. For the price of their labors serving the Eloi, the Morlocks extract a payment by periodically eating some of the Eloi. The observer of this state, known only as the Time Traveler, first observes the Eloi and believes he may be observing humanity finally achieving Utopia as they seem to live in a blissful state with all of their needs met. But later on he begins to seriously doubt whether this society is truly utopian. His doubts about utopia were not at first about cannibalism, they were about the "blissful" lives of the Eloi.

He comments on the supposedly idyllic Eloi, whereby "The too-perfect security of the Upper-worlders had led them to a slow movement of degeneration, to a general dwindling in size, strength and intelligence."[8] The Time Traveler notes that they do not ask questions, nor experiment and reminds his guests in the nineteenth century that experimenting (trial and error) is the only way man learns and develops. Ultimately, the Time Traveler begins to doubt his initial Utopia hypothesis, that freedom from want, from choice, and most particularly for our purposes, from mistakes, represents an ideal life.

The goal of those who would use behavioral economics appears to be the same as the Morlocks, to remove the ability of people to make mistakes, which simultaneously has the unwanted consequence of preventing them from learning from those mistakes. Over time, perhaps their intelligence and curiosity will dwindle and they will not question the taxes they pay and the cost of regulatory activity behind the efforts of behavioral economic planners.

We know that experimenting is natural to humans. Anyone who has ever watched a five-month-old baby sees learning by experimenting. Give the child an interesting object and she will perform hundreds of experiments with it every minute using hands, feet, and mouth to try to discern what can be done with it and what is the most satisfying way to do it.

Golf is the same way for adults. Poor golfers who don't really understand the beauty of the game will hit a shot that ends up in a bad lie and then want to move the ball. If the golfer cheats and improves his lie, he has just lost what is so great about golf: every single swing is different and you get to try different things to see what works. The variations are infinite.

After all, you must account for your own condition; are you stiff, did you lift weights the day before or lift several drinks; how strong is the wind, how constant, in what direction; is your ball on a slope, up, down left or right, and by how much; what is the consistency of the grass or whatever surface you have landed upon; how far do you need to hit, what is the ball likely to land on; where are the hazards and how can they be avoided? The combinations are endless and, although lessons help, everyone's mental ability, knowledge, and physical builds and skill levels are different. It is a game where there is no such thing as perfect, you try to both minimize and make "smaller" mistakes.

Perhaps the government doesn't care about the decision heuristics that falsely improve your golf score but suppose they did and they found that golfers in fact make mental mistakes. In the movie "The Greatest Game Ever Played" the ten-year-old caddie, Eddie Lowery, reminds the young amateur, Francis Ouimet, playing his first US Open as an amateur that the worst thing he can do is watch the pro and try and duplicate his shot, particularly as there is no way to know where the pro, Harry Vardon, has actually hit the ball. Young Eddie knows that Francis should play his own game against the course. While Eddie appears to be nudging him away from a mental mistake, mostly Eddie just encourages Francis with such pithy remarks on putting as, "Read 'em, roll 'em, and hole 'em." Eddie understands that Francis is learning by himself how to play the game at a new level.

We make countless mistakes in golf and that is why many have said the game is "90 %" mental. Given that we are making mistakes and learning constantly, could government bureaucrats nudge us into a better game? Most likely, any nudge would be one more factor the golfer would have to overcome as he continues his quest for the unattainable, the perfect game.

Adam Thierer's chapter makes the point that learning occurs at "personal, organizational and societal" levels and that "when we fail, we learn a great deal from it." But behavioral economics paternalism appears to follow the precautionary model that: "interrupts (the) learning process and leaves us more vulnerable to the most serious problems we face as individuals or a society." In fact, as Mark White points out, nudges act to prevent us from learning because: "Nudges do not engage people's rational deliberative faculties, however, but instead subvert them, relying on cognitive biases and dysfunction to circumvent rational choice." Perhaps not all nudges do this as sometimes they draw attention to something you ought to think about, such as when to opt out, but many surreptitiously do your thinking for you.

Given that we want people to learn from mistakes even when these conditions are met, we should also take into account the amount of regret that would ensue from a poor decision. That is, if a decision doesn't cause irreversible harm, and people can learn from their decisions, then an intervention is likely to make things worse by eliminating the learning component.

THE HETEROGENEOUS NATURE OF PUBLIC PREFERENCES

The next problem that afflicts all regulations (not just those motivated by behavioral economics) is the inherent differences in what we value and how we make decisions. Because we are all different with different needs, wants, and preferences, when someone proclaims that they will do the thinking for everyone, it can be a problem. As Jodi Beggs says: "As the heterogeneity of the effect of a nudge increases, the social justification for implementing such a nudge decreases." Sofie Miller and Brian Mannix quote from a National Bureau of Economic Research working paper that found that: "different consumer groups have vastly different discount rates for purchases of energy efficient appliances." This means that each consumer values energy savings over time differently, particularly as compared to other characteristics of energy products so that there is no single rule that can positively affect everyone.

But even if everyone were alike, it is still a problem for planners to know people's true preferences. A number of authors have cited the difficulty of first finding out preferences that people may not be able to accurately describe and that are constantly changing. So it's not just the fact that we are different, it is impossible to actually know what preferences people have and attempts to nudge us may have unintended consequences.

UNINTENDED CONSEQUENCES OF NUDGE POLICIES

Mark White in this volume goes back to an earlier era where John Stuart Mill proclaimed: "The strongest of all the arguments against the interference of the public with purely personal conduct is that, when it does interfere, the odds are that it interferes wrongly, and in the wrong place." Mill may have been anticipating unintended consequences. Michael Marlow provides an example of these unintended consequences where past government nudges promoting diets rich in complex carbohydrates "may have unintentionally promoted obesity." Similarly, Sherzod Abdukadirov notes that taxes on soda caused some to switch to beer. Just as with the heterogeneity problem, government planners fail far too often to examine the likely behavioral changes that result from their policies and the unintended consequences of those policies. Of course, there may be positive as well as negative consequences, but failure to analyze and consider them leads to poor policies.

THE SLIPPERY SLOPE

One of the unintended consequences of embracing nudges for every kind of personal failure is that it is perceived as a policy failure when the "right" behavior is not adopted. In fact, new or restructured information may cause people to re-enforce their original choice. Without knowing precisely why consumers choose what they do, it is impossible to distinguish a policy effort that re-enforces a choice that is consistent with true consumer preferences from a failed policy effort that does not achieve that.

In fact, there are those who favor these kinds of interventions but think that nudges are not enough, that more forceful policies are virtually always needed to change behavior. Professor Marlow distinguishes between two categories of paternalism commonly known as: "soft" paternalism and "hard" paternalism. If nudges are "easy and cheap" to avoid, they are soft paternalistic nudges. As Professor White mentions "mandates, bans, taxes and subsidies" are the traditional (hard) paternalist tools. For some, moving down the policy severity slope is automatic as Smith and Zywicki note, "Once a product or service is considered *non gratis*, policymakers quickly move from subtly changing choice architecture to outright elimination of the service."

Take one example covered in this book, the fact that far too many of us are overweight or obese, reflecting what appears to be failure to make the correct choices favoring current hunger over future fatness. What is the goal of those who would use behavioral economics to "cure" obesity, is it that everyone attains the perfect weight? As noted by Marlow in this volume, there is a $60 billion industry seeking to help us attain the enlightened weight and, in order to be profitable, they must be successful. So both the industry and, for that matter, consumers experiment to see what works. Hyper-connected consumers tell each other of their experiments to see what is working and what is not. The Eloi, of course, do not need to do so as the Morlocks control their diets. Given the government movement that goes well beyond nudges to tax offending foods, control portion sizes or, in the case of the SNAP program, disallow certain foods, perhaps we are not too far off from the dependence of the Eloi.

PRIVATE MARKETS GENERALLY PERFORM BETTER THAN GOVERNMENT NUDGES

Although some acknowledge that governments are not always perfectly rational, they continue to believe that, by using economic analysis and democratic processes, they are more likely than markets to provide people with good advice or impose measures that are good for them. Of course, while at least a few policies have the "rational" input of benefit-cost analysis, most don't.[9] Where personal decisions are concerned, the overall question is whether people (and firms) are more likely to make better decisions with government nudges (and shoves) or with market participants addressing the same issues.

Of course, there are many differences between government and market nudges. For example, Sherzod Abdukadirov points out that government nudges have no feedback mechanisms so that, when something isn't working or has unintended consequences, it can be easily altered. And, as Marlow points out: "Government choice architects do not face comparable 'market tests' and thus face greater problems overcoming their imperfections," which means that poor government products are not removed from the market. No doubt, once in place, government policies gain adherents who profit from them and lobby to keep the policies in place.

In fact, while private marketers know exactly what behavior they are trying to get people to achieve, that's not always clear with government policies. As Abdukadirov notes, what is the government trying to do when putting calorie counts on snack machines; get people to make healthier choices or walk away entirely? Or, as mentioned earlier, what is the goal overall, to make everyone's weight perfect?

In addition, as a number of authors in this volume point out, government agents exhibit the same biases as everyone else. But government agents have an additional shortcoming; they can also be under the influence of interest groups who use the government to their own advantage.

Finally, firms must live or die by success or the lack of success, and firms must experiment and they get instant feedback on those experiments. Governments do not and, even if they do, they need not heed the feedback. Trying to influence consumers to make a change in their behavior is, for business, called marketing. And, as Mark White points out: "people *expect* private companies—especially retailers, advertisers and marketers—to use whatever means they can to sell their products (outside of fraud)."

This is the primary contribution of this volume, in virtually everything that we want to do in life, a market is formed to nudge, sway, or influence us. In golf, there are countless books, programs, devices, videos, and experts all vying for your attention. It's difficult to choose between all of the different forms of influence, which gives rise to another market, a market that helps you select the best advice book. Go on the Web and search for "best _____" (fill in the blank) and there will be lots of sites that help you select the product that you want. A Google query on how to select the best retirement plan comes back with both private and public suggestions. Some are clearly identifiable as attempts to sell a company's services but not all.[10] Some come from companies that sell financial magazines[11] and some come from the government.[12]

And the fact that there are lots of sites suggests there will be meta-markets, competitive on-line sites whose goal is to help choose other sites. Most of these Websites will rise and fall as time and experience sorts them out. As with any product, there is specialization to suit individual conditions and preferences. Competition, including specialization, firms rising and falling based on merit, experimentation, and feedback, is the essence of what separates government from markets.

There is one thing that governments and markets share: conflicts of interest between the nudge supplier and consumers. There will not always be consonance between what profit-oriented firms want customers to do and what is in the best interest of those customers. Jodi Beggs refers to nudges that are not good for consumers as "predatory nudges."For example, some gyms charge a low monthly fee but then discourage people from actually using the gym. Others purposefully make it difficult to cancel a contract. Of course, when government focuses on a single element of a product or a service such as energy efficiency but ignores other attributes that could be considered a predatory nudge as well. Making government taxes less salient by hiding them could be considered just as much of a predatory nudge as shrouded bank fees. While competition in markets may ultimately drive out most predatory nudges, it is not clear that the voting process will do the same for government nudges.

The future for market nudges is machine algorithms that are tailored to us as individuals. Steve Wendel points out some of the best new devices in the consumer technology sphere that have been created to help people make better decisions concerning their health and finance. To help us make better decisions, machine algorithms that are already present on our cell phones will be vast improvements over one-size-fits-all nudges.[13]

As Tyler Cowen writes, "Imagine using machine intelligence to guide our daily decisions. The iPhone program Siri, or some new version of her, tells Mary to dump John because he is a lying bastard. Another program tells you to sell your stocks or your home."[14] It's easy to imagine that every decision flaw that behavioral economists point out could be remedied on an individualized basis vastly better by privately created algorithms. There are now dozens of apps for help with weight control and there are likely to be many more for dealing with banks, figuring out paying points versus interest rates for mortgages, and virtually any decision people make. So just as behavioral economics takes off as a government policy tool, it is likely to rapidly become obsolete, an outdated policy remedy.

A lot of behavioral economics seems to be applied to nutrition, particularly to combat obesity. While there are machine algorithms like BMI Calculator and Lose It, the real future probably lies in making healthier foods that are also tastier.[15] One example is at the UK's John Innes Centre, which created a tomato with a high level of antioxidants from snapdragon plants.[16] It has also created plants with extra vitamins, minerals, and rice with beta carotene.[17]

What we are left with is yet another decision. Should we vote to allow governments to do their best to either nudge us into doing what's best for us or, failing that, use more stringent measures to achieve these results? In some sense, it's difficult to vote for these things; candidates represent all sorts of policy choices and, even if you think voting on government intervening to correct private failures is a winner, it becomes more problematical when we have heterogeneous needs.

Or should we leave it to markets? Government and markets already compete to correct our decisions. The difference is that government policies are almost never reversible, whether they work or not, and they are coercive. On the other hand, the supply of nudges, algorithms, and technologies from the private sector is about making profits by influencing and satisfying private wants. They will not always be consistent with our true underlying preference but, importantly, they can be driven out of the market by competing products that are consistent. In the new information age, consumers will instantly evaluate and share information on what works and what doesn't. And the products developed in private markets can be individualized to a vastly greater degree than government policies.

Perhaps Lee Harris (quoted in this volume by Robert Graboyes) said it best, "The small irrationalities of our daily individual lives... can never damage society as much as the grandiose rationality of centralized planners—a vital truth that our generation seems to have forgotten…" In the end markets may simply outcompete governments to nudge us. Just like market failures, every personal failure is also a market opportunity.[18]

NOTES

1. William J. Clinton, "Executive Order 12866, Regulator Planning and Review," September 30, 1993.
2. Thaler, Richard and Cass Sunstein, *Nudge* (Yale University Press, 2008).
3. Social Security Administration, "When to Start Receiving Benefits," SSA Publication No. 05-10147, ICN 480136, January 2014.
4. F. M. Bator, "The Anatomy of Market Failure," QJE, 1958.
5. Jerry Ellig and James Broughel, "Regulation: What's the Problem?" *Mercatus on Policy*, November 21, 2011.
6. Jerry Ellig, "Ready, Fire, Aim!: A Foundational Problem with Regulations," Mercatus Research Summary.
7. Wikipedia lists 168 at https://en.wikipedia.org/wiki/List_of_cognitive_biases
8. H. G. Well, The Time Machine, 1898, p. 158.
9. Richard Williams and James Brougel, "Government Report on Benefits and Costs of Federal Regulations Fails to Capture Full Impact of Rules," Mercatus Center, December 02, 2013.
10. http://www.accountingweb.com/practice/practice-excellence/10-tips-on-selecting-the-right-retirement-plan-provider
11. http://money.cnn.com/retirement/
12. http://www.irs.gov/Retirement-Plans/Help-with-Choosing-a-Retirement-Plan
13. One site lists 25 apps that will help consumers save money: http://www.lifehack.org/articles/money/25-apps-that-will-save-you-lots-money.html
14. Tyler Cowen, *Average Is Over* (New York: Penguin Group, 2013), 72.
15. http://www.healthline.com/health-slideshow/top-iphone-android-apps-weight-loss#7
16. Michael White, "Be a Good Kid and Eat Your GMO Vegetables," Health and Behavior, Pacific Standard, July 1, 2013.

17. WebMD, "GMO's What You Need to Know," http://www.webmd. com/food-recipes/truth-about-gmos?page=2
18. See, for example, Israel M. Kirzner, Competition and Entrepreneurship, rev. ed. (Indianapolis: Liberty Fund, 2010 [1963]); Ludgwig Von Mises, Human Action: A Treatise on Economics, rev. ed. (Indianapolis: Liberty Fund, 2010 [1949]); Israel M. Kirzner, Market Theory and the Price System, rev. ed. (Indianapolis: Liberty Fund, 2011 [1963]).

INDEX

© The Editor(s) (if applicable) and The Author(s) 2016
S. Abdukadirov (ed.), *Nudge Theory in Action*,
DOI 10.1007/978-3-319-31319-1

on food sellers, 207
on mindless eating, 200, 219n32
on New York's soda ban and, 176
on weight-loss nudges, 203
Washington Post, 274
wearable products. *See also* FitBit;
    Jawbone
    exercise bands, 99, 115n14
    feedback, 100
    weight-loss nudges and, 211–12
WebMD, 307
Weight Watchers, 30, 100–101, 211
weight-loss nudges
    basics, 199–201
    conclusion, 215–16
    evidence on, 201–3
    government-sponsored, 201–5
    introduction, 195–96
    market vs. government, 212–14
    market-sponsored, 205–12
    obese understanding of their
        choices, 198–99, 218n23
    obesity causes and prevention,
        196–98
    role for government, 214–15
welfare economics, utility function
    and, 40
Wells, H.G., 321
Wendel, Steven, 5, 105, 108, 167,
    180, 326
Wengraf, Susan, 177
Wesabe, 181–82

WhichTestWon.com, 111
White, Mark D., 4, 322, 324, 325
White House Office of Information
    and Regulatory Affairs (OIRA),
    80, 171
Whitman, Glen, 26, 56
who should nudge?
    government nudges, 170–78
    market nudges, 178–82
    nudge design and, 160–70
    overview, 159–60
    regulatory nudge failure, 182–83
Why Nudge? (Sunstein), 52, 59n24,
    159
Wildavsky, Aaron, 70
Williams, Richard, 6–7
willpower, social scaffolding and, 30
Wilson, Woodrow, 298
"Wingspread Consensus Statement"
    (1998), 70
Wolfson, Julia A., 207
Wright, Joshua D., 79

Y
Yodlee, 182

Z
Zolli, Andrew, 69
Zuckerman, Laurie, 308
Zywicki, Todd, 6, 319, 324